FROMMER'S TOURING GUIDE TO PARIS

PRENTICE HALL PRESS

NEW YORK

Author
Hervé Juvin

Translation
Allison Hay and Duncan Richards

Adaptation
Times Editions, Singapore, and Hachette, Paris

Production
Times Editions, Singapore

This edition published in the United States and Canada in
1987 by Prentice Hall Press
A division of Simon & Schuster, Inc.
Gulf+Western Building
One Gulf+Western Plaza
New York, New York 10023

PRENTICE HALL PRESS is a trademark of Simon
& Schuster, Inc.

This guide is adapted from *A Paris* published by Hachette
Guides Bleus, Paris, 1986.

Library of Congress Cataloging-in-Publication Data

Juvin, Hervé
  Frommer's touring guide to Paris.

  Translation of: A Paris.
  Bibliography: p. 235
  Includes index.
  1. Paris (France) — Description — 1975- —
Tours. I. Title.
DC708.J8813   1987   914.4'36104838   86-30363
ISBN 0-13-331331-X

Printed in Singapore

CONTENTS

Photographs by Peter Tebbit, with the exception of p. 163 (Hachette photo library).

HOW TO USE YOUR GUIDE

Your *Guide to Paris* describes every feature of the city and the suburbs that a tourist may wish to visit, setting the monuments and gardens in their historical context.

Maps are provided in the opening pages to help pinpoint addresses in Paris; all maps show Metro and R.E.R. stations, and all the major monuments have accompanying map references. These are followed by basic information on the services in the city and how best to use them. Next comes a chronology of French history that traces Paris' beginnings in 52 BC as a tribal settlement to the unique metropolitan center that we know today.

The major sights of Paris are divided into 13 precise itineraries, the better to help readers plan their visits to the main districts and the city's great monuments, churches, parks and palaces. From the Louvre to the Museum of Modern Art, this section covers 4000 years of artistic creation. Each itinerary is clearly marked.

The next section offers a review of Paris' main museums, including the Louvre, the Picasso Museum and the new Orsay Museum. A number of off-the-beaten-track visits have also been included, to parks and "villages" in the city which retain their old charm and character. A special section is devoted to the Palace and grounds of Versailles.

In the final section there is a selective list of hotels, restaurants, night-spots and shops.

Note

To find an address in Paris you must first know the "arrondissement" in which it is situated. Paris is divided into 20 arrondissements, or districts, and every address in Paris indicates its arrondissement in the last two figures of its post code. In this guide, all hotels, restaurants and business establishments are classified by arrondissement.

Symbols

Monuments, museums and gardens (headings):

- ● interesting
- ●● very interesting
- ●●● exceptional

within the text, the ●●● are replaced by asterisks ***.

Maps

Map references are provided after the names of places to visit. Maps are numbered from 1–5 and precise coordinates are given for rapid location of sites.

Travel Information

Metro, R.E.R. (train) and bus travel information is given at the beginning of the different itineraries and at various points along the way.

MAPS AND PLANS

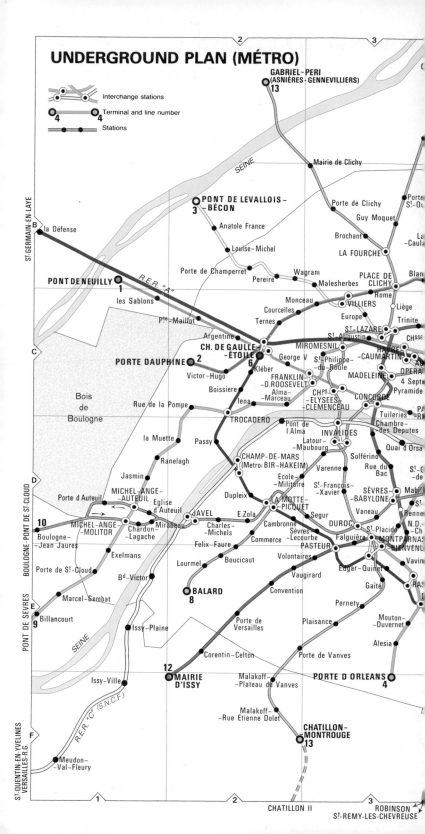

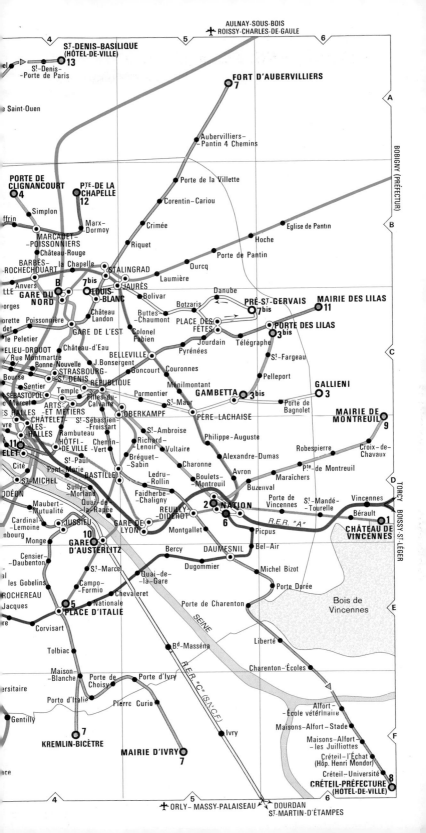

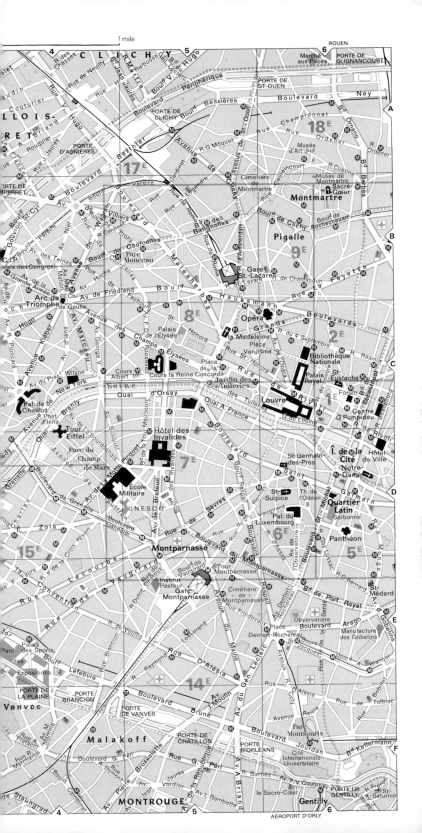

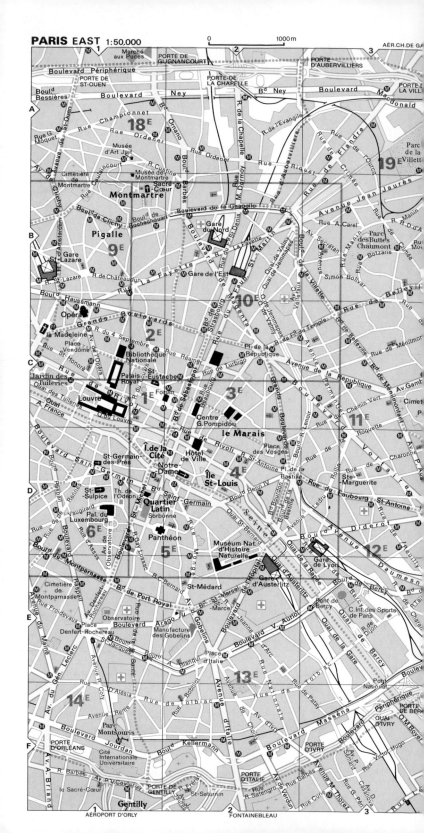

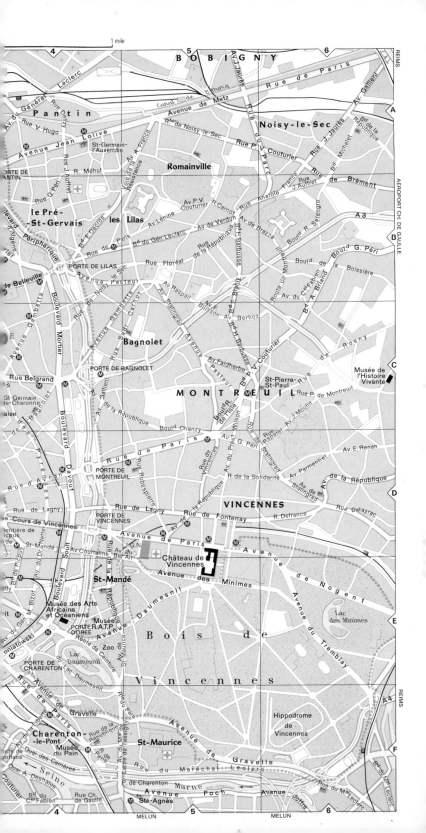

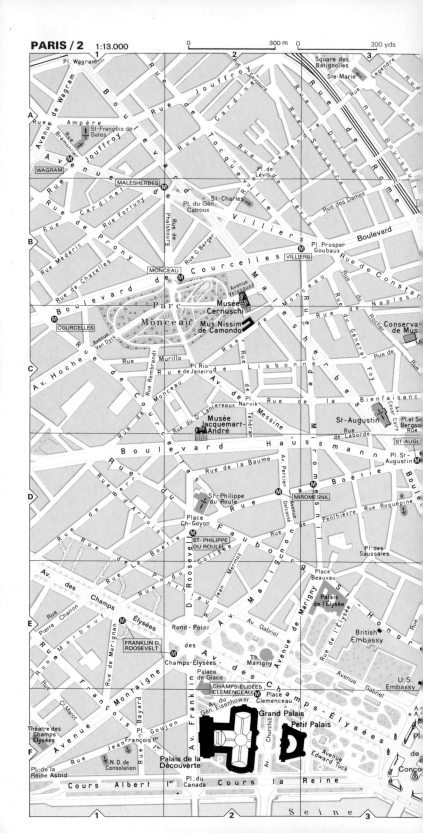

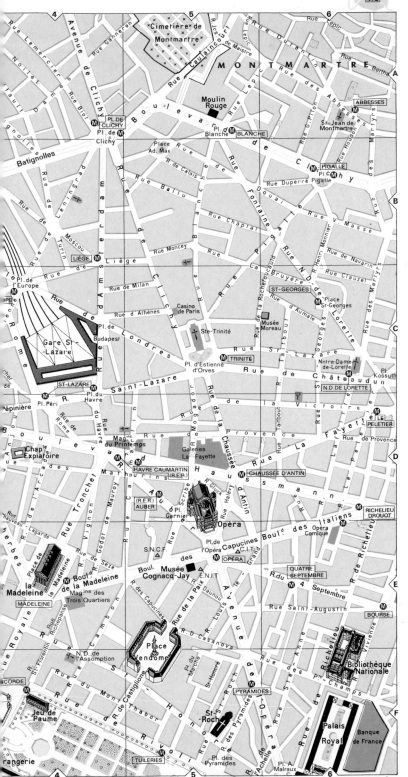

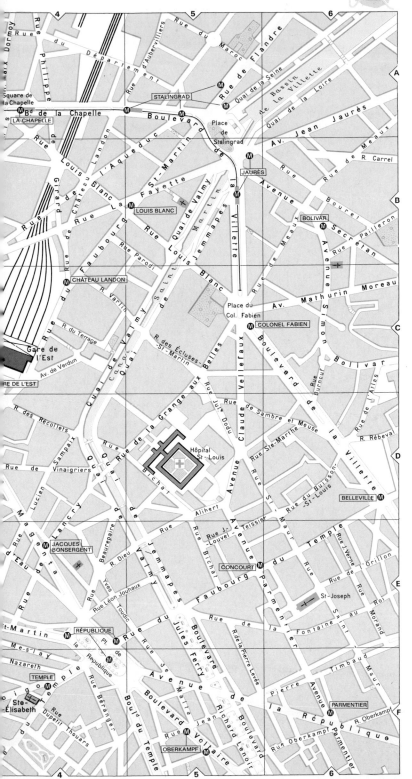

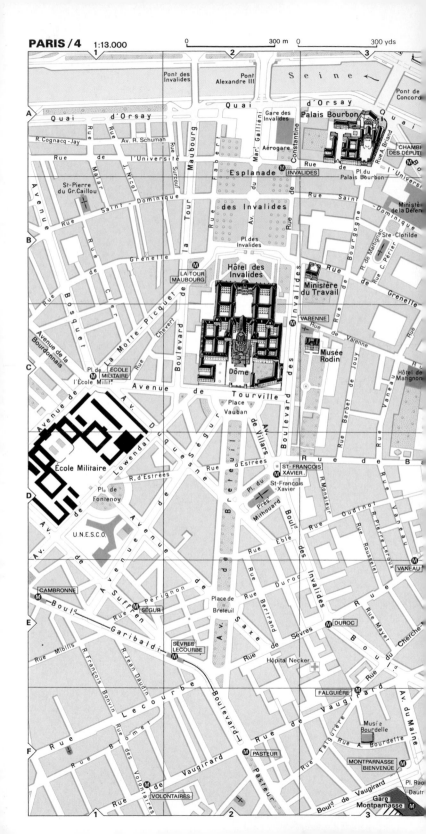

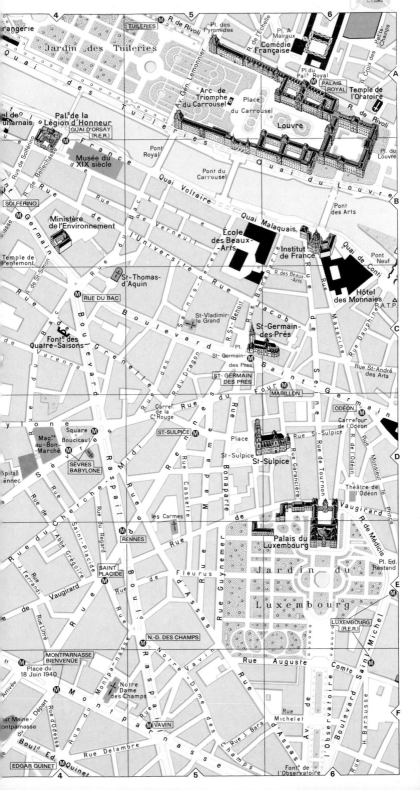

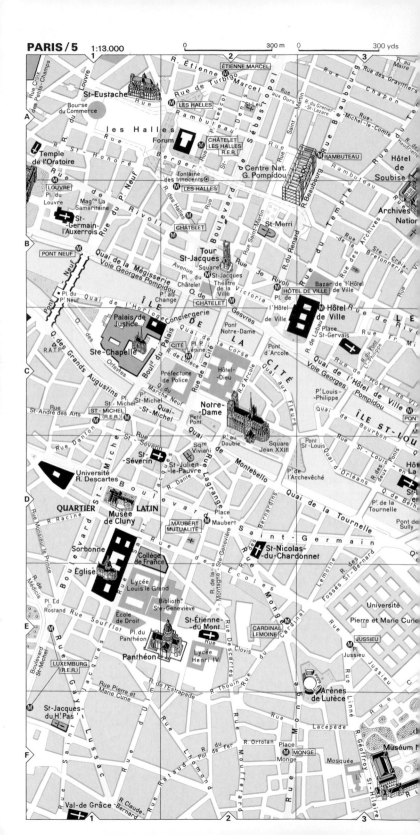

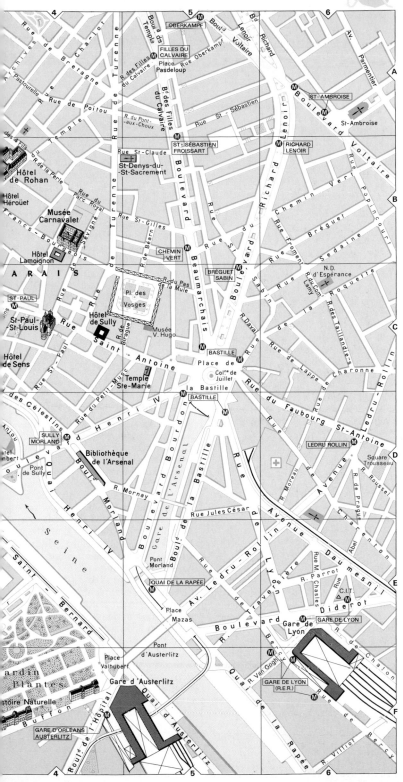

USEFUL INFORMATION

Reservations: It is advisable, if not indispensable, to book in advance, especially in season (July-August) and during trade fairs and other international meetings, Paris being the favorite venue in Europe for such gatherings. Three to four weeks' notice should be enough for hotels; for restaurants, 24 hours are generally adequate, but for large parties, arrangements should be made several weeks in advance.

Paris Tourist Office: 127 Av. des Champs-Élysées, 75008. (Metro: George V.) Tel: 47 20 88 98. Open daily in high season: Mon-Sat, 9 am − 10 pm. (Sun & public hols, 9 am − 8 pm.) Low season: Mon-Sat, 9 am − 8 pm. (Sun & public hols, 9 am − 6 pm.) *Gare du Nord Office:* tel: 45 26 94 82, international trains arrival area. *Gare de l'Est Office:* tel: 46 07 17 73, arrival hall area. *Gare de Lyon Office:* tel: 44 43 33 24, main line departures area. *Gare d'Austerlitz Office:* tel: 45 84 81 70, main line arrival area. Offices are open every day except Sun. Be prepared for lengthy queues during summer.

Maison d'information culturelle de la Ville de Paris (Paris cultural information): 1 Rue Pierre-Lescot, 75001. (Metro: Étienne-Marcel.) Tel: 42 33 75 54 (recorded information). Open daily except Sun from 10 am − 8 pm. Provides information on cultural activities in Paris.

Paris Informations Loisirs (Paris leisure information): tel: 47 20 94 94. 24-hr English language service. *Centre d'information des Musées de la Ville de Paris* (Paris museum information): tel: 42 78 73 81 (recorded information, in French).

Bureau d'Accueil de la Ville de Paris (Paris welcome office): 29 Rue de Rivoli, 75001. (Metro: Hôtel-de-Ville.) Tel: 42 77 15 40 (except Sun).

What's on in Paris: Among the Paris weeklies featuring "what's on" are: *Une Semaine de Paris; Pariscope; l'Officiel des Spectacles* and *7 à Paris.* These guides (in French) appear on Wednesdays and are on sale at most news-stands (*kiosques*); they offer complete programmes for theaters, shows, cinemas, concerts, exhibitions, fairs, etc., as well as a number of other useful addresses. The monthly English-language *Passion* is also an excellent source of information. At the *Kiosque de la Madeleine* (Metro: Madeleine), tickets still available for shows on that day can be bought at half price.

Museums: Museums usually refuse entry to visitors half an hour before closing. National museums are closed on Tuesdays. Church doors are closed between noon and 2 pm, to deter visitors during services.

Guided tours: Times and conditions of visits given in this guide may be subject to change. Readers are advised to call in advance to check schedules.

Various companies organize guided tours of monuments and particular districts; these tours are sometimes to places of special interest and may be restricted to organized groups. *Caisse nationale des monuments historiques* (Bureau of historic monuments): Hôtel de Sully, 62 Rue Saint-Antoine, 75004. (Metro: St-Paul.) Tel: 42 74 22 22. *Association pour la sauve-garde du Paris historique* (Association for the preservation of historic Paris): 44 Rue François-Miron, 75004. (Metro: St-Paul.) Tel: 48 87 74 31. *Action culturelle de la Ville de Paris* (Paris cultural activities bureau): Hôtel-de-Ville, Centre d'Information, 75004. (Metro: Hôtel-de-Ville.) Tel: 42 27 15 40. *Paris et son histoire* (History of Paris): 82 Rue Taitbout, 75009. (Metro: St-Georges.) Tel: 45 26 26 77.

When to visit Paris?

Each season has its own advantages. In summer, the city is at its quietest between July 15th and August 25th, Parisians (and their cars) having left for holiday destinations. Summer is an excellent time to roam around the streets undisturbed by crowds and traffic. The drawbacks are that there are fewer Parisians in town, many restaurants and shops are closed, and the sultry August weather can be uncomfortable without air conditioning.

Camera enthusiasts and people who like visiting monuments will find the subtle light of the Ile-de-France at its best in mid-autumn or spring. For shopping, shows and night-life, winter is the best season; but December in Paris is notorious for traffic jams. Whatever the time of year, reservations in hotels and restaurants should be made in advance, since the city's available accommodation quickly reaches saturation point at peak periods and during major exhibitions and public holidays.

Paris by Coach: *France Tourisme Paris Vision*, 214 Rue de Rivoli, 75001. (Metro: Tuileries.) Tel: 42 60 30 01 and 42 60 31 25. *Cityrama Rapid Pullman*, 4 Pl. des Pyramides, 75001. (Metro: Tuileries.) Tel: 42 60 30 14

The river boats (*Bateaux-mouches*) are an essential part of the Paris scene. They offer unforgettable sightseeing tours of the city as seen from the Seine. *Bateaux-mouches*, Pont de l'Alma, 75007. (Metro: Alma-Marceau.) Tel: 42 25 96 10. *Vedettes Paris-Tour-Eiffel*, Pont d'Iéna, 75016. (Metro: Trocadéro.) Tel: 45 51 33 08. *Vedettes du Pont Neuf*, Square du Vert-Galant, 75001. (Metro: Pont-Neuf.) Tel: 46 33 98 38. *La Patache*, known as the "Eautobus", provides unorthodox entertainment during its trips along the river and through the nostalgic canal-side scenery made famous by the classic French film *Hôtel du Nord*, the Quai de la Loire in the 19th arrondissement. This tour leaves from the Quai Anatole-France, 75007, in the morning (Metro: Solférino), or from 212 Av. Jean-Jaurès, 75019, (Metro: Porte de Pantin) in the afternoon. For times, consult *Quiztour*, 19 Rue d'Athènes, 75009. (Tel: 48 74 75 30.) *Canauxrama*, 4 Villa Blanche, 92200 Neuilly. (Tel: 46 24 86 16 for reservations.) Tours leave from the Bassin de la Villette (Metro: Jean-Jaurès) going to Port de l'Arsenal (Metro: Bastille), or vice-versa. Other tours with the same organizer include the Ourcq canal and Paris to Meaux.

Postal services: The main post office is at 52 Rue du Louvre, 75001. (Metro: Louvre.) Tel: 42 33 71 60. Open all night.

Banks: Open daily ex. Sat, Sun and hols. Money changers are usually open on Sat mornings. Banks close at noon on days preceeding Bank and public holidays.

Foreign Exchange Offices (Bureaux de change): Open daily: Gare de Lyon, tel: 43 41 52 70 (7 am – 11 pm); Gare du Nord, tel: 42 80 11 50 (6.30 am – 10 pm); Gare de l'Est, tel: 42 06 51 97 (7 am – 9 pm); Gare Saint-Lazare, tel: 43 87 72 51 (7 am – 9 m); Gare d'Austerlitz, tel: 45 84 91 40 (7.30 – 11.30 am and 1 – 9 pm Mon to Sat, 7 am – 9 pm Sun and hols.) Open daily ex. Sun: 117 Avenue des Champs-Élysées, 75008. (Metro: George V.) Tel: 47 23 27 22 (9 am – 8 pm). Open Mon-Fri: Porte Maillot, 75016, tel: 47 58 22 05 (9.30 am – 12.20 pm and 2 – 4.20 pm).

Travel services: *American Express:* 11 Rue Scribe, 75009. (Metro: Opéra.) Tel: 42 66 09 99. Open 9 am – 5 pm. Mon – Sat.

Thomas Cook: 2 Place de la Madeleine, 75008. (Metro: Madeleine.) Tel: 42 60 33 20.

Lost property: 36 Rue des Morillons, 75015. (Metro: Convention.) Tel: 43 31 14 80.

Maps: These can be purchased from most bookshops, tobacconists and some *kiosques*. The most compact is the *Plan de Paris*, published by Leconte. This excellent pocket-sized book has maps with indexes of the Paris arrondissements and suburbs, along with a Metro map.

Embassies and consulates: *Australian Embassy and Consulate:* 4 Rue Jean-Rey, 75015 (Metro: Bir-Hakeim.) Tel: 45 75 62

After dark

Contrary to popular belief, Parisians do not go out much in the evenings, provincials and visiting foreigners being the mainstay of the night-clubs and other such establishments. The so-called private clubs are accessible to guests of respectable appearance, reservations through a well-known hotel usually guaranteeing entry. Charges vary considerably, rising steeply in proportion to the degree of sophistication or adult nature of the entertainment. As in all large cities, the underworld is very active; conmen operate in the red light districts such as Pigalle and the pick-up bars; pickpockets are busy at all hours, particularly in lines for cinemas and museums, the Metro and shopping centers; and gangs of thugs, who relieve you of your wallets, jewelry and cameras, concentrate on the area behind the Champs-Élysées, and at Pigalle, Montmartre, Saint-Germain-des-Prés and near railway stations.

Entertainments end, except in a few districts, by 12.45 am, when the last Metro departs. Saturday evening crowds carry on until 2 am, except at Pigalle, where the street-walkers await customers until dawn. A full list of clubs and discotheques is given on p. 233.

00. *British Embassy:* 35 Rue du Faubourg-St-Honoré, 75008. (Metro: Concorde.) Tel: 42 66 91 42. *British Consulate:* 2 Cité du Retiro, 75008. (Metro: Madeleine.) Tel: 42 66 38 10. *Canadian Embassy and Consulate:* 35 Av. Montaigne, 75008. (Metro: F.D. Roosevelt.) Tel: 47 23 01 01. *Irish Embassy and Consulate:* 4 Rue Rude, 75016. (Metro: Étoile.) Tel: 45 00 20 87. *New Zealand Embassy and Consulate:* 9 Rue Léonard-de-Vinci, 75016. (Metro: Victor-Hugo.) Tel: 45 00 24 11. *South African Embassy and Consulate:* 59 Quai d'Orsay, 75007. (Metro: Invalides.) Tel: 45 55 93 27. *U.S. Embassy:* 2 Av. Gabriel, 75008. (Metro: Champs-Élysées-Clemenceau.) Tel: 42 96 12 02. *U.S. Consulate:* 2 Rue St-Florentine, 75008. (Metro: Concorde.) Tel: 42 96 33 10.

S.O.S.: *Samu* (emergency ambulance service): Paris: tel: 45 67 50 50; Hauts-de-Seine: tel: 47 41 79 11: Val-de-Marne: tel: 42 05 51 41. *S.O.S. Médecins* (emergency doctor service): tel: 47 07 77 77. *Poisoning emergency:* tel: 42 05 63 29. *Police:* tel: 17. *Fire:* tel: 18.

Weather: Tel: 45 55 91 90.

Airports: *Charles-de-Gaulle,* 16 mi./25 km north. Tel: 48 62 22 80. Access: R.E.R. line B, direction Roissy-Rail. Departure every 15 mins. Bus R.A.T.P. n° 350 from Gare de l'Est and Gare du Nord, n° 351 from Pl. de la Nation. Air France buses: Porte Maillot (Metro: Porte Maillot), ground floor, or Pl. de l'Étoile, opposite R.E.R. exit. Air France buses leave every 12 mins, 5.45 am – 11 pm. *Orly,* tel: 48 84 32 10. Access: R.E.R. line C direction Orly Rail. Departure every 15 mins until 9 pm. Bus R.A.T.P. n° 215 from Pl. Denfert-Rochereau, n° 183A from Porte de Choisy or n° 285 from Porte d'Italie, direction Savigny-sur-Orge. Air France buses from Les Invalides terminal leave every 12 mins.

Paris helicopters: *Hélifrance,* 4 Av. Porte-de-Sèvres 75015. (Metro: Balard.) Tel: 45 54 95 11; links Paris-Orly (6 mins); Paris-CDG (14 mins); Orly-CDG (22 mins); tourism and rental of helicopters. *Hélicap,* Paris heliport, tel: 45 57 75 51.

S.N.C.F. (French railways): Gare du Nord, (northern region), tel: 42 80 03 03. Gare de l'Est, (eastern region), tel: 42 08 49 90. Gare de Lyon, (south-eastern region), tel: 43 45 92 22. Gare d'Austerlitz, (south-western region), tel: 45 84 16 16. Gare Montparnasse, (western region), tel: 45 38 52 29. Gare Saint-Lazare, (western region),

tel: 45 38 52 29.
S.N.C.F. Central Information Office, tel: 42 61 50 50.

Metro: Main information office of the R.A.T.P., 53 Quai des Grands-Augustins, 75006. (Metro: Saint-Michel.) Tel: 43 46 14 14. Maps of the urban Metro and the regional express network are displayed and distributed in every station. The first trains start from 5 or 5.30 am on the regional express network, from 5.30 am on the urban Metro. The departure times of the last trains from the terminal vary depending on the line, leaving at intervals from 12.30 am to 1 am approx. All the trains should arrive back at their terminus by 1.15 am. Apart from some sections of Charenton-Écoles — Créteil (line n° 8) and Carrefour Pleyel — St Denis (line n° 13), the price of a ticket (1st or 2nd class) is standard, and not related to the length of the journey or the number of connecting lines used.

R.E.R. Regional Express Network consists of three lines. Line A: Saint-Germain-en-Laye — Boissy-Saint-Léger or Marne la-Vallée. Line B: Saint-Rémy-lès-Chevreuse or Robinson — Châtelet, Roissy or Mitry-Claye. Line C: Saint-Quentin-en-Yvelines — Dourdan, Massy or Étampes.

The Metro

The **Metro** is the best means of transportation in Paris, being the fastest, cheapest and most reliable. It is a network of 120 mi./192 km serving 360 stations and used by more than 4 million commuters every day. Its 3600 carriages have sacrificed aesthetic appeal to comfort, abandoning the old wooden benches for padded seats. This enormous system, which has been extensively automated, is run by the R.A.T.P. (Paris transport company) with its 15,000 employees. The decor of some stations is worth noting: in the Liège station which was built in the early days of the Metro, ceramic panels depict various tourist towns. There are reproductions of works of art at the more recently built stations of the Louvre, Varenne-Rodin and Saint-Denis-Basilique.

The bus

Parisian buses have a very respectable ancestry; their progenitors were the *fiacres*, passenger carriages, introduced in the 17th century by the philosopher Pascal. The fare at that time was 5 *sols* (a few centimes) per person. The fiacres were replaced in 1828 by a system of horse-drawn public coaches. In due course, these were superseded by the tram and then the bus. The Paris bus service, like the Metro, is run by the R.A.T.P.

There are 55 bus routes, covering 342 mi./550 km, of which 75 mi./120 km are buses-only traffic lanes. This preferential treatment does not make the buses run any faster; their average speed during the day is about 10 mi./15 km per hour, and a lot less during rush hours, a source of frustration to busy Parisians. Visitors, on the other hand, will find the bus a pleasant, sometimes surprising and always economical means of exploring the capital.

Buses run from 7 am to 8.30 or 9 pm, some until 12.30 am. There is also an all-night service from the Place du Châtelet to the suburbs every half-hour.

Buses: The map of the bus network is displayed on the platforms of Metro stations as well as in the bus terminals and at main stops on the bus routes. The routes are indicated by figures except for the PC line (*petite ceinture* or inner ring road). Price: a single 2nd class Metro ticket is valid for a journey covering 1 or 2 sections; 2 Metro tickets for all journeys covering more than 2 sections. A different price is charged on the PC line.

Tourist tickets: These tickets allow the traveler to make an unlimited number of journeys within a 2, 4 or 7-day period on any R.A.T.P. line (Metro, R.E.R. and buses). They are on sale in Metro stations, at the Paris railway stations and at the Paris Tourist Office. If you are staying in Paris for some time, it may be worth buying a *carte orange* (orange card) or *carte jaune* (yellow card). These special passes allow you to make an unlimited number of journeys within a week or a calendar month in the chosen zones on the R.A.T.P. There are also *carte orange* coupons valid for a day.

Taxis: Some recommended numbers: tel: 47 39 33 33, 42 03 99 99, 42 05 77 77, 42 70 41 41.

Limousine hire: 4 pers. max. plus a driver-guide-interpreter: *Aristo's*, tel: 47 37 53 70 and agencies.

Car rental: Airports, the Paris railway stations and most of the big garages have car rental services. Among the larger companies are: *Budget* train and auto, tel: 42 29 50 50 (central reservations); *Union Rent-a-Car*, tel 44 66 10 28 (central res.); *Avis*, tel: 46 09 92 12 (central res.); *Autorent*, tel: 45 55 53 49 (central res.); *Europcar*, tel: 40 43 82 82 (central res.); *Mattei*, tel: 43 46 11 50 (central res.); *Hertz*, tel: 47 88 51 51 (central res.); *Citer*, tel: 43 41 45 45 (central res.); *Cifa*, tel: 45 67 35 24 (central res.); *Transam*, tel: 42 06 12 29 (central res.); *Polyservices*, tel: 42 29 46 39; *Express-Assistance*, tel: 47 27 27 27; *Milleville*, (at Rungis) tel: 66 87 36 68 or 05 10 00 01 – free phone.

Hiring bicycles: in front of the Pompidou Center, and at the bungalow next to *Relais du Bois*, 9 Rue de la Faisanderie, 75116. (Metro: Porte Dauphine.) Open:

The taxi

There are about 15,000 taxis in Paris. The fact that an empty one is hard to find attests to their popularity; they are also cheaper than using your own car.

The visitor should have little difficulty with Paris taxis if he remembers that day and night fares are indicated in the vehicle; additional charges have to be paid by passengers picked up from railway stations and airports as well as for luggage exceeding two pieces; neither in Paris nor in the suburbs is a driver entitled to compensation for the return journey; most drivers will not take more than three passengers; and approximately 15 per cent of the fare is the customary tip. Private taxis are not subject to any regulations and are best avoided.

An excellent introduction to the city is to take a taxi on your first evening and drive along the Seine, doing a round trip from Place de la Concorde by way of Pont d'Austerlitz and Pont de Grenelle.

Parisian markets

A striking feature of Paris is the number and variety of its street markets. Markets play a special role in the life of the Parisian, and it is estimated that about a hundred of them operate on a regular basis throughout the capital, each with its own character and flavor.

On the twisting Rue Mouffetard, the exotic market stalls open at 6 am; Rue Lepic is known for its fish and seafood; Rue de Buci is patronized by the intellectuals and fashionable residents of Saint-Germain-des Prés; and the stalls of the La Muette market lend a rustic touch to the staid, opulent 16th arrondissement.

The main open-air food markets: *Marché Buci*, 6th arrondissement (Metro: St-Germain-des Prés), *Marché Levis*, 17th arrondissement (Metro: Villiers); *Marché Lepic*, 18th (Metro: Blanche); *Marché Maubert*, 5th (Metro: Maubert-Mutualité); *Marché Mouffetard*, 5th (Metro: Monge); *Marché Aligre*, 12th (Metro: Ledru-Rollin); *Marché La Muette*, 16th (Metro: Muette); *Marché Daguerre*, 17th (Metro: Denfert-Rochereau); *Marché Cardinet*, 17th (Metro: Courcelles).

Over forty **covered markets** were built in Paris during the 19th century, and five are still of interest:

– **Marché Saint-Quentin,** recently restored food market; *85 Bd. de Magenta, 75010,* (Metro: Gare de l'Est).

– **Marché Voltaire,** now a gym, *2 Rue Japy, 75011,* (Metro: République).

– **Marché La Chapelle food market,** completed by architect Auguste Magne in 1885, *8 Rue de la Guadeloupe, 75018,* (Metro: Marx-Dormoy).

– **Marché Secrétan food market,** a fine example of the work of architect Victor Baltard, completed in 1868. Baltard (*see p. 59*) pioneered a style of classical simplicity which was best known in his Les Halles pavilions, demolished in 1971. *46 Rue de Meaux, 75019,* (Metro: Bolivar).

– **Marché du Temple:** constructed in 1865, this is one of the earliest markets in Paris; it consists of four sections: bedding, scrap iron, odds and ends and toiletries. Originally designed by the architect Mérindol, the Marché du Temple has deteriorated badly and awaits restoration. *Rue de Picardie, 75003,* (Metro: Filles-du-Calvaire).

Wed, Sat, Sun and hols. and daily in July and August; *Locations Vertes,* Bois de Vincennes and Bois de Boulogne; tel: 42 37 39 10.

Markets: *Saint-Ouen flea market:* Sat, Sun and Mon. 9 am – 7 pm. Metro: Porte de Saint-Ouen. *Montreuil flea market:* Sat and Sun. *Flower market:* daily ex. Sun, 8 am – 7 pm. Metro: Cité. *Stamp and post card market:* Thurs, Sat and Sun and public holidays, 9 am – 6.30 pm at the corner of Av. Marigny and Av. Gabriel, near Champs-Élysées roundabout. Metro: Champs-Élysées – Clemenceau.

Auction room: Nouveau Drouot, 9 Rue Drouot, 75009, tel: 42 46 17 11 open daily (ex. Sun) 11 am – 6 pm.

Department stores: Open Mon – Sat 9 am – 6.30 pm. *Bazar de l'Hôtel-de-Ville,* 52 Rue de Rivoli, 75004. (Metro: Hôtel-de-Ville.) Tel: 42 74 90 00. *Bon Marché,* 38 Rue de Sèvres, 75007. (Metro: Sèvres-Babylone.) Tel: 42 60 33 45. *Galeries Lafayette,* 40 Bd. Haussmann, 75009 (Metro: Havre-Caumartin.) Tel: 42 82 34 56. *Printemps* 64 Bd. Haussmann, 75009, (Metro: Havre-Caumartin.) Tel: 42 85 22 22. *Samaritaine,* 19 Rue de la Monnaie, 75001, (Metro: Pont-Neuf.) Tel: 45 08 33 33. *Trois Quartiers,* Bd. de la Madeleine, opposite La Madeleine, 75001, (Metro: Madeleine.) Tel: 42 60 39 30.

Cultural events: April to May: *Paris Festival of Poetry; Traditional Arts Festival.* June: *Marais Festival.* Summer: *Paris Summer Festival; Festival of the Orangerie de Sceaux.* Sept–Dec: *Paris International Festival of Dance; Autumn Festival.* Sept: *Paris Festival of Chamber Music.* Oct: *Jazz Festival.* Nov: *Paris International Festival of Fantasy and Science-Fiction Films.*

The major annual exhibitions: Jan: *International Yacht Exhibition* (CNIT, La Défense); Feb: *Exhibition of Tourism;* March: *Exhibitions of Domestic Skills, Agriculture* (Parc des Expositions), *Exhibition of Sound;*

Sept: *Exhibition of Computer Science and Office Equipment* (SICOB at CNIT); Oct: *Automobile Exhibition* (Parc des Expositions); Nov: *Exhibition of Childhood* (CNIT).

Other events: Of course, there is insufficient space to list all the events that take place in Paris each year. Such events range from the Paris Trade Fair to the ready-to-wear fashion shows, not to mention the Paris Marathon. You will find them described in brochures published by the Paris Tourist Office, as well as in weekly publications.

Reading matter: Newsagents and *kiosques* in popular tourist areas generally offer a wide selection of English-language newspapers and magazines during the peak season. The *International Herald Tribune*, edited in Paris, is widely available, even at smaller outlets, as are the European editions of the *Financial Times* and the *Wall Street Journal*. The English-language monthly *Passion* is a good source of information on Parisian events as well as news from New York City, Los Angeles and Montreal. Recently, a slimmed-down and more expensive version of *U.S.A. Today* has appeared in Europe.

Radio: The opening of the FM waveband to local stations has considerably widened the variety of listening available to foreign visitors in France. The state-owned *France Inter* station (1829 m AM for national coverage; several regional FM stations) provides English-language news bulletins during the summer after the 9 am and 4 pm news broadcasts. *Inter's* special road information service is available, from 9 am to 6 pm, tel: 48 58 33 33 (in French).

Rooms with families: Paris Tourist Office offers up to 500 rooms with families in Paris and in the suburbs, from a room with one bed and a toilet to self-contained

Art galleries

Two districts of Paris have virtually monopolized art galleries. Around the Faubourg-Saint-Honoré and Avenue Matignon, works of art by established artists are sold by dealers of international repute. The more adventurous galleries which take risks in exhibiting work of all types and conditions, may be found on the Left Bank in the Beaux-Arts area. However, since the construction of the Pompidou Center in the Beaubourg district on the Right Bank, a number of the city's most creative and exciting galleries are to be found there.

– *Bernheim-Jeune:* (all styles since the beginning of the century), 85 Rue du Faubourg-Saint-Honoré, 75008 (Metro: Champs-Élysées-Clemenceau.) Tel: 42 66 60 31
– *Pacitti:* 174 Rue du Faubourg-Saint-Honoré, 75008. (Metro: Champs-Élysées-Clemenceau.) Tel: 45 63 75 30.
– *Présidence:* 90 Rue du Faubourg-Saint-Honoré, 75008. (Metro: Champs-Élysées-Clemenceau.) Tel: 42 65 49 60.
– *Artcurial:* (contemporary art), 9 Av. Matignon, 75008. (Metro: F.D. Roosevelt.) Tel: 42 56 32 90.
– *Wally Findlay:* (contemporary art) 2 Av. Matignon, 75008. (Metro: F. D. Roosevelt.) Tel: 42 25 70 74.
– *Daniel Malinque:* 26 Av. Matignon, 75008. (Metro: F. D. Roosevelt.) Tel: 42 66 60 33.
– *Beaubourg:* (new realism), 23 Rue du Renard, 75004. (Metro: Hôtel-de-Ville.) Tel: 42 71 20 50.
– *Regards:* 11 Rue des Blancs-Manteaux, 75004. (Metro: Rambuteau.) Tel: 42 77 19 51.
– *Daniel Templon:* (avant-garde), 30 Rue Beaubourg, 75004. (Metro: Rambuteau.) Tel: 42 74 14 10.
– *Isy Brachot:* (modern surrealists), 35 Rue Guénégaud, 75006. (Metro: Odéon.) Tel: 43 54 22 40.
– *Jeanne Bucher:* (Joru, Bissières, Tobey), 53 Rue de Seine, 75006. (Metro: Odéon.) Tel: 43 26 22 32.
– *Karl Flinker:* (modern figurative style), 25 Rue de Tournon, 75006. (Metro: Odéon.) Tel: 43 25 18 73.
– *Liliane François:* 15 Rue de Seine, 75006. (Metro: Odéon.) Tel: 43 26 94 32.
– *Furstemberg:* 8 Rue Jacob, 75006. (Metro: St. Germain des-Prés.) Tel: 43 25 89 58.
– *Proscenium:* 35 Rue de Seine, 75006. (Metro: Odéon.) Tel: 43 54 92 01. A gallery exclusively devoted to the art of the stage (costumes and decor).

studies with bathroom, which can accommodate up to 3 people.

Youth hostels: *U.C.R.I.F.* 20 Rue J-J-Rousseau, 75001. (Metro: Halles.) Tel: 42 36 88 18. *A.J.F.*, 12 Rue des Barres, 75004. (Metro: Hôtel-de-Ville.) Tel: 42 72 72 09.

Camping: ***West Paris, Bois de Boulogne, Rte du Bord-de-l'Eau (500 sites), tel: 45 06 14 98; Paris Issy-les-Moulineaux (48 sites), tel: 46 38 07 66. ***Le Tremblay-Champigny-sur-Marne (330 places N4, A4), tel: 42 83 38 24.

Of particular interest ... on your walks

Paris is full of shops, cafés and restaurants that give special character to its streets and markets. To highlight their artistic and historical importance, a list was compiled by the Ministry of Culture in 1983 and 1984. Below is a selection of them, ranging from the 1st to the 18th arrondissements; you may discover many more as you wander around. For the full list, consult the Paris Tourist Office.

1st arrondissement: *3 Rue Étienne-Marcel* (interior); *15 Rue Montmartre* (café/bar); *9 Rue Pierre-Lescot* (sign and shop window); *33 Rue du Pont-Neuf* ("Au chien qui fume") restaurant; *91 Rue Saint-Denis* (café/bar); *127 Rue Saint-Denis* ("Au beau cygne") 19th-century sign); *93 Rue Saint Honoré* (pharmacy); *95 Rue Saint-Honoré* (grocer's shop window).

2nd arrondissement: *51 Rue Montorgueil* (pastry shop); *6 Rue des Petits-Carreaux* (pork butcher); *143 Rue Saint-Denis* (café/bar).

3rd arrondissement: *29 Rue de Poitou* (bakery); *147 Rue Saint-Martin* (café/bar) and *n° 180* (pastry shop).

4th arrondissement: *37 Rue des Blancs-Manteaux* (bakery); *24 Rue Chanoinesse* (public house); *23 Rue des Francs-Bourgeois* (bakery) and *n° 29; 4 Rue Mahler* (butcher) and *n° 13* (bakery); *63 Rue Rambuteau* (milk and cheese shop).

5th arrondissement: *16 Rue des Fossés Saint-Jacques* (bakery) and *n° 18* (butcher); *9 Quai de Montebello* ("La bouteille d'or") restaurant; *6 Rue Mouffetard* (butcher's shop); *200 Rue Saint-Jacques* (pork butcher's) and *n° 202* (milk and cheese shop).

6th arrondissement: *38 Rue Bonaparte* and *n° 70* (milk and cheese shop); *1 Rue Guisarde; 13 Rue du Cherche-Midi* (shop selling wooden chests); *26 Rue de Seine* ("Au Petit Maure") and *n° 43* (café "La Palette"; don't miss the second room here).

7th arrondissement: *69 Rue du Bac* (butcher's shop); *41 Av. de La Bourdonnais* (milk and cheese shop); *13 Rue de Lille* (shop window); *64 Rue Saint-Dominique* (bakery); *n°s 93* (watchmaker's sign) and *112* (bakery).

8th arrondissement: *55 Bd. Haussmann* ("Aux Tortues") shop selling ivory and semi-precious stones.

9th arrondissement: *28 Rue du Faubourg-Montmartre* (fishmonger) and *n° 35* ("À la mère de Famille") sweet shop; *18 Rue Vignon* (Tanrade's confectionery) and *n° 24* (honey shop).

10th arrondissement: *19 Rue J.-Poulmarch* (public house); *24 rue des Messageries* (public house).

11th arrondissement: *75 Rue Amelot* (pork butchers); *28 Bd Beaumarchais* (bakery); *1 Rue Jules-Vallès* ("Chardenoux") restaurant; *153 Rue de la Roquette* (bakery).

12th arrondissement: *19 Rue Montgallet* (bakery).

14th arrondissement: *10 bis Rue Roger* (bookshop).

15th arrondissement: *108 Rue Blomet* (bakery); *10 Rue Lecourbe* (milk and cheese shop); *3 Bd. de Grenelle* (interior café/bar).

16th arrondissement: *5 Rue Mesnil* (café/bar); *25 Rue de la Pompe* (florist) and *69* (milk and cheese shop).

18th arrondissement: *48 Rue Caulaincourt* (bakery); *128 Rue Lamarck* (bakery); *22 Bd. de Clichy* (café/bar).

Chronology of historical events

52 BC — c.AD 486 Paris is conquered by the *Romans*, who name the city *Lutetia*. In *AD 250 St Denis* introduces Christianity and is martyred subsequently. Roman rule comes to an end by the close of the 4th century AD.

451 *St Geneviève* helps Paris to repel Attila's Huns and becomes Paris' patron saint.

508 *King Clovis*, first Christian king of the Franks, makes Paris the capital of his realm.

629 — 887 *Dagobert* crowned king. A tumultous period in Parisian history follows, due to repeated clashes with the Normans. In 885 — 6, following a siege of the city, the Normans are defeated by *Eudes*, crowned king in 887.

987 *Hugues Capet* crowned king at Senlis. His descendants, known as the *Capetian kings*, reign until 1328. Their domain includes Paris and a small surrounding area.

996 — 1108 Reign of the Capetian kings: *Robert the Pious*, *Henri I* and *Philippe I*.

1108 — 1137 Reign of *Louis VI*.

1137 — 1179 Reign of *Louis VII*, first husband of *Eleanor of Aquitaine*. (She later marries Henry II of England who rules Aquitaine and north-west France — an area far larger than that of the French king.)

1179 — 1223 Reign of *Philippe-Auguste*. *He builds the city walls between 1150 — 1210 and recognizes the University of Paris*.

1123 — 1285 Reigns of *Louis VIII*, *Louis IX* (St Louis) and *Philippe III*. Notre-Dame and the Sainte-Chapelle are erected.

1285 — 1314 Reign of *Philippe the Fair*. A ruthlessly cruel king — the notorious Conciergerie prison is built during his reign.

1314 — 1328 *Louis X*, *Philippe V* and *Charles IV*, last of the Capetian kings.

1328 — 1350 *Philippe VI*, first of the *Valois kings*. His reign marks a chaotic period in French history, notably the *Hundred Years War* with England, a struggle for hegemony over France.

1350 — 1364 Reign of *Jean II*. Uprising in Paris in 1358 led by Etienne Marcel.

1364 — 1380 Order is restored by new king *Charles V*. Bastille is constructed.

1380 — 1422 Reign of *Charles VII*. *Joan of Arc* relieves Orleans of English forces in 1429 but Paris remains under English rule — *Henry VI* of England crowned king of France in Notre-Dame in 1431. However the French expel the English from all of France, except Calais, by 1453.

1422 — 1461 *Louis XI*. A period of prosperity and peace for France, continued under the reigns of *Charles VIII* and *Louis XII*.

1515 — 1547 Reign of *François I*, patron of the arts and humanities. Foundation of the Collège de France and the Jesuit Order in Paris in 1534. In 1546 construction of the Louvre begins; completed in 1559.

1547 — 1559 François' successor, *Henri II*, husband of *Catherine de Médicis*, killed in a jousting match.

1559 — 1589 Reigns of the three sons of Catherine de Médecis and Henri II: *François II*; *Charles IV* and *Henri III*. Period of civil war in France between Catholics and Protestants. The *St Bartholomew's Day* massacre, ordered by the Catholic League in 1572, leaves thousands of Protestants dead. Henri III forced to flee Paris by the Catholic League and assassinated while laying siege to the city in 1589.

1589 — 1610 The Protestant Henri of Navarre recaptures Paris, accepts conversion and is crowned King *Henri IV* in Notre-Dame in 1589. A very popular king, nicknamed "Le Vert Galant"; murdered in 1610 by a fanatic.

1610 — 1643 Reign of *Louis XIII*. Beginning of the period known as "*Le Grand Siècle*". The arts flourish: Queen Marie de Médicis builds Luxembourg Palace, powerful Cardinal Richelieu establishes the Academie Française and constructs the Palais-Royal.

1643 — 1661 On the death of Louis XIII, Cardinal Mazarin and the heir's mother, the unpopular Queen Anne of Austria, rule as Regents; both are forced to flee the capital in 1648 when the *Fronde* rebellion of nobleman breaks out.

1661 — 1715 Reign of *Louis XIV*, the Sun King, and height of French prestige. Palace of Versailles built, together with Les Invalides, Gobelins and the Louvre colonnade.

1715 — 1774 *Louis XV's* reign enriches Paris with the Pantheon, the Palais-Bourbon and the Place de la Concorde. The unpopular 'Octroi' tollgates are also built, to tax goods entering Paris.

1774 — 1793 *Louis XVI*. Discontent, brewing since the reign of Louis XV, erupts in the *Revolution* of 1789. July 1789 sees the *storming of the Bastille* and August the *Declaration of the Rights of Men*. The King is forcibly brought to Paris from Versailles by the Parisian mob. In 1793, Louis XVI is executed, together with Queen *Marie-Antoinette* and the "*Ancien Régime*" ended.

1793 — 1795 The *Convention*, elected by universal male suffrage, declares France a republic. The early years of the *First Republic* are dominated by extremist leaders and the period under *Robespierre* is known as "*The reign of terror*". During this time over 16,000 people are executed. *Robespierre* himself follows his victims to the guillotine in 1794.

1795 — 1799 During this time France is governed by a committee of Convention members known as the *Directory*. This system is overturned when Napoleon Bonaparte declares himself first "Consul" and then Emperor of France.

1804 — 1815 Napoleon is crowned Emperor in Notre-Dame. He introduces the Civil Code in 1804, the Code still forms the basis of French law today. The power and prestige of France is unparalleled until Napoleon's defeat by the English and Prussian allies at *Waterloo* in 1815.

1815 — 1848 After Napoleon's defeat and banishment to St. Helena, the Bourbon *Louis XVIII* is crowned king. He is succeeded by *Charles X*, ousted by *Louis-Philippe* from the Orleans faction after the July Revolution. There follows a period of modernization for Paris: the first French railway line is opened, running between Paris and Saint-Germain-en-Laye, as well as the new canals of Ourcq, Saint-Denis and Saint-Martin.

1848 — 1870 The workers' Revolution of 1848 declares the short-lived *Second Republic* and Louis-Philippe, last of the Bourbon kings is ousted in the wave of revolutions sweeping Europe. He is succeeded by Napoleon's nephew, *Louis-Napoleon* in 1851, who dissolves the Second Republic and founds the *Second Empire*. *Napoleon III* is crowned in 1852. The next twenty years is a time of prosperity for Paris and development for Paris. *Baron Haussmann* carries out huge changes in the city: the Opera and Les Halles are built and the Grands Boulevards created. The *Franco-Prussian War* and subsequent defeat and hardship provoke a further rebellion in the capital in 1870: the *Paris Commune*.

1870 — 1945 Napoleon III flees to England; his successors crush the Parisian rebellion and established the *Third Republic*. The Third Republic spans the early years of the 20th century, known as "La Belle Epoque". Paris becomes the show piece of Europe: in 1889, the Eiffel Tower is erected and numerous "Universal Exhibitions" are held in the capital. The Third Republic was to survive *World War I* and German occupation of 1914 — 1918. With the occupation under Nazi forces in *World War II* the Fourth Republic is dissolved and *Marshall Pétain* declared head of state.

1946 — 1986 *General de Gaulle*, head of the French Resistance, takes control of post-war France but relinquishes power to the Fourth Republic in 1946.

1954 — 1962 The *Algerian War of Independence* nearly causes civil war in France. In 1959, De Gaulle is reinstated as President and the *Fifth Republic* is founded.

1968 Widespread strikes and student demonstrations lead to the resignation of De Gaulle and the election of Georges Pompidou as President.

1974 Valéry Giscard d'Estaing is elected President.

1981 François Mitterand is elected President.

HISTORY OF PARIS

Paris grew up at the point where a number of rivers, including the Marne, pour into the river Seine. Its location has made it a major crossroads on the north-south and east-west trade route since ancient times. The Seine was most easily forded at the Ile de la Cité, and Paris developed on this natural island stronghold.

The site's commercial and strategic advantages, added to the fertile soil of the region and its mineral resources (stone and gypsum), were perhaps not lost on a Celtic tribe, the **Parisii**. This tribe settled in the region, probably in the mid-3rd century BC, at what was then called **Lutetia**. The Parisii were both prosperous and adaptable; they sent a contingent of 8000 men to help the Gaul, Vercingetorix, repulse the Romans, but soon came to terms with the Roman conquerors. Lutetia was split into two cities — Gallic on the Ile de la Cité and Roman on the Left Bank, where villas, arenas, baths and a forum were built.

52 BC

This era of peace and prosperity was shattered by the barbarian invasions of the mid-3rd century; the 10,000 inhabitants of Lutetia sought refuge on the Ile de la Cité and barricaded themselves behind its strong ramparts.

St Denis, first bishop of Paris, who was to become patron saint of France, was sent to convert Gaul at the time of the Emperor Decius. His martyrdom at the village of Catulliacus, the modern Saint-Denis, marked the advent of Christianity in France. A milestone, dated 307, bears the name "civitas Parisiorum" (city of the Parisii) and may be considered authentic proof of the birth of the city. As a portent of its future glory, Julian the Apostate was proclaimed Emperor in the old palace of the Cité in 360. For a short period, the Cité became the capital of what remained of the Roman Empire and the Emperor rejoiced over this "town blessed by God" and the limpid waters of the Seine.

250

360

The Paris water supply

Until the Roman conquest, **water drawn from the Seine** was sufficient for the Cité; but it was not enough for the new districts of the Left Bank and an aqueduct crossing the Bièvre Valley at Arcueil had to be built to bring water from Rungis to Cluny. To meet the Right Bank's increasing needs, two more aqueducts were later built, while the Left Bank continued to rely on the wells of the Montagne Sainte-Geneviève. By that time, the Seine had already become so polluted that it was forbidden to sweep the streets in the rain to avoid soiling it any further.

A radical improvement in the water supply was the construction, in 1605 during the reign of Henri IV, of a pump known as **La Samaritaine** (the Samaritan), at the Pont Neuf. A similar installation was set up at the Pont Notre-Dame in 1673.

Marie de Médicis' renovation of the old Roman aqueduct (principally to water the Luxembourg Gardens) might have improved the city's water supply had the privileged classes not diverted it to their own mansions via private culverts. At the time of the Revolution in 1789, Parisians were limited to an average of one litre (less than two pints) of water per day. At the beginning of the 19th century, when **Napoleon** asked what would be the best gift he could make to the Parisians, the prefect, Chaptal, replied: "Give them water, sire". The Emperor ordered the digging of the Ourcq canal, which provided an abundant supply to the Right Bank; he also laid the basis for a modern network of water supply and drainage which

A gargoyle of Notre-Dame Cathedral.

began to function after the restoration of Louis XVIII in 1814. Paris had to wait another century before every building had running water. Even today, turn-of-the-century hotels display the traditional notice: "water and gas on every floor".

The night of the barbarians

During the fifth century, repeated barbarian invasions swept across the ruins of the Roman Empire. At that time, Paris was confined to the walls of the fortress of the "Cité". Two names are remembered from this period: **Bishop St Marcel,** and **St Geneviève** who, in 451, rallied the population to resist Attila's Huns and thus prevented the pillage of the town. Roman domination was clearly at an end.

451

In 508, **Clovis,** the first Christian king of the Franks, decided to make Paris the seat of his realm, and the early Merovingian kings followed his example, embellishing the town with a number of churches. In the 7th century, **King Dagobert** decreed that he be buried in the basilica built over the tomb of St Denis, thus inaugurating a tradition that was followed by the kings of France for 12 centuries.

508

The prosperity of Paris was short-lived since **Charlemagne** chose Rome and Aix-la-Chapelle (Aachen) as the capitals of his empire. The town was attacked by the Normans in 845, 846 and 861. In 885, the fierce resistance put up by Eudes, the Count of Paris, won for him the elected title of King of France. The Roman town on the Left Bank was, however, laid waste by the Normans and, for over a century, Paris was again confined to the "Cité".

800

The kings of Paris

The first of the Capetian kings, **Hugues Capet,** spent much of his time in Paris, but Orleans, Laon and Sens were more prosperous centers. An embryonic administration came into being. The Seine's natural ports made Paris a city of tradesmen and merchants who expanded their business to the Right Bank. The **boatmen** of the Seine were organized into a powerful corporation and they gave the town its coat of arms: a ship with a silver sail and the motto *Fluctuat nec mergitur* ("it rocks but does not sink").

987

Around 1137, Louis IV built **Les Halles,** the city's central market area, on the site known as "des Champeaux" (meadows), and there they remained for eight centuries. The expansion of trade was coupled with an intellectual and architectural renaissance: **Abbot Suger** had the basilica of Saint-Denis rebuilt, **Maurice de Sully** began the construction of Notre-Dame Cathedral, and Abélard drew crowds of pupils to the episcopal school in the church of Notre-Dame.

1137

Philippe-Auguste was the first truly Parisian king. He built the stout rampart that bears his name between 1180 and 1210, considerably strengthening the city's perimeter defenses. Philippe-Auguste also laid the foundations of the first good roads, paved some streets, erected the keep of the Louvre, gave the University an official charter and bestowed various privileges on it. In addition, he took the municipal administration in hand; during his reign, market regulations were drawn up for the first time and burghers and merchants became seriously involved with the running of the city.

1179

Paris, the capital

Gradually, between the 12th and 13th centuries, Paris came to be recognized as the capital of France. In the achievement of this status, the reputation of its university, the beauty of its churches and the prestige of Louis IX (St Louis) were important factors. Notre-Dame was completed, and the **Sainte-Chapelle** erected by Pierre de Montreuil. The nobility built luxurious mansions, and St Louis extended his Palais de la Cité. The Quinze-Vingt hospital was founded in 1254, and the **Sorbonne** in 1257. For the first time, contemporary writers mention Paris as the most beautiful town they had ever known. Houses were built outside Philippe-Auguste's rampart and began to cluster on all the bridges, obscuring the river that flowed below.

1254

During the reign of **Philippe le Bel** ("the Fair"), the population of Paris probably exceeded 20,000, four-fifths of whom lived on the Right Bank. This increase in population stimulated commercial, financial and intellectual activity and also gave the city a new political consciousness; the Hundred Years' War saw the first Parisian revolution when **Étienne Marcel** forced Charles V to flee the capital.

1358

However, in other respects the war was a disaster. Despite the rampart built by Charles V, English troops entered Paris, and Joan of Arc failed to take it back. Henry VI of England was crowned King of France in Notre-Dame in 1431. The devastation suffered by the city — burned-out houses, trees felled to provide fuel for the English occupants and a population reduced to abject poverty — compelled Charles VII, when the French reoccupied Paris, to abandon it for his magnificent Loire Valley residences.

1436

The rebirth of Paris

Louis XI (1423–1483) patiently and resolutely rebuilt Paris after his succession in 1461. **François I,** who came to the throne in 1515, resumed work on the Louvre and laid the first stone of the Hôtel-de-Ville. His generosity to poets and humanists was much praised by the 16th-century poet, Ronsard.

In 1530, François I founded the Collège de France and four years later, Ignatius Loyola established the Jesuit Order. These two events illustrate the dual role of Paris; it had become the intellectual and religious capital of the **Counter-Reformation.** By the end of the century, the people of Paris were in violent opposition to the Protestant ideas favored by the humanists and aristocrats. The St Bartholomew's Day massacre of thousands of Protestants in Paris was the climax of a bloody struggle that seemed about to end with victory for the Catholic League. The Catholic triumph, however, was short-lived; the Protestant, Henri de Navarre, laid siege to Paris but finally negotiated a peaceful takeover of the capital and became king, in return for agreeing to convert to Catholicism. He was crowned **Henri IV** at Notre-Dame in 1594.

1530

1572

1594

The king, ably assisted by his minister, Maximilien Sully, and by the Provost of merchants, François Miron, took upon himself the role of

town planner. He extended the Louvre and the Tuileries, improved the
Place des Vosges and Place Dauphine, undertook the redevelopment of
1610 the Marais and Saint-Germain districts as well as the Ile de la Cité, and
inaugurated the Pont Neuf. Henri IV's assassination put an end to his
projects, but many of them were continued by others under his son
Louis XIII (1601–1643), most notably by the engineer Christophe Marie
who developed the Ile Saint-Louis from two marshy islands upstream of
the Ile de la Cité in the middle of the Seine.

Louis XIII's great minister **Cardinal Richelieu** (1585–1642)
pushed Charles V's rampart far to the north on the Right Bank. Land
speculators developed new districts around the Cardinal's palace and in
the Marais. Meanwhile, religious communities multiplied on the Left
Bank; between 1600 and 1640, about 60 **convents** opened, mainly in the
vicinity of Val-de-Grâce, their domes rising high into the Paris sky.

Traffic in Paris

In the Middle Ages, the free movement of pedestrians and
horsemen was regarded as a potential menace to law and order in
that it allowed criminals to escape the city without difficulty and
agitators to stir up trouble. Consequently, until the end of the 18th
century, streets could be hastily sealed off with heavy **chains**
stretched between hooks embedded in the walls of the houses; a few
of these hooks still remain in the Montagne Sainte-Geneviève area.
The keys to the padlocks were entrusted to neighboring shopkeepers. In times of trouble, the chains were rolled out to hamper the
passage of the populace. Efforts to dispense with these impediments
were made under Charles VI (1368–1422) during the upheavals
following the killing of Louis d'Orléans by his cousin Jean sans Peur
("the Fearless") in 1407. Not only were the chains reinstalled but
600 more were added in ten days; the locksmiths of Paris were forced
to work overtime. Films set in the period tend to show Paris streets
jammed with horses and carriages. The reality was quite different;
the majority went on foot and wealthy burghers rode mules rather
than horses. As to **carriages,** in 1550 there were only three in the
whole of Paris, and even these were too many for the pedestrians
who petitioned the king to prohibit them. Only in the 17th century
did the means of transport diversify; sedan chairs appeared in 1620,
the hackney carriage in 1640, the omnibus in 1662 and the
two-wheeled sedan in 1669. The speedy one-horse cabriolet became
the terror of Paris streets at the beginning of the 18th century.

Classical Paris

1643 On the death of **Louis XIII,** the former king's most powerful general,
Prince Condé, led an uprising which was known as **La Fronde.** Thus
commenced a grim period during which the Regent Cardinal Mazarin,
the heir's mother, Queen Anne of Austria, and the young Louis XIV
were forced to flee Paris. Understandably, the **Sun King** was ever
afterwards highly suspicious of Paris. He left the administration of the
capital to his able and trusted minister Colbert and concentrated his
creative genius on the Palace of Versailles. However, Paris was far from
neglected during the reign of Louis XIV. We owe the Louvre

colonnade, Les Invalides, Les Gobelins, the Observatory, La Salpêtrière, l'hospice des Enfants Trouvés (orphanage) and the Paupers' hospital to the Sun King, fine statues of whom were erected in the Place Vendôme and the Place des Victoires. Even more than this artistic flowering, the people of Paris appreciated the re-establishment of street lighting and the various effective measures taken against beggars, thieves and other criminal elements.

Despite the transfer of the Court and government to Versailles, Paris maintained its intellectual supremacy. Under **Louis XV,** whose reign lasted from 1715 to 1774, the arts prospered as never before. Philosophers, artists and encyclopaedists gathered in the **salons** of the Faubourg Saint-Honoré, and the Marais was extended to the west, the population of the city having grown to 650,000. The École de Médecine, the Church of Sainte-Geneviève, later to become the Panthéon, and the foundation of the Church of Saint-Sulpice all date from this time. In addition, a broad esplanade facing the river was built by the architect Gabriel for state celebrations. This esplanade was named Place Louis XV and is now known as Place de la Concorde.

1715

Domestic **comforts** increased. Rooms became smaller and easier to heat, small apartments made their appearance, and toilets and bathrooms were occasionally installed.

Louis XVI, beheaded in 1791 during the Revolution, seems to have been luckless even in his architecture. Built during his reign, the hated **Fermiers-Généraux wall,** a perimeter wall at which a toll was levied on goods entering or leaving the city, caused much resentment. Nonetheless, Louis did attempt to modernize the city; a market replaced the pestilential Cimetière des Innocents and the Concorde and Neuilly bridges were completed. The style of Louis XVI's new public buildings — the Mint, the Théâtre Français and the Palais de Justice — was admirably sober and dignified.

A crucial municipal regulation passed at this time related the height of buildings to the width of the streets in which they were situated.

Street lighting in Paris

Paris is proud to be known as the "City of Light", but the title is a recent one. For centuries, the streets were dark and dangerous. In the 13th century, under Philippe le Bel, only three lamps burned all night: at the Cimetière des Innocents, the Nesle Tower, and the Grand Châtelet. Although the law required one candle to burn until daylight at the window of every house as a precaution against "the wicked youths who roam the streets at night", this measure was not enforced until the end of the 17th century. In 1662, mobile street lighting was introduced by **Abbot Caraffe** in the form of torch bearers stationed at crossroads to see home the burghers of Paris. These men were paid three *sols* (a few centimes) an hour and were equipped with hourglasses to determine the length of time they spent accompanying their clients. In 1667, **Gabriel Nicolas de la Reynie,** chief of the Paris police, distributed 6000 lanterns to be kept lit on window sills. Three years later, these lanterns were strung out over the streets on ropes and pulleys. The oil lamps which had existed since 1745 were tested for the first time in Rue Dauphine in 1763; a few years later they were to be found at 200 ft/60 metre intervals hanging over all the streets of Paris. There they remained, despite Lebon's invention of gas lighting in 1791, until 1829 when gas lighting became widespread.

Revolution in the city ...

1789

Paris dominated the Revolution. It was as if the city's unanimity against the King was its way of reasserting its role as the undisputed capital of France. The spirit of revolt was widespread; the Bastille was stormed by a united confederacy of all the capital's social classes. After the fall of the Bastille, Bailly (an astronomer and member of the Académie des Sciences) was made mayor, and the King was brought back from Versailles to be imprisoned in the Tuileries.

Later, the Jacobin and Cordelier factions in Paris executed the dictates of Robespierre and, as delegates of the Paris regime, their power in the provinces was absolute.

The **Thermidor revolution** (1794) brought down Robespierre and ended Paris' stranglehold on the rest of France. As for the city itself, it emerged from this upheaval with its monuments and mansions damaged and a large number of religious establishments razed to the ground. Under the Directory government of 1795–1799, projects such as the Odéon district and the Chausée d'Antin were completed.

Napoleon's triumphal return from Egypt in 1799 brought with it a wave of fascination for all things Egyptian. Paris became the capital of

The different enclosures of Paris since the Gallo-Roman era.

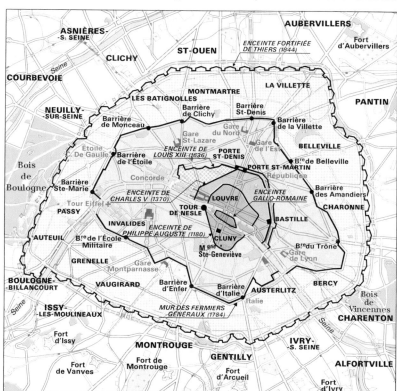

1:125.000

Napoleon's empire, and treasures from all over Europe flowed into the city, under the close scrutiny of Fouché, Minister of Police. Napoleon's organizational genius was soon applied to the capital; Paris was dotted with Roman-style monuments — triumphal arches at Carrousel and Étoile, the Stock Exchange (Bourse) and La Madeleine. These were less important, however, than his regulations on road building and urban development. He improved the water supply by the excavation of the Ourcq canal, constructed a sewage system, introduced street numbering, set up cemeteries on the outskirts of the city, and was responsible for the construction of the first major urban arterial road in Paris, the Rue de Rivoli.

1804

Under the Restoration, private initiative took over the development of the **new districts,** covered shopping arcades and places of entertainment. The political establishment was still largely indifferent to the poverty and suffering of the poor who lived in the crowded central districts. Their condition was described by the contemporary writers Eugène Sue and Victor Hugo. In 1832, of a population of 700,000 in Paris, 44,000 died of cholera as living conditions deteriorated. The **industrial revolution** created a new bourgeoisie and ruined the small independent artisans who subsequently became a driving force in the **riots** that erupted in the reign of Louis-Philippe (1830–1848).

1815

1830

Saint-Lazare railway station, the city's first, was opened in 1837. Queen Marie-Amélie consented to travel on the inaugural Paris–Saint-Germain-en-Laye train, but not so King Louis-Philippe who preferred to put safety first.

... the city in revolution

The revolutions of 1789 and 1848 did not lead to drastic changes in Paris. Rather, it was **Napoleon III** who, between 1852 and 1870, transformed the capital from the mediaeval to the industrial age, uprooting in the process thousands of Parisians.

1852

The architect of this change was Baron Haussmann who, in the course of two decades, altered the face of the city beyond recognition. Entire districts were demolished to execute his vast programme; steel was used for the building of railway stations and for the central food market, Les Halles. On the new wide boulevards, luxurious stone apartments were built where the wealthy came to live (and still do). Alphand landscaped parks in the woods of Vincennes and Boulogne and scattered squares and stretches of greenery all over the city. Belgrand improved the water supply and trebled the capacity of the sewage system. In 1860, **Paris annexed the parishes** that lay within the outer fortifications: Auteuil, Vaugirard, Grenelle, Montmartre, La Chapelle, Belleville, Charonne and Bercy were all swallowed up by a city that had doubled its population in 20 years.

Paris had never known such brilliance and splendor as it did on the eve of the disastrous war with Prussia in 1870. Its exhibitions, great restaurants and social life were incomparable. The cognoscenti who flocked there from all over the world left fortunes at the feet of its demi-mondaines and paid court to its ladies of fashion. Trade and credit expanded and department stores developed. Paris became "Gay Paree", the capital of pleasure and entertainment, an image which has endured.

The prisons of Paris

The fortress of **Grand Châtelet**, of which the Conciergerie was an annex, was the main prison in pre-revolutionary France and the seat of the provosts who dispensed justice in Paris. The fortress was demolished in 1802, and the site is known today as the Place du Châtelet. Within the 9th-century walls of the Grand Châtelet, the inmates were distributed on the various floors according to their resources; at the top of the keep were the "gold rooms" for prisoners who could pay for their room and board; the floor below for those who could only afford the straw on which they slept (these dungeons went under such hair-raising names as "Barbary", "End of Ease" and "The Ditch"); lowest of all was the gruesome "Oubliette", prisoners being lowered into it with ropes and pulleys. The poets François Villon and Clément Marot swore that their terms there were worse than hell. The Petit Châtelet, an extension of the prison, was so badly ventilated that prisoners frequently died within a few days in the underground dungeons. The other prisons were no better. The dungeons in the Abbé prison on the Quai de la Mégisserie were below the level of the Seine, the waters of which seeped through the walls periodically, drowning the occupants when the river flooded. Measures taken against beggars and vagrants by Louis XIV so multiplied the number of inmates that the Hôpital Général was established to absorb the overflow. Prostitutes, female prisoners, and women who had been declared insane, were kept in the Salpêtrière almshouse, and male offenders at Bicêtre.

Modern times

1871
In the winter of 1870–1871, after four months of seige by the Prussian armies, Paris surrendered, yielding at last to the severe cold and the prospect of impending famine. The population saw the capitulation as a betrayal by the government, and out of this sense of outrage, the **Paris Commune** arose. La "semaine sanglante", or **bloody week,** saw the burning of the Tuileries, the Hôtel-de-Ville and many great private mansions. Troops loyal to the Republic advanced from Versailles and methodically recovered Paris, barricade by barricade. In the ruthless repression that followed, thousands were massacred. In commemoration of this episode, the government erected a monument, the basilica of Sacré-Coeur on the heights of Montmartre.

1889
The Universal Exhibition of 1889 was marked by the building of the **Eiffel Tower,** while the Grand and Petit Palais as well as the Pont Alexandre III were constructed for the 1900 Exhibition. The **Metro** was inaugurated at the same time, the work of engineer Bienvenüe; the famous Art Nouveau entrances were designed by Guimard.

By the turn of the century, Paris was the undisputed **art center of the world.** Picasso and Braque originated Cubism in about 1907; this was succeeded by Dada, Surrealism, Expressionism and Abstract art. Paris celebrated the end of World War I — "les années folles" — to the exotic rhythms of jazz. A subsidized housing scheme was introduced, streets had electric lighting for the first time, and advertizing appeared on the walls. The modern age had dawned in Paris.

The Great Depression of the thirties began a decade of crisis which the left-wing Popular Front Government could do little to alleviate. The

German occupation in June 1940 imposed a new discipline on the capital, characterized by a curfew, ration tickets and the sound of wooden clogs. After four years of occupation, General Leclerc's tanks entered Paris in August 1944, and Charles de Gaulle rode in triumph down the Champs-Élysées. A long and difficult process of modernization was about to begin.

Paris today

The most significant phenomenon in post-1945 France has been the gravitational pull of the capital. About 10,000,000 people, or one-fifth of the country's total population, now live in Paris (although the population of central Paris has fallen slightly in the past decade). In the 50s and 60s, the expansion of public facilities was the principal concern. The opening of the river port of Gennevilliers in 1950, and the removal of the Les Halles market to Rungis in 1969 facilitated the city's provisioning. Increased housing was provided by the large-scale building of low-priced subsidized flats and the growth of the suburbs. Transportation was improved by the construction of the outer ring road (*boulevard périphérique*), the modernization of the Metro and bus services, the extension of the suburban railways and the opening of the R.E.R. (regional express network). Cultural facilities were broadened in scope by the building of the CNIT exhibition center at La Défense, the Maison de la Radio and the UNESCO headquarters.

1970

The exceptional growth and prosperity enjoyed under the Fifth Republic have enabled the Paris Municipality to undertake projects such as the huge new La Défense office district, the Montparnasse Tower, the 13 autonomous branches of the Université, the Palais des Congrès complex, the Pompidou Center and the Forum complex in the old Halles district ; these projects have transformed the skyline of Paris.

Paris developments

By the end of the 1980s, several districts of Paris will have been totally changed.
The La Villette Park and Museum, located on the 136-acre/55-hectare site of the former municipal slaughterhouse, will include a museum of Science and Technology and the National Music Conservatory.
The Bastille Opera, designed by Carlos Ott, is planned to open in 1989 in eastern Paris which, until now, has been sadly deficient in cultural facilities.
The district of La Défense will acquire a monumental cubic arch and buildings for the Ministries of Town Planning and Environment as well as an International Communication Center by 1988.
The long-postponed **Arab World Institute** was scheduled for completion in 1987 on the Quai Saint-Bernard, near the university branch at Jussieu. The project includes facades equipped with photocells that react to the prevailing light to produce different motifs of Islamic art.

L'ILE DE LA CITÉ

The island cradle of Paris, symbolized by the ship riding the Seine on the city's coat-of-arms (a reminder not only of the island but also of the main profession of its earliest inhabitants), was a bustling, overcrowded town in the Middle Ages. It possessed churches, a palace, a hospital, a school in the cloisters of Notre-Dame, and the cathedral itself, hemmed in by wood-paneled houses stretching down to the water's edge. Much of this has disappeared, and today Notre-Dame is fronted by a large square, popular with tourists of every age and nationality. In the background there are shops selling picture postcards and souvenirs, often hidden by the lines of tour buses. All this activity somewhat vitiates the beauty of the Square de l'Ile de France. A touch of severity is imparted by the nearby Palais de Justice (law courts) with the preoccupied lawyers and stony-faced guards.

Today's visitor will do well to follow the example of the pilgrims of the past by melting into the crowds in the nave of Notre-Dame and simply absorbing the atmosphere of the river and the quays. The sunset over the Pont des Arts, as seen from the little green park at the downstream end of the Ile de la Cité, Square du Vert-Galant, is unforgettably beautiful.

Notre-Dame

Metro: Cité ●●●
Bus: nᵒˢ 21, 24, 38, 47, 81, 85, 96 **Map 5, (C 2)**

The parvis (or square) of Notre-Dame is considered "kilomètre zéro", the point from which all distances in France are measured, a telling reminder of the cathedral's overwhelming importance in the history of the capital. More than the structure's much-praised harmony and balance of strength and finesse, it is the character of Notre-Dame that makes it unique; the poet and playwright Paul Claudel thought of it more as a person than a monument.

▬▬ HISTORY

The eastern point of the Ile de la Cité seems to have inspired piety down through the ages. The Gauls and the Romans built altars there to worship their gods. **A Christian basilica** replaced them in the 6th century. Destroyed by the Normans in 857, it was immediately rebuilt with embellishments. In the middle of the 12th century, the bishop of Paris, Maurice de Sully, following the example of Abbot Suger, who had a basilica built at Saint-Denis over the tombs of the kings of France, decided to give the capital a cathedral worthy of it. Work began in 1163 (the high altar was consecrated in 1196), when the old Romanesque style of religious architecture was giving way to the new Gothic. **Notre-Dame** is the last of the great galleried cathedrals like Saint-Denis, Noyon, Senlis and Laon, and the first to use flying buttresses; this innovation was later imitated by the cathedrals of Strasbourg, Rheims and Chartres.

The construction was a community effort. It was financed by the king, the clergy and nobles as well as by the city guilds and corporations, and the poorer people provided the labor under the supervision of the two master-builders, Jean de Chelles and Pierre de Montreuil. Progress was slow, the four stages taking almost a century. As early as 1260, the original plans were modified to allow more light into the nave through

The view of Notre-Dame from the Quai Montebello.

enlarged windows, and to add a screen in front of the choir and chapels to the side-aisles. Jean Ravy, in charge of the work from 1318 to 1344, completed the cathedral by raising the 50 feet/15 metre flying buttresses at the choir, a revolutionary solution at the time.

Centuries were to pass before this **Gothic masterpiece**, which served as an example of structures in the Ile-de-France and throughout Europe as far as Sweden, was altered. One of Louis XIII's lesser inspirations led architect Robert de Cotte, in the 14th century, to remodel the interior, replacing the altar and adding new bronze and marble embellishments. In order to allow free passage to the royal canopy during processions, Soufflot mutilated the central doorway by widening it; furthermore, the cathedral's canons themselves replaced the stained glass of the windows with plain glass. During the Revolution, there was further damage when the statues were prised from the doorways.

When Napoleon returned Notre-Dame to the Church in 1802, it was in such a sorry state that the organisers of his coronation — magnificently depicted in the painting by David (*see Louvre, p. 170*) — were obliged to hide the walls behind draperies and hangings. Victor Hugo led the outcry against this situation, and after the publication of his best-selling masterpiece, *Notre-Dame de Paris*, artists, politicians and men of letters petitioned Louis-Philippe for a complete restoration, which was eventually carried out by the architect Viollet-le-Duc. The changes he made were drastic, but he was able to retain the original Gothic elan although some details may be open to criticism.

The 19th-century historian Jules Michelet described Notre-Dame as **"the Parish of French History"**, and the cathedral's immense historical importance certainly reaches well beyond the capital. In 1430, Henry VI of England was crowned King of France at Notre-Dame; fifteen years later, Charles VII had a Te Deum sung there to celebrate the recovery of Paris; in 1594, Henri IV paid homage there as the price of his entry into the capital; the Te Deum for Louis XIV's marriage was heard in the cathedral, and the Maréchal de Luxembourg later hung flags on the walls captured from his enemies, earning himself the nickname of "the tapestry-hanger" of Notre-Dame. The great orator-priest Bossuet preached there, and it was at Notre-Dame that Napoleon was crowned Emperor in 1804. The marriage of Napoleon III followed in 1853; since then, the cathedral has been used for the state funerals of writers such as Barrès and Claudel, and the heroes of the two world wars, Marshals Foch and Leclerc. Charles de Gaulle's state funeral took place on November 12th, 1970. Pope John-Paul II said Mass at Notre-Dame in May 1980.

VISIT

The layout of Notre-Dame is starkly simple; a long nave leading to the choir, crossed by a wide transept and flanked on both sides by double aisles. Although it is by no means the largest or the tallest example of Gothic architecture, it is certainly the most harmonious. Notre-Dame measures 427 feet/130 metres in overall length, 115 feet/35 metres in width, and is 115 feet/35 metres high under the vaults. The towers are 226 feet/69 metres high. About 9000 people can gather in its 59,200 square feet/5500 square metres of floor space.

The main façade of Notre-Dame de Paris has always been considered a definitive masterpiece of French Gothic art. It is, in fact, the only French cathedral to possess perfect unity combined with a total clarity of composition. Three superimposed levels are capped by two quadrangular towers; the whole can be "read" like a book.

The first level contains the three great

entrances, surmounted by the Gallery of Kings. In the center is the **Portal of Judgement,** dominated by the huge statue of Christ teaching, surrounded by the twelve Apostles. The anonymous sculptor of this work could not have been lacking in humor — near St Matthew, one of the figures is parting his long hair, the better to hear the divine speech. The twelve Virtues are opposite the twelve Vices in bas-relief; on two side-posts the Wise and Foolish Virgins can be seen on either side of Christ. Overhead the Last Judgement is depicted; the dead are leaving their tombs to have their souls weighed by St Michael, while the elect are admitted to heaven and the damned are led away by demons; among the damned, the sculptor has included a bishop. The upper section of the tympanum depicts the Redemption.

On the left, what is known as **The Virgin's Entrance** is remarkable in its composition. Dating from the early 13th century, the three kings and the three prophets of the tympanum, along with the death and coronation of the Virgin, reveal a peerless perfection of style and execution. The bas-reliefs illustrating the monthly tasks of both rich and poor provide a real insight into the daily life of the time.

On the right, **Saint Anne's Entrance** consists in part of sculptures from the 11th-century church that preceded Notre-Dame.

The tympanum, near the Virgin and the angels, probably portrays Louis VII and Maurice de Sully in the guise of a king and a bishop.

The wrought-iron hinges (especially on the Saint-Anne Entrance) are masterpieces of mediaeval ironwork. Above the portals runs the Gallery of the Kings of Judea. Here, 28 statues were mistaken by the revolutionaries for those of the kings of France and destroyed in 1793. Replacements were made to Viollet-le-Duc's specifications. The heads of the original statues were found in 1975 and are now in the Cluny Museum (see p. 123).

The rose window, 31 feet 6 inches/9.6 metres in diameter, is the largest made in the 13th century. The exquisite quality of the light and the colors that radiate from the much-photographed window have inspired a multitude of imitations.

A fine openwork gallery runs between the twin towers, which were to have been capped by two spires, subsequently considered superfluous. Viollet-le-Duc filled the angles of the buttresses with a strange assortment of chimera and gargoyles. (*The towers can be climbed — 387 steps. Daily ex. Tue 9 am – 4 pm winter; 5 pm summer. Entry payable at foot of N tower. Rue du Cloître Notre-Dame.*) From the top, there is a superb view of the Cité, the Seine, the Montagne Sainte-Geneviève, the Panthéon to the south, and Montmartre to the north. In the south tower there is a huge wooden beam strong enough to support the great 16-ton/16,256-kg bell in full peal (electrically driven since 1953).

> "**F**rench architecture of the Middle Ages was a synthesis of the functional and the decorative. It is to be seen not only in the decorative roofing, pipes, windows, galleries, but even in the minor fittings such as iron work, drainage, supports, heating and ventilation. Nothing was concealed as is so often the case with post-16th century buildings; on the contrary, they are emphasized and, through the ingenious combinations and the impeccable taste that controls their execution, they contribute to the architectural richness. In a fine 13th-century building, however grand, no ornament is dispensable as each fulfils a need."
>
> **Viollet-le-Duc**

Notre-Dame's lateral facades and apse consist of three levels backing on to each other.

To the south, opening onto the Square Jean XXIII, **Saint Stephen's Entrance** was begun in 1257 by Jean de Chelles. (Latin inscription on the base). The tympanum depicts the life and martyrdom of St Stephen; under the modern statues of apostles can be found curious bas-relief scenes of student life (12th century).

To the north, is the **Cloister Entrance,** used by canons to reach the cloister; also built by Jean de Chelles around 1255, this doorway retains a pier with a fine statue of the Virgin Mary holding the Infant Jesus in both arms. The portal is crowned by a beautiful 43 feet/13 metre window.

Nearby, the small red door, built by Pierre de Montreuil and reserved for the canons' use, carries seven 14th-century bas-reliefs illustrating the life of the Virgin Mary. The **flying buttresses** constructed by Jean Ravy are among the most original and powerful features of the cathedral; they were built on a principle entirely new to the 14th century and provided a perfect crown for this stately edifice. (You should stand away from them to appreciate their uniqueness.) The weight of the vaults is so finely balanced, that they seem to dissolve into air and the whole cathedral appears weightless. Rising over the entire structure, the spire restored by Viollet-le-Duc is 295 feet/90 metres high.

Inside Notre-Dame, the stained glass and rose windows diffuse a celestial light; the windows of the nave were made in the 1960s according to mediaeval techniques, but the glass in the rose windows of the facade and the transept dates, at least in part, back to the 13th century.

Large religious paintings known as "mays" hang in the side-chapels. These were offered by the Corporation of Silversmiths every May 1st from 1630 to 1707. In the transept, two statues flank the entrance to the choir: St Denis by Nicolas Coustou (17th–18th century), and a 14th-century Virgin Mary.

The decoration of the **choir,** renovated according to Louis XIII's wishes, is exquisite, especially the woodwork in the stalls, which were carved in the early 18th century. Behind the high-altar, a fine statue of the Virgin by Coustou (1723) stands between the statues of Louis XIII and Louis XIV.

On either side of the choir are remnants of a previous enclosure, decorated with bas-reliefs by Jean Ravy (14th century). The apse chapels house the tombs of former archbishops or patrons of Notre-Dame.

The treasury (*open 9 am – 5 pm ex. Sun and national hols*) contains precious religious objects, ancient manuscripts, relics and the Palatine Cross, which is said to contain a fragment of the True Cross.

Music at Notre-Dame

For those interested in music, the Sunday afternoon organ concerts given at 5.30 pm are strongly recommended. You can hear the largest organ in Paris played in a unique and moving setting. This magnificent instrument, constructed by Clicquot in the 18th century and rebuilt about 100 years later by Cavaillé-Coll, is as suited to classical French music as it is to the romantic masters. Notre-Dame has always influenced French music through its great organists and chapel masters, such as Léonin and Pérotin le Grand, who founded the French polyphonic school in the late 15th and early 16th centuries. Some of the greatest French musicians such as Clérambault and Louis Vierne played at Notre-Dame, and, until his death in 1984, Pierre Cochereau regularly enraptured congregations with his improvisations.

Around Notre-Dame

Baron Haussmann's 19th-century urban projects changed Paris for better and for worse. Some feel, for example, that his extensive demolition of the mediaeval area facing Notre-Dame was a mistake, since the cathedral facade was intended to be viewed at close quarters, not from the other side of a broad square.

In the middle of this open space, a bronze slab, engraved with the coat-of-arms of the city, designates the starting point ("kilomètre zéro") of all French roads. On the Rue de la Cité side is the access to the **archaeological crypt** of Notre-Dame (*open daily 10 am – 5 pm*). An area of 263 feet/80 metres has been excavated, revealing remains of the ancient Cité buildings: Gallo-Roman chambers, foundations from the Roman ramparts, mediaeval cellars and the foundations of the 18th-century orphanage, the Hospice des Enfants Trouvés.

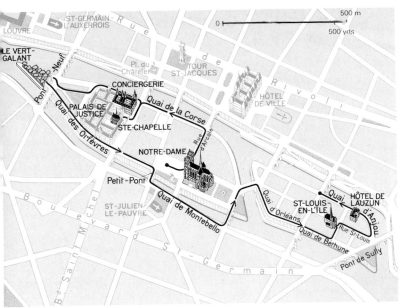

L'Ile de la Cité.

VISIT

The Hôtel-Dieu hospital stands on the north side of the parvis and the Rue d'Arcole runs along its flank as far as the quays. This massive building dates from the late 19th century; the original Hôtel-Dieu, founded in the Middle Ages following an epidemic in the Cité, was so overcrowded that each bed was said to contain "one sick, one dying and one dead"!

To the east of the Rue d'Arcole, the **Rue Chanoinesse** leads through the only part of the Cité to have survived Haussmann intact. The Rue de la Colombe has probably remained almost unchanged since the 13th and 14th centuries, evoking great names of the past who taught at the Notre-Dame School: Abélard, St Dominique, St Bonaventure. On the corner of the Rue des Ursins, at n° 19, are the remains of the **Saint-Aignan Chapel** that date from 1118, where St Bernard preached piety and morality to his students — in vain, it would seem, in view of the salacious reputation that the area was later to acquire.

In the flower market on the Place Lépine, the flimsy wooden stores that date back to 1808 (although recently renovated) offer splendid displays of cut flowers, plants and shrubs. On Sundays, this square is converted into a bird market. Access is by way of the Quai de Corse, which runs along the west side of the Hôtel-Dieu. The Quai aux Fleurs itself leads to the eastern extremity of the Cité, providing fine views of the Right Bank, the Hôtel-de-Ville and the Ile Saint-Louis on the way. Behind this stands the massive building of the Trade Court (1874).

At the back of Notre-Dame is the recently laid-out garden dedicated to Pope John XXIII. Until the 19th century, the area between the cathedral and the Seine was covered with houses.

The Ile-de-France square, however, facing east on the other side of the Quai de l'Archevêché, was a wasteland until a morgue was established there under the Second Empire, attracting the morbid interest of Parisians who flocked to hear the details of the latest hideous death or sensational crime. The memorial to the Martyrs of the Deportation (1940–1944), which stands at the tip of the Cité, on the Seine's edge, resembles a modern crypt. The memorial is decorated with sculptures and contains the tomb of the Unknown Deportee.

Le Palais de Justice
(Law Courts)

Map 5,   Metro: Cité, Châtelet, Saint-Michel   Bus: nᵒˢ 21, 24, 81, 85, 96
(C 1)

Between the Pont-au-Change and the Pont Saint-Michel is the labyrinth of the Palais de Justice. Miles of underground corridors link the cells with the judges' chambers, the "P.J" (crime squad) headquarters, lair of Simenon's Inspector Maigret, and to the courts themselves. In the history of the Palais de Justice, probably the most curious scenes took place during the Revolution, when the sinister old ladies known as "tricoteuses" or "the knitters" brought their knitting along to the trials where their cries of "to the guillotine!" sent shivers down the bravest spines. Most visitors will probably find the **Sainte-Chapelle** or the **Conciergerie** of greater interest, one for its deeply religious beauty, the other for its tragic history.

▬▬ *VISIT*

(Open daily 9 am – 6 pm ex. Sat, Sun. Free admittance to hearings.)

Access to the Palais is via the **Cour du Mai,** named after the May tree that the law students planted every May 1st. Behind handsome 18th-century iron gates, the courtyard leads to the sober buildings, rebuilt after a fire in 1755.

The wide Palais staircase leads to the merchants' gallery. To the right, after crossing the long prisoners' gallery, you come to the **Salle des Pas-Perdus** or waiting hall. This Gothic hall dates from the time of Philippe le Bel (1268–1314) and has been burned down several times and rebuilt. An amusing detail to look for on the monument erected to the memory of the 19th-century lawyer Berryer is the tortoise at the feet of the figure symbolizing the Law, a reminder of the slow but steady pace of justice. At the end of the hall, on the left, the **Première Chambre Civile,** or civil chamber, occupies what was once St Louis' apartment, with an elegant ceiling dating from the reign of Louis XII (1461–1483). To the left, a succession of galleries and spiral staircases leads to the Tour d'Argent ("silver tower"), which offers a superb view over the Seine. Visitors interested in legal matters can while away the hours in the Galerie des Bustes or admire the lush Second Empire decor of the Cour de Cassation (the Supreme Court of Appeal), visit the Vestibule de Harlay by way of the Galerie Lamoignon, or mingle with the crowds at the Assises. The 20 mi./30 kilometres of corridors that run beneath the Palais and through which prisoners are brought to trial are not open to the public.

●●● The Sainte-Chapelle

In the courtyard of the Palais de Justice stands the chapel of the Sainte-Chapelle, one of the purest works of high Gothic art. Such is the consonance of its lines, its light and its colors that it hardly seems to touch the ground. St Louis, its builder, wished to create a setting as precious as the relics it was to enclose; the result is a miracle wrought in stone and stained glass.

▬▬ *HISTORY*

St Louis (Louis IX, 1214–1270) was deeply religious and, throughout his life, he sought out and purchased the most venerated relics of Christianity, whatever the price. Thus, around 1230, when the Emperor of the East, John III, let it be known that he would be prepared to sell the True Crown of Thorns, then in his possession, in order to settle his debts, St Louis acquired it in spite of the stupendous asking price and the doubts about its authenticity. It was bought in 1239, and Pierre de Montreuil was charged to make the most splendid of **reliquaries.** The master builder and masons worked at great speed and, three years later, the **Sainte-Chapelle** stood in the royal courtyard, linked by a gallery to the king's apartments.

▬ VISIT

(Open 10 am – 5 pm, Oct – Mar, then 10 am – 6 pm. Access through door at left in Cour du Mai. Closed Jan 1st, May 1st, Nov 1st, 2nd, Dec 25th, tel: 43 54 30 09.)

The exterior of the Sainte-Chapelle reveals one of the simplest possible structures; groups of shafts support the vaults, themselves so light as to require only simple buttresses to balance their thrust; the 50-foot/15-metre high windows replace any form of wall between the pillars. The gracious spire, survivor of numerous fires, is 246 feet/75 metres high; in the distant past, the angel at the back of the roof rotated in order to display the Cross to every point on the compass.

The lower chapel, the vaults of which reach a height of only 23 feet/7 metres, was originally designed for the use of the Palace guards and servants. The rich decoration combines gold and cabochons (polished, unfaceted gems) with colored glass, and was further enriched during the 19th century. The floor is studded with the fine tombstones of generations of Sainte-Chapelle clergy. Note especially that of P. de Rully, dating from 1440.

The upper chapel, at the top of the spiral staircase, explodes with color. One of St Louis' contemporaries found it to be of such transcendent beauty that he felt on entering it "as if transported to heaven and ... introduced into one of the most beautiful chambers of paradise".

The chapel, with its ribbed and filleted vaults, is surrounded by a low wall decorated with arcatures; twelve apostles stand with their backs to the pillars. In the center of the apse, two small spiral staircases lead to the gallery which bore the shrine containing the relics. St Louis himself used to climb the left-hand staircase to open up the reliquary in front of his assistants and show them the Crown of Thorns. In the last row of the choir, to the right, a door leads to a private chapel built by Louis XI (1423–1483), from which the king was able to watch services through a latticed window without being seen himself. Even in his own chapel, Louis XI lived in constant fear of assassination.

The stained glass windows of the Sainte-Chapelle, the oldest in Paris, are also the finest existing examples of 13th-century stained glass. Of the 1134 scenes from religious history that are depicted, only 720 are original, but the 19th-century restoration work is so skilled as to be undetectable. In the pre-Gutenberg world, this glasswork served an educational and sermonic purpose; thus from one pane to another, from left to right and top to bottom, are shown scenes from the Bible rendered with naiveté, simplicity and freshness combined with a certain technical virtuosity. The congregation was captivated by the almost supernatural atmosphere which must have given the most hardened soul the impression of being already half-way to heaven.

Conciergerie ●●

From the Quai de la Mégisserie on the Right Bank, the Conciergerie, with its four massive towers and solid walls, gives the impression of an authentic mediaeval fortress. Certainly it is the oldest palace of the Capetian kings: the Bonbec tower (on the right) dates from the 11th century and the l'Horloge (Clock) tower from the 14th. The Conciergerie owes much of its forbidding aspect to the 19th-century renovators who embellished the time-worn walls with much Gothic detail. The clock of the Tour de l'Horloge has also been restored, but with far greater respect for authenticity; it is the oldest in Paris, dating from 1370.

▬▬ *HISTORY*

Built by Philippe le Bel, the **Conciergerie** consists of three Gothic halls which were soon transformed into a prison. The word "concierge" in those days did not mean a caretaker or doorkeeper, as now, but was the title of a much sought-after post in the king's entourage. Before the Revolution, the Conciergerie was reserved for those who had committed heinous crimes such as Ravaillac who stabbed Henri IV to death, the Marquise de Brinvilliers, an accomplished poisoner, and Cartouche, the celebrated brigand. During the Revolution, about 2600 prisoners spent their last days here on their way to the guillotines of Place de la Concorde or Place de la Nation. Marie-Antoinette was held at the Conciergerie from August 2nd to October 16th, 1793, the day of her execution, in a dungeon which she shared with her guards. Coincidence or poetic justice ensured that first Danton and then Robespierre were kept in the adjacent dungeon a few months later before following the queen to the scaffold.

Other well-known inmates of the prison, victims of the Terror and, later, of the month of Thermidor, were: Charlotte Corday who murdered Marat, the so-called "Friend of the People"; the scientist

Quai de l'Horloge, alongside the Conciergerie.

Lavoisier; the poet André Chénier; Prince Philippe d'Orléans, known as Philippe "Égalité" because of his belief in the new ideas, Fouquier Tinville, a former prosecutor; and finally the judges of the Revolutionary Tribunal themselves, who sat only a few yards away in the chambers of the Palais de Justice.

By the Revolution, the position of Concierge had lost much of its former prestige but it still retained considerable powers over the condition of prisoners. Thus it was that "citoyenne (female citizen) Richard", concierge at the Conciergerie, bought carnations and other blossoms at the flower market every morning to decorate Marie-Antoinette's cell.

▬ *VISIT*

(I Quai de l' Horloge: open daily 10 am – 5 pm, tel: 43 54 30 06.)

The entrance to the Conciergerie leads to a square courtyard; below, to the right, is the **Salle des Gardes** (guard-room), dim and murky since the quay was built. Before this, the Seine used to lap the walls up to the base of the towers, and the prisons were regularly flooded.

To the left, a small staircase leads to the room known as the Salle des Gens d'Armes ("armed people", thus "gendarme"), the most interesting in the Palais, and one of the finest Gothic halls ever built. The four rib-vaulted naves cover 5900 square feet/1800 square metres and the pillars added by Viollet-le-Duc do not detract from the perfection of their proportion and rhythm. At the end, to the right, are the kitchens with their enormous chimneys and original fittings intact. The severe beauty of the Gothic vaults makes a perfect setting for the concerts that are often held there. The last row in the hall is known as the **Rue de Paris;** this was the path taken by Monsieur de Paris, also known as Samson the executioner. This passage leads to the sinister prison world of the Revolution: Marie-Antoinette's dungeon, the chapel where the Girondins, the pioneers of the Revolution, ousted by Robespierre, were held, and the Womens' Courtyard where prisoners could exercise during the day. There was a wide variation in the way of life of the prisoners; the wretched "straw" prisoners huddled together on their litters in the rue de Paris, while the affluent "gold coin" prisoners spent their last nights in revelry.

Place Dauphine and Square du Vert-Galant ●●

Map 5, (B-C 1)

The **Place Dauphine** is reached by following the Quai de l'Horloge, then taking the Rue de l'Horloge. It was built on the initiative of Maximilien de Sully, Henri IV's minister and steward, on the site of the old royal gardens, where Philippe le Bel had Jacques de Molay, Grand Master of the Templars, burned at the stake. The square was named Dauphine in honor of the Dauphin, the future Louis XIII. It originally formed an enclosed triangle of stone and brick houses of similar design with slate roofing. The eastern side of the square succumbed to the 19th-century taste for pomp, and its houses were demolished to make room for the Palais staircase. Even though the only remaining original dwellings are n[os] 14 and 26, the square still retains an immense charm with its tiny restaurants, art galleries and rustic calm, which even the oppressive traffic of the nearby Pont Neuf cannot quite destroy.

VISIT

The Square du Vert-Galant juts into the Seine to the west of the Pont Neuf like the prow of some stately vessel. The square is so called because of an affectionate nickname given to Henri IV, whose equestrian statue can be seen overlooking it. The promontory, which is a starting point for some of the Bateaux-Mouches and a favorite meeting-place on summer evenings, gives an idea of the original elevation of the Seine islands before the works which raised the level of the Cité in the 16th century. This pleasant shady site invites contemplation of the Louvre and the old Mint building as well as the receding lines of the quays to the west, which border the Seine and its constant barge traffic.

The Quai des Orfèvres, on the south side of the Palais, was once the center of the jewel trade (*orfèvre:* goldsmith) before becoming the headquarters of the Paris police. Some of the old craftsmen have bequeathed their names to posterity, like Strasser, the inventor of *strass*, or paste jewelry, and Boehmer and Bassenge, who made Marie-Antoinette's fabulous necklace.

A leisurely stroll along the Quai de Montebello on the Left Bank, before crossing over to the Ile Saint-Louis, will give you a splendid view of Notre-Dame.

Ile Saint-Louis

Map 5, (C-D, 3-4) Metro: Cite, Pont-Marie, Hôtel-de-Ville   Bus: n°s 24, 47, 67, 86, 87

Ile Saint-Louis is a haven of privacy and elegance and should not be rushed through but absorbed step by step, house by house, without disturbing the tranquillity of the island or its residents. The Ile is at its best early in the morning, in spring or autumn when the light falls on the facades of the old mansions, and wisps of mist from the Seine isolate the island, restoring the enchantment of the 17th century. Later, the sun dissolves both the mist and the illusion. Smoke rises from the ovens of the pseudo-mediaeval restaurants, ice cream aficionados queue up in front of the famous Berthillon shop, and tour buses grind noisily along the quays. To savor the serenity of the Ile Saint-Louis, an early start is strongly recommended.

HISTORY

Before 1614, **l'Ile aux Vaches** and **l'Ile Notre-Dame** were two separate islands, just upstream from the Cité. At that time, the entrepreneurs Marie, Poulleyier and Le Regrattier joined in a venture to fill the channel and divide the resulting island into lots for development. The slow rate of progress led the owners to transfer the project to another architect, Louis Le Vau; all the buildings were completed by 1664, and very little has changed since, which accounts for the island's remarkable architectural unity.

VISIT

Pont Saint-Louis, one of the local children's favorite playgrounds, leads to the **Quai de Bourbon,** which curls round the western tip of the island. Anglers sit in silence in the shade of the poplars that line this cobbled quay with its stone bollards and magnificent view of the right bank, the Church of Saint-Gervais and the roofs of Hôtel-de-Ville. The corner mansion, at n° 45, dates from 1659 and is known as the Maison du Centaure, in reference to one of the medallions on the facade. The north side of the island consists of nobly-proportioned mansions, whose elaborate and often grotesque sculptures and finely-worked mansard roofs attest to the status of their owners, past and present. Parliamentary counsellors are lodged at n°s 19 and 15 while n° 1 has retained the charming grille from the old *le Franc Pinot* cabaret.

The Quai d'Anjou, on the other side of

the Pont-Marie, doubles back on itself to follow the narrow arm of the Seine; at n° 17, the **Hôtel Lauzun** was built in 1650 by Le Vau for Charles Gruÿn, who apparently made such exorbitant profits as a supplier to the army that he found himself in prison before his mansion was finished! It was subsequently bought by the Comte de Lauzun, hence the name. Charles Baudelaire once lived here and was introduced by the painter Joseph Broissard into the famous "Club des Haschichins", which was founded by poet Théophile Gauthier, and counted Alexandre Dumas and Eugène Delacroix among its members. The club met regularly in the Ile Saint-Louis to seek new forms of perception. The mansion's exterior is hardly extravagant, but the luxury and opulence of the interior make this one of the finest 17th-century dwellings to have been preserved. Unfortunately, as it is used by the Mayor of Paris for official receptions, it is often difficult to visit. (Guided visits only. Tel: 42 76 54 04, or inquire at the Hôtel-de-Ville reception bureau.) The same is true for the **Hôtel Lambert,** at n° 1 (or n° 2 Rue Saint-Louis-en-Ile), which was built in 1640. Voltaire, then Jean-Jacques Rousseau, courted the successive mistresses of the house, Madame Dupin and the Marquise de Châtelet. The mansion's ancient shaded walls and elegant rotunda are seen to best advantage from the Boulevard Henri IV or the Square Barye.

On the Quai de Béthune and Quai d'Orléans in the south of the island, there are houses with elegant balconies which command attractive views. Those with a feel for history or poetry will particularly enjoy passing by n° 16 Quai de Béthune, home of the Maréchal-duc de Richelieu (1696–1788) and later President Pompidou (1911–1974) and n° 18 where 20th-century poet and novelist Francis Carco died. **Rue Saint-Louis-en-l'Ile,** with its village high-street atmosphere, acts as a magnet for visitors; sadly, many of the shopkeepers and craftsmen have sold out to luxury boutiques, businesses and restaurants; yet Paris celebrities are still to be found here, as were Marie Curie, President Léon Blum and radical politician Jules Guesde before them.

The exterior of the **Church of Saint-Louis** is distinguished only by its iron clock and openwork spire, but the Jesuit-style interior is superb. Twinned with the Cathedral of Carthage in Tunisia, where St Louis is buried, the church has retained a statue of this most Christian of kings, as well as a curious painting by Ary Scheffer depicting Louis' last communion. The luxurious **woodwork,** 17th-century goldwork, and a 14th-century alabaster high-relief of The Birth of the Virgin Mary are also worthy of the visitor's attention.

More sights

At n°6 Quai d'Orléans, the Polish library houses a small museum dedicated to 19th-century poet and Polish nationalist, Adam Mickiewicz, who lived here for several years (open on Thursday, 3 – 6 pm). A stroll along the quays is rewarding because of the graffiti scratched on the walls and parapets by the 18th-century chronicler, Restif de la Bretonne, who could never resist inscribing his thoughts and comments on them after his morning walks around the island.

=== *RECOMMENDED FOR REFRESHMENT* ===

Taverne Henri IV, 13 Place du Pont-Neuf, 75001 (tel: 43 54 27 90). Open 11.30 am – 9.30 pm. Closed Sat eve, Sun, Aug, Christmas, Easter, Public hols. Excellent wine and home-made *charcuterie* (cooked meat specialities).

Le Satay, 19 Rue Saint-Julien-le-Pauvre, 75005 (tel: 43 54 31 33). Open 4 pm – 2 am; closed Sun. Selection of teas, Indian cuisine and sorbets by Berthillon.

Berthillon, 31 Rue Saint-Louis-en-l'Ile, 75004 (tel: 43 54 31 61). Open 10 am – 8 pm Wed to Sun. The best ice cream in Paris.

LES HALLES AND THE BEAUBOURG DISTRICT

On the Right Bank, one of the most interesting districts is Les Halles on the Plateau Beaubourg which is distinguished by the Pompidou Center. The character of the area has undergone a revolutionary change ever since the *halles* (market halls) were removed. The motley crowd of porters, wholesale butchers, tramps, owners of small hotels and well-heeled patrons of the all-night gourmet restaurants, have all vanished.

This gaudy, uniquely Parisian world has been replaced by the modern world of punk rockers haunting the Square des Innocents, art galleries, seed and exotic fruit stores in Rue Berger, and surburbanites who scour the Forum in search of the latest fashion. Les Halles is also one of the new centers of Paris chic: fashion designers, actors, film stars and rock idols all congregate here.

▬ VISIT

The Place du Châtelet is flanked by two large theaters, built by the architect Davioud in 1862. "Le Châtelet", one of the largest theaters in Paris, was long associated almost exclusively with comic operetta, before considerable renovation transformed it into the **Théâtre Musical de Paris,** presenting a wide range of entertainment including concerts, musicals and ballet. Across the square, the facade of the neo-Renaissance **Théâtre de la Ville** has a thoroughly modern hall, and the stage is built on the spot where the mystical poet, Gérard de Nerval, was found hanged one morning in 1855.

Tour Saint-Jacques

(Map 5, B 2 Metro & R.E.R.: Châtelet.)

The bell-tower of the Church of Saint-Jacques-de-la-Boucherie, built during the reign of François I, still soars above the corner of the Rue de Rivoli and the Boulevard de Sébastopol. It seems sadly out of place in this cramped square, especially since none of the fine mediaeval dwellings adjacent to it, belonging to the rich corporation of skinners, tanners and offal merchants of the Grand Châtelet, has survived. As its name implies, Saint-Jacques-de-la-Boucherie was the head quarters of the powerful guild of butchers, in addition to being the starting point for Ile-de-France **pilgrims** on their way to Santiago de Compostela.
The church was sold during the Revolution as a national asset, and demolished in 1802; only the bell-tower, henceforth named the

Tour Saint-Jacques, was reprieved to be used as a shot tower: drops of molten lead were allowed to fall from the top into vats of cold water 170 feet/52 metres below, where they hardened into musket bullets. A statue of the 17th-century philosopher Blaise Pascal commemorates the experiments he performed there.

The tower, often under-estimated in terms of architectural importance, is, in fact, an important landmark in the evolution of French art. It belongs to the **flamboyant Gothic** period; the sculptures on the upper portion by the pictorialist Rault, the vaults, ribs, and the entire robust and opulent decoration attest to this. Nevertheless, Jean de Felin did not complete its construction until 1522. The tower can therefore be said to symbolize the persistence of the Gothic style, renewed, simplified and ready to evolve towards a Classical form, at a time when the Italian school was beginning to dominate the capital with its elaborate, sophisticated lines.
The Tour Saint-Jacques stands erect, the rearguard of Gothic architecture in a century indifferent to its concepts. Perhaps this is the underlying cause of the solitary, rather pathetic appearance of the bell-tower-without-a-church that so delighted the Surrealists.

Church of Saint-Merri

On the opposite side of the Rue de Rivoli, the Beaubourg development project has saved the ancient streets of the parish of Saint-Merri from the motorcar. After forming a charming pedestrian square for its first few yards, the **Rue Saint-Martin** crosses the Rue des Lombards, named after the Lombardy financiers who were established here from the Middle Ages onwards. At n° 76 Rue de la Verrerie stands the handsome **presbytery** of the Church Saint-Merri.

The 18th-century porch leads to the transept, one of the finest examples of **flamboyant Gothic,** which attests, like the Tour Saint-Jacques, to the vitality of this art form right up to the end of the 16th century. Work on the present-day church was, in fact, only begun in 1520 and completed in 1612 in the finest 15th-century style. The exterior has remained the same, particularly that of the right flank surrounded by ancient houses, but the interior was considerably **remodeled in the 18th century.** This interesting Baroque transformation of a Gothic choir provides an idea of what the choir of Notre-Dame could have looked like in the 18th century. Particularly worthy of attention is the beautiful applied stucco that masks its pillars and Gothic archways, which were executed by the architect Germain Boffrand under Louis XV. The sculptures adorning the keystones, the network of ribs above the intersection of the transept, and the **stained glass** of the first three bays of the choir have all, in contrast, retained their original splendor. The woodwork in the choir dates from the 18th century.

The organ, which once resounded to the masterly touch of composer Camille Saint-Saëns (1835 – 1921), is located behind a magnificent organ case, and is still frequently used for concerts.
Following the Rue Saint-Martin to the right, with its old houses and newly-installed boutiques, you reach the vast plaza that opens onto the Plateau Beaubourg, in front of the Georges Pompidou Center.

●●● # Georges Pompidou Center

Map 5,   Metro: Châtelet, Les Halles, Hôtel-de-Ville, Rambuteau,
(A-B 2)   R.E.R.: Châtelet-Les Halles   Bus: n°^{os} 38, 47, 58, 67, 69, 70, 72, 74, 85, 96

▬▬ *HISTORY*

The Plateau Beaubourg owes its name to typically Parisian irony: calling this "bourg" (village), "beau" (beautiful), when it was one of the most notoriously squalid districts of the city, where refuse from Les Halles was allowed to accumulate unchecked. Degenerating even further over the centuries, it had become one of the most unsanitary parts of Paris when, in 1936, the demolition of its more dangerously decrepit buildings began.

In 1968, the area was scheduled for redevelopment along with the old market halls; President Pompidou's decision to build a huge contemporary art exhibition and creation center was about to change the entire district.

The daringly unusual architecture of the **Georges Pompidou National Art and Culture Center,** inaugurated in 1977, met with instantaneous approval from the public, and now attracts more visitors than the Eiffel Tower.

The principal characteristic of the center, designed by architects Renzo Piano and Richard Rogers, is the transparency of its functions: all the floors, galleries and escalators are visible from the exterior. Using modern materials — steel beams, synthetic glass and colored plastic — the structure has relegated all its functional elements such as escalators, elevators, ventilation and heating ducts to the outer walls; these elements are color-coded: red for the walkways, green for the water supply, blue for ventilation, yellow for electricity.

VISIT

(Open daily ex. Tue, May 1st, Dec 25th; 12 – 10 pm, 10 am – 10 pm Sat & Sun. Day passes available, offering access to all exhibitions and activities.)

The main entrance of the Pompidou Center is at the piazza level; there is another on the street level, which forms a mezzanine on the Rue Beaubourg side. The **reception desk** at the entrance, provides information on all the center's activities and temporary exhibitions. Beneath the portrait of President Pompidou by Vasarely, escalators rise to the mezzanine, and to the famous glass "snake" that winds to the fifth floor, where a panoramic alleyway provides fine **views** over the roofs of Paris, Montmartre, the Church of Saint-Eustache, the Eiffel Tower, the towers of Notre-Dame, the Panthéon and nearby Saint-Merri.

In front of the Center, a wide, open space has been left to the right of the Rue Saint-Martin where pedestrians gather and the numerous street musicians, jugglers, fire-eaters and mime artists perform, reviving something of the cacophonous atmosphere of the mediaeval fair.

On the piazza itself there is a replica of the **studio** of Constantin Brancusi (1876 – 1957), one of the first truly modern sculptors *(open 12 – 6 pm).*

The Quartier de l'Horloge, the district to the north of the Center, is bounded by the Rues Saint-Martin, Beaubourg and du Grenier-Saint-Lazare. **A huge animated clock,** "Le Défenseur du Temps" or "Defender of Time", by Jacques Monestier, looks down upon the Rue Bernard-de-Clairvaux. On the hour, a man armed with a spear confronts a dragon, a ferocious bird and a crab.

Rising from the corner of the Rue Rambuteau and the Rue Brantôme is a 20th-century **statue by Ossip Zadkine,** depicting Prometheus' flight from heaven after stealing fire. The exquisite interplay of sculptures by Niki de Saint Phalle and Jean Tinguely adorns the fountain dedicated to Stravinsky between the Rue Saint-Merri and the Rue du Renard.

Rue Berger, conveniently widened along the stretch that leads from the Center, across the Boulevard de Sébastopol and on to the Forum, is crossed by several of the main thoroughfares of mediaeval Paris.

Main features of the Georges Pompidou Center

Activities are divided into five sections:

The Public Information Library (BPI), reached from the second floor, contains over one million books, slides, video tapes, records and various documents available for free public consultation within the library's 49,230 square feet/15,000 square metres of floor space, spread over three levels. But such is its popularity that this space is often found inadequate. On the first floor we have art, literature, sport, leisure and travel; on the second, newspapers and magazines; and on the third, social and physical sciences from economics to computers. The ground floor Galerie de l'Actualité (current affairs) provides all the latest in books, newspapers, magazines and records.

The Industrial Creation Center (CCI) organizes exhibitions dedicated to "places, objects and signs of the daily life of modern society".

The Institute of Musical Acoustic Research and Coordination (IRCAM), under the direction of composer Pierre Boulez, is a veritable research laboratory situated underground between the Center and the Church of Saint-Merri. A vast field of study is offered to composers, the results of whose work can be judged at the numerous workshops and concerts *(visits not allowed).*

The film library on the fifth floor offers around 20 films per week, in addition to organizing debates and seminars *(see programme at ground-level reception desk, and in the press; tel: 42 78 35 57).*

The National Museum of Modern Art covers 56,000 square feet/17,000 square metres on the third and fourth floors *(see description p. 185).*

In addition to these five sections, there is a children's library and children's workshop.

Rue Saint-Martin was the old Right Bank extension of the Saint-Jacques Way on the Left Bank, and followed the ancient Roman road that led to Senlis. (Fine old houses at n°s 92, 100 and 111 – 133.)

Rue Quincampoix, first mentioned in 1203, is almost entirely lined with handsome 17th- and 18th-century houses. There is an overhanging house at n° 2, a superb doorway crowned by a head of Bacchus at n° 10, a studded door at n° 12, a rocaille-style door at 14; La Reynie, first Prefect of Police of Paris, is said to have lived at n°s 22, 27 and 29. There is also a fine monumental door at n° 36, and an 18th-century mansion at n° 56 – 58.

Rue Saint-Denis remains, despite the removal of the old market buildings, one of the youngest and most diversified centers of Paris night-life.

History

Rue Saint-Denis, tracing the ancient Roman way leading to Saint-Denis, Pontoise and Rouen, first gained importance in the 18th century, and became one of the liveliest and richest streets in the capital. The kings of France used the Rue Saint-Denis for their **triumphal processions** into Paris and down to Notre-Dame. Triumphal arches were erected all along the route, and the fountains flowed with milk and wine, particularly the latter, to ensure the goodwill and enthusiasm of the populace. Louis XI certainly made the most spectacular entrance. Despite this sovereign's austere reputation, the city authorities commissioned naked maidens to dance in the fountains as water-goddesses. The gloomiest was perhaps that of Louis XVIII, in 1815: the soldiers in the procession were mainly veterans of Napoleon's defeated army and were seen to weep on hearing the cries of "Long live the King!"

Nowadays, Rue Saint-Denis is shared by art galleries, fashion boutiques, trendy hairdressers and interior decorators and the perennial prostitutes, more recent sex shops and ubiquitous fast-food stores. The street has managed to bring together business concerns which had hitherto existed in separate areas (fashion, advertising, show business), while retaining its less reputable residents and their tough protectors.

This explosive blend should be sampled with a certain amount of caution: it can get rough at night, and the very ancient Rue de la Grande Truanderie (*truand:* crook, swindler, gangster) still lives up to its name.

The Church of Saint-Leu-Saint-Gilles* opens onto the Boulevard de Sébastopol. Frequently rebuilt, notably by 19th-century architect Victor Baltard, it is a quaint combination of everything from early Gothic to Baroque architecture. Note the interior buttresses (an unusual feature), the group of *St Anne and the Virgin** by Jean Bullant (16th century), and the 15th-century alabaster bas-reliefs.

La Fontaine des Innocents**: After crossing the Rue Saint-Denis, the Rue Berger runs on the left of a tree-lined square containing the superb fountain built in the 16th century, by Pierre Lescot and Jean Goujon. This was the site of the former Cimetière des Innocents, and is separated from the adjacent market by a covered walk.

History

The Innocents charnel house, or morgue, was apparently not as macabre as the name suggests. Public scribes, idlers, prostitutes and adventurers gathered here, and its nocturnal life was so notorious that it became necessary to prohibit entry after dark. The danger to public health posed by two million corpses was finally perceived in 1786 and the bones were transferred by night to the **catacombs** (see p. 116), over a period of three years. A fruit and vegetable market then replaced the cemetery.

The fountain, designed by Pierre Lescot and carved by Jean Goujon in 1549, backed onto a wall at the corner of the Rue Saint-Denis. The 18th-century sculptor Augustin Pajou added a fourth side when it was removed to its present site in 1788. This is one of the masterpieces of Renaissance art; the elegance of the female form, the art of the draperies and the natural ease of the pose all combine to make it one of the finest examples of French sculpture. The bas-reliefs around the fountain are now preserved in the Louvre. The house at n°s 1 – 15 Rue des Innocents, built in 1669, was, with its four floors, 52 windows and 394-foot/120-metre facade, for a long time the largest in Paris.

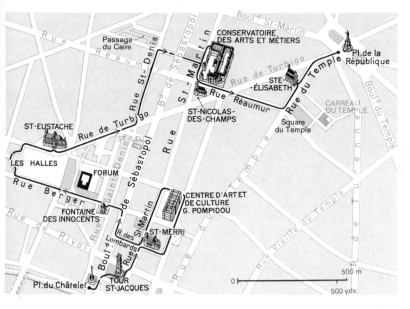

Les Halles and the Beaubourg district.

Les Halles

Metro: Châtelet, Les Halles, Etienne-Marcel
R.E.R.: Châtelet-les-Halles
Bus: n°s 21, 29, 38, 47, 58, 67, 69, 70, 72, 74, 81, 85

**Map 5,
(A 1-2)**

As part of the greatest urban development project undertaken in Paris since the Second Empire, the demolition of the central Halles, or wholesale food markets, has enabled the construction of a gigantic complex consisting of shopping arcades, residential buildings, leisure areas and entertainment facilities, all linked by extensive pedestrian zones.

▬▬ HISTORY

The history of Les Halles is, in fact, the history of the whole Right Bank; even more than the Louvre, Les Halles influenced the development of the entire area.

The original market on the Ile de la Cité soon became over-crowded, and a second market was opened on the Place de la Grève (the present Place de l'Hôtel-de-Ville), then a third in the fields which supplied the parish of Saint-Germain l'Auxerrois. In 1181, Philippe-Auguste added to this the fairground of Saint-Lazare, at the tip of Saint-Eustache, and two covered market halls, or "halles", built to protect the produce.

Les Halles at the time must have offered the bustling, clamorous spectacle of an immense bazaar, with no two buildings alike, but where everyone knew what he was looking for and where to find it. At the end of the 13th century, Louis IX added three halls, one for drapers, and one each for sea and freshwater fish. The organization of the transport and sale of fish was a major advance of the time, and the *harengères* or fish wives stuck in the popular imagination. Fish, namely herring, soon became the staple diet of the poor, meat being reserved for the richer classes.

All transactions were carefully supervised by officials. Forgers, and those who sold short could be pilloried at Saint-Eustache, while dealers in butter who cheated on the weight were exposed to public ridicule by being made to stand with the offending slab on their heads.

With the rapid rise in the population of Paris, Les Halles soon became inadequate for the huge quantities of goods that passed through every day, and Napoleon had the **leather and wine trade** transferred to the Left Bank. The mediaeval alleys were transformed into wider streets, first by Rambuteau and then by Haussmann. Eventually, Napoleon III commissioned Victor Baltard to erect metal structures for the market halls that bore his name (one remains at Nogent-sur-Seine, where it was transferred for use as an exhibition and concert hall). Ten of these strange, umbrella-like structures were erected between 1854 and 1866, using cast iron, steel and glass; they became the rage, and it was considered stylish to go there in the early hours of the morning to enjoy a bowl of onion soup or chew on a grilled pig's trotter in one of the colorful Les Halles restaurants, where the early-rising fishmongers and market porters mingled with the late revellers.

An anachronism from the Middle Ages in the heart of modern Paris, unable any longer to ensure the efficient distribution of food to the millions of Parisians and suburban dwellers, and a source of endless traffic jams, Les Halles had to go. In 1969 the wholesale markets were transferred to **Rungis,** 6 mi./10 km south of the capital. A new, stimulating period was opening for this time-honored district: cellar discotheques, modern art galleries, fashion boutiques, design centers and advertising studios took over from the old food stores.

▬▬ *VISIT*

Forum des Halles

Monster cranes have been standing for the past 15 years over what was commonly known as "the hole of Les Halles". The project is still incomplete, but its essential part is now functioning, namely the Forum, which was opened in 1979. The Forum des Halles forms a four-level underground complex, complete with streets, avenues, cinemas, restaurants and a pleasant patio, La Place Basse. The architects Vasconi and Penchréac'h have organized the Forum around a huge central crater; the glass arches of the arcades provide a profusion of natural light and offer a magnificent view upwards to the Church of Saint-Eustache. In the middle of the Place Basse, the Argentine sculptor Julio Silva created a strange, **pink marble composition** entitled *Pygmalion.*

Displayed on the same level, near the Porte Lescot, there is a gilded bronze bas-relief by the artist P.M. Trémois, *La Lumière nous arrive du fond des âges* (Light coming from the depths of time).

Higher up, on level 3 (Rue de l'Arc-en-ciel), the painter Attila has painted imaginary porticoes opening onto infinity; next to them is a **fresco** on which Moretti traces the Evolution of Man from the 320,000 year-old Tautavel mask to Victor Hugo and Louis Armstrong.

On level 2, the painter, Cueco, has decorated the pillars with a fantastic **mosaic** bestiary, as has Rieti on level 1.

The Grévin Waxworks, on level 1 (*open daily 10.30 am – 8.30 pm, 1 – 7pm Sun & Public hols; tel: 42 61 28 50*) commemorates the brilliant Paris of the *Belle Epoque* (turn-of-the-century), the Eiffel Tower, the cabarets and public balls.

The Holographic Museum, also on level 1 (*open daily, ex. Mon, 11 am – 7 pm; tel: 42 96 96 05*) displays some of the most astounding applications of the three-dimensional viewing process invented by Dennis Gabor in 1947. Laser technology has opened new vistas in holography, where figures come to life in their plexiglass half-cylinders.

Above the Forum, a tiny leafy mall leads to a garden surrounding a semi-circular courtyard, between Saint-Eustache and the Rue

Baltard's "umbrellas"

Iron made its definitive mark upon the world of architecture under the Second Empire. It had previously been quite widely used in the roofing of large buildings, in the columns of shopping arcades and passages, and in the greenhouses of the Jardin des Plantes, which date from 1833. However, its large-scale use represented a major innovation for the Parisian landscape. Baltard's famous umbrellas are probably the best-known example.

Iron had been looked down upon as being too utilitarian and industrial: Napoleon III had to intervene personally to overcome Baltard's relucance. The Emperor, delighted with the newly completed Gare de l'Est (1847), imagined the central markets along the lines of this hall, roofed with an iron framework filled with glass panes: "what I want are vast umbrellas, nothing more." Haussmann had great difficulty in persuading Baltard to give up the solid stone wall with protruding pillars that he wanted as a surround for each pavilion.

Berger. On the corner of the Rue Pierre Lescot and the Rue Rambuteau, the Hôtel-de-Ville has opened a cultural center, combining workshops, exhibition rooms and especially a fully computerized **information bureau** capable of replying to any questions concerning the capital's cultural life.

Photographic exhibitions

The **Espace Photographique de Paris** holds temporary photographic exhibitions and is a permanent multi-media library. Understandably, the works most prominently displayed are those of such immortalizers of Paris as Lartigue, Doisneau, Brassai and Kertesz.

La Bourse du Commerce (Commodities Exchange), reached by the Rue Berger, is a round building dating from 1889. In the high circular room, brokers of wheat, corn, sugar, alcohol and such commodities trade according to the same rules as those of the Stock Exchange. From here, walk to the Church of Saint-Eustache along the Rue Coquillière, where the numerous restaurants are open late into the night, and still maintain the old Les Halles traditions (the *Pied de Cochon* restaurant never closes!)

Church of Saint-Eustache

Metro: Les Halles   **Map 5,**
R.E.R.: Châtelet-les Halles   Bus: n⁰ˢ 67, 74, 85   **(A 1)**

Saint-Eustache, far from having suffered from the upheaval in its neighborhood, has acquired new authority. The south-facing perspectives are now untrammeled, and the church seems to stand as a link between a modern, agitated and disconcerting age and the reassuring permanence of a rich past. Inspired by Notre-Dame, this is the last great Gothic church, and one of the major religious centers of Paris, particularly noted for its sacred music.

▬▬ HISTORY

A small chapel dedicated to St Eustache had been in existence since the 13th century, just to the north of Les Halles. However, as the parish had become one of the richest and most populous in Paris, the chapel was soon too small for the congregation. Financed by generous donations, the first stone of what was to become a **great Gothic vessel** was laid in 1532. Due to a subsequent lack of funds, the church was only completed when the French Renaissance was at its zenith, a century later, but the original plans were carefully respected, and the church that was consecrated in 1637 is comparable with the great Gothic cathedrals.

In the mid-18th century, the main facade was replaced by a cold, characterless Classical version. The church was severely damaged by fire in 1844 but was restored by Baltard. Its musical tradition stretches far back in history and is perpetuated by the Saint-Eustache Master's Award, and by organist Louis Guillou; Liszt, Berlioz and Verdi played some of their works for the first time in public at Saint-Eustache.

Several famous Parisians are linked to the **Church of Saint-Eustache.** Molière was baptized here and also buried here at night in the guise of "King's Tapestry Maker", religious ceremonies being forbidden for actors. Jean-Baptiste Lully, the 17th-century composer and violinist, was married at Saint-Eustache, and the Duc de Richelieu was baptized under its roof. The poets La Fontaine and Voiture, the statesmen Mirabeau and Colbert and the composer Rameau all lie buried here, along with Mozart's mother, Maria Anna.

▬ VISIT

To appreciate the **exterior of Saint-Eustache,** make a detour along the Rue du Jour, where the fine 15th-century house at n° 4 affords a marvelous view of the flying buttresses and the roofs, then by the Rue Montmartre. N° 3 on this street faces the delightful north portal of the transept. The facade of this typical Renaissance transept, flanked by the turrets of two staircases, is crowned by the head of a deer with the Cross, the vision leading, so it was said, to St Eustache's conversion.

The interior of the church is vast — 328 feet/100 metres long, 144 feet/44 metres wide, and 12 feet/34 metres high under the vaults — and simple; there are double side-aisles, but no projecting transept as at Notre-Dame. The height of the archways precludes any sizeable galleries: there is merely a small Renaissance gallery running beneath the lofty windows. The hanging keystones in the nave, transept and choir, introduce an almost Baroque note in this flamboyant interior, and the beautiful **stained glass** in the choir from a sketch by Philippe de Champaigne (1631), depicts St Eustache in the midst of the Apostles. Among the numerous tombs and works of art in the church, particularly worthy of note are the *Martyrdom of St Eustache* by Simon Vouet (17th century) and **Colbert's tomb,** designed by Le Brun, in the

Church of Saint-Eustache seen from the Forum of Les Halles.

ast chapel to the left of the choir. Also to be seen are *The Pilgrims of Emmaüs*, an early Rubens, and the 19th-century frescoes by Thomas Couture.

Behind the church, the border of the district is marked by the Rue de Turbigo, which leads off to the left from the Rue Rambuteau. The picturesque **Rue Montorgueil,** with its handsome 18th-century facades, has remained authentically Parisian and its colorful daily street market is one of the liveliest in the city. At n° 20 Rue Étienne-Marcel, the **Tower of Jean-sans Peur** (1408) is one of the last vestiges of feudal Paris.

After crossing the Rue Saint-Denis and the Boulevard de Sébastopol, the Rue de Turbigo leads on towards the **Church of Saint-Nicolas-des-Champs.** The first five rows in the choir date from the 15th century, while the rest of the structure is mainly 16th and 17th century. This fact is attested to by the fine **South Doorway*** (a copy of a door by 16th-century architect Philibert Delorme), the semicircular vaults that replace the Gothic in the choir, the increased height of the sideaisles, and the fluted columns. In the choir and the side-chapels, a number of fine 17th- and 18th-century **paintings** surround the high altar, with its 17th-century altarpiece painted by Simon Vouet. A forest of pillars forms a double cloister. Note also the magnificent Classical **organ,** built by F.H. Clicquot in the 18th century.

The Church of Saint-Martin-des-Champs*, on the other side of the Rue Réaumur, combines a Romanesque apse with a Gothic nave, and is now part of the *Conservatoire National des Arts et Métiers* (Technical College), itself due to be transferred to the Centre des Sciences et Techniques at La Villette. The college consists of a technical education department, laboratories and an industrial museum on the site where, in the 6th century, the Benedictine **Abbaye Saint-Martin-des-Champs** was established.

Pierre de Montreuil brought Gothic art to perfection with the **former monk's refectory*,** the most remarkable vestige of the old abbey. A mere seven columns divide the great hall into two naves; the beauty of the decorative motifs, the purity of line and the harmony of the proportions unite to make this one of the finest masterpieces of Notre-Dame's great architect.

National Technical Museum

(Entrance: 270 Rue Saint-Martin; open daily ex. Mon. & Public hols 1 – 5.30 pm, 10 am – 5.15 pm Sun; tel: 42 71 24 14.)

Like the Conservatoire itself, the national Technical Museum was established by the Revolutionary Convention (1794). Many of the exhibits were taken from the royal apartments, such as the magnificent *Drummer Girl*, Queen Marie-Antoinette's favorrite mechanical toy which plays eight different tunes (room 13). Next door, in rooms 15 to 19, are the magnificent 18th-century **clockwork pieces,** craftsmanship at its peak: the engraving and chasing is worthy of priceless jewelry. In rooms 5, 8 and 9, which trace the evolution of the **railway,** the scale models are a delight for enthusiasts. The Church of Saint-Martin-des-Champs itself is given over to the history of locomotion from Cugnot's 1770 truck to Clément Ader's huge bat-like airplane. On the first floor can be found optical (room 30), musical (room 31), mechanical (room 32), and acoustic (room 33–37) instruments. Still and movie cameras, by such pioneers as Niepce, Daguerre and the Lumière brothers, are displayed in rooms 38–40; the latter room also houses graphic and household arts exhibits.

RECOMMENDED FOR REFRESHMENT

Olsson's, 26 Rue de la Reynie, 75001 (tel: 42 33 03 37). Open 11 am – 8 pm Tues, Wed, Fri, Sat. Open Thurs 1 – 9 pm. Swedish pastries and salads.

Pacific Palissades, 51 Rue Quincampoix, 75004 (tel: 42 77 01 17). Open 8 pm – 2 am Mon to Sun. Trendy but good.

Café Costes, 45 Rue St Denis, 75001 (tel: 45 08 54 38). Open 10 am – 2 am Mon to Sun. An inspiring tribute to fifties decor. Traditional café/bar.

Côté cour, côté jardin, 22 Rue Mondétour, 75001 (tel: 45 08 11 35). Open 8 am – 2 pm Mon to Sun.

FROM THE LOUVRE TO THE ARC DE TRIOMPHE

Paris is at its grandest and most formal in the area between the Louvre and the Place de l'Étoile. Here there is none of the quaintness of the old quarters with their narrow winding streets. Instead, we have palaces, monuments and well-planned gardens set along the major thoroughfares. La Voie Triomphale or "Triumphal Way" starts at the Louvre, passes under the Arc du Carrousel and crosses the Tuileries gardens, its geometric layout in striking contrast to the voluptuous statues of Maillol. It opens out at the Place de la Concorde under the towering obelisk, cuts through the shady gardens of the Champs-Élysées and moves on to the Étoile where it divides into twelve broad avenues which lead to the prosperous districts of western Paris.

•• Saint-Germain-l'Auxerrois

Map 5,   Metro: Louvre   Bus: nᵒˢ 21, 24, 27, 69, 72, 74, 81
(B 1)

Across from the Louvre's majestic colonnades, the Church of Saint-Germain-l'Auxerrois, once the parish of the kings of France and the artists of the Louvre, remains, despite mutilations and transformations, one of the major Gothic monuments of Paris.

▬▬ HISTORY

The present building is the sum of five centuries of architecture. It retains its 12th-century belfry, 13th-century central porch, choir and apse, and 15th-century doorway and nave. The 18th century has left its mark on these Romanesque, flamboyant Gothic and Renaissance parts, demolishing tympanum and pier to allow the passage of the enormous royal **processional canopy.** Another victim was the splendid rood screen by the Jean Goujon and Germain Pilon (16th century), of which five bas-reliefs are preserved in the Louvre. The Revolution turned the church into a fodder store; then Baltard and Lassus, in the 19th century, further ruined what was left of its unity.

It is believed that the **St Bartholomew's Day Massacre** of the Protestants, which broke out when the clock struck midnight on August 24th, 1572 started from this church; happier associations are provided by the numerous artists who lived in the Louvre area and are buried here: architects Le Vau and Soufflot, painters Boucher, Nattier, Chardin and Van Loo, and sculptors Coustou and Coysevox.

▬▬ VISIT

The porch, erected in Flamboyant style by Jean Gaussel in 1539, lends great originality to the church's exterior. It consists of three bays with keyed vaults; the parish archives and treasures were placed in small chambers over the left and right-hand bays. The sculptor of the 13th-century central doorway has depicted an amusing scene on the right: St Geneviève being provoked by a demon, who is trying to put her candle out.

The interior has lost much of its charm since the 18th-century restoration mutilated the arches and pillars of the nave and the double side-aisles. The 15th-century **stained glass** in the transept has been preserved, as has been the magnificent 17th-century organ case, originally from the Sainte-Chapelle. Opposite the pulpit, the elaborately carved **churchwarden's pew** belonged to the royal family; behind this are a carved 15th-century triptych and a 16th-century Flemish altarpiece (in the chapel). A wrought-iron grill dating from 1767 surrounds the choir; the two superb 13th- and 15th-century statues in the 14th-century parish chapel were originally from the doorway.

The Louvre   ●●●

Metro: Louvre, Palais-Royal   **Map 4,**
Bus: n°s 21, 24, 27, 39, 48, 67, 69, 72, 74, 76, 81, 85, 95 **(A-B 5-6)**

The Louvre attracts superlatives. It was the "largest royal palace" and is claimed to be the "most beautiful museum in the world"; it is also said to represent "the fulfilment of a dream that unites five centuries of French history in a common vision of power and glory". Yet Parisians are ambivalent about it. The Palace, they feel, is too big and too closed off from the outside world and lacks the wit, the charm, the variety and the elegance typical of the mansions or *Hôtels* of the Marais or Faubourg Saint-Germain, the old quarters and even certain churches. The Louvre has also developed under many influences, which has made Parisians reluctant to accept it as truly "Parisian".

Such local prejudice notwithstanding, the Louvre deserves all the attention that a visitor is able to give it.

▬▬ HISTORY

The foundations of the original Louvre Castle have been excavated in the Cour Carrée (Seine side). This strong, four-square fort was, in fact, the keep of Philippe-Auguste's ramparts.

This defensive structure became a combination of prison, treasury and royal archives. Charles V pushed the ramparts farther north and also made it a proper palace by decorating it with statues and paintings (the first royal collection) as well as installing a library.

François I, the most Italian of French kings, would have preferred his Loire valley residences to this sinister and decrepit dwelling, but the Parisians insisted on his presence. Before moving in, François had the old fort renovated and brightened up; the keep was demolished and a vast area cleared for tournaments.

In 1546, Pierre Lescot was commissioned to embellish the Louvre. The original plans called for a central mansion surrounded by long porticos, but only the Henri II staircase and the two wings decorated by Jean Goujon (who executed the Salle des Caryatides in 1550) were completed. Shortly before the Wars of Religion, the west and south wings were constructed in the Renaissance style, in marked contrast to the Gothic northern and eastern wings.

Catherine de Médicis, refusing to live any longer in the Hôtel des Tournelles, where her husband Henri II was killed while jousting, took up residence in the Louvre. The château was far too cramped and uncomfortable to accommodate the Queen Mother and her retinue, and a second palace, Les Tuileries, had to be built 550 yards/500 metres farther down the banks of the Seine.

In 1556, the architect Philibert Delorme set to work on the clayfields where tiles were formerly manufactured (tiles: *tuiles*; hence Tuileries). Construction was halted several times by the tragic events of the Wars of Religion. Fighting broke out in the Louvre during St

Bartholomew's night, and Protestants were subsequently hanged in the Salle des Caryatides.

It was left to that great builder Henri IV to complete Catherine de Médicis' projects; the **Pavillon de Flore** and the **Galerie du Bord-de-l'Eau** were both finished in 1608. In the reign of Louis XIII, Jacques Lemercier built the **Pavillon de l'Horloge,** extending it by a wing designed to match that of Pierre Lescot; lack of funds prevented any further development.

In 1659, Louis XIV personally made the completion of Le Vau's plans a top priority. **The Galerie d'Apollon** was rebuilt and Perrault's Colonnade (1673) provided a resplendent exterior; the Cour Carrée was closed off by three new wings, and the old houses that had remained were demolished. It all happened in such a short time that a contemporary chronicler was able to write "one can already make out the great pavilions, galleries, apartments and courtyards, and in two years a perfect work should be visible". In fact, not two years but two centuries were to pass, the delay being caused by the construction of the Palace of Versailles, where Louis XIV kept the great artists of the day busy, before transferring the court there in 1682. The unoccupied palace was then taken over by a motley crowd: the sculptors Coustou and Bouchardon and the painter Boucher set up apartments for their families, even knocking holes in the walls and ceilings to accommodate stove pipes. Less desirable tenants soon moved in who pilfered objects and defaced the buildings; jugglers practiced their acts in the galleries; grog shops were set up under the Colonnade. At this time, the king was in such dire financial straits that he even let out the princely apartments to tenants.

By the mid-18th century, the Louvre had reached such a state of deterioration that demolition was considered. It was saved by Louis XVI's minister, Marigny; the architects Soufflot and Gabriel restored the Colonnade and the shopkeepers were thrown out but the tenants remained. It was not until October 5th, 1789, that the palace was completely evacuated — this time to accommodate the king who had been dragged back from Versailles by the starving Parisians.

On June 20th, 1792, rioting Parisians broke into the palace and placed a Phrygian cap, the symbol of liberty, on the king's head, forcing him to drink to the nation's health. On August 10th, the king forbade

From the Louvre to the Arc de Triomphe.

Arc de Triomphe.

his Swiss Guards to disperse the mob gathered in the courtyard, and almost all the guards were massacred in the palace and gardens. The Convention and the sinister Committee of Public Safety then sat in the royal apartments and the Grande Galerie was opened to the public; the Convention had effectively created the Louvre Museum. After a century of neglect, the Emperor Napoleon revived the old royal ambition of building a **"Grand Louvre"**.

He had the royal apartments put in order and commissioned architects Percier and Fontaine to erect the Arc du Carrousel, finish the Cour Carrée and build the Galerie Nord. Louis XVIII took up residence in the Tuileries after the Restoration. Royal occupants were twice driven from the Louvre and from the throne — Charles X in 1830 and Louis-Philippe in 1848 — but these bloodless coups did no harm to the architecture itself, and Napoleon III was at last able to install the **imperial house** in the "Grand Louvre" completed by Visconti and Lefuel. After the burning of the Tuileries by the Paris Commune, the Third Republic decided to erase the remains and allowed Lefuel to simply rebuild the Flore and Marsan pavilions.

In our own day, the Louvre, finally living up to the hopes of the Renaissance kings, is to face its most stunning transformation with the creation of a glass pyramid in front of the Pavillon de l'Horloge by the architect, I.M. Pei.

VISIT

A first glimpse of this huge palace, from the banks of the Seine or the Tuileries gardens gives an impression of unity that is astonishing for a building so often enlarged and modified; on closer examination, however, it is easy to distinguish between the older sections, around the Cour Carrée and along the Seine, and the more recent 19th-century additions.

The old Louvre

A visit to the Louvre is best started at the old Louvre, which surrounds the Cour Carrée.

Most people regard the **Colonnade**** as an important work by Claude Perrault but, in fact, it is not at all certain who is responsible for it since its essentially decorative conception differs from the rest of the palace. It seems most likely that Perrault inspired it, while François d'Orbay drew up the plans and then supervised the construction. The size of the Colonnade — which Perrault wanted as wide as possible and without raised pavilions at each end — and the height of the columns necessitated the use of iron. Work was suspended in 1678, and the facade was restored in 1756.

The 23-foot/7-metre deep **moat** was only excavated in 1964, thanks to André Malraux; it reveals the monumental substructure of the Colonnade and places its proportions in their true context. The area

had already been cleared of the buildings which cluttered its perspective in the mid-18th century; a stone bridge crosses the moat and leads to the main entrance, opening onto the **Cour Carrée**** in the heart of the old Louvre. Compared to the majesty of the Colonnade, the prevailing impression here is one of elegance and poise. The **west wing,** opposite the entrance, is divided into three parts. To the left of the Pavillon de l'Horloge, the oldest section, started under François I, is the work of Pierre Lescot. Three projections provide the rhythm and are flanked by handsome fluted columns; Jean Goujon was responsible for the decoration, consisting of allegorical figures, statues between the columns, and heads surrounded by dogs over the windows. A frieze depicting children with garlands runs along the top. The three pediments, adorned with figures representing War, Plenty and Science, are most expressive. In the center of the west wing, the **Pavillon de l'Horloge** was built in 1624 by Lemercier, who was also the creator of the northern part of this wing. The other three wings are the work of Le Vau, who had the remarkable gift of adhering both to the spirit and the precepts of his predecessor, Pierre Lescot. Until the 19th century, only the west wing had three floors; under the First Empire, Percier and Fontaine added an extra floor to the others, lending a deceptive appear-

Royal monograms

Succeeding monarchs had their initials engraved in the sections of the Cour Carrée for which they were responsible allowing us to identify them. We have K for Charles X, H for Henri II, HDB and HG for Henri IV on the south wing; LA for Louis XIII and LB or LMT for Louis XIV. In these initials, the kings' romantic entanglements arc sometimes concealed. For example, the H for Henri II entwined with the C for Catherine de Médicis (the Queen) can be read as D for Diane de Poitiers, his mentor and mistress. The Cour Carrée is an ideal site for various public spectacles. In July and August, concerts, dances, opera, theatrical presentations and fashion displays are staged there.

ance of unity to the whole. The subtle grace of the Renaissance masters was thus replaced by the proficiency of Classical art.

The Louvre viewed from the Seine

Claude Perrault's facade borders the Quai du Louvre, facing the Pont des Arts and the Institute. It can best be admired from the passage that opens onto the Jardins de l'Infante, to the south of the Cour Carrée. The majestic arrangement of the Colonnade has been continued, the columns replaced by simple pilasters surrounding the windows. The Petite Galerie, perpendicular to the Seine, was erected by Catherine de Médicis in 1556, and fitted out as apartments for Queen Maria Theresa, the young Spanish wife of Louis XIV. It contains the famous **Galerie d'Apollon,** much restored since the fire of 1871. Le Brun was responsible for most of its decoration. Downstream the **Grande Galerie,** or Galerie du Bord-de-l'Eau, commences. Its various sections, built under Henri IV, were either restored under Napoléon III (up to the Carrousel archways) or rebuilt after the fire of 1871. Parts of the decoration are quite charming, like the sea cherubs riding in a frieze over the ground floor, but the 19th-century restorers added some pedestrian rhetoric such as trophies, figures from the Arts, Sciences and Agriculture and 86 famous men; on the garden side are Maillol's beautiful nudes.

Between the wings of the Louvre

It is from the Pavillon de l'Horloge (clock pavilion) rather than from the Arc du Carrousel that the visitor can best appreciate the spread of the Louvre's wings. It commands a superb perspective of the Tuileries gardens and the Concorde-Champs-Élysées axis.

The Jardins du Carrousel, within the Louvre itself, owe their name to the carousels — gigantic parades in celebration of important events — given by the kings. During the party given by Louis XIV in 1662 in honor of Louise de La Vallière, the King took part in the dancing and competitions, for which sumptuous diamonds were awarded as prizes. These were quite probably the happiest days of his reign.

L'Arc de Triomphe du Carrousel was erected by Percier and Fontaine in honor of Napoleon's victories during the 1805 campaign and was modeled with great flair and skill on the arch of Roman emperor Septimus Severus. The arch was originally crowned by a flight of four gilded horses taken from the Basilica of St Mark in Venice; they were returned in 1815 and replaced by an allegorical carving by François de Bosio celebrating the Restoration. The majority of the decorative carvings dating from the 19th-century remodeling are somewhat mediocre, being copies of ancient motifs. A notable exception is the *Triomphe de Flore* by Jean-Baptiste Carpeaux, on the south face of the Pavillon Flore (fine view from the Pont-Royal).

The flowerbeds, or "parterres", were laid out following the destruction of the Tuileries. The striking sensuality of Maillol's eighteen statues which decorate the lawns is in distinct contrast to the sober decor of the wings rebuilt after 1871.

The Palais des Tuileries rose between the Flore and Marsan pavilions, its terrace looking out over the gardens on the site of the present Avenue du Général Lemonnier. The popular image of the Tuileries collapsing amidst the flames lit by the Commune is quite erroneous; the main structure was left practically unscathed by the fire of 1871, and both Lefuel and Viollet-le-Duc offered to restore it. However, the newly-established Third Republic wished to see an end to all trace of the royal palace, and the demolition was completed in 1884.

The Tuileries

Map 4, Metro: Concorde, Palais-Royal, Tuileries
(A 4-5) Bus: n°s 21, 24, 27, 39, 48, 68, 69, 72, 81, 95

The Tuileries gardens invite leisure, encouraging you just to stroll around, enjoy a drink or an ice cream, or watch the children on the merry-go-rounds. On clear days, tourists with their cameras flock there looking for a "creative shot" in the reflections of the fountains; others just stop over on their way from the Champs-Élysées to the Louvre. In summer, sun-bathers stretch out on the banks of the Seine as if on a Parisian Riviera, oblivious to the incessant hum of traffic on the embankment motorways.

HISTORY

Catherine de Médicis desired that elegant walks of the type she had known in Italy should be laid out in front of the **Tuileries Palace,** and the landscape architect, Le Nôtre, responded with the prototype of the **French formal garden.**

The Jardin des Tuileries, as it came to be known, remained open to the public throughout the 17th and 18th centuries. Charles Perrault is said to have found inspiration for his celebrated fairy tales when mingling with the crowds there, and the gardens were the scene of the bizarre **Fête of the Supreme Being** organized by Louis David during the Revolution (June, 1794).

VISIT

The Terrasse du Bord-de-l'Eau, running along the banks of the Seine, offers a panoramic view of the Left Bank. The terrace ends at the Pavillon de l'Orangerie, opposite the Jeu de Paume. These Second Empire pavilions house exhibitions, although the Jeu de Paume is temporarily closed for alterations. Its collection of Impressionist paintings has been moved to the Orsay Museum.

The Bassin Octagonal* (to the west near Concorde), is adorned with statues and lined by flowerbeds and trees which combine to provide a superb example of open-air architecture. On each side of the gates that close off the garden from the Place de la Concorde stand copies of Coysevox's magnificent winged horses transferred from the Château de Marly in 1719.

Place de la Concorde

Map 2, Metro: Concorde Bus: n°s 24, 42, 52, 72, 73, 84, 94
(F 3-4)

The Place de la Concorde, which has changed its name as often as France has changed its regimes, was the scene of many major upheavals between 1750 and 1850. Nowadays its peace is only disturbed by the monstrous traffic jams on week-days. On Sunday mornings and summer evenings the Concorde, almost deserted, returns to its original splendor, art and nature blending together to create an impression of grandeur.

HISTORY

Like the Place des Victoires, the Place des Vosges or the Place Vendôme, the Place de la Concorde is a **royal square** designed and executed to provide a setting for the statue of a reigning sovereign — Louis XV in this case. The Concorde is distinguished by its vast area — 20 acres/almost 8 hectares — and by the nature and environment of the site. Gabriel, the architect of this least built-up space in Paris, could be called an ecologist before his time. Built between 1755 and 1775, at the request of the aldermen of Paris on swamps situated beyond the town walls to avoid the demolition of any existing structures, the Place de la Concorde seemed ill-fated from the start. Panic spread through the crowds gathered there to celebrate the marriage of the Dauphin to Marie-Antoinette in 1770, and more than 100 people were trampled to death.

On January 21st, 1793, the guillotine was set up for the execution of Louis XVI and the 1500 other victims who followed him in the next two years. After the Revolution, the Directoire had the grim scaffold dismantled and gave the square the conciliatory name of Concorde.

The name deterred Louis-Philippe from erecting any statue or monument of political significance here. Instead, he had the 3000-year-old **pink granite obelisk** from the Temple of Luxor installed in the square. (The obelisk had been offered to Charles X by Mehemet Ali but it was only received in the reign of Louis-Philippe.) This superb monolith, 75 feet/23 metres high and weighing 3230 tons, was erected in 1836 and, so the story goes, was saved from toppling over and disintegrating by a sailor who advised wetting the overstrained ropes that were being used to haul it upright.

The two great **fountains** (1840) are inspired by those of St Peter's Square in Rome. Around the edges of the square are statues representing eight great towns of France, in the shape of female figures, set upon pedestals built by Gabriel. The most remarkable are those of Rouen and Brest by Cortot, and Lille and Strasbourg by Pradier.

VISIT

The views from the obelisk pedestal are incomparable: the Louvre-Champs-Élysées axis, the Pont de la Concorde to the south, and the sober facade of the Church of La Madeleine to the north. This is the only side of the square with mansions (hôtels) by Gabriel. Both the Hôtel de la Marine, where Marie-Antoinette once kept small apartments for her incognito visits to Paris, and the Hôtel de Crillon now shared by the Automobile Club de France and the luxurious Crillon Hotel, have the stately look of great palaces. Completed in 1770, they form one of the the finest examples of the Louis XV style. They are framed on each side by the United States Embassy (to the left) and Consulate (to the right), installed in the magnificent Hôtel de la Vrillière. This mansion, at n° 2 Rue Saint-Florentin, was bought in 1806 by the great statesman Talleyrand, then at the height of his wealth and influence. He died there in 1838, after having diplomatically lent the house to the Czar Alexander during the 1815 occupation of Paris. The United States authorities carried out a full restoration, and the result is one of the richest and most complete Empire decorative suites in France. The famous "Eagles' salon", with its extraordinary ceiling and the finely restored furniture, shows how Empire motifs were invariably drawn from antiquity.

●●● Champs-Élysées

Map 1,   Metro: Étoile, George-V, Champs-Élysées-Clemenceau, Concorde
(B 6)   R.E.R.: Étoile   Bus: nᵒˢ 28, 30, 31, 32, 42, 49, 52, 73, 80, 83, 92
Map 2,
(E-F 1-3) When a Parisian announces his intention to go to "Les Champs" (*champs* meaning field), nothing is further from his mind than a visit to the country. He intends to go to the bars, cinemas and shopping arcades of France's most prestigious avenue. From the Rond-Point to the Étoile, the Champs-Élysées is certainly one of Paris' most radically transformed avenues; in the course of a century, boutiques and arcades, company headquarters, showrooms, cafés and cinemas have fought bitterly over every square foot of space, driving out almost every one of the fine old mansions that once lined the avenue. Only the "green belt", from the Rond-Point to the Concorde, gives an idea of what the "Champs" was like in an older, less commercial age.

▬▬ HISTORY

The Champs-Élysées was nothing but a vast patch of fields and swamps when Marie de Médicis, in 1616, created a wide tree-lined alley known as the **Cours de la Reine,** running on from the Tuileries garden. Soon afterwards, Le Nôtre planted rows of trees along the fields of the Grand Cours, further extending this already popular promenade. Becoming known as the Champs-Élysées (Elysian Fields), the avenue was continually widened and extended, first by the Duc d'Antin, then by his successor Marigny (both Superintendents of Buildings to the king), who ran it on as far as the Seine at Neuilly. A favorite haunt for muggers and other doubtful characters, the groves and bushes of the Champs were never very safe. (Lebon, the inventor of gas lighting, was murdered here on the night of Napoleon's coronation.)

The Cossack occupants of the early 19th century did much damage to the avenue, chopping down its trees for fuel. The subsequent introduction of sidewalks and gas lighting, along with the installation of fountains and entertainment halls — restaurants-*cum*-ballrooms — attracted a rich, elegant, pleasure-seeking public. Fine mansions proliferated under the Second Empire, and members of high society drove down the Champs in open carriages on their way to the Bois de Boulogne.

With the approach of the 20th century, the avenue shed its aristocratic character to become a center of Republican demonstrations. Over a million Parisians followed the funeral procession of Victor Hugo. The French army paraded down the Champs-Élysées before leaving for the front in 1914, while July 14th, 1919 saw probably the world's greatest victory parade in celebration of the armistice (November 11th, 1918) when French and Allied troops marched down the Avenue, wildly cheered by vast enraptured crowds. On August 26th, 1944, the day after the Liberation of Paris, Charles de Gaulle took the same route, cheered by equally enthusiastic hordes. Today's Champs-Élysées has lost its past magic in a medley of fast-food joints, banks and cinemas.

Yet the Champs is still unique, representing a maelstrom of peoples, cultures and social classes which is difficult to match anywhere else in the world. Here, the affluent clientele of the luxury hotels come to sip their drinks on Fouquet's famous terrace or sample the creations of some of the world's finest chefs; here also are the youthful representatives of every trend from rockers to ultra-chic. Towards the end of the week, queues form at the entrances of exclusive clubs such as *Régine's* on the Rue de Ponthieu or the *Élysées Matignon* on the street of the same name, matching the serpentine crowds which wait outside the Champs' famous cinemas, the finest in Paris. The stream of tourists starts early in the morning and rapidly swells to a river, submerging the few inhabitants of the district and the businessmen, models and show-biz executives going about their daily business.

▬▬ VISIT

From Concorde to the Rond-Point

For those who have just left the Tuileries gardens, the contrast is obvious: the gardens off the Champs-Élysées are what the French call **English Gardens** (*jardins à l'anglaise*), of a type which was in vogue during the Second Empire; the accent is on going along with nature, rather than bending it to the human will as in the French style. The scenery to the right has hardly changed in a century: the restaurant *Ledoyen* has been there since the days of Louis XVI; the fountains date from the Second Empire, like the Pavillon Gabriel and the Pavillon de l'Élysée. Across from the Théâtre Marigny, on the corner of avenues Marigny and Gabriel, an open-air stamp market is held on Thursdays and Sundays.

To the left, between the avenue and the quays of the Seine, stand the Grand Palais and the Petit Palais. Built for the Universal Exhibition of 1900 in the rather opulent style of the time, their architecture combines steel with stone and discards conventional roofing in favor of glass canopies.

The Petit Palais, with its monumental dome-crowned porch, houses the **Museum of Fine Arts of the City of Paris*** (*open 10 am – 5.30 pm ex. Mon & Public hols; tel: 42 65 12 73*) which, itself, consists of three collections: the Dutuit (Greek, Roman, Egyptian art and antiquities, mediaeval and Renaissance tapestries, statues, books, ivories and art objects, Dutch and Flemish School paintings from the 16th and 17th centuries, and French School from the 18th century, porcelain and pottery); the Tuck (a fine collection of furniture, tapestry and art objects from the 18th century), and the Municipal (19th-century French painters: Courbet**, Degas*, Cézanne*, Bonnard, et al.).

In the Grand Palais, behind the Ionic colonnade and mosaic frieze, a superb staircase unfolds under the immense, 140-foot/43-metre high glass canopied roof. Nothing was spared — from the statue on the corner steps, to the Art Nouveau (or more precisely "modern style") figures — to make of this hall "the monument consecrated by the Republic to the Glory of French Art". Long relegated to varied events ranging from the Automobile show to home improvement exhibitions, the Grand Palais has been reinstated as a cultural center where a number of amazingly successful temporary art exhibitions have been held.

The Palais de la Découverte*, in the west wing of the Grand Palais (*entry Avenue Franklin-Roosevelt; open 10 am – 6 pm ex. Mon, Jan 1st, May 1st, Jul 14th, Aug 15th, Dec 25th; planetarium 5 approx 1-hr shows per day; tel: 43 59 16 65*) is simultaneously a scientific education center and a museum of popular science. Created for the International Exhibition of Technical Arts in 1937, its success led to its becoming a permanent fixture. Physics, chemistry, biology, mathematics, medicine and other sciences are made accessible to the layman, who can also enjoy the delights of space travel under the 82-feet/25-metre diameter vault of the **planetarium,** which seats 300 people.

The Rond-Point des Champs-Élysées, designed by Le Nôtre, occupies the intersection of the Champs-Élysées and the Avenue Franklin-Roosevelt. This is the only part of the Champs-Élysées to have retained several fine original buildings, in particular the **Palais de Glace** (Ice Palace) a former skating rink now transformed into the *Théâtre du Rond-Point Renaud-Barrault* (the restaurant alone makes it one of the most pleasant meeting places in the district), and the *Jours de France* mansion, standing in grand style behind its gilded gates at the corner of the Avenue Montaigne. Across from the Rond-Point, the facade of the old *Figaro* building contrasts with modern cinemas and drug-stores. The **flowerbeds** around the Rond Point are among the prettiest in the capital. Some of the world's most prestigious art galleries line the Avenue Matignon between here and the Faubourg Saint-Honoré. The **Avenue Montaigne** is the home of high fashion and luxury, with the houses of Dior, Givenchy, Nina Ricci, and the sumptuous *Hôtel Plaza-Athénée*. The *Théâtre des Champs-Élysées*, where the Perrault brothers first used reinforced concrete construction methods (1912), should not be overlooked.

From the Rond-Point to the Étoile

Between the Rond-Point des Champs-Élysées and the Place Charles-de-Gaulle (Parisians still call it the Place de l'Étoile), runs the avenue which has the reputation of being the finest in the world. It is split into two unequal parts; on the sunny side, the terrace cafés encroach on the pavement in summer to the inconvenience of pedestrians, and the boutiques, cafés and coffee-shops in the arcades do a thriving trade all year round, some in genuinely luxurious style (*Galeries du Rond-Point, Élysées 26, Claridge's*), others in a more typically "Parisian" setting (the Art Deco *Lido* gallery). The shady side, less favored by the crowds, is lined with automobile showrooms, banks, and airline offices, although *Fouquet's* famous café and terrace (corner Av. George-V), with its celebrated clientele, and the *Publicis Drugstore* (at the top of the Avenue) give it a certain animation. A remaining vestige of the great era of the Champs-Élysées is the **Hôtel de la Païva**, at n° 25. Built around 1860, this was the home of the amazing Thérèse Lachman who, from humble Polish origins, went from husband to husband and lover to lover, becoming first a marquess then a countess. All the time, she was an accomplished international spy. The literary Goncourt brothers, writers Renan and Sainte-Beuve, and the statesman Gambetta were all frequent visitors to her house and salon.

●●
The Arc de Triomphe

Map 1,   Metro and R.E.R.: Étoile-Charles-de-Gaulle   Bus: n°s 22, 30, 31, 43, 52, 73, 83
(A-B 5)

The Place Charles-de-Gaulle, after more than a decade still commonly known as the Place de l'Étoile, provides a fitting crown to the Avenue des Champs-Élysées. The Arc de Triomphe, in addition to its architectural and historical interest, represents, with the Tomb of the Unknown Soldier which lies beneath the arch, a proud symbol of national unity.

=== *HISTORY*

The Place de l'Étoile first took shape in the late 18th century, when the architect Soufflot leveled the summit of the Chaillot Hill to reduce the slope of the Avenue des Champs-Élysées. Five avenues were originally planned to radiate from here, and Napoleon ordered the construction of a gigantic triumphal arch in honor of the Grande Armée. From among the many incredible projects submitted to him — including a statue of Liberty, pyramids to match those of Egypt, and gigantic conference rooms — the Emperor chose Jean Chalgrin's conventional plan. Work was ordered to start in 1806, after the victory of Austerlitz, but construction proved to be slower and costlier than foreseen. When Empress Marie-Louise formally entered Paris by the Champs-Élysées in 1810, painted tarpaulins and plaster statues were hastily improvised to give the impression of a completed arch. The monument shared the misfortune of Napoleon's empire: abandoned under the Restoration, the Arc de Triomphe was, for 30 years, the laughing stock of Paris, the citizens joking that only one solitary mason was ever to be seen at work on the "Altar of the Homeland"! The Arc de Triomphe was finally completed in 1836, and Napoleon's ashes passed under the arch on their return from St Helena in 1840. The Place de l'Étoile assumed its present guise under the Second Empire; Baron Haussmann opened seven new avenues leading away from the Place, while the architect Jacques Hittorf designed all the surrounding facades, which explains their remarkable unity of style.

On July 14th, 1919 the traditional parade of soldiers and generals was also one of victory. In 1920, the body of an unknown soldier was buried under the Arc de Triomphe, and on November 11th, 1923, the **remembrance flame** on the tomb was set alight for the first time. All important national events since, such as the Liberation of Paris in 1944, have been celebrated on the Champs-Élysées.

VISIT

A walk around the Place Charles-de-Gaulle demonstrates the power of the arch's proportions, and brings to life the sculpted groups and the gigantic figures of the frieze. The pedestrian underpass (at the top of the Champs-Élysées, on the right, or at the top of the Avenue de la Grande-Armée, to the left) leads to the central platform. Chalgrin took ancient Roman arches as a model for the Arc de Triomphe. Its dimensions, 164 feet/50 metres high and 148 feet/45 metres wide, make it the largest arch ever built.

A tour of the Arc de Triomphe

Facing the Champs-Élysées is François Rude's masterpiece, *The Departure of the Volunteers*, better known as **La Marseillaise.** The dynamic vitality of this group makes it a matter for regret that President Thiers commissioned other renowned, but less inspired, artists to execute the other three groups. To the left is *The Triumph of 1810* by Cortot.

Facing the Avenue de la Grande-Armée: To the right stands *Resistance* and, to the left, *Peace* both by Etex and both lacking the touch of genius that characterizes *La Marseillaise*. Above these groups are high reliefs representing great events of the Empire: the Funeral of Marceau, the Battle of Aboukir, the Battle of Austerlitz and, on the sides, the Battle of Jemmapes, the Crossing of the Arcole Bridge and the Capture of Alexandria. A 440-foot/135-metre **frieze** runs under the pediment; Rude and five other sculptors have peopled it with 6.5-foot/2-metre tall giants, representing heroes of the Republic (this work was paid for on a per-metre basis).

The interior walls of the arch (*access by underpass*) carry the names of hundreds of generals of the Empire; the **Tomb of the Unknown Soldier** lies under a large slab. Access to the platform at the top of the arch is gained by an elevator (where long queues may be expected) or by a steep staircase. (*Open daily 10 am – 6 pm ex. Tue & Public hols.*) The **panorama** at the top is magnificent, overlooking the twelve radiating, symmetrical avenues. The view over the rich districts of the Right Bank from this high point of the Louvre-La Défense axis is probably of more interest than the modest museum (documents and souvenirs of the arch's construction and history and a film). Visitors may attend the ceremony of the relighting of the flame over the Tomb of the Unknown Soldier every evening at 6 pm.

RECOMMENDED FOR REFRESHMENT

Boulangerie Saint-Philippe, 73 Avenue Franklin-Roosevelt, 75008 (tel: 43 59 78 76). Open 7.30 am – 7.30 pm every day but Sat. Appetizing luncheon dishes.

Chez Mélanie, 27 Rue du Colisée, 75008 (tel: 43 59 42 76). Open 11.30 am – 3 pm Mon to Fri; closed Sat & Sun. A small restaurant with a regular clientele.

FROM PALAIS-ROYAL TO THE PLACE VENDÔME

The area of the Palais-Royal, Place des Victoires and the Place Vendôme was originally dedicated to the glories of the kings of France. Today, the Rue de la Paix and the Place Vendôme house Paris' most elegant jewelers, fashion houses and hotels.

VISIT

The Palais Royal district

The Place du Théâtre-Français, renamed Place André-Malraux, dates from the Second Empire. Two fountains, adorned with cherubs and nymphs and surrounded by a few trees, frame the impressive view up the Avenue de l'Opéra. To the right, the stern facade of the Comédie-Française, and the passage to the arcades of the **Palais Royal,** together with the tiny **Place Colette,** remind the visitor by their irregular aspect that two different ages co-exist here: the age of kings and the age of Haussmann, one looking inwards to dreams of past splendor, the other outwards to trade and international travel.

In the Place Colette, at n° 157, *La Civette,* opened in the mid-18th century, sold the tobacco and cigars made famous by the Duchess of Chartres. This shop subsequently attracted a large clientele of snuff-takers; Casanova draws an amusing picture of it in his *Memoirs.* More recently, the *Louvre des Antiquaires,* opened in 1978 on the site of an old department store, offers 250 antique shops spread over three floors; Art Nouveau, Art Deco and Fifties art take pride of place (*open daily ex. Sun & Mon: 11 am – 7 pm; temporary exhibitions*).

The Théâtre Français, built between 1786 and 1790 by Victor Louis — already famous for his Grand Théâtre at Bordeaux — is home to the company of the Comédie-Française.
Theater-goers can admire the superb, expressive bust of Voltaire* by Houdon in the foyer, as well as the armchair in which Molière died while playing *Le Malade Imaginaire* one afternoon in 1673.

The column in Place Vendôme.

The Comédie Française

In 1680, Louis XIV ordered the actors of the Hôtel de Bourgogne, who were based in the Rue Mauconseil, to join Molière's actors from the Rue Mazarine and form a single company.
The various schemes of well-wishers and factions at the Sorbonne led the fledgling Comédie Française to move from the Théâtre Guénégaud to the Rue de l'Ancienne-Comédie, then to the Odéon. Under the Revolution, the company, led by François Joseph Talma, became established in the Victor Louis hall, then known as the "Théâtre des Variétés-Amusantes".
The talent of Talma and the charms of the actress Anne Mars came to the attention of Napoleon, and the Moscow Decree of 1812 conferred the Statute of Association of Actors on the Comédie-Française, placing *sociétaires* (actor-shareholders), *pensionnaires* (ordinary company members) and *élèves* (pupils) under the direction of an administrator appointed by the government. Headed today by Jean-Pierre Vincent, the Comédie-Française's repertoire consists mainly of the great French classics (Molière, Corneille and Racine), but is also open to foreign playwrights as well, from Shakespeare to Pirandello, and to the modern works of Ionesco and Beckett. None of these has ever provoked a scandal comparable to that which broke out on the evening of February 21st, 1830, when a pitched battle was fought between protagonists of the Classical and Romantic schools over the merits of Victor Hugo's *Hernani*.

••• The Palais-Royal

Map 2, Metro: Palais-Royal Bus: n°s 21, 27, 29, 39, 48, 67, 69, 72, 74, 81, 95
(F6)
Map 4, The Palais-Royal is a quadrangle closed off by its arcades from the outer
(A6) world, a cloistered universe in the center of Paris. The nearby
attractions of the Louvre, Les Halles and the Opéra, do not disturb its
peace and quiet. Neither do the occasional visitors and tourists, who
peer into the showcase windows, nor the local children playing around
the fountains. The calm of the café terraces and the tea-rooms masks
some of the seamier aspects of the "ancien régime" and the birth of the
Revolution.

▬▬▬ HISTORY

Religion preceded royalty within the walls of this ancient palace. To live
as near as possible to Louis XIII, Cardinal Richelieu, in 1624, purchased
a tract of land adjacent to the city walls built by Charles V, and
commissioned the architect Jacques Lemercier to build a vast, but
"modest" palace. This "modesty" can be discerned in the relative
simplicity and lack of pomp of the present-day buildings.

On his death, **Richelieu** bequeathed the palace to Louis XIII; a few
months later, the King followed his counsellor to the grave, and the
Regent, Anne of Austria, and the infant Louis XIV moved in. This
move could hardly be described as innocent, as **Cardinal Mazarin**
owned the Hôtel Tuboeuf in the neighboring Rue Neuve-des-Petits-
Champs, and only the garden separated the two buildings. The cardinal
had a gateway built between the two, and was able to visit his royal
mistress unobserved.

The Fronde rebellion forced the queen to flee Paris with Louis
XIV. On his return, the young King opted for the Louvre as the royal
residence; the Palais-Royal went to the King's brother, **Philippe
d'Orléans,** and from him to his eldest son, Philippe the Regent, whose
name became synonymous with a period of depravity and scandal.

Cafés proliferated in the **Galeries des Proues,** attracting an
affluent crowd. Encyclopaedist Diderot "took his thoughts for a walk"
every day in the gardens and probably crossed the path of the young
Casanova, who hurried to this fashionable spot on his arrival in Paris in
1750.

Fire twice ravaged the **Palace Opera House** (1763 and 1781) and
led to the building of the two wings that line the **Cour de l'Horloge.** In
1781, the Palace became the property of Louis-Philippe d'Orléans who,
being short of money, had apartment houses with ground level shopping
centers and uniform arcades built by Victor Louis; the three sides of the
garden contained sixty shops. The precincts of the Palace became the
most popular resort of idle Parisians who went there to gamble and
otherwise amuse themselves. This provided a ready-made audience for
the protagonists of the revolution. On the evening of July 13th, 1789,
the unknown journalist Camille Desmoulins leaped on a table in the
Café de Foy, called all patriots to arms and exhorted them to wear a
chestnut leaf from the garden as an insignia; the chestnut leaf became
one of the most popular emblems of the Revolution.

Under the Revolution and the Restoration, the gambling frenzy
reached new heights. Cheating and violence got so out of hand that
Louis-Philippe decreed the closing of all gambling houses. The
Palais-Royal was given a new lease of life in the 20th century by Jean
Cocteau and Colette, who chose to live in Galerie de Montpensier and
Galerie de Beaujolais respectively.

VISIT

The Palais-Royal consists of two sections: **the palace** itself, which houses the Conseil d'Etat, and the **arcades** which surround the gardens. The imposing facade of the palace overlooks the Cour d'Honneur with its two groups of four allegorical figures, while the elegant double colonnade separates it from the garden. Surrounding the fountain is the recent work of sculptor Buren which has seriously divided opinion in the Parisian art world. Installed in 1986, the work consists of a series of columns, painted with black-and-white stripes. The quaint gallery shops of the Galerie de Montpensier are also worth a visit. Here, second-hand medals and decorations are sold beside Palais-Royal porcelain. In the Galerie de Beaujolais, the renowned and venerable restaurant *Le Grand Véfour* has two puppet and musical box boutiques as neighbors, while decorators and engravers have set up shop in the Galerie de Valois. Leave the palace by the Galerie de Valois. At n° 6 *Rue de Valois*, the present-day Ministry of Culture, Richelieu, presided over the first meetings of the Académie Francaise. The Passage Verite leads to the tiny **Place de Valois,** with its fine well-restored 18th-century facades, then to the Rue Croix-des-Petits-Champs, which runs along the immense facade of the Bank of France.

A curiously turreted house (1685) stands on the crossroads of the Rue de la Vrilliere. At n°s 1 and 3, the Bank of France occupies the old Hôtel de la Vrilliere (1640), a palatial edifice built by Mansart, with one of the finest 17th-century arcades, the Galerie Dorée.

From Palais-Royal to the Place Vendôme.

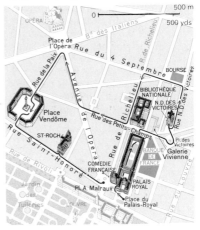

The Palais-Royal.

●● Place des Victoires

Map 3, Metro: Bourse   Bus: n°s 20, 21, 29, 39, 48, 67, 74, 85
(F 1)

The Place des Victoires, a perfect example of the royal squares designed to provide a setting for the statue of the reigning sovereign, has retained its fine layout with practically no modifications despite the opening of the Rue Étienne-Marcel in 1883.

▬▬ HISTORY

In 1681, the **Duc de la Feuillade,** a zealous courtier and an intrepid soldier, commissioned a statue of Louis XIV at his own expense. The problem of its location was solved by having the architect Hardouin-Mansart clear the present square of its old houses and design the facades of the new surrounding mansions. These were quickly snapped up by rich financiers such as Samuel Bernard (n° 7), a great bailer-out of kings. Louis XIV expressed his gratitude by allocating the sum of 120,000 *livres* to de la Feuillade, who nevertheless died bankrupt.

    The statue of the Sun King was melted down in 1792 and replaced by a statue of General Desaix which met the same fate in 1815. The present equestrian statue of Louis XIV is the work of Bosio (19th century).

▬▬ VISIT

Some of Paris' most sought-after fashion designers are today established around the Place des Victoires, which has become one of the world's top design centers.

The short Rue Vide-Gousset leads to the charming Place des Petits-Pères and the **Church of Notre-Dame-des-Victoires*,** erected by Louis XIII to celebrate his victory over the Protestant citadel of La Rochelle. In 1836, the church became the center of an annual mass pilgrimage to the Virgin Mary; over **36,000 votive offerings** cover its walls. In the choir, above the fine 17th-century paneling, hang six large paintings by Van Loo, which illustrate the life of St Augustine. To the left, the second chapel houses the tomb of the 17th-century composer **Lully,** by Coysevox. Also worthy of note is the fine **organ** by Kern, in its 18th-century casing.

The Stock Exchange (La Bourse)
Map 3 (E 1)   Metro: Bourse

Opposite the church, to the right, the Rue Notre-Dame-des-Victoires leads to the bustling Rue Réaumur and the Stock Exchange. Despite its resemblance to an antique temple, the building, built by the architect **Brongniart** between 1808 and 1826, is the scene of feverish activity at quotation time (*daily, 12.30 – 2.30 pm*). Stock brokers, exchange agents, repre-

sentatives and messengers crowd the surrounding square and its restaurants, especially the *Gallopin*, well known as the headquarters of the Paris Stock Exchange milieu.

The Company of Exchange Agents organizes half-hourly audio-visual presentations of the activities of the Exchange (*daily ex. Sat, Sun & Public hols*).

The Rue Vivienne, which runs parallel to the Rue Notre-Dame-des-Victoires appears at first sight to have few attractions. Nevertheless, it contains a remarkable row of 17th- and 18th-century mansions, often colorfully named after the old trading houses. During the week when the doorways are open, it is possible to slip inside and admire the fine facades overlooking the courtyards. Especially noteworthy are n°18 (1660), the door of n° 16, n°s 6 (1640), 4 and 2 (1640, designed by Le Vau). From n° 1 to n° 9, there is a succession of late 19th-century buildings, and, after the garden, the Hôtel Tuboeuf. Mazarin's collection, from which the Bibliothèque Nationale stemmed, was kept here in the 17th century. From 1666 onwards, at n° 6 Colbert assembled the Royal library, which rose from 10,000 to 20,000 volumes, as well as medals from the Louvre and the Cabinet d'Estampes. The mansion belonged to the minister's brother, whose family owned a good half of the district.

●

The Bibliothèque Nationale

The original royal libraries were inherited by "La Nationale", which is supposed to possess a copy of everything published in France since the 16th century. The library occupies the **old Mazarin Palace,** which has been repeatedly enlarged and altered to contain the ever-growing collection. Except for the occasional public exhibition, the Bibliothèque Nationale (National Library) is accessible only to authorized scholars.

HISTORY

France's first book-loving king was probably **Charles V** whose Louvre **collection** amounted to over 1000 volumes. With the invention of the printing press, the royal libraries of François I grew rapidly under the direction of humanist scholar **Guillaume Budé.** The importance of printed books was soon recognized, and the Montpellier decree of 1537 stated that a copy of every publication in France should henceforth be stored in the Louvre collection; this decree still forms the basis of the French **copyright system.**

By 1720, several hundreds of thousands of works had accumulated in the Hôtel Tuboeuf. The constant replenishment of the collection led to the annexation of the Hôtel de Nevers and the Hôtel de Chivry. By the 19th century, the Bibliothèque Nationale had reached its modern-day proportions, occupying 57,000 sq feet/16,000 sq metres of floor space, with 75 mi./120 km of shelves over 10 floors. Today, the library contains about 10,000,000 volumes, the oldest dating back to the 15th century (two Gutenberg bibles), while the most modern editions arrive daily from French publishers.

The manuscript section is even more valuable than the printed works department, including papyrus and parchments together with letters by famous modern authors (Victor Hugo, Flaubert, Proust, Céline). Equally interesting are the Phonotèque Nationale, with its 380,000 records; the 700,000 items in the Cabinet des Médailles; the maps, navigators' logs and globes in the Maps and Plans section; and, lastly, the 2,000,000 photographs and 12,000,000 engravings in the Cabinet des Estampes et Photographies.

VISIT

Without an official library card, there is little to see at the Bibliothèque Nationale; even the reading rooms are screened off to ensure peace and quiet for scholars, although **temporary exhibitions** do succeed in opening the Mansart and splendid Mazarin galleries. However, the Cabinet des Médailles et Antiques is open to the public (*daily 1 – 5 pm*); the famous throne of King Dagobert is displayed here.

The Rue des Petits-Champs, to the right at the end of the Rue Vivienne, runs on towards the Avenue de l'Opéra.

Molière lived near here, at n° 40 Rue Richelieu; a **fountain** by Visconti and Pradier is dedicated to this great playwright whose sudden death released composer Jean-Baptiste Lully from the obligation to repay a debt of 10,000 *livres*.

The Avenue de l'Opéra, with its generous width and luxurious buildings, has become a center of the travel and tourist industry. **The Rue de la Paix** is highly prestigious and far more discreet. The street is the acknowledged headquarters of the luxury jewelry and gem trade.

●●
Place Vendôme

Map 2, Metro: Pyramides, Tuileries   Bus: nᵒˢ 24, 42, 52, 84, 94
(E-F 5)

The Place Vendôme, at the end of Rue de la Paix, is one of the finest examples of French 17th-century architecture: majestic, rigorous and brilliantly laid out.

▬▬ HISTORY

Like the Place des Victoires, the Place Vendôme was conceived as a tribute to Louis XIV by one of his courtiers, François Louvois, who commissioned the architect Jules Hardouin-Mansart to design it.

The square was cleared and an equestrian statue of the King erected at its center in 1715. The land around the square was then sold to rich buyers and gradually the square took shape, displaying a remarkable respect for the overall harmony of the site.

The statue was torn down during the Revolution and, in 1810, the **Austerlitz Column** was erected, crowned by a statue of Napoleon in the guise of Caesar. This was demolished when the Bourbons returned to power and replaced by their emblem, the fleur-de-lys. In a conciliatory gesture, Louis-Philippe reinstated Napoleon, this time in the modest uniform of a corporal; the Commune then pulled the statue down at the instigation of the painter Courbet (*see box*). With the advent of the Third Republic, the column was replaced and has remained undisturbed ever since.

▬▬ VISIT

The magnificent yet stern Place Vendôme narrowly misses being a square: at 700 feet/214 metres by 735 feet/224 metres it can only be termed a rectangle. Its oblique corners, and the projecting facades of its buildings, relieve any underlying monotony of its masterly design. The present Ministry of Justice is housed in the old Royal Chancellery; the glamorous Ritz Hotel stands at n° 15; Chopin died at n° 12, in 1849.

The Rue Saint-Honoré cuts across the Rue de Castiglione, the fine arcades of which link the Place Vendôme to the Rue de Rivoli (equestrian statue of Joan of Arc). Fashion and luxury goods have always held sway here; the suppliers to the court of Versailles were already established in the vicinity at the time of Louis XIV.

The 18th-century patroness of the arts, Mme. Geoffrin, held her salon at n° 374. A block of flats built by the monks of the Feuillants convent runs from n° 229 to n° 235; in 1791 the revolutionary club founded by La Fayette, Sieyès and Talleyrand, was established here. David painted his monumental *Serment du Jeu de Paume* ("The Tennis Court Oath", 1789, now at the Louvre), in the old church.

Courbet and the Vendôme Column

On April 12, 1871, at the instigation of the painter Gustave Courbet and the playwright Félix Pyat, the Paris Commune decreed the demolition of the column that supported the statue of Napoleon in Place Vendôme. On the morning of May 16, all Paris, or so it seemed, temporarily forgot the enemy besieging the city and turned their fury against the Vendôme column.

Twelve days later, the Republican troops from Versailles regained control of the capital.

Courbet was deemed responsible for the column's destruction; he was sentenced to six months in prison and ordered to pay for the entire cost of its restoration. This ruined him, and in 1873 he fled to Switzerland to escape his debts. During his absence, his paintings were seized and sold off at bargain prices. Four years later he died, aged 58, an impoverished exile.

●

Church of Saint-Roch

The Church of Saint-Roch, a fine example of Baroque architecture, boasts a remarkable collection of funerary sculptures.

HISTORY

Although begun in 1653 according to **Lemercier's** plans, work on the Church of Saint-Roch was delayed by lack of funds, and by the hillock that forced the nave to be oriented to the north instead of the east. In the early 18th century, **Hardouin-Mansart** decided to add a series of chapels, which extended the length of the church to over 410 feet/125 metres. Only a large donation by banker John Law, a recent convert to Catholicism, permitted the completion of the vaults; Robert de Cotte designed the facade in an unexpectedly Jesuit style.

General Bonaparte repulsed an attack by Royalist rebels in 1795 on the steps of this church, and gained a reputation as a defender of the Republic which proved invaluable to his later career.

VISIT

The design of the church is quite exceptional. To the Classical 17th-century nave and choir, two circular 18th-century chapels have been added, one behind the other, with cupola roofs. The end chapel was rebuilt in the 19th century. Of particular interest, in the side chapels to the right, are the bust of Maréchal de Créqui by Coysevox, and the statue of Cardinal Dubois by Coustou; and to the left, in the Chapelle des Fonts, the **Chassériau frescoes.** Behind the chancel are two paintings by Vignon and Le Sueur; over the altar of the Chapelle de la Vierge is a magnificent **Nativity** originally from Val-de-Grâce.

The district that spreads from the Avenue de l'Opéra, between the Place Vendôme and the Place des Victoires requires a brief comment. Nowhere else in Paris did Haussmann's development projects have such an impact as here. Not only were many old buildings demolished but even the topography of the area was changed. The Church of Saint-Roch was no exception. During the construction of the Avenue de l'Opéra the Saint-Roch hillside was leveled. Originally, it had been high enough to enable several windmills to operate on its crest, hence the **Rue des Moulins (Mill Street),** near the **Rue Sainte-Anne.** One of these mills was to have an unusual career; it was dismantled and rebuilt on another hill, or *butte*, that no one has, so far, considered levelling – the Butte Montmartre, where the mill (now the Moulin Radet) still spreads its vanes over the sign of the famous *Moulin de la Galette.* The Butte Saint-Roch has now completely disappeared; over the 15 years between 1864 and 1879, thousands of tons of soil were carted away from here and hundreds of houses demolished.

The Rue de l'Échelle, on the way to the Place André-Malraux, evokes the bloody past of the Butte Saint-Roch. The ladder (*échelle*) in question was used by the ecclesiastical authorities to convey offenders and blasphemers to the scaffold.

RECOMMENDED FOR REFRESHMENT

Gallopin, 40 Rue N-D.-des-Victoires, 75002 (tel: 42 36 45 38). Open 11 am – 3 pm, 7 pm – midnight Mon to Fri. The Stock Exchange's traditional rendezvous.
A Priori Thé, 35-37 Galerie Vivienne, 75002 (tel. 42 97 48 75). Open noon – 7 pm Mon to Sat. Sweet and savory pies under the arcades.
The Ritz Bar, 15 Place Vendôme, 75001 (tel 42 60 38 30). Open 11 am – 1 am Mon to Sun. Affordable for breakfast or afternoon tea!
Le Rubis, 10 Rue du Marché-Saint-Honoré, 75001 (tel: 42 61 03 34). Open 7 am – 11 pm Mon to Fri; closed during Aug; good wine bar.

FROM SAINT-HONORÉ TO THE DEPARTMENT STORE DISTRICT

This area is an object lesson in French "art de vivre": from *Maxim's* to the early 1900s tea-room of the Printemps department store, by way of the luxury shops on the Faubourg-Saint-Honoré and the Louis XV furniture at the André-Jacquemart museum. There is a sense of discreet pleasure in the good things of life that money can buy, a feeling that is palpable in the showrooms of the great fashion houses, in the department stores of the Boulevard Haussmann, and among the well-behaved children of the Parc Monceau.

Saint-Honoré district

Metro: Concorde, Madeleine   Bus: nos 24, 42, 84, 94   **Map 2 (D-E 1-3)**

The short, broad **Rue Royale** which passes between Gabriel's magnificent colonnades, frames the church of the Madeleine to fine advantage. Its 18th-century buildings, also designed by Gabriel, are worth special attention, despite the fact that the street's former private residents — Gabriel himself at n° 8, Mme de Staël, the writer, at n° 6 — have been replaced by plush company headquarters and luxury shops. Among the most illustrious addresses here is *Maxim's* restaurant, as much a part of history as it is of gastronomy.

The **Rue du Faubourg-Saint-Honoré** leads off to the left from the Rue Royale along the route that led from the Porte Saint-Honoré (Rue Royale) to the village of Roule in mediaeval times.

▬▬ *HISTORY*

Under Louis XIV, and particularly under **Louis XV,** the low price of land led to the construction of a number of mansions, whose gardens spread as far as the Avenue Gabriel. This new, aristocratic quarter rivaled the Faubourg Saint-Germain with its elegance, its salons, and its fêtes. Today, numerous **luxury boutiques**, embassies, and the Ministère de l'Intérieur (Ministry of Home Affairs) occupy the buildings around the residence of the President of the Republic. The luxury trade was established here with the opening of the *A la Pensée* boutique at n° 5, in 1809; *Aux Montagnes Russes* followed at n° 9, in 1831, then Thierry Hermès transferred his saddlery shop to n° 24 in 1880, just 10 years before Jeanne Lanvin established, at n° 22, her haute-couture boutique.

▬▬ *VISIT*

Rue du Faubourg-Saint-Honoré: Yves Saint-Laurent, Chloé, Sonya Rykiel, Ungaro, Tarlazzi, De Luca, Walter Steiger, Stéphanie Kélian and nearby Dior (Rue Boissy-d'Anglas), Maurice Segoura's antiques and *Maxim's* Art Nouveau boutique are all here. The Rue du Faubourg-Saint-Honoré also has a number of fine townhouses, which tend to be overlooked in this profusion of luxury shops.

The Town Hall of the 1st arrondissement was originally established in 1811, at n° 14. A perfume store was opened in 1774 at n° 19, forerunner of the numerous present-day shops. The houses at nos 21 and 23 date from 1776. The handsome facade of

The entrance of the Ritz Hotel close to Rue du Faubourg-Saint-Honoré.

the Hôtel de Rohan-Montbazon has been remodeled since its construction in 1719. Nᵒˢ 33 and 35 date from the early 18th century as does the Hôtel de Charost at nᵒ 39. This belonged to the rebellious Pauline Bonaparte, who sold it to George III of England in 1815, when she became Princess Borghese; the fine mansion is now the British Embassy. The palace at nᵒ 41 next door was built by Visconti in the mid-19th century; it was later taken over by the Rothschild family who leased it to the United States for use as an embassy.

L'Élysée

Map 2 (E-3)
Metro: Champs-Élysées-Clemenceau

The Élysée Palace, residence of the French President, is still protected by resplendent Republican guards in their sentry boxes; less decorative, but far more effective, are the police and "gardes mobiles" (intervention forces) who prohibit curious visitors from watching the endless coming and going of official cars through the palace gates, which are usually closed.

HISTORY

The palace was built by Claude Molet in 1718 for the Count of Évreux, then purchased by the Marquise de Pompadour, the mistress of Louis XV, in 1753. The greedy marquise wheedled the plot of land that juts into the Avenue Gabriel from the enamored king; it was filched from the public promenade of the Champs-Elysées, and has unfortunately never been returned.

During the Revolution the confiscated palace was rented out as apartments (the writer Alfred de Vigny spent part of his youth here), and the gardens were opened to the public. Marshal Murat had the site restored and gave it to Napoleon, who signed his second abdication here on June 22nd, 1815, before leaving for St Helena. Returned to the royal family, the palace was used to accommodate visiting sovereigns before the Third Republic made it the presidential palace.

After the Élysée, the Rue du Faubourg-Saint-Honoré leaves behind the world of high fashion to enter that of art galleries and antique dealers. To the right, in the **Place Beauvau,** opened in 1836, the Ministère de l'Intérieur (Ministry of Home Affairs) hides behind Doric columns which frame the magnificent wrought iron gates.

The 19 tenants of the Élysée Palace

The Élysée Palace has been the residence of 19 French presidents since 1873. They are: Mac-Mahon, Jules Grévy, Sadi-Carnot, Casimir-Périer, Félix Faure, Émile Loubet, Armand Fallières, Raymond Poincaré, Paul Deschanel, Alexandre Millerand, Gaston Doumergue, Paul Doumer, Albert Lebrun, Vincent Auriol, René Coty, Charles de Gaulle, Georges Pompidou, Valéry Giscard d'Estaing, and, since May 10th, 1981, François Mitterrand. The only president to die in the Élysée Palace was Félix Faure, who died in the arms of the beautiful Mme. Steinheil, who was then hastily ushered out through the tradesmen's entrance.

As it nears the Avenue Matignon, the Rue du Faubourg-Saint-Honoré loses much of its commercial look. On the corner of the avenue stands the *Julien Cornic* book-store, specializing in fashion and its history, under a row of quaint, low pavilions reminiscent of a 1900 seaside resort. Some of the world's most famous **art galleries** are to be found along the stretch of the avenue which runs to the Rond-Point-des-Champs-Élysées.

The Church of Saint-Philippe-du-Roule rises at the corner of the Rue du Faubourg-Saint-Honoré and the Rue La Boétie. This imitation Romanesque basilica was built by Chalgrin between 1774 and 1784 on the site of the chapel of a leper colony, and is the parish church of one of the capital's most fashionable congregations. Note the powerful fresco of the *Descent from the Cross* by Chassériau (1855) over the chancel. On leaving the church, take the Rue Myron-T.-Herrick to join the Rue de Courcelles, which leads to the broad **Boulevard Haussmann.**

Jacquemart-André Museum**
Map 2 (C-D, 2) Metro: Saint-Philippe-du-Roule, Miromesnil

The Jacquemart-André Museum is housed in a late 19th-century mansion at nᵒ 158 Bd. Haussmann (*open 1.30 – 5.30 pm ex. Mon, Tue, Public hols, Aug; tel: 45 62 39 94*). The exhibits form an elegant *pot-pourri*, the results of the ceaseless efforts of collectors

Édouard André (1835–1894) and his wife Nélie Jacquemart (1841–1912). Botticelli is juxtaposed with François Boucher, and Tuscan primitives with Canaletto's *Venise en Fête*, Palissy ceramics and Louis XV tables.

André and Jacquemart scoured **Italy** to bring back treasures from the **Florentine quattrocentro** (Donatello, Della Robbia, Botticelli), from the **Venetian Renaissance** (Titian, Mantegna, Tintoretto) and masterpieces such as the bust of Pope Gregory XV by Bernini, or the small but exquisite *St George Slaying the Dragon* by Paolo Uccello.

The museum's ground floor has numerous fine pieces of furniture and *objets d'art*, sculptures by Lemoyne and Pigalle, tapestries, and paintings and drawings by Watteau, Greuze, Boucher and Fragonard that recall the blossoming of French art under Louis XV. 17th- and 18th-century European art is represented by works of varying importance by Reynolds, Rembrandt, Canaletto, Van Dyck, Frans Hals, Murillo and, above all, by the superb **Tiepolo frescoes** which cover the ceilings of rooms 4, 5 and 13. Note also the beautiful 16th-century Limoges enamels.

Parc Monceau

Metro: Monceau   Bus: nᵒˢ 30, 84, 94   **Map 2, (B-C, 1-2)**

Leave the Boulevard Haussmann and climb the Rue de Courcelles. To your right, off the Place de Pérou, the Rue Rembrandt leads to the gates of Parc Monceau. The park itself is surrounded by fine **Napoleon III mansions.** The beautiful house at n°5 Rue Van Dyck was built by M. Menier, who made a fortune from the manufacture of chocolate.

═══ *HISTORY*

The Parc Monceau is a favorite haunt of both joggers and children; the contrast between the natural setting and the Baroque fantasies of the neighboring houses is delightful.

From Saint-Honoré to the department store district.

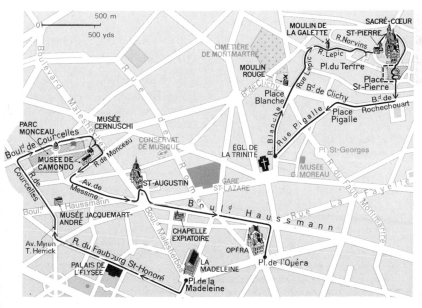

The present park covers only a modest part of the immense estate of the Duc d'Orléans, the future Philippe Egalité, who, in 1778, commissioned the architect, painter and writer **Carmontelle** to design a garden in the then-fashionable "Anglo-Chinese" style. Carmontelle's creation rivaled the landscapes of pre-Romantic painter Hubert Robert: grottoes, waterfalls, hillocks, pools, and thickets provided the setting for an imitation pyramid, a pagoda, a Roman temple, Dutch windmills and mediaeval ruins. The building of the Octroi wall added a further ornament: **Nicolas Ledoux's rotunda** toll-house, with its later dome.

The Second Empire gave the park its present look, reducing it to half its original size. The financier, Péreire, pulled off one of his most spectacular real estate operations here, selling off 25 acres/10 hectares of the park as building plots. The engineer Alphand later restored the park's buildings which had fallen into ruin, and today the park remains a fitting adornment to one of the capital's most affluent districts.

FROM PARC MONCEAU TO THE DEPARTMENT STORE DISTRICT

In the vicinity of Parc Monceau there are a number of small museums **The Cernuschi Museum***, the City of Paris' Chinese art museum at n° 7 Avenue Vélasquez, has the collection of one of the first Frenchmen to take an interest in the art of the Far East, the banker Enrico Cernuschi (*open daily 10 am – 5.30 pm ex. Mon & Public hols; tel: 45 63 50 75*). Most of his personal collection was brought back from a two-year voyage to China in 1871–1873; the museum has since been enriched by several donations.

On the ground floor, are the Han Dynasty funerary objects, the T'ang clay figures and, in the left-hand room, Shang and Chou bronzes, jewelry, buckles and mirrors. In the foyer, the painted silk *Horses and Grooms* is one of the T'ang Dynasty's finest masterpieces (*temporary exhibitions on the first floor*).

The Nissim de Camondo Museum*, at n° 63 Rue de Monceau (*open 10 am – noon; 2 – 5 pm daily ex. Mon, Tue & Public hols; tel: 45 63 26 32*), was offered as an annex to the Decorative Arts Museum by Count Moïse de Camondo, in memory of his son Nissim, who was killed in an air battle during WWI. In this mansion, rebuilt in 1910, the Camondo family had assembled an exceptional collection of 18th-century *objets d'art*, furniture, Aubusson tapestries, Savonnerie carpets, paintings by Guardi, Hubert Robert and Jongkind, Sèvres porcelain and silver services, furniture signed by Riesener, Martin Carlin and Leleu. All of this is displayed in fine paneled rooms. On the first floor, the magnificent tapestries based on sketches by Oudry, which illustrate the fables of La Fontaine, are worth special attention. Don't miss the room with panels painted by J.-B. Huet, and the "Buffon" service, of which every dish is painted with a different bird.

The Jean-Jacques Henner Museum, 43 Avenue de Villiers (*open daily ex. Mon, 10 – noon; 2 – 5 pm; tel: 47 63 42 73*), has paintings, studies and drawings by this Alsatian artist who won the Prix de Rome in 1868, and who drew his inspiration from such Italian masters as Titian and Correggio. Henner was much appreciated in his life-time; serious in style, his work was far removed from that of the Impressionist school which was soon to flourish.

The Boulevard Malesherbes, at the other end of the Avenue Vélasquez, which leads to the Parc Monceau, is the model Parisian boulevard as conceived by Haussmann. Note the superb 1860–1880 buildings with their stone balconies, their skylights and pilasters, and the sculptures adorning their majestic facades. On the corner of the Rue des Mathurins is an early 20th-century building with a conservatory.

The Church of Saint-Augustin, massive and ponderous under its 164-foot/50-metre dome, conceals a complex idea beneath its apparent banality; in 1866, Baltard, who had just used iron to build Les Halles on Napoleon III's insistence, employed a cast-iron framework to support this Italian Renaissance-*cum*-Byzantine structure.

Church of Saint-Augustin.

From the Place Saint-Augustin, the Boulevard Haussmann curves slightly. To the right, the Square Louis XVI encloses an **expiatory chapel.** This necropolis-like monument was built over the old Madeleine cemetery where a number of the Revolution's victims were buried, among them Louis XVI and Marie-Antoinette. Their remains were exhumed in 1815 and transferred to Saint-Denis, while Percier and Fontaine undertook the construction of the neo-Gothic chapel. In the vaults, Louis XVI appears prostrated in prayer, while Cortot has depicted Marie-Antoinette upheld by the figure of Religion.

All around are impressive buildings representing financial and commercial interests: the dome of the Union and Phoenix insurance company on the corner of the Rue Pasquier, and the massive Wagons-Lits headquarters at the crossroads of the Rue de l'Arcade and the Rue des Mathurins.

The bustle and flurry generated by the adjacent Gare Saint-Lazare and the shops of Rue Tronchet give a foretaste of the permanent agitation around two nearby shrines of Parisian chic: the "Grands Magasins" (department stores) *Le Printemps* and *Les Galeries Lafayette.* Note the sculptures that decorate the rotunda and the

Haussmann's Paris

Baron Haussmann made radical changes in the appearance of the capital. All through the Second Empire (1852–1870), he demolished whole districts to make room for new avenues, freeing Paris from the stifling entanglement of its old districts. Some contemporary observers had nothing but praise for Haussmann's gigantic labors. Théophile Gautier wrote in 1855:

"Modern Paris could not exist within the old Paris. Civilization cuts broad avenues through the somber mazes, crossroads and blind alleys of the old town; it chops down houses just as the American pioneers chopped down trees. Decayed walls crumble to allow dwellings fit for Man to rise from their ruins, where health is borne in with the air, and serene thought with the sunlight."

Others, like Baudelaire, were more nostalgic: "Le vieux Paris n'est plus ... la forme d'une ville change plus vite, hélas! Que le coeur d'un mortel." ("Old Paris is no more ... the shape of a town changes more quickly, alas, than the heart of a mortal.")

fine late 19th-century mosaics of *Le Printemps;* also the Art Nouveau wrought-iron work of *Les Galeries Lafayette.*

The **Gare Saint-Lazare** is the world's third-largest railway station, after Tokyo and Chicago. 110,000,000 travelers and harassed commuters travel annually through its portals, forcing the locality to live according to their office hours: five days per week, there are traffic jams every morning between eight and nine and every evening between five and six, while the shops, snack-bars and restaurants are crowded at lunch-time. Nightfall brings comparative calm, and brings to life the porno cinemas and the doubtful pleasures of the Rue de Budapest.

The **Rue de Rome,** to the left of the station, climbs towards the Boulevard des Batignolles between the shopfronts of its numerous musical instrument stores. The **Conservatoire National Supérieur de la Musique** stands nearby in the Rue

---

Also worth seeing ...

The Russian church** in the Rue Daru (17th arrondissement, Metro: Courcelles) is dedicated to St Alexander-Nevsky. It is built on traditional Orthodox lines, with an onion dome and a profusion of vividly-colored arches and much goldwork. Five cupolas crown the building which is classified as a cathedral. Erected in 1860, it was financed by Czar Alexander II and the flourishing Russian community in Paris.

---

de Madrid, although it will soon be transferred to the La Villette Center; a small museum (*open: 2 – 6 pm Wed to Sat, ex. Aug & Public hols*) displays the instruments and various souvenirs of famous composers and musicians.

From the Grands Boulevards to Montmartre

Few of the cabarets and music halls that made Paris the world's capital of pleasure and entertainment in the 19th century and during *La Belle Époque* have survived. The great amusement parks — the Tivolis, Vauxhalls, Olympic Circuses, the Ruggieri Gardens in the Rue Saint-Lazare, the *Jeux Chevaleresques* at the Porte Maillot, the *Montagnes Russes* at Ternes and the race-course at the Place Clichy — are but distant memories, sacrificed under the reign of Louis-Philippe and the Second Empire to real estate speculation.

The theaters were better able to adapt to changing fashions and still line the boulevards: *l'Ambigu*, at n° 2 Bd Saint-Martin (founded by Audinot in 1769, rebuilt in 1827) staged the premiere of Dumas' *Three Musketeers*; the *Théâtre de la Porte-Saint-Martin*, at n° 16, drew crowds from all over Paris to see Frederick Lemaître and Marie Dorval in the 1850s; the *Théâtre de la Renaissance*, at n° 20, founded in 1872, under the directorship of Sarah Bernhardt, who created *Lorenzaccio* by Musset here; the *Théâtre des Nouveautés* was rebuilt in 1920, at n° 24 Bd Poissonnière, and the *Théâtre des Variétés* (1807) occupies the site of the old Panorama gardens at n° 7 Bd Montmartre. At n° 1 Bd des Capucines, the *Vaudeville* has been replaced by the Paramount cinema; at n° 28 *Les Montagnes Russes* is now the famous *Olympia* music-hall.

The "Gay Paree" of the music hall and the sequinned and feathered "revues" are not found in the boulevards but in streets like the Rue Richer, where n° 32 is the famous *Folies Bergère*, established in 1869, or at the foot of the Montmartre slopes, home to the *Casino de Paris*, the *Élysées Montmartre* and the legendary *Chat Noir*.

CASINO DE PARIS

The *Casino de Paris* opened at n° 38 Rue de Clichy in 1890. Long before then, this site was the setting for the Folie Richelieu, regarded in its time as the choicest place for risqué entertainment. Even Louis XV and Madame de Pompadour are rumored to have rarely turned down the Duc de Richelieu's erotic suppers there. The Revolution put an end to such goings-on; Citizen Desrivières bought the Folie and turned it into an indoor amusement park called **"Tivoli"**, which had acrobats, showmen in balloons, fireworks by the Ruggieri brothers (creators of the Royal Fireworks for which Handel composed music); it also had the tight-rope walker Madame Saqui who fired the heart of at least one spectator: Napoleon Bonaparte. The *Tivoli* was sold off in 1851 and converted into an enormous skating ring called the *Pole Nord*. The first *Casino de Paris* was a vast and florid Second Empire ballroom; burned down in 1895, it was rebuilt with superb Art Nouveau glass panels. From 1920 it became the quintessential Parisian revue, with stars such as Mistinguett, Maurice Chevalier, Joséphine Baker, Line Renaud and Zizi Jeanmaire heading the bill.

═══ RECOMMENDED FOR REFRESHMENT ═══

Near Parc Monceau:
Sucre et Sel, 30 Rue Salneuve, 75017 (tel: 42 27 77 47). Open noon – 6.30 pm Mon to Sat; noon – 3 pm Sun. Midway between a restaurant and a tea room.
Near the department stores:
La Clairière, 43 Rue Saint-Lazare, 75008 (tel: 48 74 32 94). Open 7 am – 7.30 pm Mon to Fri. A good, traditional bistro.
Le Roi du Pot-au-Feu, 34 Rue Vignon, 75009 (tel: 47 42 37 10). Open noon – 9 pm Mon to Sat. Old-fashioned décor, traditional cuisine, reasonable prices.
Ma Bourgogne, 133 Boulevard Haussmann, 75008 (tel: 45 63 50 61). Open 7 am – 9 pm Mon to Fri. Extensive luncheon menu.

THE SAINT-GERMAIN DISTRICT

The Faubourg-Saint-Germain falls in the 6th and 7th arrondissements of modern Paris, although in the 17th to 19th centuries, when L'Ile de la Cité was the center of Paris, it was a suburb (*faubourg*). Geographically, it straddles the very contrasting worlds of Les Invalides and Saint-Germain-des-Prés: the former was the elegant Paris of the Sun King, the latter the Paris of cafés, literary bars and jazz cellars. The Faubourg-Saint-Germain has an atmosphere of aloofness and privacy, achieved by being the sanctuary of the Establishment for over two centuries. Even today, the large number of police patrols make this district of ministries and the National Assembly resemble a well-protected garrison. Gone are the days when, with the concierge's permission, you could peer through the half-open doors into private courtyards or even visit a family mansion on a guided tour. Now, so many of the private mansions have been commandeered as government ministries that their doors are kept guarded with all the paraphernalia of security systems and cameras, and there is strictly no entry.

HISTORY

In accordance with the wishes of the nobility of the kingdom, the Faubourg-Saint-Germain gradually superseded the Marais as the district of high society towards the end of the 17th century and the beginning of the 18th century. During a period of 50 years, from 1680 to 1730, most of the large mansions in the area around Grenelle were constructed or nearing completion. This gave it an incredible unity but made it lose its old character, now only to be found in a few streets, particularly around Les Invalides, Rue Saint-Dominique and Rue de Grenelle. For more than a century, the Faubourg was the most fashionable district of Paris. Mme. du Deffand and, later, Mme. Récamier held court here, and bankers such as Samuel Bernard or politicians like Barras and Talleyrand gave sumptuous parties. A century later, the area is still the home of elegance and class in contrast to the easy-going life and mixed society of the Champs-Élysées or the great boulevards.

VISIT

The Pont de la Concorde is the most "republican" of all Parisian bridges. Building was begun in 1787 (by the engineer Perronet) and was completed in 1791, with stones taken from the ruins of the Bastille — "so that the population would always be able to trample on the old fortress". Millions of hurrying drivers are scarcely aware of the patriotic act they perform each day when they cross the Seine between the Concorde and the Quai d'Orsay.

The Palais-Bourbon
Map 4 (A3) Metro: Chambre-des-Députés,
Bus: n°s 84, 63, 94.
(*Visit on request: 126 Rue de l'Université; tel: 42 97 64 08. To attend a session, apply in person at 33, Quai d'Orsay.*)

La Chambre des Députés (Chamber of Deputies) with the Senate comprises the French Parliament. Today the parliament meets in the mansion built in 1722 for the Duchesse de Bourbon, daughter of Louis XIV and Madame de Montespan; later it was enlarged and embellished by the Prince de Condé. During the Revolution, the Committee of Five Hundred used it for meetings and afterwards the National Archives were stored there. Later, they were transferred to Rue des Archives (p.135) Napoleon added a Classical facade, with a colonnade designed to match that of the Madeleine.
Viewed from the Seine side, the Palais-Bourbon is rigid and austere. However, the original facade overlooking the **Place du Palais-Bourbon** has retained some of

The Pont des Arts and the Institut de France.

the character of its century, although spoiled by extensions. The ornate facade of the portico, sculpted by Corton in 1842, and the bas-reliefs on the walls of the wings by Rude and Pradier may be viewed from the outside; but admission to the palace requires written permission.

If you do manage to enter, note the waiting room ("la salle des pas-perdus") with its ceiling painted by Vernet. The library is decorated by a history of civilization, painted by Delacroix; Houdon's busts of Voltaire and Diderot are also to be found there.

The art of conversation

The art of conversation is supposed to have reached its pinnacle in the salons of the 18th century. A Wednesday visitor at Madame Geoffrin's had this to say about it: "At her house, you are not allowed to talk about the business of the court or the city, of war and peace, theology or metaphysics or, in general, of any worldly subject!" What there was left to talk about is left to our imagination, though perhaps it may be found in the voluminous writings of the age. We will content ourselves by naming some of the immortals in whose salons this inimitable talk was heard: Madame du Deffand and Madame Geoffrin; Madame de Staël and Madame Récamier; and, in the 19th century, Princesse de Mathilde, Madame de Caillavet, Polignac and Madame de la Rochefoucauld.

The Rue de Bourgogne, with its plush restaurants and luxurious apartments, would be well detailed in guides to parliamentary life if such guides existed. The visitor, however, would do better to head towards the **Rue de Grenelle** where, on the right at n°s 138–140, one can see the elaborate portal and the noble facade in the courtyard of the 18th-century **Hôtel de Sens,** the last residence of Marshal Foch, now occupied by the National Geographic Institute. Next door, at n° 142, the **Hôtel de Chanac** (1750), offers its current resident, the Swiss Ambassador, the luxury of an incomparable bathroom designed by Brongniart in 1782. Opposite, at n° 127, is the luxurious **Hôtel du**

Châtelet (1770), the front of which is decorated with huge Greek columns. It now contains the offices of the Ministère du Travail (Ministry of Labor).

Along the Boulevard des Invalides, you join **Rue de Varenne**. The vast garden, which is hidden behind the iron fence at the end of the boulevard, belongs to the Rodin Museum. The former **Hôtel de Biron**, set in some of the capital's most beautiful gardens, contains the major works of Rodin.

Rodin Museum **

(Map 4, C 3; 77, Rue de Varenne. Metro: Varenne. Bus: n°s 69, 87. *Open 10 am – 5.30 pm and 10 am – 5 pm Oct – Mar ex. Tue, Public hols; tel: 47 05 01 34.*) A shrewd barber had this mansion built in 1728 by Jacques Gabriel, who was the father of Louis XV's favorite architect. It was bought by the Duchesse du Maine, then by Marshal Biron and the ambitious and scandalous courtesan Lauzun; a religious boarding school altered its rather risqué decor prior to Matisse, Cocteau and Rodin moving into the mansion, which had been singled out for demolition. Rodin's growing fame changed these plans, and the government of the time purchased the building, to

"Eve" in the Rodin Museum.

which the sculptor donated all his work before his death. The Rodin Museum has retained the original collection of Rodin's work, which is distributed between the mansion's rooms and its beautiful gardens. In the main courtyard, on the right, *The Thinker***; on the left, *The Burghers of Calais*** and *The Gates of Hell*. The English-style gardens, with their collection of statues, are also open to the public. Works representing all the different phases of Rodin's art, such as *The Kiss***, the *Walking Man** and *The Cathedral** are grouped together on the ground floor of the mansion. The quality of the seductive female portraits displayed around the salons should not eclipse the beauty of the 18th-century paneling on which they hang; *Eve* and *The Age of Bronze* carry on a silent conversation here, while the first floor is reserved for works done by Rodin in his youth and for sketches by Balzac and Victor Hugo. In this setting of bronze and white marble, often in almost crude form, the colors of the paintings by Van Gogh (*Les Moissonneurs****, *Le Père Tanguy****), by Renoir (*Nu**) and by Monet (*Paysage de Belle Ile***) burst forth with an exuberance which contrasts sharply with the dramatic tension suggested in the works of Rodin.

The Rue de Varenne was built on the site of the former abbey of Saint-German des-Prés, as was the Rue de Grenelle.

Hôtel de Broglie, at n° 73, built by Boffrand in 1735, was the American headquarters during World War I. N°s 74, the small Castries house (1760) and 78, the simple facade of which hides the beautiful **Hôtel de Villeroy** (1725), are now occupied by the Ministry of Agriculture. Note the spectacular portal of n° 72, the **Hôtel de Castries**, built in 1709.
A bit farther on, at n° 69, you can see the two magnificent courtyards of the **Hôtel de Seissac**, modified under Louis XVI, now used as an annex to the Hôtel Matignon at n° 57.

The Hôtel Matignon is, without question, the most beautiful mansion in the area. Begun in 1721 by Courtonne, sold unfinished, then improved by the Comtesse de Matignon, it became the property of Talleyrand who held magnificent parties there between 1808 and 1811. Since 1958, the mansion has been the residence of the prime minister. Only his guests are able to appreciate the panels painted by Fragonard and the tranquility of Paris's largest private park. Note the portal of the **Hôtel**

Gouffier de Thoix (1719) surmounted by its sculpted shell, and the Hôtel de Gallifet at n° 50. Then rejoin the Rue de Grenelle via the Boulevard Raspail or the Rue du Bac, arriving at n° 59, the Hôtel Bouchardon.

The Dina Vierny Museum is installed in what used to be the home of 19th-century man-of-letters Alfred de Musset. Before seeing the modern works of art within, pause in front of the Fontaine des Quatre Saisons* **(The Fountain of the Four Seasons)**, sculpted by Bouchardon between 1739 and 1748. This fountain illustrates the early problems of providing the capital with water, not really solved until Napoleon III; until then, the area did not have a satisfactory water supply. Images of Paris, the Seine, the Marne and cupids in bas-relief decorate this fountain. Voltaire dismissed it as "a lot of stone for a little water".

The Rue de Grenelle offers a row of beautiful 18th-century houses: n° 79, the Hôtel d' Estrées, belonged to Czar Nicholas II and is now the Soviet Embassy. At n° 85, the Hôtel d'Avaray has been excellently restored by the Dutch Embassy. The long facade of the Hôtel de Courteilles at n° 110, obscures, behind its ten Corinthian columns, the Ministry of Education. You may prefer the **Hôtel de Villars**, built by

The Saint-Germain district.

La Vie Parisienne 1848 – 1914

This was the period during which Paris reached its apogee. This status was due to Napoleon III's empire and to the projects realized by Haussmann, as well as to the Universal Exhibitions held in the capital in 1889 and 1900. This was a time of fabulous parties, from which no one — gangster, banker, English lord or working girl — was turned away. It was also the era of the courtesans, over whom grand-dukes and princes fought in the *Café Anglais* and *Maxim's*, and for whom more than one rich man went to ruin. Their names still retain their seductive power: Cora Pearl, La Païva, Liane de Pougy, Émilienne d'Alençon, La Belle Otero, Cléo de Mérode ... The quest for pleasure was not restricted to high society. The 1860s were the golden age of the café-concert. Among the most popular were those held at the **Eldorado**, n° 3 Bd. de Strasbourg. Built in 1858, and recently renovated, this theater presented a succession of the stars of the day: Theresa, Judic, Yvette Guilbert, and, in particular, Dranem, notorious for his absurd and saucy songs. At the **Alcazar d'Été**, on the Champs-Élysées, Paulus achieved fame with his song "En revenant de la revue" ("Coming home from the show"), while Polin staged *The Comical Soldier* at the **Ambassadeurs** (located near the Hôtel de Crillon). To cater to a more artistic audience, Rudolphe Salis opened the renowned **Chat Noir**, on the Bd. Rochechouart, where Aristide Bruant, with his black felt hat and red scarf, was immortalized by Toulouse-Lautrec. From the 1870s, the whole of Paris flocked there, as they did in 1889, when the famous **Moulin-Rouge** was opened at the Place Blanche. The "quadrille naturaliste", otherwise known as the French can-can, was pioneered at the **Elysée-Montmartre**, and created a new music-hall show, where music, song, dance and strip-tease were the forerunners of today's Parisian cabaret. Among the hot-spots were, and still remain, the **Folies-Bergère** in Rue Richer, the **Casino de Paris** in Rue de Clichy, the **Ba-Ta-Clan** in Bd Voltaire and the **Concert Mayol**. Paris began to have a reputation for its daring: the first known public strip-tease performed by some artists' models for the Quat-Z-Arts ball in 1893 earned the performers several days in prison. This reputation for "risqué" entertainment endures to the present day.

Boffrand in 1713, where two exquisite oval windows decorated with garlands open on to n° 118; or perhaps the house at n° 134 which is somewhat incongruous since it is an example of Art Nouveau by Lavirotte. **Via the Rue de Bellechasse**, you rejoin the Bd. Saint-Germain, passing the huge Ministry of Defense on the left. Its rather dull 1877 facade contrasts with the old area of Rue Saint-Dominique (n°s 16, 14, 12, 10, 8). The Rue de Bellechasse then crosses the main road (going towards the Seine), **Rue de l'Université**. Lamartine lived at n° 82; the **Hôtel de Soyecourt,** n° 51, is one of the finest mansions of the area. Following an interesting row of 18th-century mansions at n°s 15, 13, 11 and 5, Rue de Bellechasse ends at the Seine, between the Gare d'Orsay and the Palace of the Legion of Honor.

The Museum of the Legion of Honor across from the Musée d'Orsay (*entrance — 2 Rue de Bellechasse. Open 2 – 5 pm ex Mon.*) was established in the superb Hôtel de Salm. Built in 1786, it was bought by Napoleon from Mme de Staël. After the building was destroyed by fire in 1871, an exact replica was erected in its place. The severity of this mansion suits the spirit of the museum which portrays history through uniforms, arms, paintings and manuscripts of the orders of chivalry and nobility under the *Ancien Régime*, and celebrates the creation of the Order of the Légion d'Honneur by the Emperor in 1802. At n°s 80 and 78 Rue de Lille, you will find the Seignelay and Beauharnais mansions, now the Ministry of Works and the West German Embassy respectively. From here, you rejoin the Bd. Saint-Germain and the

Metro Chambre-des-Députés, unless you prefer to follow the **Quai Anatole-France**, a favorite walk for those who work nearby. Boats, launches and barges which ply the Seine enhance the magnificent view of the Tuileries gardens. On the opposite bank, and at the Deligny swimming pool, young Parisians gather in summer to sunbathe.

The Gare d'Orsay was constructed between 1898–1900 by Laloux and demonstrates the reluctance of contemporary architects to show iron work: the metal frame is completely hidden under the stone walls.

The Orsay Museum. Saved from demolition, the station has been converted into a museum which contains works of art and documents, notably from the Jeu de Paume and the Orangerie, which retrace the evolution of art and French society between 1848 and 1914.

RECOMMENDED FOR REFRESHMENT

La Petite Chaise, 36 Rue de Grenelle, 75007 (tel: 42 22 13 35). Open noon – 2 pm, 7 – 11 pm Mon to Sun. The oldest restaurant in Paris.
Le Pied de Fouet, 45 Rue de Babylone, 75007 (tel: 47 05 12 27). Open noon – 2 pm, 7 – 9 pm Mon to Fri; open for lunch Sat.
Chez Germaine, 30 Rue Pierre-Leroux, 75007 (tel: 42 73 28 34). Open 11.30 am – 2.30 pm, 6.30 – 9 pm Mon to Fri; open for lunch Sat.
Le Sauvignon, 80 Rue des Saints-Pères, 75007 (tel: 45 48 49 02). Open 9 am – 11 pm, Mon to Sat. Left Bank wine bar.
Christian Constant, 26 Rue du Bac, 75007 (tel: 42 96 53 53). Open 8 am – 8 pm, Mon to Sun. The tea-room of a famous pastry chef.

TROCADÉRO-EIFFEL TOWER-INVALIDES

This area, which extends from the Chaillot hill to the Eiffel Tower, and from the École Militaire (Military Academy) to Les Invalides, is one of large open spaces and groupings of monuments. There is a striking contrast in the spirit of the buildings to be found here, the Eiffel Tower proudly proclaiming the birth of the industrial age, and the dome of Les Invalides magnificently reminding us of the days of glory and military triumph.

Chaillot hill

The Chaillot hill was once a handful of humble dwellings. Because of the fine view that it gave of the capital, the village of Grenelle and the fields on the Left Bank, Catherine de Médicis had a country house built there. This was later bought by Marshal Bassompierre, renowned as much for his love affairs as for his military exploits, at the beginning of the 17th century. His heirs sold the mansion to Queen Henrietta of England, wife of the unfortunate Charles I, who established the Convent of the Visitation of Mary there. A number of aristocratic ladies who took refuge with the nuns were irreverently called "Bassompierre's girlfriends" by Parisians. In the first few years of the 19th century, Chaillot hill was disrupted by enormous public works: the convent was demolished, the summit leveled off, the slopes made less steep and the Pont d'Iéna completed, since Napoleon had chosen this site on which to build the palace of his son, the King of Rome. The architects Percier and Fontaine promised him that they would construct "the biggest and most impressive palace in the world". However, the fall of the Empire ruined those plans.

In 1827, the Chaillot hill acquired the name Trocadéro to commemorate the capture of the Trocadéro fort in Spain (1823). A square was laid out in 1858; a building designed to promote Muslim art was constructed for the Universal Exhibition of 1878 and was finally replaced by the present Palais de Chaillot in which the 1937 exhibition was held.

▬ VISIT

Place Trocadéro, partly encircling the equestrian statue of Marshal Foch, is the point from which six beautiful avenues fan out towards the Étoile, Passy and the Bois de Boulogne. Here people from the wealthy neighborhoods around enjoy the delicacies of the Carette tea-room and congregate on the cafe terraces. To the west,

behind a high wall, is the small cemetery of Passy where a number of celebrities, all of whom died after 1850, are buried (including Manet, Debussy, Fauré).

A wide terrace separates the two pavilions of the Palais de Chaillot and offers one of the finest views of the Left Bank.

Church of the Dôme, Les Invalides.

• Map I, Palais de Chaillot
(D-E 4-5) Metro: Trocadéro   Bus: nᵒˢ 22, 30, 32, 63, 72, 82

Built for the exhibition of 1937, the Palais de Chaillot consists of two pavilions extending from long curved wings and a very large theater situated under the terrace.
The National Theater of Chaillot, today completely renovated and fitted with a revolving stage, was one of the centers of dramatic art during the time that Jean Vilar was directing the popular National Theater there; it has found new inspiration with the stage management of Antoine Vitez.

On the terraces today, the acrobatics of the young roller-skaters often attract large audiences.

The Chaillot gardens are arranged around a large pool surrounded by ornate stone and bronze sculptures and set with powerful water jets. At night the pool, fountains and palace are all lit up to provide one of Paris' most beautiful evening spectacles.

The Trocadéro Aquarium*
(*Entrance through the gardens; open daily 10 am – 5.30 pm; tel: 47 23 62 95.*)
On the left, going down into the gardens, an artificial grotto conceals the entrance to an aquarium, reserved for the main species of fish from France's rivers.

The Museum of French Monuments**
(*Open 9.45 am – noon and 2 – 5.15 pm, ex Wed and Public holidays; tel: 47 27 35 74.*)
The Museum of French Monuments, founded by Viollet-le Duc in the old Palais de Chaillot in 1882, was completely reno-

---

The Museums of the Palais de Tokyo and Palais de Galliera

The Palais de Tokyo on the Avenue du President Wilson comprises two wings linked by a portico. It was built for the Universal Exhibition of 1937, and today the Musée d'Art Moderne de la Ville de Paris occupies its east wing, beside the Place de l'Alma.
The Musée de l'Art Moderne**
(*Av. du President Wilson. Open daily 10 am – 7.30 pm, 10 am – 8.30 pm on Wed. Closed Mon, Jan 1st, May 1st and Dec 25th. Tel: 47 23 61 27.*)
This museum has been refurbished since the National Museum's collection was moved to the Pompidou Center, which is better adapted for exhibitions of contemporary art. The collection groups 20th-century works from different schools: Cubism is represented by Jacques Villon, Léger, Picabia, Delaunay, Picasso, Braque and Juan Gris; Expressionism and Fauvism by Vlaminck, Rouault and Matisse (Matisse's famous triptych *La Danse* is here); the Paris school is represented by Modigliani, Soutine, and Gromaire. The mural *Fée Electricité* by Raoul Dufy, created for the Electricity Pavilion at the Exhibition of 1937, is,

at 197 feet/60 metres long and 33 feet/10 metres high, one of the largest murals ever painted. The ARC section of the museum (Art-Research-Confrontation) organizes concerts, exhibitions of contemporary painting and cultural events. There is also a museum for children, to encourage interest in the plastic arts.
Palais de Tokyo: west wing (*entry: 13 Av. du President Wilson; open 10 am – 5.15 pm, ex. Tue and Public hols; tel: 47 23 36 53*).
This part of the museum is now reserved for photography, and exhibitions from the National Center of Photography are held here.
Opposite the Palais de Tokyo is the **Palais de Galliera**, named after the Italian duchess who had it built in the 1880s. This Renaissance-style building displays the collections of the Museum of Fashion and Costume. (*Entry: 1 Av. Pierre-1ᵉʳ de-Serbie; open 10 am – 5.40 pm ex. Mon and when there are no exhibitions; tel: 47 20 85 46*). More than 400 complete costumes trace the evolution of male and female dress, from 1750 to the present day.

ated in 1937. It contains copies of sculptures and reproductions of murals which retrace the history of France's monuments. It is primarily of interest to all those who have given up straining their necks to see statues perched on columns or who are tired of examining the decorations in a multitude of churches where viewing is difficult. **Sculpture**: in the left wing of the palace, in the double gallery on the ground floor Rooms 2-4: Romanesque (Moissac, Conques, Vézelay, Cluny, Autun); Room 7: art of the Crusades. Rooms 8-13: Gothic art of the 11th and 12th centuries. (Saint-Denis, Chartres, Paris, *Beau Dieu*** from Amiens, *Ange au Sourire*** (*Smiling Angel*) from Rheims. Rooms 14 to 21: the evolution of sculpture from the 14th to 16th century (tombs* by Michel Colombe; decor has an Italian influence). In the upper gallery, on the second floor, the rooms are devoted to the **great French sculptors**: Jean Goujon, Ligier Richier, Germain Pilon, Rude, Carpeaux. Room 25: Sculpture of 17th century (collection from the Versailles park). Rooms 26 and 27: 18th-century sculptures and paintings (Bouchardon, Houdon, Pigalle). **Murals**: in the pavilion, reproductions of the most famous Romanesque and Gothic murals, from the oldest (crypt of Saint-Germain d'Auxerre) to the largest (Saint-Savin-sur-Gartempe), from the Catalan school (Saint-Martin-de-Fenollar) to the *Dances of Death* from La Chaise-Dieu.

The Naval Museum**
(*Entrance: Place de Trocadéro; open 10 am - 6 pm ex. Tue and Public holidays; tel: 45 53 31 70.*)
Founded by Charles X in 1827, this museum retraces the history of the French Navy. Paintings, navigational instruments, figureheads and scale models portraying various aspects of exploration and maritime navigation are on display. In the hall of the museum, there is a large model of the fine 1810 vessel, *Ocean*. In the main gallery, there are 17th- and 18th-century models of vessels; the original sculpture of the poop of the *Réale*, an admiral's flagship of

1680. The museum contains Napoleon's barge (1811), numerous models of the first French battleships, a series of paintings by Vernet, *Ports of France**, and several rooms devoted to aeronautics, fishing, sailing and underwater exploration.

Musée de l'Homme**
(*Entrance: Place du Trocadéro; open 9.45 am – 5.15 pm ex. Wed and Public hols; tel: 45 53 70 60.*)
This anthropological museum portrays the evolution of Man and shows many different human societies in their traditional environments. Some temporary exhibitions display the discoveries of particular missions and explorations. On the first floor, after seeing the copy of the *Hottentot Venus* and the famous *Venus of Laspugue* in ivory, one may linger over some outstanding pieces of African art, statues, masks, pottery and bronzes. On the second floor are exhibits showing the way of life of peoples in Asia, Oceania, America and the Arctic zone.

The Henri Langlois Museum of the Cinema and Film-Making
(*Guided tours at 10 am, 11 am, 2 pm, 3 pm and 4 pm, lasting 1½ hrs. Closed Tue. Tel: 45 53 74 39. Program of films in the press, or tel: 47 04 24 24.*)
The memory of Henri Langlois, pioneer in film-making and passionate advocate of the artistic value of the cinema is rekindled in this museum. The permanent exhibition traces the history of world cinema from the very first animated images of optic theater and Edison's Kinetoscope (1894) to the costumes of Greta Garbo, Rudolph Valentino and Catherine Deneuve, continuing through the film-making of the Lumière brothers and the famous special effects of Méliès, Fritz Lang and Eisenstein. The evolution and progress of photography and projection equipment are explained and include a commentary. The magic of the big screen may be appreciated in the cinema, which is across the garden and approached from the left wing of the palace. Every day four or five films from different eras and from many countries are shown.

The Champ-de-Mars ●

Metro: École Militaire, Bir-Hakeim R.E.R.: Champ-de-Mars **Map 1,**
Bus: nᵒˢ 28, 42, 49, 69, 80, 82, 87, 92 **(F 5-6)**

The Champ-de-Mars is a vast formal garden with the École Militaire at one end and the Eiffel Tower at the other. In the area around the École Militaire, the garden looks like a cross between a race-course and a fair: it is full of cars, ice-cream and postcard sellers, along with the crowds who have come from all over the world to see the Eiffel Tower.

▬▬ HISTORY

The Champ-de-Mars was laid out in 1765, by Gabriel, as **a training ground** for the military academy. It was here that Napoleon Bonaparte drilled his first armies. In 1780, it was used as the first race-course and in 1783 and 1784, it was the site of the first aeronautical experiments. The Champ-de-Mars was the setting for the great festival on July 14th, 1790, celebrating the first anniversary of the storming of the Bastille.

Napoleon as Emperor used the Champs-de-Mars to decorate his most valiant soldiers. Then it was used as a site for exhibitions. The Universal Exhibitions of 1867 and 1878 were held here; the exhibition of 1889 ruined, it was alleged, the Parisian landscape and made the Champ-de-Mars the center of a fierce controversy about whether the Eiffel Tower should be constructed, and, if so, whether it should be retained permanently. The present design of the Champ-de-Mars — one section an English-style garden and the other French — dates from 1908. Today, children play and joggers take their exercise there.

●●●
The Eiffel Tower

Map I, 　Metro: Bir-Hakeim,　R.E.R.: Champ-de-Mars　Bus: nᵒˢ 42, 69, 82, 87
(E 5)

The Eiffel Tower was the highest building in Paris when it was completed in 1889 and continued to be so until 1930. It symbolized the glory of modern industry, the triumph of the iron age and the skill of

Trocadéro-Eiffel Tower-Invalides.

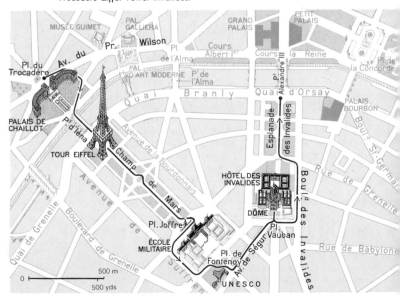

Statistics of the Eiffel Tower

— 986 feet/300.51 metres high at its inauguration.

— 1053 feet/320.76 metres high with the television transmitter.

— 7000 tons of iron in the structure.

— 1652 steps up to the 3rd platform.

— 12,000 pieces of metal in the structure.

— 2,500,000 rivets fastened by 300 fitters.

— 40 tons of paint to repaint the tower (every seven years).

— 42 mi./67 km extent of the view from the top of the tower.

— 187 feet/57 metres: height of the 1st platform which covers 45,209 sq. ft/4200 sq. m.

— 377 feet/115 metres: height of the 2nd platform.

— 899 feet/274 metres: height of the 3rd platform, and the apartment that its engineer, G. Eiffel, had reserved there.

— 15,000 visitors per day during the tourist season.

— 3,000,000 visitors a year.

— 27 suicides from the top of the tower.

Eiffel Tower.

engineers who would, in the future, replace architects and artisans in the conceiving and building of monuments. It was ten years ahead of its time and heralded the 20th century before becoming the symbol of Paris. It has played an important role in history, poetry and music but, before going over this well-trodden ground, you might prefer to familiarize yourself with a few bare facts, listed above.

HISTORY

One of the most famous monuments in the world was originally an entry in a competition, open to all the engineers in France, in May 1886 for the opening of the Universal Exhibition of 1889. The competitors had to submit a design for an iron tower with a square base, with the width of each side at ground level to measure 410 feet/125 metres and reaching a height of 985 feet/300 metres It was to be erected on the Champ-de-Mars. The successful plan was drawn up by Maurice Koechlin and Émile Nouguier who worked for **Gustave Eiffel,** an engineer already famous for his viaducts, bridges and experiments in metal construction. The tower took two years to build, from January 1887 to May 1889. The exceptional speed of its construction was due to the precision of the plans, the lightness of the structure and the basic principle of the construction. It was an achievement in advance of its time.

This engineering feat aroused interest not only in France but all over the world. National morale, at a low ebb after the Franco-Prussian

War and defeat of 1870, seized upon the tower as a **metaphor** of French recovery which allowed Eiffel to exclaim: "France will be the only nation whose flag will have a 985-foot/300-metre staff". Intended to last only for the duration of the exhibition, the tower soon became indispensable for wireless and military communications, which saved it from being demolished when its original life-span expired in 1909. Meteorological observation devices, warning-lights for aircraft, television and radio antennae were added to the tower and its height increased by 69 feet/21 metres with the installation, in 1957, of a television transmitter. Since 1981, it has been used as an antenna for a local Paris radio station which is, naturally, called Radio Eiffel Tower.

Artists and the Eiffel Tower

The artists of the 19th century fiercely opposed Eiffel's plans to build a tower. "We come," they wrote, "writers, painters, sculptors, passionate lovers of the beauty of Paris, until now unspoiled, to protest with all our strength, all our indignation, against the erection, in the heart of our capital, of this useless and monstrous Eiffel Tower ... Is the city of Paris going to accept the wild ideas, the mercenary aspirations of a machine-maker and allow itself to be shamefully disfigured and dishonored?" The 300 signatures under which the protest was made included those of Garnier, the architect of the Opera, Maupassant, Gounod, Verlaine, Huysmans and Van Dongen, the great luminaries of art, literature and music.

"Paris? Mais c'est la tour Eiffel, Avec sa pointe qui monte au ciel." ("Paris? Paris is the Eiffel Tower, with its spire reaching to the heavens.")

This verse by **Michel Emer,** sung by **Maurice Chevalier,** says enough about the Parisians' love for "their" tower, which has been painted by Utrillo, Delaunay, Vuillard, Pissarro, Dufy, Marquet, Bryen and Dubuffet; filmed by Renoir, Carné, Prévert and Cocteau. The latter wrote, "The Eiffel Tower is a world like Notre-Dame. It is the Notre-Dame of the Left Bank; it is the Queen of Paris." As for **Roland Barthes,** he used to refer to the tower as a "natural phenomenon": "The tower is known to the whole world. Not only the universal symbol of Paris, but wherever Paris is pictured from the American Mid-West to Australia; every trip undertaken to France is also somehow in the name of the Tower."

▬ VISIT

(Open 10 am – 11 pm and 10.30 am – 11 pm from Nov to Mar. Every evening, dinner-show on the second level of the tower. Other sights: audio-visual presentations on the history of the tower, 1st level; visit to the elevator machinery, west pillar.)

The top of the Tower offers an incomparable view of Paris. The best time is just after rain has washed away the dust and smoke and cleared the sky (the worst being early summer mornings before the mists have lifted, or in autumn and winter when the skies are gray). Under ideal conditions, from the third-floor glass enclosure, the view extends, it is said, to 42 mi./67 km beyond the Ile de France; but the best view of the monuments and districts of Paris is from the second level. Just before sunset, seen from the first level, Paris lies in an immense halo of vibrant light.

The feeling that the Tower moves is purely illusory; even in the strongest wind, movement is not more than 3 ins/12 cm in any direction.

The École Militaire ●●

The École Militaire (military academy) is French Classicism at its best. Situated at the end of the Champ-de-Mars, it preserves in lavish detail all the hallowed traditions of a great institution.

HISTORY

Emulating his grandfather Louis XIV, who had founded the Hôtel des Invalides for his disabled soldiers, Louis XV established a college where young gentlemen without means could be trained to become officers. The original plans for the building drawn up by the architect Gabriel were found to be too extravagant. After modifying them, he succeeded, in three years (1769–1772), in producing a magnificent complex of buildings. In 1784, the École accepted Napoleon Bonaparte, a thin, sensitive, fifteen-year-old Corsican, who was expected to "make an excellent sailor". He was commissioned as a lieutenant in the artillery and his report made the sibylline prediction that he would "go far in favorable circumstances".

VISIT

The imposing north facade of the École Militaire, with its central pavilion decorated by eight Corinthian columns surmounted by a quadrangular dome, decorated with symbols of Peace, Power, France and Victory, and framed by its long wings, blocks out the Champ-de-Mars. Before visiting the building's tower on the right (Avenues de Suffren and Lowendal), note the entablature representing Victory, in the image of Louis XV, which is one of the few royal effigies to have survived the Revolution. To the right, at 78 Av. de Suffren, the "Swiss Village" contains antique and second-hand dealers.

The southern facade of the academy is on the **Place de Fontenoy.** Two porticos surround the main courtyard in front of the main pavilion. The buildings have outstanding grace and finesse of detail. Note the important use of rigorous horizontal lines. The lavishly-decorated **chapel** is open to worshippers. (*Services at noon during the week, 6 pm on Sat, 9.30 and noon Sun.*)

UNESCO

Place de Fontenoy is surrounded on all sides by vast public buildings of varying interest. The headquarters of UNESCO (United Nations Educational, Scientific and Cultural Organization) is in the shape of a big Y supported by pillars. A second building, with a ribbed copper roof resting on fluted concrete walls, contains the conference rooms. The UNESCO building was inaugurated in 1958 and is an example of international architecture and engineering, bringing together an American, **Breuer**, an Italian, **Nervi** and a Frenchman, **Zehrfuss**. UNESCO drew on the great artists of the 156 member nations to decorate the buildings which for a long time have been the symbol of "modern" architecture in Paris (a statue by Henry Moore and a mobile by Calder are visible from the Avenue de Suffren; there are also frescoes by Picasso and Tamayo, ceramics by Miró, tapestries by Lurçat and Le Corbusier). The recent withdrawal of the United States, the United Kingdom and Japan has called the organization's methods of operation into question.

(Visit: 7 Place de Fontenoy, 75007. Open Mon to Fri 9 am – noon and 2 – 5 pm, ex. during conferences. Tel: 45 68 10 00.)

●●
Les Invalides

Map 4, Metro: Invalides, Varenne, Latour-Maubourg.   R.E.R.: Invalides
(B-C 2) Bus: n⁰ˢ 28, 49, 63, 69, 82, 83, 92

The Hôtel des Invalides is situated in an area seemingly consecrated to the army and its honor. All the names of the avenues in the district between the Champ-de-Mars, the École Militaire and the Faubourg-Saint-Germain, commemorate military heroes. The two buildings of the Musée de l'Armée (Army Museum) illustrate the surprising, often terrifying, development of the art of war, while the tomb of Napoleon, under its royal dome, attracts large crowds. In these surroundings, one cannot help reflecting on Napoleon's particular vision of France, its grandeur and its destiny.

▬▬ HISTORY

Until the time of Louis XIV, soldiers who were disabled or too old to serve, were reduced to begging or forced to depend on the benevolence of religious institutions. In 1670, the King ordered an immense mansion built for them on the Grenelle Plain.

Around a main courtyard and ten other small courtyards, the buildings were quickly erected under the supervision of architect Libéral-Bruant. They were completed in 1676, by which time the earliest residents had already moved in.

The King then ordered the young architect, Jules Hardouin-Mansart, to design a second church, the "Dome", which was to share an altar with the Church of Saint-Louis. About 70 years later, in an effort to develop a strong sense of national unity, Louis-Philippe had Napoleon's coffin brought back from St Helena on December 15th, 1840. It was carried through a heavy snowstorm under the Arc de Triomphe and down the Champs-Élysées before being placed under the dome of the Invalides and exhibited for three months. Visconti was commissioned to build Napoleon's tomb and the reinterment ceremony, presided over by Napoleon III, took place on April 2nd, 1861.

▬▬ VISIT

For an overall view of Les Invalides, it is best to go down the esplanade towards the Seine, as far as the Pont Alexandre III. The whole is harmonious; the general effect is of regal simplicity; the contours of the dome seem to unite and complete the symmetry of the buildings, at last freed from the surrounding development which once disfigured them. The grass esplanade has been returfed, the trees along the mall replanted and the caretakers' gardens reorganized.

The Esplanade des Invalides*, measuring 1,640 feet/500 metres by 820 feet/250 metres was laid out by Robert de Cotte between 1704 and 1720. Looking towards the Seine and the Right Bank, it offers a superb view and since the completion of works for the underground parking and the airport link station (aerogare), its lawns and trees are once again flourishing. A wide moat in front of the garden of the Hôtel des Invalides points its cannon at the *boules*-players and pedestrians.

The facade of Les Invalides, 643 feet/196 metres long, is a perfect example of the austere simplicity of Classical architecture. Between the two pavilions adorned with trophies, the decoration is concentrated on the unusual dormer windows and especially on the magnificent portal which acts as a frame for the equestrian statue of Louis XIV, accompanied by Prudence and Justice.

The main courtyard, designed by Libéral-Bruant, is noted for its balance, sobriety and austerity, qualities equally applicable to a monastery or a convent, which convey a sense of discipline. They act as a reminder that, before becoming a major work of Classical art, Les Invalides was a hospice, with a reputation for harshness. Two tiers of arches extend on four sides, four pavilions with sculpted pediments break their horizontal lines, and at each angle of the roof, horses rear up, trampling on the trappings of War. An attentive visitor will not miss the fifth dormer window, to the right of the main pavilion (the left side on entering). Between the paws of a wolf is a round window, a sculptor's pun on the name of Louvois (loup voit — "the wolf sees"), the former Superintendent of Buildings.

The Church of Saint-Louis, also called the Soldiers' Church, was completed by architect Hardouin-Mansart to the design of Libéral-Bruant. Its interior is spartan, decorated only by captured flags hanging from the cornices, some of which have since gone to the Army Museum. Nearly 500 flags were burned to prevent them from falling into the hands of the Allies in 1815. The small hidden cellars of the Church contain the remains of many military leaders; also buried here is Rouget-de-l'Isle, composer of the Marseillaise. The magnificent 17th-century **organ** attracts music-lovers. In 1837, the first performance of Berlioz's Requiem was given here.

The Church of the Dôme** (Joint visit with the Army Museum: 10 am – 6 pm; 7 pm in June, July, Aug. Tickets valid on two consecutive days also give access to the Museum of Relief Maps and Plans.) One of the best examples of the French Classical style, this church took more than 50 years to attain its perfection. Louis XIV built it to bear witness to the greatness of his reign, and the Church of the Dôme is the religious counterpart of the Château of Versailles. The Baroque influence remains; the three successive buttresses of its facade are those of a **Jesuit Church**. Its layout, in the shape of a Greek cross, is copied from St Peter's in Rome. Above its facade, which superimposes Doric and Corinthian columns (in the niches, statues of St Louis by Coustou and of Charlemagne by Coyse-

vox), **the dome** rises up with authority and great flair. The first-floor windows are framed by 40 columns, side by side, and the whole is crowned with a pierced lantern and a spire of 557 feet/170 metres.

The interior of the Church of the Dôme may be a disappointment today, owing to its excessive decoration. The magnificence of the marble pavements, the bas-reliefs by Jouvenet and De la Fosse, the profusion of gilding and the skilful marquetry can be overpowering. However, the purity of the **cupola's** contours is admirable, as is the virtuosity of the craftsmen who roofed it with gilded lead strips which have had to be regilded many times since.

Museum of Relief Maps and Plans

(Open 10 am – 6 pm from May to Aug, 10 am – 5 pm the rest of the year. Access: via the Army Museum.) The Museum displays models of strongholds and French and Belgian ports, formerly classified as "secret documents". Many of these were produced with microscopic precision between 1660 and 1870. Especially noteworthy are the plans of the fortifications by the great military architect Vauban.

Museum of the Order of Liberation

(Open daily ex. Sun and public hols, 2 – 5 pm. Access: 51 bis Bd. de Latour-Maubourg.) The Ordre de la Libération was created by De Gaulle in 1940 in recognition of those who made outstanding contributions to the war effort against the Germans. Various documents retrace the deeds of the "Compagnons", as well as the battles of the Resistance and the Normandy-Niémen squadron.

The Emperor's tomb is in the crypt overlooked by a circular gallery, designed by the architect Visconti to allow visitors to lean over the marble balustrade. In the crypt itself, a base of green granite supports the enormous **sarcophagus** of red porphyry which contains six encased coffins: one in white tinplate, one in mahogany, two in lead, and the last two in ebony and oak. At the far end of the crypt lies the son

The Pagoda, or Japan in Paris

The Pagoda, its pointed roofs recalling a drawing, is situated at 57 Rue de Babylone in the middle of the 7th arrondissement, a long way from the Japanese quarter with its restaurants, bookshops and fashion boutiques around Avenue de l'Opéra. The building, built in the late 19th century for the very fashionable and extremely rich wife of Doctor Morin, head of the nearby department store, *Au Bon Marché*, portrays the amazing vogue in the early years of the Third Republic for things Japanese — curios , kimonos, vases, tapestries, screens and *netsukes*. The story, perhaps apocryphal, is that the architect, Alexandre Marcel, bought a pagoda in Japan, had it dismantled and transported back by boat, then reconstructed brick by brick in the Rue de Babylone. The artist Bernet was commissioned to repaint the dragons and samurai in their original brilliance. The new Republican bourgeoisie, with its history of bankruptcies and scandals, flocked to Madame Morin's masquerades, fancy-dress balls and transvestite parties. These were so exciting that many rented, at great expense, rooms with balconies or windows overlooking the Pagoda, for a good view of the proceedings. However, this phase was short-lived and with the coming of the 20th century, Japan was soon forgotten. The Pagoda was sold and would have become the Chinese Embassy but for the paintings depicting the defeat of the Celestial Empire. The transaction was called off and the building was converted into a cinema in March 1931; it remains so today.

of Napoleon, "the King of Rome", who died as the Duke of Reichstadt, in 1832. The statues by Pradier symbolize the Emperor's victories.

In the side chapels all around the Church of the Dôme are the bodies of military leaders and the emperor's closest companions. On either side of the entrance of the crypt are the tombs of generals Duroc and Bertrand, who followed Napoleon to St Helena. The tombs of Joseph Bonaparte and Foch are on the right and those of Jérôme Bonaparte, Turenne and Marshal Lyautey are on the left. There is also a monument to Vauban.

The religious architecture of the 17th and 18th centuries is inspired by the magnificent basilica of St Peter's in Rome. The imposing sight of the cupola, the majestic design of its facade and the richness and luxury of its decor obsessed French architects who, following the example of Poussin, went to study in Italy. Initially, they were content to copy the Church of Gesù in Rome; the most characteristic example is seen in the church of Saint-Paul-Saint-Louis (see p. 141). Later, when the architects had assimilated the Italian style, they freed themselves from its influence, renounced the use of heavy decoration and gave new importance to elegance and finesse of the domes they were then building. This is seen in the Institut, the Sorbonne, Val-de-Grâce and, at its finest, in Les Invalides. Its success is based on the use of a simple design: a central circle, a cross and small circles at each arm; a two-tier cube serving as a plinth to a double drum, then the cupola and the spire. The bareness of the lateral walls enhances the portico of the facade which is made of three tiers of gilded columns of different styles, first Doric, then Ionic and finally Corinthian. This ordered sequence, which gives an impression of lightness, is reproduced in the horizontal layout, in the projections of the entablature and in the staggered columns which frame the central axis. A harmony of style permeates Hardouin-Mansart's masterpiece, a quality which Soufflot tried to emulate in the Panthéon and Servandoni in the Church of Saint-Sulpice.

The Army Museum* *(Open daily, ex. Jan 1st, May 1st, Nov 1st, Dec 25th. April to Sept: 10 am – 6 pm; Oct to March: 10 am – 5 pm. Tickets valid for two days.)*

The Army Museum contains the world's richest collection of military art. Its two buildings, referred to as "East" and "West", overlook the main courtyard. Here you can marvel at the skill that went into the creation of the cross-bow, arquebus, musket, stone-thrower and pistol, as well as swords, armor and parade weapons.

Some pieces merit special mention: in the François I room, hunting horns sculpted in ivory; 16th-century armor and the splendid sword belonging to François I (display 20).

The Emperor's Tomb in the crypt of the Church of the Dôme.

On Henri II's sable and silver-decorated armor (display 40) are engraved the initials of the king, "H", the queen, Catherine de Médicis, "C", and the royal favorite, Diane de Poitiers, "D". In the Henri IV room, there is an impressive display of armor for battles and tournaments, especially the "ensemble à la chimère" (display 15). In the Louvois room is a display of regimental arms of the 18th to 20th centuries as illustrated by artist Caran d'Ache. The second floor on the east side of the museum is devoted to the military history of France up to the 18th century. Among the displays are the cannonball that killed Turenne and various personal mementoes of Napoleon. On the third floor, east side, the colonial history of the Second Empire and the 1870–71 Franco-Prussian War is documented. The west side is devoted to World War I and life during the 1939–45 occupation (including a scale model of the Normandy landing). The west side also has a display of all the uniforms of France's allies in the two World Wars and a history of artillery.

═══ *RECOMMENDED FOR REFRESHMENT* ═══

Carette, 4 Pl. du Trocadéro (tel: 47 27 88 56). Open 8 am to 7 pm every day except Tue. A traditional tea-room.

HÔTEL LUTÉTIA
45 Boulevard Raspail
— 75006
Paris
Dali, Picasso, Miro

July 2 - 31 August

Metro Sèvres - Babylone

FROM SAINT-GERMAIN-DES-PRÉS TO MONTPARNASSE

The districts of Saint Germain-des-Prés and Montparnasse represent two different periods of French history. The first, with its jazz cellars and Existentialist atmosphere still evokes, 30 years later, memories of the post-World War II period, while in the second, the presence of painters and models, the *Dôme* of the "Années Folles" and the restaurant *La Coupole* remain as symbols of the carefree post-World War I years of the 1920s.

The same Saturday evening fever resounds in the Odéon area and Boulevard du Montparnasse; cinemas, night-clubs, bars and all types of restaurants attract crowds of all ages and origins, younger and more cosmopolitan in Saint-Germain, more staid in Montparnasse.

The painters, writers and bohemians have more or less disappeared from these areas, taking refuge in their studios, still numerous near Notre-Dame-des-Champs.

The Odéon Intersection

Metro: Odéon   Bus: n⁰ˢ 63, 96   **Map 4, (C-D 5-6)**

Cafés, cinemas and university bookshops enliven the Odéon intersection, a favorite place for a rendezvous. Opposite the statue of Danton, the courtyards of the Commerce-Saint-André open onto n° 130 Boulevard Saint-Germain. This courtyard was one of the popular meeting places in revolutionary Paris. It was here that Marat's newspaper *l'Ami du Peuple* (Friend of the People) was printed and Dr Guillotin experimented on sheep with his terrible machine. On the right, in a passage with open wrought iron gates, a tower in the old enclosure of Philippe-Auguste forms the corner of a workshop; and three beautiful courtyards of the 15th-century Hôtel de Rohan lead into the quiet Rue du Jardinet. Going back to the courtyards of the Commerce-Saint-André, you will find, on the right, a passage leading into Rue de l'Ancienne-Comédie. At n° 13, the **Café Procope**, established in 1684 by a Sicilian, Francesco Procopio, made its fortune by selling a "new aroma" — coffee — at the Saint-Germain Fair, charging two and a half *sous* (a few centimes) per cup. Opposite the Comédie-Française, behind the Saint-German *boules* ground, the *Procope* quickly became the meeting place of artists, authors and actors. The encyclopaedists Diderot, Voltaire and Rousseau patronized it as did the revolutionaries Marat, Danton and Robespierre; Musset and George Sand accompanied Balzac there, and it was also in the *Procope* that Gambetta introduced the fashion of smoking a pipe in public.

The Buci Intersection, once a popular area on the Left Bank with its sedan chairs and its guardsmen, is today a lively market. Nearly all the houses on **Rue Mazarine** are old (handsome 18th-century mansion at n° 51). On the right, the **Rue Guénégaud** is lined with numerous art and antique galleries. On the left, the long and austere wall is part of Hôtel des Monnaies, n⁰ˢ 11–25 on the Quai de Conti.

Saint-Germain-des-Prés from the terrace of Les Deux Magots.

Hôtel des Monnaies

Map 4, (C 6)   Entrance: 11, Quai de Conti   Metro: Pont-neuf   Bus: nᵒˢ 24, 27, 58, 70

The Hôtel des Monnaies was constructed on the site of the Hôtel de Nesle which bordered on the fortifications of Philippe-Auguste. Louis XV ordered the building of new workshops on this site to serve as a mint. The design chosen was that of an unknown architect, Antoine, who, with his simple forms and minimalist decorations created the first work in the Louis XVI style.

━━ *VISIT*

The entrance archway to the mint, supported by elegant fluted columns, leads to a double staircase. On the first floor — **Money Museum,** "Musée Monétaire" (*Open 11 am – 6 pm ex. Mon, tel: 43 29 12 48*), a room **selling medals** is open to the public in the other wing (*9 am – 5.30 pm, 9 am – noon on Sat, closed Sun and Public hols.*). Only telephone tokens are made at the mint now; the minting of coins has since moved to Pessac.
(*Guided tours of the medals and decorations workshops, Mon and Wed at 2 pm ex. Jul. – Aug.*)

Institut de France

Map 4, (B 6)

The Institut de France, with its appropriately solemn dome, is situated on the Quai de Conti opposite the Pont des Arts. The harmony of the Classical building is better appreciated from the Pont des Arts than the Place de l'Institut, which is no place for pedestrians.

The Institut covers the site of the Nesle Tower which used to defend the river bastion of Philippe-Auguste. This tower, according to a Parisian legend, was the scene of the somewhat gruesome affairs of three beautiful princesses who lived there at the time of Philip le Bel (about 1310). It was their practice to have their lovers of the night thrown into the Seine in the morning. More importantly, in 1661, three days before his death, Cardinal Mazarin bequeathed a share of his immense wealth for the construction of a college for sixty gentlemen from the four French provinces which he had united (Alsace, Artois, Piémont, Roussillon). In 1805, Napoleon had the Institut de France, founded ten years earlier and formerly situated in the Louvre, transferred here. The Institut is composed of five academies: the *Académie Française* (French Academy) founded by Richelieu in 1635, *Les Inscriptions et Belles-lettres* (Writing and the Humanities, 1663), *Les Sciences* (1666), *Les Sciences Morales et Politiques* (Moral and Political Sciences, 1832) and the *Académie des Beaux-Arts* (Academy of Fine Arts, 1795).

━━ *VISIT*

The facade of the Institute Palace (**Palais de l'Institut**), which faces the Seine and the Louvre, has a theatrical air about it. The pitch of the dome dominates a forecourt flanked by curved wings decorated with Classical colonnades, and terminates in two large pavilions.

The palace itself consists of a main courtyard, from which the arched portico of the two forecourts to the right and left open on one side to the former Church of the Quatre-Nations, where the Institute's public sessions take place, and on the other to the Mazarine Library. Beyond that, a second, more spacious courtyard is where the Academicians meet every Thursday.

The charming courtyard of the the kitchen in the old college, with its well and walls covered with ivy, is open to the public.

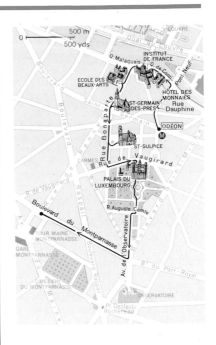

From Saint-Germain-des-Prés to Montparnasse.

The forty members of the Académie Française (French Academy), are elected by their peers. After being thoroughly screened and accepted by the head of State, the Patron of the Academy, they work slowly to update their famous dictionary. Their immortality is relative, but the reception ceremony is a major event in Paris. The newly elected member, wearing the bicorn hat, the cape, the sword and the famous green jacket, sings the praises of his deceased predecessor. Fiction, poetry, theater, the church, diplomacy, cinema, journalism and medicine are represented by such famous names as H. Troyat (1959), C. Levi-Strauss and J. d'Ormesson (1973), M. Yourcenar, the only woman "immortal" (1980) and finally J. Soustelle and L.S. Senghor, former president of Senegal (1983).

The Mazarine Library

(Open daily 10 am – 6 pm ex. Sat and Sun.)

The Mazarine Library was Cardinal Mazarin's personal collection before becoming the first public library in France. Today, it has half a million volumes and a vast collection of manuscripts and incunabula, displayed in a perfect 17th-century setting.

On the other side of the Institute, the Quai Malaquais widens at the opening of the narrow Rue de Seine, crowded with art galleries and bookshops specializing in antique books. Beyond that, at the corner of the Rue Bonaparte, stands a beautiful brick and stone house, built in the 17th century, which, in the 18th century became the Hôtel de Transylvanie, a popular gambling house. The facade and arcades which extend along the quay belong to the École des Beaux-Arts (School of Fine Arts) the entrance of which is at n° 14 Rue Bonaparte.

The School of Fine Arts

**Map 4,
(B-C,
5-6)**

The National School of Fine Arts (*École des Beaux-Arts*), which unfortunately is not open to the public, owes much of its local reputation to the rowdiness of its students. Its origin is more respectable: until the Revolution, it was a convent founded by Marguerite de Valois, the wife of Henri IV, in fulfilment of her vow to the patriarch Jacob. Only the chapel survives from Jacob's convent, and its dome is the oldest in Paris.

Around the School of Fine Arts, small restaurants and colorful boutiques stand next to beautiful art galleries and shops selling prints and old engravings. At the corner of Rues Bonaparte and Jacob, it is sometimes possible to watch a weaver at work on a carpet. There are some beautiful 16th-century mansions in **Rue Bonaparte**, with sculpted portals and generous courtyards. To the left is **Rue des Beaux-Arts,** home to writers and artists Nerval, Corot and Fantin-Latour. Oscar Wilde died at n° 13 "... beyond my means", as he is reported to have said. (Note plaque.) Farther up, Rue Visconti has retained all its 17th-century houses, as well as its privacy, which made it a refuge for hunted Protestants during the St Bartholomew's Day Massacre.

Rue Jacob, with its numerous 18th-century mansions, leads into **Rue des Saint-Pères** which, together with the Rues de Verneuil, Université and du Bac and the prestigious Quai Voltaire, is one of the main Paris centers for antiques and *objets d'art*. Taking the Boulevard Saint-Germain, one comes to the intersection of Saint-Germain-des-Prés. At *Lipp*, the famous brasserie, politicians forget their differences over dinner, side-by-side with theatrical stars and artists. A labyrinthine store (*Le Drugstore*) offers many diversions, videos, books and all the latest gadgets. In the *Café de Flore* and the famous café *Les Deux Magots*, favorite haunts of the 1950s, memories of personalities like Sartre, Juliette Gréco, Mac Orlan, Prévert and Camus still linger. These cafés have a literary heritage; annual prizes are announced at *Les Deux Magots*, and *Le Flore* is where Guillaume Apollinaire developed his melancholy writing style. Between the two cafés is *La Hune*, a bookshop with a unique range of books on the plastic arts, both architectural and decorative; this store is also one of the few to stay open until midnight.

> *"Ah! la charmante chose*
> *Quitter un pays morose*
> *Pour Paris*
> *Paris joli*
> *Qu'un jour*
> *Dut créer l'Amour!"*
>
>   **Apollinaire**
>
> ("How lovely to
> Leave a cheerless place
> For Paris,
> Delightful Paris,
> Which must once have been
> Created
> By Love itself.")

●●   # Saint-Germain-des-Prés

Map 4,   Metro: St-Germain-des-Prés   Bus: nᵒˢ 39, 48, 63, 70, 86, 87, 95, 96
(C 5-6)

The church of Saint-Germain-des-Prés, behind its monumental bell-tower porch, represents 15 centuries of uninterrupted sanctity, undisturbed by the crowds outside who, in good weather, gather to watch the jugglers perform.

▬▬ *HISTORY*

This place was the site of the camp of the Gauls of Camulogene, opposite that of the Romans on the Right Bank. The day before the battle that decided the fate of Lutèce, Childebert, the son of Clovis, ordered the building of a monastery to house the fragment of the True Cross and St Vincent's tunic, which he had brought back from Spain.

From the 9th century, Saint Germain-des-Prés was a link in the chain of Benedictine abbeys and priories and was a rich foundation. It was sacked four times in 40 years by the Normans. Nonetheless, the abbey was reconstructed as a church between 990 and 1021. The tower has survived and is the oldest in France. In 1163, the chancel was enlarged and consecrated by Pope Innocent III in person; in 1245 Pierre de Montreuil, who built the cloister and refectory, added the Chapel of the Virgin.

In the 14th century, the abbey was in its heydey, its domain extending over the present neighborhood of Saint-Germain and beyond the Champ-de-Mars. After the 16th century, the monks pursued scholarly activities, making them the founders in France of studies on archaeology, mediaeval history and religion.

VISIT

The façade has diverse characteristics; the arches on the top level of the huge tower, the only relic of the original building, were rebuilt in the last century and a spire was added at the same time. A 1607 portal hides the old porch; the presbytery dates back to the 18th century. The choir is of the same date as Notre-Dame, but its small 12th-century buttresses have been reinforced by a more spectacular series of arched buttresses.

The interior of the church, so important in history yet surprisingly small in size, was planned as a monastery, not as a parish church. It is 213 feet/65 metres long and 68 feet/21 metres high and was profusely covered with exuberant murals to the glory of the 19th century, which destroyed the harmony of the Romanesque style. To the right, under the porch, is the Chapel of Saint Symphorien which has been closed to the public since excavations uncovered a sarcophagus and the ruins of the ancient foundations. Notice the **capitals** in the nave and transept, which are copies of the originals exhibited at the Cluny Museum. Their vigor contrasts with the austere sacred scenes painted on each arch by Flandrin.

On the right, in the side aisle, there is a large 15th-century statue of the **Virgin and Child** which came from Notre-Dame. In the left transept is the handsome tomb of Jean-Casimir, king of Poland, by the Maszy brothers, and a statue of St Francis-Xavier by Coustou; on the right side is the tomb of O. and L. de Castellan, by Girardon.

The choir and cloisters are vantage points from which to admire the 12th-century architecture which is almost intact. Notice particularly the decorations in the naive tradition with images of monsters, birds and animals which demonstrate so well the beauty of the native white stone of Paris. Also notice the arches which form a decorative triforium; their marble bases are from the basilica of Childebert (6th century).

Around Saint-Germain-des-Prés

In the little garden which borders Rue de l'Abbaye, there are fragments from the great Lady Chapel and cloister built by Pierre de Montreuil, surrounding a **sculpture by Picasso:** the Monument to Guillaume Apollinaire. **The Abbot's Palace,** erected in 1586, has recently been restored. To the left, Rue de Fürstenberg leads to the site of one of the miracles of modern Paris: a square from a far province, frozen in time, its history almost forgotten. It is the small, delightful **Place de Fürstenberg***. In it there is nothing but a street lamp and four catalpa trees in a small circle around a green-painted bench, but the atmosphere takes you back to the 17th century. There are a few art galleries, a decorator's shop and the sober facades of handsome bourgeois buildings: n° 6 was the studio where Delacroix lived and worked from 1857 until his death in 1863. **Delacroix Museum*** (Map 4, C 6; 6 Rue de Fürstenberg. Open 9.45 am – 5.15 pm, daily ex. Tues and Public hols; tel: 43 54 04 87). One of the most appealing corners of old Saint-Germain-des-Prés.

Walks at night

Those who like to walk at night should try the Rue de Seine; halfway down this street is the Café la Palette, covered with paintings by hard-up students from the Beaux-Arts.

On the opposite side of Rue de Rennes, around Rue du Dragon, Rue du Sabot and Rue Bernard-Palissy, the area has hardly changed since the 17th century. The London Tavern (3 Rue du Sabot) and the Twickenham (70 Rue des Saints-Pères) are particularly appealing. This is the principal haunt of Paris' so-called "new philosophers". The dragon at the corner of the road of the same name (at the Croix-Rouge intersection) and the medallions on the facade of n° 24 which commemorate Bernard Palissy, famous for his ceramic and enamel work, also deserve notice.

Rue de Rennes, designed by Baron Haussmann, starts from the Place Saint-Germain-des-Prés among the ready-to-wear and fashion boutiques and runs straight to the foot of the Montparnasse tower. To the left, Rue du Vieux-Colombier leads to Saint-Sulpice.

Place Saint-Sulpice resembles a large Italian square with chestnut trees casting a shadow over its fountain and town hall, right up to the severe facade of the seminary (on the right). Calm, almost asleep next to Saint-Germain-des-Prés or Montparnasse, the cafe terraces, the immense open central spaces and the Italian-style facade of the church have a slightly southern flavor on sunny days.

•• Saint-Sulpice

Map 4,
(D 5-6)
Metro: Saint-Sulpice, Mabillon

The church of Saint-Sulpice was founded by the abbey of Saint-Germain-des-Prés as a parish church for the peasants of its domain. Rebuilt several times, the present building was begun in 1646, six architects being in charge successively over a period of nearly one and a half centuries. In 1732, the Classical style in which the nave was built no longer being in fashion, a competition was organized and won by the Florentine architect Servandoni, who proposed a fine Italian-style facade. The mural decorations are by Delacroix.

▬▬ *VISIT*

The unusual dimensions of the church interior are as impressive (377 feet/115 metres long, 184 feet/56 metres wide and 125 feet/38 metres high) as the majesty of its nave with its massive arches. On each side of the entrance, there are two enormous holy-water spouts, presents given by the Republic of Venice to François I, that rest on marble rocks sculpted by Pigalle. In its magnificent Chalgrin case, the **organ** is one of Paris' favorite instruments. The power of **Delacroix's** creation dominates all the other works in this church: the first chapel in the side aisle to the south (on the right looking at the choir), contains, beside two tableaux and four lively angels, one of the most famous paintings by the leader of the Romantic school, *Jacob's Fight With the Angel***, which Baudelaire interpreted as the painter's terrible struggle with life.

From the **Place Saint-Sulpice**, Rue Bonaparte continues up to Rue de Vaugirard which, on the left, goes around the Luxembourg gardens and along the facade of the Palace. Rather than these quiet, residential streets, one may prefer the narrow and busier **Rue Saint-Sulpice**, long proud of its shops selling religious objects; then, to the right, is Rue de Tournon, where several well-known dress shops and galleries are to be found, a thriving center of "la mode Parisienne".

•• Luxembourg Palace and gardens

Map 4,
(D-E 6)
R.E.R.: Luxembourg   Bus: nᵒˢ 21, 27, 38, 58, 82, 84, 85, 89

Once resplendent with the villas of the colonial Romans, this site caught the fancy of Queen Marie de Médicis, who was languishing in the Louvre and anxious to live in a palace which would recreate the lively atmosphere of the house of her youth in Tuscany. After the assassination of her husband Henri IV, she bought the mansion of Duke François of

Luxembourg gardens.

Luxembourg and all the area around it in 1612. In 1615, her architect, Saloman de Brosse, taking the Pitti Palace of Florence as a model, created the Luxembourg Palace. In 1621, Rubens was commissioned to paint 24 large pictures allegorically depicting the life of the Queen. The Palace remained royal property after her death until the Revolution, when the gardens were expanded, opening the superb perspective of the Avenue de l'Observatoire. The Luxembourg Palace was used for various official purposes, its two chief functions being the seat of Government and the Senate, (the architect Chalgrin remodeled the interior for this purpose) a role it continues to play today. The German High Command built fortified shelters under the gardens during World War II. (*Visit the palace: Sun ex. when there are Senate receptions, 10 – 11 am, then 2.30 – 3.30 pm. Tel. 42 34 20 60.*)

━━ *VISIT*

To recall his royal patron's Pitti Palace, **Salomon de Brosse** used elements of **Italian decor** — embossing, ringed columns and Tuscan capitals — but he retained a very French design, with a central body, two interconnecting wings and a gallery with arches enclosing the court. The former Luxembourg mansion, named Petit-Luxembourg, is situated in front of the Palace. It serves as the residence of the President of the Senate. The 18th and 19th centuries saw an increase in the number of official statues and paintings. The paintings and wood panels which decorated the apartments of Marie de Médicis are preserved in a room called the *Livre d'Or* (the Golden Book); the library has been decorated with two large paintings by **Delacroix.**

The National Theater of the Odéon, opposite the Luxembourg Palace, extends over a district in which almost every street has been named after a writer: Racine, Corneille, Crébillon and Régnard are honored here, as they were on the stage at the first theater worthy of the name built in Paris. Until its completion in 1782, the best companies, such as Molière's, had only been able to act as best they could in markets or festival halls, or even on tennis courts. Named the Odéon, by virtue of the passion for Classicism in the 1800s, this theater was a hall for concerts, balls and even a circus before being reserved for the dramatic repertoire. The general effect is austere, despite the Doric peristyle and surrounding arches. It burned down several times and was rebuilt identically. Inside, the ceiling was painted by **André Masson** (1965).

The Luxembourg gardens** which show less of the French taste for geometric order than that of the Tuileries, were for a long time the favorite gardens of artists and poets. The painter Watteau used to like walking there at twilight. Nerval may well have crossed young Baudelaire's path there, and Théophile Gautier once thumbed his nose at convention by walking a lobster tied to a blue ribbon.

When there is the slightest hope of sunshine, crowds flock to the Luxembourg gardens; students spread out their books and papers, children enjoy sandpits, slides, roundabouts, roller skating, go-carting, donkey rides and even model boats to rent. Everyone should visit the Théâtre des Marionnettes (*Wed, Sat, Sun: 2.30 – 3.30 pm*) where the young writer André Gide came to laugh and cry in front of the puppet show.

The Médicis fountain* (1624), with its attractive sculpture and greenery, owes its Italian style to Salomon de Brosse, although the sculptures and bas-reliefs are 19th-century. Everywhere else, the lawns are scattered with statues from Louis-Philippe's reign. Unfortunately, the caretakers maintain a strict time-table and close the gates every evening after the statutory bugle call half an hour before sunset.

The Paris Observatory (Observatoire) with its characteristic dome, can be seen from the Place A.-Honorat, at the end of the Avenue de l'Observatoire which is divided by a long garden linking the Luxembourg gardens. From the Place Jullian, where the statue* by Rude recalls the execution on this site of Marshal Ney in 1815, this spot offers an impressive view of the Parisian landscape, which seems to crown the Luxembourg Palace with the enormous Sacré-Coeur of Montmartre. To the right, at the corner of the Boulevard du Montparnasse, behind the hedges, is the restaurant *Closerie des Lilas* which has a friendly bar and congenial brasserie, a haunt of writers and artists.

The Avenue de l'Observatoire, to the south, ends at the Observatoire de Paris, the oldest astronomical establishment of its kind. Work began there, appropriately, on June 21st, 1667, the day of the summer solstice. However, the plans given to Claude Perrault by Colbert were more to cater to the taste of the "Grand siècle" for solemn buildings, than to meet the needs of astronomy, even though the use of iron was banned to avoid affecting the magnetic needle. The four sides of this massive rectangle, 102 feet/31 metres by 92 feet/28 metres, face each point of the compass and

a line down the middle is the meridian of Paris; the dome and the wings were added in the 19th century. The major work of the new observatory was to determine longitudes. The width of France from east to west was calculated, and was found to be greatly reduced, much to the chagrin of Louis XIV, who accused the astronomers of having stolen some of his land. Today the main function of the "Bureau international de l'heure" is to determine and broadcast the official time, especially by its "speaking clock" (tel: 46 99 84 00). A small museum exhibits various old instruments, prisms, spheres and astrolabes. (*Open first Sat of every month at 2.30 pm; apply in advance at 61 Av. de l'Observatoire; tel: 43 20 12 10*). Behind the Observatory, at n° 38 Rue du Faubourg-Saint-Jacques, is the **Hôtel Massa*** which is occupied by the Society of Men of Letters.

At the Observatory exit, Rue Cassini on the left, leads into Av. Denfert-Rochereau which goes down to Place Denfert-Rochereau, a large crossroads in the south of Paris (*arrivals and departures of bus 215 for Orly airport*). **The Lion of Bartholdi** recalls the heroism of soldiers commanded by Colonel Denfert-Rochereau who successfully defended Belfort when the Germans invaded in 1870.

The catacombs
Map: West Paris (E 5); Metro and R.E.R. Denfert-Rochereau Bus: n°s 38, 68. *Open Jul 1st – Oct 15th every Sat afternoon, and the 1st and 2nd Sat of all other months. Take a pocket-torch.*

The pavilion at n° 1, on the left, gives access to the Paris catacombs, a real underground empire of the dead. The catacombs were the underground stone galleries created by the excavation, since Gallo-Roman times, of the so-called "mountains" of Montparnasse, Montrouge and Montsouris. In 1785, the remains of 30 generations of Parisians were brought from the Cimetière des Innocents, where they had become a risk to public health, and then piled in the ossuaries. This place inspired the freakish imagination of the Comte d'Artois, the future Charles X, who invited the beautiful ladies of the court there just before the 1789 Revolution. The grim atmosphere of the place was enlivened by generous doses of music and wine, and the parties ended in great gaiety. In August 1944, the Resistance chose this shelter to direct the uprising of Paris against the German occupiers.

Montparnasse

Metro: Montparnasse-Bienvenüe, Vavin

Bus: n⁰ˢ 28, 48, 58, 68, 82, 89, 91, 92, 94, 95, 96

**Map 4,
(F 4-5)**

The original grass-covered mound in this area was nicknamed "Mount Parnassus" by the students, who gave outdoor readings of their poems on its open spaces. The mound was leveled in the 18th century but the boulevard laid across it kept the name alive. Around the boulevard today the old Paris district survives, with its artistic and popular traditions and its rich night life; behind the tower is its new face: shopping arcades, hotels and masses of buildings.

▬ HISTORY

The wall of the Fermiers-Généraux (tax collectors) earned Montparnasse its popularity; cabarets and small suburban taverns multiplied on the other side of the toll barrier, serving the tax-free local wine of Suresnes. For over a century, the *Bal Bullier, L'Élysée-Montparnasse, la Grande Chaumière* and *l'Arc-en-Ciel* attracted fun-seeking Parisians. The district drew painters down from Paris' other hill, Montmartre: Modigliani, Soutine, Léger and Zadkine shared their misery and genius there. Refugees from central Europe, notably Lenin and Trotsky, enlivened discussions on the terraces of the popular cafés, the *Dôme*, the *Coupole, Sélect* and the *Rotonde*, and artists' models came out of studios to set the carefree 1920s ablaze.

The names associated with Montparnasse make a list of the most outstanding writers, musicians and painters (primarily, but not exclusively, French) of the last century: writing with Apollinaire, Max Jacob, Cocteau, Breton, Léon-Paul Fargue and Blaise Cendrars; music with Satie's Groupe des Six and Stravinsky; painting with Picasso, Matisse, Miró, Giacometti and Max Ernst. Hemingway and Henry Miller watched the Parisian world pass by from the small hotels and countless bars in the district. Montparnasse still remains a place of art and culture with its many theaters, café-theaters and artists' studios.

▬ VISIT

Boulevard Raspail leads down from the Place Denfert-Rochereau towards Boulevard du Montparnasse; on the corner of Boulevard Edgar-Quinet, the trees to the left mark the **Montparnasse Cemetery** where a number of well-known people are buried, including sculptors Houdon and Rude, musicians César Franck, Saint-Saëns and d'Indy and writers Baudelaire, Maupassant, Bourget and Sartre.

At the intersection of these two boulevards, are some of the hottest night spots in the city. On the left side of Boulevard Raspail are rows of terraces — a microcosm of activity, life and light, colored by the carefree bohemian attitude and a touch of artistic chic which is so typically Parisian. After the **Church of Notre-Dame-des-Champs,** the boulevard takes on a garish look. Multi screen cinemas, bookshops and all kinds of bars

and *crêperies* are found in front of the Place du 18 Juin 1940, where the old Montparnasse station used to be.

The Maine-Montparnasse tower
(Open daily 9.30 am – 11.30 pm, from Apr – Sept; 10 am – 10 pm, from Oct – Mar.)
This commercial center and station have completely transformed the appearance of what used to be a working-people's district. The tower, never fully accepted by Parisians, is now a permanent feature of the Paris skyline with its rigorous geometry and the steepness of its vertical lines tempered by the curve of its walls. The tallest building in Europe, the tower is 686 feet/209 metres high, accommodates more than 7000 people a day in its 52 floors of offices and has 7200 windows. Completed in 1974, the top of the tower has a splendid open-air terrace.

In 40 seconds, the lift takes visitors up to the **56th floor** where there is an illuminated map of the city, and a bar and restaurant from which, in pleasant surroundings, you can admire the full panorama of Paris.

A terrace in pink granite separates the tower from the **station,** comprising three buildings of aluminum, stone and concrete. The station and its predecessor, is the chief link between Paris and Brittany and, for centuries, the alighting point of Bretons arriving in the capital. Thus roads are named after Breton towns: Rennes, Maine, Croisic. Brittany "chouchen" (honeyed wine) is still served in the cafés which hoist the traditional flag of Brittany and, in countless crêperies, cider from Brittany still washes down "galettes de blé noir" (traditional pancakes) and shellfish. Montparnasse is often jokingly referred to as the unofficial capital of Brittany as its population of Bretons exceeds that of Brittany's regional capital, Rennes.

Behind the station, the railway tracks separate two very different districts. On the right, the Boulevard de Vaugirard leads up to the wide and rather solemn Boulevard Pasteur; from here extend the Rues Falguière and Vaugirard (14,270 feet/4350 metres and the longest in Paris), not only the most heavily populated area in the 15th arrondissement but in the whole of Paris. The 15th arrondissement's 500,000 or so inhabitants make it equivalent to the size of a provincial French city such as Bordeaux. On the left, between the Avenue du Maine and the railway tracks, Paris experienced one of its most radical transformations during the years 1970–1980. The old blocks of buildings and workshops, a large number of which harbored workmen since the beginning of the century, were destroyed to make room for vast new complexes, in particular, those along Rue du Cdt-Mouchotte. Squatters and alternative communities were more or less chased out of their homes in Rues Vercingétorix, de l'Ouest and Raymond-Losserand. However, the inquisitive visitor can still find some villas, artisans' houses, gardens, artists' studios, old bistros and shops whose appearance is unchanged. On each side of Rue d'Alésia, contemporary houses and old buildings stand side by side in harmony. On sunny days, hitchhikers can be seen at the Porte d'Orléans heading south. The face of the district will once again be altered when green lawns and a vast garden open to the public (which should cover the railway tracks from the station to the Place des Cinq Martyrs) is completed in 1988.

Also worth seeing

Musee Zadkine — 100 *bis* Rue d'Assas. Metro: Notre-Dame-des-Champs, Vavin. (*Open Wed-Sat 10 am – 5.30 pm, tel: 43 26 91 90.*) The sculptor Zadkine lived in this house, with its attractive little garden, from 1928 until his death in 1967. The 300 pieces of work exhibited portray his progression from the Cubism of the 1920s to a very personal, lyrical style.

Musee Bourdelle — 16 Rue Bourdelle. Metro: Falguière. (*Open daily ex. Mon and Public hols, 10 am – 5.30 pm, tel: 45 48 67 27.*) The artistic interest of this small museum centers around the contemporary busts and the series of figures of Beethoven. The sculptor Bourdelle worked here from 1884 until his death in 1929. The most interesting section is undoubtedly the old family house with its garden and workshops, particularly the sculptor's own, which is preserved with his tools and sketches, and left just as they were when he died.

Musée de la Poste (Postal Museum), in the Maison de la Poste et de la Philatélie, 34 Boulevard de Vaugirard. (*Open daily ex. Sun and Public hols, 10 am – 5 pm, tel: 43 20 15 30.*) This museum will astonish stamp collectors who can follow the complete history of the postal service, from parchments carried by monks and the horse post created by Louis XI to modern-day airmail services. A printing workshop producing stamps in copperplate engraving can also be visited and its stamps can be purchased. Their everyday use all too often makes us forget their beauty.

AROUND MONTPARNASSE

La Coupole, 102 Bd du Montparnasse (tel: 43 20 14 20). Open 10 am – 2 am Mon to Sun. Still a monument to Parisian life. Fashionable Parisians lived their most fervent hours here during the carefree years after World War I. You can still enjoy a warm, relaxed and pleasant atmosphere with good food and always plenty of people.

La Closerie des Lilas, 171 Bd du Montparnasse (tel: 43 26 70 50). Open 10 am – 1.30 am Mon to Sun. Between Montparnasse and the Latin Quarter — the heartland of Parisian literature. Hemingway was a regular visitor to this bar.

Le Dôme, 108 Bd du Montparnasse (tel: 43 35 25 81). Open noon – 3 pm, 5 pm – 1 am daily ex. Mon. One of the big names for old-time Montparnos, it offers excellent seafood and fish in modern surroundings.

RECOMMENDED FOR REFRESHMENT

Restaurant des Beaux-Arts, 11 Rue Bonaparte, 75006 (tel: 43 26 92 64). Open noon – 2.30 pm, 7 – 10.30 pm Mon to Sun.

Le Bar de l'Hotel, 13 Rue des Beaux-Arts, 75006 (tel: 43 25 27 22). Open 7 – 11 pm Mon to Sun. One of the most original hotel bars in Paris.
The most original bar of Parisian luxury hotels.

Millésimes, 7 Rue Lobineau, 75006 (tel: 46 34 22 15). Open 11 am – 3 pm, 5 – 10 pm daily ex. Sun.
Pleasant wine bar.

La Petite Cour, 8 Rue Mabillion, 75006 (tel: 43 26 52 26). Open noon – 2 pm, 8 – 10.30 pm daily ex. Sun, Mon.

Sunset, 35 Quai de la Tournelle, 75005 (tel: 43 25 44 42). Open noon – 2 pm, 7.45 – 10.15 pm. Closed Sat noon and Sun.

THE LATIN QUARTER

The demise of the Latin Quarter has been proclaimed since the last century, when students lamented the change in the area which had traditionally been their own. Now the scholars, who gave the district its name, are dispersed throughout Paris, since prices in the area have become prohibitively high. All the same, the area retains its bohemian charm: its bookshops, cafés and cinemas showing art films seem to be resisting the onslaught of fast-food outlets, the aggressive sales patter of the shop-keepers on the Rue de la Huchette and Rue Saint-André-des-Arts and the outlandish clothes shops of Boulevard Saint-Michel. Discerning visitors will realize that although times have changed, the Latin Quarter lives on.

Place Saint-Michel

Metro: Saint-Michel   Bus: n°ˢ 21, 27, 38, 85, 96   **Map 5, (C 1)**

The **Place Saint-Michel** was built at the beginning of the 19th century, absorbing the tiny mediaeval alleys such as Rue de l'Hirondelle, where the surgeon Ambroise Paré lived in the 14th century. In 1860, Davioud erected a fountain to hide the ugly wall of the building which forms the corner of the boulevard of the same name. The young people who meet there now give it a certain charm.

Those with a taste for old Parisian homes will be attracted by the small houses which have cafés with terraces encroaching on the pavement. Also of interest, at n° 5 in the narrow and winding Rue Hautefeuille, is the attractive turret of the Abbots of Fécamp's mansion (16th century). Along the Quai Saint-Michel (fine view of the facade of Notre-Dame), there is a tiny square lined with old houses like the restaurant-tearoom of *La Bûcherie* or the English-language bookshop *Shakespeare and Co.*, which offer a more intimate atmosphere than the surrounding cafés. To the right, Rue Saint-Julien-le-Pauvre leads to the small, tree-encircled Church of Saint-Julien.

Saint-Julien-le-Pauvre

Metro: Maubert-Mutualité, Saint-Michel   Bus: n°ˢ 21, 24, 27, 38, 47   **Map 5, (D 2)**

This ancient stop-over of the pilgrims bound for Santiago de Compostela documents the transition from Romanesque to Gothic styles and contains some superb capitals.

▬ HISTORY

The present church, built from 1165 to 1220, is a contemporary of Notre-Dame. It followed several chapels, established from the 6th century and devoted to various St Juliens in history: the Martyr, the Confessor, the Hospitable and, lastly, the Poor, a charitable bishop of Le Mans. For a long time, the church was the seat of the University congregations. However, these became very riotous and, following the wrecking of the church's interior in 1524, students were banned and the

Cafés on Place de la Sorbonne.

church became a chapel of the Hôtel Dieu hospital before being transferred to the Byzantine rite in 1889. Its facade was rebuilt in the 17th century.

▬ VISIT

The **Gothic style** is at its very beginnings, and the solidity and simplicity are still primarily Romanesque. Humble and un-assuming, it blends in perfectly with the surrounding roads, old houses and irregular roofs. Saint-Julien-le-Pauvre has all the charm of a country church. Even though the nave was covered by a heavy barrel-vault in 1650, the **northern lower side** has remained intact, with its attractive **capitals** sculpted with acanthus leaves and harpies. The screen cuts through the **choir**, which was set up in accordance with the Byzantine rite to display icons and sacred pictures.

In Square Viviani, formerly the church enclosure, a crutch supports an ancient type of acacia planted in 1680, and one of Paris' oldest trees. Sculpted stones and a sarcophagus decorate the paths of this small garden, barely shaded by the acacias and linden trees. This square attracts tourists because of the splendid **view** of Notre-Dame and of the Ile de la Cité from behind the trees and book stalls on the quay.

●● Saint-Séverin

Map 5,   Metro: Saint-Michel   Bus: n°⁵ 21, 24, 27, 38, 47, 63, 81, 85, 86, 87, 96
(D 1)

Saint-Séverin is situated in one of Paris' most authentically mediaeval districts. This is the district which is bounded by the busy, noisy Boulevards Saint-Michel and Saint-Germain, the Quai Saint-Michel and the Rue Saint-Jacques. The names of the roads which surround the church are old and colorful such as Le Chat-qui-Pêche (The Fishing Cat). The shops selling kebabs and spring rolls, the experimental cinemas and the jazz cellars could be passed over in favor of the wonderfully confused facades and crooked 12th-century houses. N° 12 Rue Saint-Séverin is perhaps the narrowest house in Paris, and was the home of Abbot Prevost, author of *Manon Lescaut*.

The **church of Saint-Séverin** is one of the bastions of the old Paris on the Left Bank; it is also one of the masterpieces of the end of the Gothic era which summarizes, in a single column, the perfection of its technique.

▬ HISTORY

The church of Saint-Séverin took its name from a hermit who lived in the 6th century. From the 12th century onwards, the population of the Left Bank grew and Saint-Séverin became the parish for the whole of this part of Paris. The present church was begun in the early 13th century. Around a Romanesque bell-tower, the first three bays of the nave were added in Gothic style. In the 15th century, the building had to be enlarged, resulting in its unusual interior proportions. Construction was completed around 1530 in flamboyant style of which the church represents one of the most beautiful examples. The golden years of 1638–1758 transformed the interior layout, following a whim of the "Grande Mademoiselle", Louis XIV's eccentric cousin, who fell out with her own parish, Saint-Sulpice, and paid for the alterations to the choir (by Le Brun), and the dressing of the choir's columns and Gothic arches in marble and painted wood. Classical music and organ recitals are given here regularly from March to October.

VISIT

'The church is closed from 1 – 3.30 pm and on Mon.)

The lower part of **the facade** dates from the 13th century and the upper section from the 15th. The portal comes from the Church of Saint-Pierre-aux-Boeufs in the Ile de la Cité, demolished at the beginning of the 19th century. On each side, the chapels are covered with gabled roofs with jutting gargoyles. The varied style is very noticeable, the first three bays being 13th century, the following five, 15th century.

The double ambulatory is, without doubt, the most remarkable feature of the church. With the ease and skill of Gothic genius, the sculptor's imagination multiplied the ribs of its vault, which join together in a spiral around the marvelous **central pillar** supporting what appears to be a whole world of vegetation. The exotic appearance of this extraordinary pillar with its abundance of "foliage" has been compared to a grove of palm trees.

In the **Saint-Séverin Church,** behind a Louis XV casing, there is a remarkable organ with 18th-century stops which makes the church one of the most important centers of religious music in Paris. In the chapel there is the **Tree of Jesse,** a 16th-century fresco.

The **Rue des Prêtres-Saint-Séverin** which encircles the church enables one to look into the garden and the galleries of the **"charniers"** (charnel-houses) which used to surround the church's cemetery. Here, the bones taken from the tombs were heaped. These are the only mediaeval galleries (rebuilt) which still exist in Paris. Nothing else remains of the old mediaeval thoroughfare.

Cluny Museum

●●

Metro: Odéon, Maubert-Mutualité   R.E.R.: Saint-Michel
Bus: n⁰ˢ 21, 24, 27, 38, 63, 85, 86, 87, 96

Map 5, (D 1)

On the site of the thermal baths of Lutetia, built by the Seine boatmen's corporation in the 2nd and 3rd centuries, the 14th-century abbots of Cluny built a luxurious Paris residence. The modern-day Cluny Museum is unquestionably the finest example of French domestic architecture that Paris has retained from the 15th century.

HISTORY

The Cluny Museum covers an immense site of Roman baths, built between the 2nd and 3rd centuries and sacked by the Barbarians a century later. Around 1330, Pierre de Châlus bought the ruined site and the surrounding land for the powerful Cluny Abbey in Burgundy. His successors built the colleges surrounding the abbot's residence, designed by Jacques d'Amboise (1485-1500).

After the Revolution, the building was turned over to gardeners who cultivated fruit and vegetables over the ruins of the baths. At the instigation of Alexandre du Sommerard, a prominent collector of artifacts from the Middle Ages, the present building was bought by the State and converted into a museum in 1844.

VISIT

(Open daily ex. Tue 9.45 am – 12.30 pm and 2 – 5.15 pm, tel: 43 25 62 00.)

The **exterior** of the Cluny Museum is characterized by the survival of its mediaeval defenses, including **crenellation** and turrets. The height and number of windows and the finesse of the decoration show the affluence of its original inhabitants.

A **handsome portal** opens onto the main **courtyard,** from which you can see the five-sided staircase tower, protruding mullion windows, roof-timbers decorated with a frieze, a flamboyant balustrade on which gargoyles grimace, and dormer-windows emblazoned with coats-of-arms. The interior is well-lit and remarkably laid-out, enhancing the works of art and, in particular, the objects which recreate mediaeval life, in the rooms reserved for skilled crafts (furniture, illuminated manuscripts, armor, gold and silversmiths' work, pottery, ironmongery).

The tapestries form the museum's most remarkable collection. In room IV is a famous collection illustrating, in five scenes, the *Vie Seigneuriale*** (the activites of a nobleman's household, 16th century). On the first floor, the rotunda of room XI has been specially arranged for the series of six works known as *La Dame à la Licorne**** (Lady with Unicorn). On a red floral background, the same blue island has one or two richly-dressed women, flanked by a lion and a unicorn. The precise meaning of the tapestries is not known, but they are thought to represent the five senses. The beautifully-drawn animals and flowers evoke an earthly paradise. Among the major works of mediaeval decorative art, two of great value should be noted: in room III, **English embroidery** — *Les Léopards d'Angleterre** (The Leopards of England, 16th century); **wooden sculptures** in room VIII, particularly *La Vierge au Froment**, *La Déploration du Christ** and *La Vierge de Pitié**; and four superb statues of the apostles which came from the Sainte-Chapelle (13th century) in room IX.

The chapel* used to serve as an oratory for the abbots of Cluny. Its vault rests on one central column and the decor preserved in its alcoves makes it a flamboyant Gothic jewel. The walls are lined with the tapestry of *La Légende de Saint-Étienne*** woven around 1490.

The "Thermes" ** ** (baths) date from the beginning of the 3rd century. The Frigidarium is the only room which has kept its vaults; it includes a swimming pool for which water came from Rungis by an aqueduct 7½ miles/12 km long! In the room named "Notre-Dame de Paris" are the **21 heads of the Kings of Judah* from the *Galerie des Rois* above the portals of Notre-Dame. They were torn down from the cathedral during the Revolution.

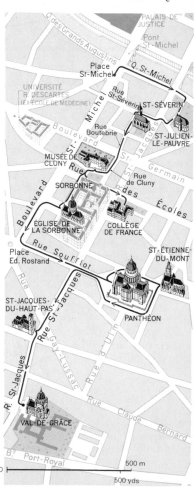

The Latin Quarter.

A Cluny tale ...

The young and comely Mary Tudor, married at the age of sixteen to King Louis XII, once stayed here. She had the misfortune of losing her husband only three months after the wedding. The successor, François I, fearing that she might bear a posthumous child as heir to the throne, set his spies on her. They had the good fortune of surprising the Queen in a compromising situation with the Duke of Suffolk. François I forced the couple to marry immediately in the chapel and then deported them to England.

Collège de France

The Collège de France dominates the little Place Marcelin-Berthelot, behind the Sorbonne at the junction of Rue Saint-Jacques and Rue des Écoles. It was founded by François I on the advice of one of the greatest French humanists, Guillaume Budé. The college continued the tradition of free education for all and some of the most celebrated philosophers, sociologists and historians attended it. Among them are: Jacques Lacan, Claude Lévi-Strauss, Raymond Aron, Fernand Braudel, Michel Foucault, Pierre Boulez and Roland Barthes.

Entrance to the Cluny Museum.

The Sorbonne

Metro: Odéon, Maubert-Mutualité   R.E.R.: Luxembourg   Bus: n° 36   **Map 5, (D-E 1)**

From the Cluny Museum follow the Rue du Sommerard to the right and continue up Boulevard Saint-Michel to the Sorbonne, seat of the University of Paris.

HISTORY

Founded in 1253 by the chaplain of St Louis, Canon **Robert de Sorbon,** the Sorbonne made Paris the intellectual capital of the Christian world. Abélard, St Bonaventure, St Albert le Grand, St Thomas Aquinas and other famed scholars studied there. The students were always boisterous, almost by tradition, and increasingly protected by the special jurisdiction of the Sorbonne, which constituted an actual state within the State.

The Sorbonne's decline began in the 16th century. Its staunch opposition to the ideas of the Protestants and then to the 18th-century philosophers made it an anachronism to all liberal and tolerant thinkers. In 1806, Napoleon created an imperial university, composed of academies which hardly changed until **May 1968.**

In 1968, an explosive dispute erupted over a political crisis and terminated a venerable tradition: for the first time in its history, the Sorbonne was invaded by the police. The University is now totally transformed; today it spreads its 300,000 students over 13 universities which are dispersed all over the Paris area.

VISIT

The interior — 22 amphitheaters, examination and lecture rooms, two museums and some laboratories are concealed behind the austere walls; rooms and corridors are decorated with allegorical murals; the great lecture hall contains the famous composition by Puvis de Chavannes, *Le Bois Sacré* (The Sacred Wood).*

The Church of the Sorbonne is only open for exhibitions and concerts. Constructed at the beginning of the 17th century, its very beautiful lateral facade looks out onto the main courtyard of the Sorbonne. Inside is the **tomb of Richelieu***, in white marble, sculpted by Girardon in 1694 from designs by Le Brun.

•• # The Panthéon

Map 5,   Metro: Cardinal-Lemoine   R.E.R.: Luxembourg
(E 1-2)   Bus: n°ˢ 21, 24, 27, 38, 84, 85, 89

From the Sorbonne, via Rue Victor-Cousin, rejoin Rue Soufflot which opens on the left to the Place du Panthéon. This street seems to dissociate itself from the hurly-burly of the neighborhood — it does not even have the inevitable cafés or shops.

The Marseillaise by Rude on the Arc de Triomphe and *Liberty Guiding the People* by Delacroix at the Louvre both evoke a proud and flamboyant image of the Republic; by contrast, the Panthéon is an austere and cold monument, built to commemorate France's heroes and testify to their virtues.

▬ HISTORY

The Panthéon does not have a happy history. In 1744, Louis XV, lying seriously ill at Metz, vowed that if he recovered he would build a magnificent church to replace the Sainte-Geneviève Abbey. He did recover, and Soufflot was set to design an enormous dome crowning a sanctuary in the shape of a Greek cross. In 1778, the erection of the dome, and possibly some minor ground subsidence, caused cracks in the walls; the luckless architect died broken-hearted two years later.

In 1791, the Assembly decided that the church should henceforth "receive the ashes of distinguished men who lived during the period of the Liberty of France". The temple of the Republic's heroes was named after the abode of the Greek gods of Olympus, the Panthéon. Under the Restoration, it was again used as a church but, with the burial of Victor Hugo (1885), it reverted to its Republican role.

▬ VISIT

(Open daily, ex. Tue and Public hols. Apr – Sept, 10 am – 6 pm, Oct – Mar, 10 am – 4 pm.)
Seen from the Place du Panthéon, the Panthéon is very impressive, with its **peristyle** copied from the Pantheon in Rome and a dome of such great height that its architect, Soufflot, had to use an iron support for it. The austerity of the walls was intensified when the Assembly ordered 42 of the building's windows to be walled-in, but that provided large interior surfaces for the artists of the Third Republic to decorate. The painters Laurens, Sicard, Detaille, Hébert, Cabanel, Bonnat and especially **Puvis de Chavannes,** found spaces suitable to their individual talents; the latter became the only renowned fresco painter of the 19th century, heir to the Italians of the *Quattrocento.*

The Crypt *(guided tours every 15 mins)* extends under the whole building. Set in a funereal atmosphere is the shrine containing Gambetta's heart, the cenotaph of J.-J.

Rousseau, and a statue and monument to Voltaire, as well as the tombs of distinguished men of the Republic, from Rousseau to Victor Hugo, Jaurès to Jean Moulin. The crypt is a fortress of the national memory; President Mitterrand went there to pay homage the day after his election in May 1981.

The Sainte-Geneviève library, on the north side of the Place du Panthéon, is one of the richest in Paris, particularly in its manuscripts and ancient engravings. On the site of the strict Montaigu College where Loyola, Rabelais, Erasmus and Calvin studied, the architect **Labrouste** used, for the first time, a metallic structure to cover the building, constructed in 1850. At n° 4 Rue Valette, the **Sainte-Barbe College,** founded in 1460, is the oldest private school in Paris. Behind the Panthéon, the small Place Sainte-Geneviève opens out in front of the Church of Saint-Étienne-du-Mont.

Saint-Étienne-du-Mont

The Church of Saint-Étienne-du-Mont is the only example in Paris of the transition from a Gothic structure to the new decorative elements of the Italian Renaissance.

Map 5, (E 2)

HISTORY

In 1492, this church was built to replace an earlier church which had become too small for the district's parishioners. The bell-tower and apse were constructed first, followed by the choir and the magnificent rood screen (1545), then finally the side chapels.

VISIT

(The church is open 7.30 – 11.45 am and from 2.15 – 7.15 pm during the week, on Sun 4 – 7.15 pm.)
The design of the **facade** announces the originality of this church. Its portal is composed of three superimposed pediments, each of different shape and decoration. The Gothic **choir** bays contrast with the arched windows of the Renaissance **nave.** Inside, the pure Gothic architecture was decorated in a style directly inspired by the Italian Renaissance; note the exquisite **stained-glass windows*** of the apse (16th and 17th century) and particularly the **rood screen****, erected by Antoine Beaucorps to Philibert Delorme's designs. Joining two open stairways which spiral around pillars right up to the balustrade of the choir, this is the only screen of its kind in Paris today. On the right of the choir is the church's most venerated monument, the **Shrine of Sainte-Geneviève,** patron saint of Paris.

By taking Rue Saint-Jacques, you will emerge in front of the **Church of Val-de-Grâce**** which, together with its adjoining buildings, is the best-preserved 17th-century ensemble in Paris.

Val-de-Grâce

R.E.R.: Port-Royal   Bus: n⁰ˢ 89, 91, 21, 27   **Map 5, (F 1)**

Married to Louis XIII for 23 years without producing an heir, Queen Anne of Austria vowed to build a church if she gave birth to a son. In 1638, the future Louis XIV was born and it was he who, in 1645, laid the first stone of the church, designed by Mansart. Lemercier was brought in to expedite the work which was completed in 1665. In 1793, Val-de-Grâce became a military hospital.

VISIT

The church strongly resembles those in Rome; its two-level Jesuit-style facade is dominated by the famous decorative dome, its architects Le Muet and Le Duc having been inspired by the dome of St Peter's in Rome.
The same Baroque style was used in the superb interior decoration, as well as in the sculpted arch of the altar and in the baldachin supported by six twisted columns which, once again, is reminiscent of the altar of St Peter's. **Mignard** decorated the **cupola** with a huge painting, *Le Séjour des Bienheureux*.

RECOMMENDED FOR REFRESHMENT

La Cour de Rohan, 59 Passage du Commerce-Saint-André-des-Arts, 75006 (tel: 43 25 79 67). Open noon – 8 pm, Mon to Fri. A delightful tea-room at the Odéon.
Bernard Pontonnier, 19 Rue des Fossés-Saint-Jacques, 75006 (tel: 43 26 80 18). Open 11.30 am – 11 pm Mon to Sat. Good wine bar next to the Panthéon.

MAUBERT, THE GOBELINS

Metro: Maubert-Mutualité   Bus: n⁰ˢ 24, 63, 86, 87   **Map 5, (D 2)**

T his area is a jumble of incongruities: the market of the Place
 Maubert, old houses with grey roofs, a mosque with a minaret
towering over the neighborhood, the Gobelins factory and the well-kept
flower beds and hothouses of the Jardin des Plantes. Notwithstanding
this diversity, there is a harmony to be found here, not in the
monuments and buildings — nothing relates the "Maube" to the Paris
Mosque or the Gobelins to the Botanical Gardens — but in the perennial
scenes of Parisian life which have endured.

▬ VISIT

The Place Maubert, despite all the
renovations, has retained some of its
picturesque character. Its popular and lively
fruit and vegetable market is highly regarded by experts in such matters. In the
warm summer evenings, visitors to the city
enjoy strolling through the attractive
square. Like the whole of the 5th arrondissement, the Place Maubert has seen the
minor artisans, merchants, small-wage ear-
ners of the arts and of publishing increasingly driven away by an intellectual
bourgeoisie with liberal ideas and casual
dress. Nevertheless, the atmosphere of the
square, where the tramps formerly held
their famous "cigarette butt exchange", has
remained very characteristic of the spirit of
the Left Bank.

The **Salle de la Mutualité,** Rue Saint-
Victor, sometimes comes to life when
there are political meetings, attracting supporters and opponents. The **Church of
Saint-Nicolas-du-Chardonnet**   (late
17th-century facade) also has its troubles
due to its occupation by "integrist" Catholics, who continue to celebrate Mass in
Latin. It contains the tomb of the architect
Le Brun.

Rue Monge crosses the Rue des Écoles
and heads towards the Gobelins (both laid
out by Haussmann). In the small Square
Monge, at n° 20, there is a beautiful early
18th-century fountain; the two Renaissance
niches come from the Hôtel-de-Ville.

The Lutèce arenas* Map 5, (E–F, 2–3);
Metro: Cardinal-Lemoine, Jussieu, Monge;
Bus: n⁰ˢ 47, 89.

Lively market at the bottom of Rue Mouffetard.

This **Gallo-Roman** arena, together with
the baths of Cluny, are the only Roman
remains still visible in Paris.

From Rue Monge, Rue Rollin leads to the

Maubert, the Gobelins.

right on to the **Place de la Contres-
carpe**, which has been famous since the
Middle Ages; Rabelais used to frequent the
cabaret of the *Pomme de Pin* at n° 1. People
of dubious morals held rowdy shows here
for centuries, before being replaced by
today's lovers of Greek cuisine or
"authentic" cabarets.

Gobelins factory

Metro: Gobelins   Bus: n⁰ˢ 27, 47, 83, 91

▬▬ HISTORY

In 1440, Jean Gobelin, a dyer who specialized in scarlet, opened his workshop on the banks of the Bièvre. Henri IV, desiring to set up a royal tapestry industry in Paris, commissioned two Flemish tapestry-makers to begin it. In 1662, the statesman Colbert created the royal factory of Crown Tapestries and placed it under the direction of Le Brun. The royal furniture factory was transferred there, soon to be joined by the best tapestry-weavers, goldsmiths and cabinet-makers in the kingdom. These craftsmen, inspired by painters such as Boucher, Poussin, Mignard and Van Loo, produced, first in the style of Louis XIV and then of the Regency, some of the most beautiful examples. The factories of the Savonnerie and of Beauvais have since been installed at the Gobelins.

▬▬ VISIT

(Open Wed, Thur, Fri 2 – 3.30 pm, tel: 45 70 12 60.)
A visit to the workshops reveals the different weaving techniques on looms with vertical warps (high-warp) or by knotting (Savonnerie).
On the first floor, there are temporary exhibits devoted particularly to modern tapestries created from designs of great artists such as Lurçat, Picasso, Picart Le Doux, et al.; in the chapel, 18th-century tapestries.

The National furniture factory (*Mobilier National*), n° 1 Rue Berbier-du-Mets, on the corner of Rue Croulebarbe, is where the furniture for French kings, emperors and the Republic's presidents has been made. Continue down to the Place D'Italie to the Boulevard de l'Hôpital which ends in front of the Seine by the Place Valhubert; the entrance to the Jardin des Plantes (Botanical gardens; *see following page*) is opposite the Gare d'Austerlitz, which dates from 1869.

The Pitié-Salpêtrière

Metro: Saint-Marcel   Bus: n⁰ˢ 57, 91

▬▬ HISTORY

The hospital, in Boulevard de l'Hôpital, owes its name to the arsenal, established under Louis XIII, where gunpowder was made with saltpeter. Louis XIV decided to open a hospital there in 1654, as "a general hospital for the poor".

In 1662, 10,000 pensioners were crowded in there; for recalcitrants, the alternative was a convict-ship. A workhouse for women of ill repute, set up in 1690, later admitted the mentally ill. Freud came here to study under Professor Charcot who used hypnosis to treat hysteria.

▬▬ VISIT

On the boulevard is a French-style garden in front of the building which reminds one of Les Invalides. In the center, the chapel of Saint-Louis-de-la-Salpêtrière supports its octagonal dome surmounted by a lantern. Built 1657-77 by the architect Libéral-Bruant, it owes its unusual geometric arrangement to the need to separate the different types of inmates, which led to its having nine naves.

At n° 42 **Avenue des Gobelins,** there is a building with a square cupola, built in 1914 for the Gobelins factory (*see above*).

Jardin des Plantes

The Jardin des Plantes (Botanical gardens), with its pavilions, conservatories, paleozoology rooms and an amazing variety of trees, plants and flowers once enjoyed a great reputation. Lack of funds in the past caused some deterioration, but, with new grants, it has recovered its former prestige.

HISTORY

The first "royal garden of medicinal plants", created in 1626 by Hérouard and Guy de la Brosse, was opened to the public in 1640. It was **Buffon,** manager from 1739–88, who made the garden a center for the fashionable, aristocratic study of botany. The zoo was opened during the Revolution, but the animals were slaughtered for food when Paris ran short of it during the Siege of 1870. However, thanks to Geoffroy Saint-Hilaire, Lamarck, Lacépède and Cuvier, the Botanical museum acquired an international reputation.

VISIT

Open daily 7.30 or 8 am to sunset.
Zoo and Vivarium: *daily 9 am – 6 pm.*
Hothouses: *daily ex. Tue, Public hols., 1.30 – 5 pm.*
Botany school: *daily ex. Sat, Sun & Public hols, 9 – 11.30 am and 1.30 – 5pm.*
Alpine garden: *Apr – Sept, daily ex. Public hols. 10 – 11.30 am and 1 – 5.30 pm.*
Museums of palaeontology, paleobotany and minerology: *daily ex. Tue, Public hols., 1.30 – 5 pm, weekdays 10.30 am – 5 pm Sun.*

Paris mosque*
Map 5, (F 3); Metro: Monge   Bus: n°s 24, 47, 57, 61, 63, 67, 89 — *Entrance: Place du Puits-de-l'Ermite, Guided tours daily* — 9 am – noon and 2 – 6 pm, ex. Fri and Muslim feast days, tel: 45 35 97 33.

Rue Mouffetard is wonderfully lively with its little shops and regular food market offering provincial specialties. Notice the old shop sign at n° 6, which declares itself to be "The House of Confidence" (18th century). At n° 60, the fountain of Pot-de-Fer dates back to Marie de Médicis; at n° 69, the sign of the *Vieux Chêne* marks the site of a revolutionary club, later a popular dance hall.

The Church Saint-Médard, at n° 141 *(Open daily ex. Mon and Sun after 4 pm; concerts)*, was erected in memory of the bishop who advised the Mérovingian kings. On this spot the Rue Mouffetard used to cross the small river, Bièvre, which has since disappeared. The nave and the facade, of Flamboyant style, date back to the 15th century. For want of funds, the choir retained its temporary wooden vaulting and was only completed at the beginning of the 17th century.
Inside are paintings by Natoire, Restout, and a superb **16th-century triptych** behind the pulpit.

RECOMMENDED FOR REFRESHMENT

Marty, 20 Av. des Gobelins, 75013 (tel: 43 31 39 51). Open noon – 3 pm, 7 – 10.30 pm Mon to Sat. A real brasserie.
Le Traiteur, 28 Rue de la Glacière, 75013 (tel: 43 31 64 17). Open noon – 2.30 pm, 7.30 – 11 pm Mon to Fri.
La Mosquée, 1 Rue Daubenton, 75005 (tel: 43 31 18 14). Open 11 am – 9 pm Mon to Sun. Muslim tea-room.
Buvette du Jardin de Plantes, 57 Rue Cuvier, 75005 (tel: 43 36 14 41). Open 11 am – 5.30 pm Mon to Sun. Crêpes and grills, next to the zoo.

THE MARAIS

The Marais district fell on hard times at the end of the 17th century but, following extensive restoration work, has now regained some of its splendor. Mansions dating from the 16th and 17th centuries display their homogeneous facades or conceal large courtyards. By some miracle, some of the ancient houses still stand. The Marais should be seen slowly; the richness of the architecture is best taken in small doses : the Archives and the Carnavalet Museum should be visited first; next the Place des Vosges and finally the streets near the Seine.

▬▬ HISTORY

As its name implies, **the Marais** (or marsh) was built on a stretch of marshy land where a branch of the Seine used to flow.

From the 13th century, monks and Knights Templar made the Marais one of Paris' **kitchen gardens,** but it was only the protection offered by its high wall, built by Charles V at the end of the 14th century, that persuaded Parisians to come and live in this area. Charles V himself, fleeing from the old Cité Palace, came to live in the **Hôtel Saint-Paul.** In 1393, at a fancy dress ball, four of Charles VI's friends smeared themselves with pitch to disguise themselves as savages and were accidentally burned alive. The king narrowly escaped death, and the infamous **"Bal des Ardents"** (Ball of the Burning) precipitated the madness which cast such a pall over his reign. The name Rue des Lions-Saint-Paul is the only reminder of the zoo which he had installed there.

François 1 demolished the Hôtel Saint-Paul but subsequent kings did not leave the Marais. Charles VIII, Louis XII and Henri II lived in the Palace of Tournelles, but Catherine de Médicis then abandoned it because it reminded her of the death of her husband, Henri II, killed there in 1559 during a tournament. In 1605, Henri IV entrusted Sully, his finance minister, with the building of a square which introduced town-planning to the area. Entirely symmetrical, the Place Royale (today's **Place des Vosges**) attracted great lords and courtiers who had splendid mansions built there.

The "hôtel", a Classical building set between an entrance court and garden, became at this time a unique feature of French architecture. Another feature of French society also developed at this time : conversation in the "salons" of these great houses. Free thinkers, philosophers and musicians brilliantly aired their views in the company of sophisticated women. By the end of the 17th century, however, the Marais had lost out to the Faubourgs Saint-Honoré and Saint-Germain, and merchants and successful craftsmen took over the abandoned mansions. A long period of decline followed, lasting for over a hundred and fifty years.

At the beginning of the 1960s, the inhabitants of the Marais set up a preservation committee which prevented the district from sinking into the oblivion toward which it was heading. At the end of 1964, the Malraux Law on the protection of heritage was applied to the Marais, making it the largest protected district in France. The handsome 17th-century mansions were restored, and the courts and gardens regained the charm and Classical elegance which make today's Marais not only a tourist attraction but a much-favored residential area of wealthy Parisians.

Place des Vosges.

The Hôtel-de-Ville

Map 5, Metro: Hôtel-de-Ville   Bus: n⁰ˢ 38, 47, 58, 67, 69, 70, 72, 74, 75, 76, 96
(B-C,
2-3)   Paris, like even the smallest commune in France, has its elected mayor,
and this is his office and official residence. Here, in the square decorated
with fountains, Parisians take their constitutionals, strolling in front of
the Hôtel, almost surreal in its newfound cleanliness. The idyllic scene
at present should not obscure from memory the tempestuous events that
the Hôtel-de-Ville has known in its many centuries of existence.

HISTORY

The original Hôtel was built in 1260 by St Louis at a place on the Seine
where the unemployed gathered to air their grievances. It was also used
for the punishment of criminals. Municipal government was introduced
in 1260, and the municipal assembly was moved there at the suggestion
of Étienne Marcel, a rich draper and leader of the States General. In
1357, Marcel revolted against the royal power, allying himself with the
disaffected peasantry and even letting the English into the city. Finally
Charles V got the better of him and he was put to death. But it was the
Revolution which gave the Hôtel-de-Ville its position of importance.

On July 17th, 1789 Louis XVI was brought here and made to pass
through an arch formed by crossed swords and forced to kiss the new
tricolor cockade of red and blue, the colors of Paris, to which La Fayette
added white, the color of the monarchy. Three years later, the
Hôtel-de-Ville became the seat of the ruling body during the Revolution.

In 1848, when King Louis-Philippe was overthrown, the Hôtel-de-
Ville became the seat of the provisional government. In 1871, the leaders
of the Paris Commune uprising made the building their headquarters. In
May 1871, along with the Tuileries and many other monuments, the
Hôtel-de-Ville was totally destroyed. It was later rebuilt to a design by
Ballu. The exterior of the building is neo-Renaissance, but its interior,
lavishly decorated (sometimes to excess), reflects the Third Republic's
taste for pomp.

VISIT

*(Group visits on request at: Accueil de la Ville
de Paris, 49 Rue de Rivoli, tel: 42 76 40 40.)*
The **facade** is full of character, with its two
corner pavilions, Corinthian columns which
support a group of 146 statues, its bell-
tower adorned with four chimeras, the
ridge of the roof bristling with heralds, and,
finally, the statue representing "The City of
Paris" sitting on a throne above the clock
flanked by Education and Work.
Seven types of wood were used for the
dining-room floor, 24 crystal chandeliers
by Baccarat decorate the ballroom, and
Jean-Paul Laurens, Benjamin Constant and
Puvis de Chavannes depicted not only the
whole history of Paris, but also feminine
beauty, with a certain naive eroticism. You
may prefer the magisterial purity of the
grand staircase of honor* by Philibert

Delorme which was spared by the fire of
1871.
The mayor's office is adorned with works
recalling his more famous predecessors —
the provosts Étienne Marcel and François
Miron, Bailly, Lamartine and Clemenceau,
mayor of Montmartre in 1870.

From the Place de l'Hôtel-de-Ville,
follow Rue de Rivoli on the right which
runs beside the facade of the Bazar de
l'Hôtel-de-Ville, a paradise for do-it-
yourself enthusiasts, then take Rue des
Archives on the left.

The Cloister of the Billettes*, at n⁰ˢ
22–26, is the only Middle Ages cloister that
has been preserved in Paris. With the

adjoining church, it was built on the ruins of a house belonging to an unfortunate Jewish money-lender who was accused in 1290 of having stabbed, then burned, a consecrated host.

A small door to the left of the church, which became Lutheran in 1812, opens onto a pretty cloister of very simple architecture, with Flamboyant arches and solid pillars. Numerous concerts are held here today.

At n° 40, the renovation of a building in 1971 led to the rediscovery of a very beautiful house called the **"Maison de Jacques Coeur"**, which was occupied by a famous 16th-century merchant and financier. Characteristic of the period, with its mullioned windows and red and black brick construction, it is one of the oldest houses in Paris.

Macabre memories

The Place de l'Hôtel-de-Ville, formerly the Place de Grève, was the equivalent of London's Tyburn Hill: from the 14th century to the Revolution, bourgeois and commoners were hanged from the permanently erected gallows, nobles beheaded, and heretics or sorcerers burned at the stake. There was much popular excitement on these occasions, with hundreds of Parisians turning out to witness them.

There was a full house when the notorious highwayman, Cartouche, was tortured. Women of the court paid in gold to rent space on balconies to see the quartering of Damiens who had stabbed Louis XV.

The National Archives

Metro: Rambuteau. **Map 5, (A-B, 3-4)**

At the crossing of Rue des Archives and Rue des Francs-Bourgeois, a group of mansions has recently been added to the Palais Soubise; together, they form the Palais des Archives.

HISTORY

The palace was originally the manor of Olivier de Clisson, Supreme Commander of the Royal Army, built in 1375 on land belonging to the Knights Templar. In 1553, the Guise family bought the manor and had it considerably enlarged. During the Wars of Religion, it was the headquarters of the Catholics.

The decision to carry out the massacre on St Bartholomew's Day was made here by the Duc de Guise, known as "Le Balafré" ("Scarface").

In 1697, the Princesse de Soubise bought the building, her royal lover, Louis XIV, footing the bill. The architect Delamair was commissioned to build a new mansion, for which he created a splendid main courtyard and added, on the other side, a vast garden and another house for the Cardinal de Rohan. Following the death of the Princesse de Soubise (1709), Boffrand, who succeeded Delamair, designed the incomparable interior decoration of the palace, on which he worked continuously until 1745.

From 1808, the **National Archives** gathered all the documents acquired from the territories conquered by the Imperial Armies, particularly those from the Vatican and Holland.

Today, there are more than 6 million documents of all kinds which take up 173 miles/280 km of shelf space. Having filled the Palais Soubise, they spilled over into the Hôtel Rohan, then into nos 58, 56 and 54 of Rue des Francs-Bourgeois as well as the Hôtels Assy, Le Tonnelier de Breteuil and de Jaucourt.

▰ *VISIT*

The entrance door, with the tympanum decorated by Delacroix, opens onto the beautiful horseshoe-shaped **courtyard** surrounded by a gallery of 56 columns in pairs.

The facade of the palace is very attractive, featuring a pediment on which the statues of Prudence and Wisdom are seated.

The Interior — the magnificent apartments can be viewed on guided tours. From Boucher to Van Loo, from Natoire to Lemoyne, the finest artists of the early 18th century vied with each other to produce, with the highest imagination, paneling, paintings and reliefs.

Museum of French history *(Open daily ex. Tue, Public hols, 2 – 5 pm, tel: 42 77 11 30)* – situated in the apartments of the Prince and Princesse de Soubise. In the former guard room, various antique documents are displayed (but in a very modern setting), such as one of Joan of Arc's letters, the Edict of Nantes and the wills of Louis XIV and Napoleon.

The Hôtel Guénégaud, opposite, at n° 60 Rue des Archives, contains the museum of "hunting and nature".

The Hôtel Rohan, n° 87 Rue Vieille-du-Temple, was built by Delamair. It is only open for exhibitions and conferences. Above the entrance of its old stables, in the right-hand courtyard, there is a unique work by Robert le Lorrain, *The Horses of Apollo**.

The Church of Notre-Dame-des-Blancs-Manteaux, opposite the Hôtel Jaucourt is also part of the Archives. Its name preserves the memory of a convent where St Louis housed the mendicant monks, the Serfs of the Virgin Mary, who went begging dressed in long white coats. It is better known for its remarkable **organ** than for its architecture — it was reconstructed in 1685 — and is an important center of sacred music.
Beside the church, at n° 57 *bis*, there is a massive tower behind the gate; this was erected at the same time as Philippe-Auguste's enclosure, about 1200.

A Gothic turret, at the corner of Rues des Francs-Bourgeois and Vieille-du-Temple, marks the **beautiful house of Jean Herouët,** who was Louis XII's treasurer.

Asia in the heart of the Marais

Standing in the midst of some of the finest examples of French civil architecture, the Kwok-On Museum, at n° 41 Rue des Francs-Bourgeois, appears even more exotic. The museum was set up by a wealthy resident of Hong Kong who donated all the costumes, musical instruments, puppets and masks used by the different types and traditions of Asiatic theater. It illustrates the refinement of the shadow theatre of South-East Asia (particularly Indonesia), the stylized Japanese dances and Noh theater, and the more popular Kabuki drama or Bunraku marionettes. *(Open noon – 6 pm, ex. Sat, Sun and Public hols, tel: 42 72 99 42.)*

The Marais Cultural Center holds some marvelous exhibitions. A little farther on, the 1630 Hôtel Sandreville is at n° 26; at n° 35, the **Hôtel Coulanges,** which dates back to the beginning of the 18th century; at n° 33, the 1634 Hôtel Barbes. This exceptional row of houses represents the richest and most interesting part of **Rue des Francs-Bourgeois,** where the Royal Court used to meet.

The Hôtel Lamoignon, on the left-hand corner of Rue Pavée, was constructed in 1584 for Diane of France, King Henri II's legitimate daughter. It is one of the largest and oldest houses in the Marais. Since 1868, it has housed the collections of the **History library of the City of Paris** (Bibliothèque historique de la Ville de Paris; *open daily ex. Sun, 2 – 6 pm)*. On **Rues Payenne** and **Parc-Royal** there is a row of very beautiful mansions to admire before entering the Hôtel Carnavalet via Rue de Sévigné. Mansart lived and died at n° 5 Rue Payenne. At n° 11, the **Hôtel de Marle** is distinguished by a mask above the doorway and its unusual keel-shaped roof by Philibert Delorme; it is now the Swedish Cultural Center. Opposite, the Georges Cain garden lies in front of the elegant **Hôtel de Saint-Fargeau** (1689). In Rue de Parc-Royal on the right, the general effect presented is one of remarkable unity, with all the mansions dating back to the 17th century.

The Carnavalet Museum ●●

Metro: Saint-Paul, Chemin-Vert   Bus: nᵒˢ 29, 69, 76, 96   **Map 5, (B 4)**

At n° 23 Rue de Sévigné, the Hôtel Carnavalet is one of the major examples of 16th and 17th-century French architecture, as well as an enthralling museum.

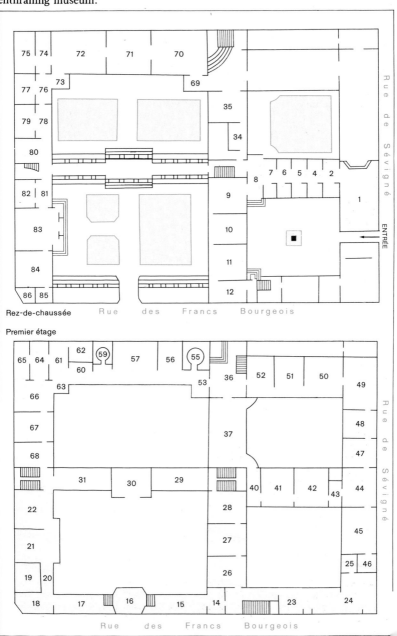

Plan of the Hôtel Carnavalet.

HISTORY

The Hôtel Carnavalet is a combination of two mansions, one built by Pierre Lescot in 1544, Italian in style, and the other by Mansart in the middle of the 17th century. The place derived its name, somewhat corrupted, from a Madame de Kernevenoy who briefly occupied it. Madame de Sévigné, who lived here from 1676 to 1694, wrote her famous letters to her daughter on the premises and also received the greatest philosophers of the age. The École des Ponts et Chaussées was situated here for a while before it became, after much restoration by Baltard, the Museum of History of the City of Paris.

VISIT

The city of Paris would not be able to find a more suitable place to house its **museum of history** than the Hôtel Carnavalet which, in the 17th century, was one of the prominent centers of wit, elegance and Parisian life. It was restored haphazardly, yet with some attempt at retaining its spirit, and was later annexed to its neighboring mansion, Le Peletier de Saint-Fargeau. The museum owes much of its charm to its style and unusual atmosphere which is rather whimsical though typically Parisian. Rather than impressive major works, important events or prominent people, the Carnavalet Museum has chosen to portray the daily life of Parisians from all ages and all backgrounds; the barber's sign-board has its place, as do models of bridges, prints popularizing the storming of the Bastille and apothecaries' equipment. By moving from room to room, visitors cover a five-century period of history, skirting the porters of Les Halles, discovering fairs, bargemen's contests, then some of the beautiful collections of French furniture, all of which recall the life-style of the 17th and 18th centuries.

The entrance to the mansion is through the 17th-century portal adorned with lions; on the keystone, there is a **statue of Plenty** by Jean Goujon. In the center of the courtyard, there is a statue of Louis XIV on a throne, by Coysevox. Note the Gothic appearance of the main building, the lower part contrasting with the Four Seasons (Renaissance) and the 17th-century wings. Through the door opening onto Rue des Francs-Bourgeois, the mansion's garden can be seen, framed by the 16th-century arch of Nazareth.

The Carnavalet Museum — (Entrance 23 Rue de Sévigné, 3rd floor. Open daily ex. Mon & Public hols. 10 am – 5.30 pm. Certain rooms are closed from 12.30 – 2 pm, tel: 42 72 21 13) — portrays **Parisian life-**

styles from François I to the Belle Epoque, from Renaissance to Art Nouveau; it makes this daily life alive and interesting. The magic of the Carnavalet is that it brings back to life Parisians of the past through its countless paintings and engravings which depict the **minor trades**, the construction of a bridge, a fire, an execution on the Place de Grève, the solemn entrance of the king. Also on display are the shop and tavern signs beside the furnishings of an apothecary's shop and the wainscotting from the Café Militaire (1752); the series of Views of Paris by the Raguenets offer an unequaled panorama of the city in the 18th century.

The furniture collections of Louis XIV, Regency, Louis XV and Louis XVI, displayed in settings appropriate to the era (tapestries and wainscotting) many of which come from the great 18th-century Parisian mansions, are worth studying, before delving into the revolutionary fever of **1789–1794**. An exceptional tableau of military and civil life under the Revolution has actually been reconstructed in the Hôtel Le Pelletier de Saint-Fargeau. It also includes the laundry book of the Royal family who were imprisoned in the Temple, as well as miniature guillotines, models of the Bastille, Robespierre's moustache cup and even his last letter.

At the entrance of the museum — Rms. 4–7: temporary exhibitions.
To the right, rooms devoted to trades and signs.
Rms. 8–12: Paris in the 16th century and under the reign of Henri IV — paintings from French and Flemish schools. The Provost of Traders and Paris Councillors (Rm. 13) — this is the first collective portrait of Parisian town councillors. The staircase leading to the first floor is dominated by Michel Bourdin's bust of Henri IV. On the landing, there is a statue of Marie-Adélaïde

de Savoire, dressed as the huntress Diane, by Coysevox.

Rms. 14–22: 17th-century Paris.

Rms. 14 & 15: Parisian sights, including the Pont Neuf, the Quai de la Tournelle, the Ile Saint-Louis.

Rm. 16: below the ceiling painted by Bon de Boullogne, there are engravings representing the monuments constructed under Louis XIII and Louis XIV.

Rm. 17: views of the Paris of Louis XIV.

Rm. 18: miniature paintings and scenes of working life.

Rm. 19: the painted woodwork (enriched with gold) and the ceiling came from the Hôtel Colbert.

Rm. 20: decorations from Parisian churches.

Rm. 21: large study from the Hôtel de la Rivière, ceiling painted by Le Brun — Remarkable wall-clock.

Rm. 22: room from the Hôtel de la Rivière.

Rms. 23–25: Madame de Sévigné lived here for 18 years. — Numerous portraits, pieces of furniture and crockery.

Rms. 26–28: souvenirs of the City of Paris.

Ground floor

Rms. 34 and 35: paneling from *Café Militaire* by Ledoux — staircase by Luynes — Busts of Liszt and Marie d'Agoult.

Rm. 69: bust by Mirabeau — Declaration of the Rights of Man and Citizens.

Rm. 70: The States-General; crockery with revolutionary designs.

Rm. 71: the storming of the Bastille and the Fête de la Fédération.

Rm. 72: the Convention — model of the guillotine — last letter from Robespierre

"the Incorruptible", a moving appeal to the Commune, stained with its author's blood.

Rm. 75: royal family's furnishings during their imprisonment in the Temple.

Rms. 76 and 77: civil and military life under the Revolution.

First floor

Rm. 37: a large room in which Regency furniture provides a replica of an aristocratic home at the beginning of the 18th century.

Rms. 40–48: Regency furniture — gilded study (Rm. 40) — Blue room (Rm. 41) and Grey room (Rm. 42) — Polychrome room (Rm. 43) — Turquoise room (Rm. 47) — Louis XV's Yellow room (Rm. 48).

Rms. 49 and 50: beautiful Louis XV woodwork.

Rm. 51: Parisian theater in the 18th century.

Rm. 52: the philosophers Voltaire, Diderot, J.-J. Rousseau, Montesquieu, Franklin.

Rm. 55: delightful Louis XVI circular drawing room.

Rms. 56 and 57: Louis XVI salons.

Rm. 60: picturesque scenes of Paris.

Rm. 62: room painted by Boucher and Fragonard in 1765 — Delightful rural scenes.

Rms. 63–68: scenes of Paris, especially by Hubert Robert (demolition of the houses on the bridges).

Leaving the Hôtel Carnavalet, take Rue des Francs-Bougeois which crosses Rue de Turenne and leads on to the Place des Vosges. The Place des Vosges was the first royal square; it is also one of the most beautiful monumental squares in Paris.

The Place des Vosges ●●●

Metro: Chemin-Vert, Bastille **Map 5, (C 4-5)**

Henri IV was so obsessed with building that a contemporary noted, "throughout his reign all one could see was masons at work". On a site in the Marais, he decided to have pavilions, similar in design, built around a quadrangle. They were to be two-storied and supported by arches which would form galleries. The work was meticulously carried out under the direction of Sully, and completed in 1612.

Louis XIII inaugurated the square by celebrating his marriage to Anne of Austria there. Place Royale, as it was then called, became the center of court activities, particularly its festivities. Duels were also fought here despite Richelieu's ban on them. Renamed "Indivisibilité" under the Revolution, the Place finally honored the Vosges region, the first to pay its taxes. The square suffered no great damage but was forgotten over a century. Now it has become a popular residential area and a place much favored for walks.

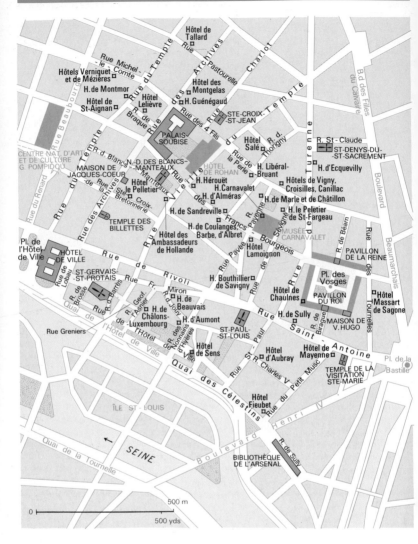

The Marais.

═══ *VISIT*

The **36 pavilions** of the Place des Vosges are arranged around two taller buildings which face each other at each end of the garden: the **King's pavilion** (on the side of Rue de Biragrue) and the **Queen's pavilion** (on the side of Rue des Francs-Bourgeois). It is rigorously symmetrical but not monotonous, due to the uneven roofs and the contours of the cornices and dormer windows. Notice the different treatments used on the arcades of the houses; the facades have retained their original refined harmony: the whiteness of the stone, the red of the false bricks, and the blue of the slate blend wonderfully with the changing Parisian sky.

Madame de Sévigné was born at 1 *bis;* at n° 11, the beautiful Marion Delorme attracted crowds of wooers; Bossuet was a lodger at n° 17; Richelieu may have lived at n° 21. Particularly remembered is **Victor Hugo** who lived in the Hôtel Rohan-Guémenée at n° 6. A small **museum** contains a replica of his study, where his famous works *Les Misérables* and *La Legende des Siècles* were written. *(10 am – 5.30 pm, closed Mon).*

The Hôtel Béthune-Sully✱✱ is reached by taking Rue de Birague, then Rue Saint-Antoine on the right. It was built in 1624, and bought by Béthune, who was better known as Henri IV's minister, Sully. A **remarkable restoration** has taken place in the buildings overlooking the main courtyard, which now appear in their original splendour. Notice the decoration of the sculpted dormer windows and the symbols of the Elements and Seasons. This is the portal under which Voltaire was beaten up by the servants of a nobleman whom he had ridiculed, an experience which made him a determined opponent of nobles and the court. Guided tours provide the opportunity to admire the **painted ceilings** and the wainscotting in Sully's apartments. Today, the mansion is occupied by the Caisse Nationale des Monuments Historiques et des Sites, (National Historical Monuments and Sites Commission, *tel: 48 87 24 14 or 42 74 22 22*).

The Church of Saint-Paul-Saint-Louis✱, situated farther up, on the opposite side of Rue Saint-Antoine, was built by the Jesuits between 1627–1641, near their house (the present Lycée Charlemagne). The facade conceals the dome, which was the principal innovation of the Jesuit style.

The interior has a layout copied from the Gesù church in Rome; the well-lit nave boasts an exceptionally rich decoration. Of note are: the shell-shaped holy-water stoups, donated by Victor Hugo; at the transept, *Christ in the Olive Gardens,* by Delacroix; to the left of the main altar, in the chapel, the *Virgin of Sorrows✱* by Germain Pilon (1586).

The Hôtel Fieubet, the most unusual in the Marais, is situated at n° 1, the extreme end of Rue du Petit-Musc (the old French *la pute y muse* — "the prostitute loitering there" — gives an indication of the street's former character). Planned by Hardouin-Mansart, it was built in 1680. A lover of Baroque decoration acquired it in 1860 and transformed the sober facade into the Rococo style.

The Hôtel de Sens ●

Metro: Pont-Marie **Map 5, (C 4)**

The Hôtel de Sens at 1 Rue du Figuier is one of the only great private residences from mediaeval times to be seen today. Its recent restoration

Hôtel de Sens, now home of the Forney Library.

is considered by some to have been too radical. It is occupied by the Forney Library, devoted primarily to decorative and fine arts. It also has a fine collection of wallpapers and posters.

HISTORY

Built between 1475 and 1500 for the bishops of Sens, this mansion was one of the meeting places of the Catholic League. One of their number, Monseigneur de Pellevé, was so fervently attached to the cause that he died of apoplexy when a Te Deum at Notre-Dame saluted the entrance of Henri of Navarre, a Protestant convert, who was crowned King Henri IV. The building then passed to Queen Margot, former wife of Henri IV, before becoming a post house for the Lyons mail coaches. These were so often attacked by highwaymen that travelers used to write their wills before taking them.

VISIT

(Open Tues–Fri: 1.30 – 8.30 pm, Sat: 10 am – 8.30 pm, tel: 42 78 14 60).

Corner turrets frame the facade which has two doors set in two pointed arches. The flamboyant Gothic-style porch gives access to the courtyard; a square tower retains the defensive solidity of mediaeval works and is reminiscent of a sturdy, provincial castle.

The Schweitzer Square, on the opposite side of Rue du Figuier, offers an unimpeded view of the long, Classical facade of the **Hôtel Aumont,** n° 7 Rue de Jouy. Le Vau built it at the beginning of the 17th century, and François Mansart enlarged it. He made it into a comfortable home, well-lit by high windows, opening onto a French-style garden designed by Le Nôtre. The Hôtel Aumont is now the Administrative Court of Paris.

The International City of Arts — beside the Quai de l'Hôtel-de-Ville, is a modern building where artists from all over the world stay. You may prefer to follow the Rue François-Miron, behind the Hôtel Aumont.

The Hôtel de Beauvais is situated at n° 68. This mansion was constructed for Catherine Bellier, better known as Cateau-la-Borgnesse, Anne of Austria's first chambermaid to whom she confided the sexual initiation of the 16-year old Louis XIV. When the seven-year old Mozart was invited to Paris to play for the Court, he stayed here. Unfortunately, the main part of the mansion's decoration has deteriorated.

The Rue François-Miron, which is named after one of the guild's Provosts, follows the path of an ancient Roman road. Notice the restored houses at n° 44–46 and the timber-frames of n° 11 and 13, dating back to Louis XI, which are rarely found in Paris.

●● Saint-Gervais-Saint Protais Church

Map 5, (C 3)   Metro: Hôtel-de-Ville

Behind an unusual Classical facade in which appear, for the first time in France, the combination of the three classical orders (Doric, Ionic and Corinthian), this church is one of the masterpieces completed towards the end of the Gothic period *(closed Mon.).*

HISTORY

The construction of the church began in 1494 based on plans by **Martin Chambiges,** on the site of a basilica dedicated, in the 7th century, to two Roman officers, St Gervais and St Protais, who were martyred in the reign of Nero. Not completed until 1660, it was converted into a "Temple of Youth" during the Revolution, having formerly been the center of a parish. Madame de Sévigné was married here.

▬ VISIT

The Classical facade, attributed to Métezeau or Salomon de Brosse, was the first of its kind in Paris, superimposing the three different orders. In the interior of the long nave, 246 feet/75 metres, the **Flamboyant Gothic style** proffers the splendor of its vaults and the refined interplay of the ribbing and arches. The stained glass in both the nave and choir dates from the 16th and 17th centuries.

The Organ — most of the organ-stops date back to 1601, the oldest in Paris.

Also Worth Visiting:

The **Hôtel Guénégaud,** opposite Rue des Haudriettes, at n° 60 Rue des Archives, was built by François Mansart between 1648 and 1651. Its simplicity and the quality of its construction makes it one of the Marais' most beautiful houses. The garden and the rear facade can be seen from Rue des Quatre-Fils. To visit the interior, enter **The Museum of Hunting and Nature** (Musée de la Chasse et de la Nature; *open daily, ex. Tue and Public hols. 10 am – 5.30 pm, tel: 42 72 86 43).* On the ground floor, the paintings by Bruegel, Cranach and Rubens provide an amazing decor for collections of antique arms, dating from prehistoric times to the 17th century. On the first floor, there are remarkable hunting weapons from the 16th to 19th centuries, while on the second, there are hunting scenes painted by Vernet, Desportes, Oudry, Chardin, Claude Monet.

The Hôtel Salé*, n° 5 Rue Thorigny, constructed in 1656 by Aubert de Fontenay, was financed by revenue collected from an unpopular tax on salt. It has been superbly restored and it is now the Picasso Museum *(Open daily 10 am – 5.30 pm. ex. Tue).* Here, in a refined decor with furnishings by Diego Giacometti, the most complete collection of the artist's work is to be seen. Picasso's private collection, exhibited at the Louvre since 1978, has also been transferred here.

The Hôtel Libéral-Bruant, n° 1 Rue de la Perle, is named after the architect of Les Invalides who designed it and lived there in 1685. Very sober, almost severe, it contains curiosities from the **Bricard Lock Museum:** *(Open daily ex. Sun, Mon, Public hols. and Aug 10 am – noon, 2 – 5 pm).* Here, you can follow the evolution of keys and locks, slide-bolts and Gothic door knockers to magnificent chamberlains' keys and the decorated locks from the Palais-Royal and the Tuileries.

▬ RECOMMENDED FOR REFRESHMENT ▬

Le Temps des Cerises, 31 Rue de la Cerisaie, 75004 (tel: 42 72 08 63). Open 7.30 am – 8 pm Mon to Fri. Near the Bastille.

La Bourgogne, 19 Pl. des Vosges, 75004 (tel: 42 78 44 64). Open 8 – 1 am Mon to Sun; or **La Chope des Vosges,** 22 Pl. des Vosges, 75004 (tel: 42 72 64 04), Open noon – midnight Mon to Sat. Facing each other across the square. Traditional cooking.

La Tartine, 24 Rue de Rivoli, 75004 (tel: 42 72 76 85). Open 8 am – 10 pm daily ex. Tues, Wed morning. Wine and cheese.

4th Sans Ascenseur, 8 Rue des Ecouffes, 75004 (tel: 48 87 39 26). Open noon – 5.30 pm, 6.30 – 11.30 pm Tues to Fri, noon – 4 pm at weekends. Sweet and savory pies.

THE OPÉRA AND THE GRANDS BOULEVARDS

The Grands Boulevards are among the showpieces of Paris. Their association, in the 19th century, with such dazzling personalities as Balzac, Chopin, Musset, Georges Sand, Victor Hugo and Émile Zola evokes a great and not-so-distant past.

The chic, the zest and the spirit of Paris are all to be found here. There are famous buildings, beautiful vistas lined by trees, smart café terraces spilling onto the sidewalks, intriguing shopping arcades, theaters which provide light amusement, cinemas, and a blaze of lights and advertisements.

▬ HISTORY

In 1660, Louis XIV used his army to pull down the **ramparts built by Charles V,** and fill in the ditches. Along the slightly-curved line of the old enclosure, wide thoroughfares and side-roads were opened to traffic, and **triumphal arches** replaced the fortified gates. In the middle of the 18th century, the new roads (called **boulevards** after the military term for rampart terrace) became walks; in the summer, Parisians would come and rent chairs and sit under the trees. Several handsome mansions give a certain elegance to the west side, while the east side, near the working peoples' district, is thronged with street entertainers.

The footpaths were paved in 1778 and from 1825 the first street lights replaced gas lighting. The boulevard was now ready to provide the setting for the **meeting place of chic Parisians,** of high-spirited crowds, which it maintained with varying degrees of success until the outbreak of World War I.

Since the 1920s, the Grands Boulevards have remained the principal area of entertainment and popular music. The neon lights of *La Scala, ABC, Midi-Minuit, Eldorado,* and the *Casino Saint-Martin* have shone throughout the history of the **music hall,** associated with names like Édith Piaf, Maurice Chevalier, Charles Trénet and Yves Montand. The *Opéra-Comique, Ambigu, Gymnase, Porte Saint-Martin, Marivaux* and the *Nouveautés* retain the atmosphere of the **Boulevard theater.** And, as before, the whole social range is represented, from the exclusive boutiques of La Madeleine to the popular and crowded Place de la République.

La Madeleine

Metro: Madeleine   Bus: nᵒˢ 24, 42, 52, 84, 94   **Map 2, (E 4)**

The Church of La Madeleine is most notable for its striking resemblance to a Greek temple and its commanding position at the junction of the Rue Royale and Boulevard de la Madeleine. Another facade of a neo-Greek temple, the Palais Bourbon, may be seen from here on the opposite bank of the Seine.

Galeries Lafayette, a triumph of the Iron Age.

HISTORY

Few churches have had such a tumultuous history. Begun by Constant d'Ivry in 1764 as a simplified version of the Church of Saint-Louis-des-Invalides, it was changed radically by his successor, Couture, who wanted to build a second Panthéon. All work ceased from 1790, and the Revolutionaries knocked the tops off the still-unfinished columns. In 1806, Napoleon decided to dedicate this edifice to the glory of his Grand Army and, for a third time, the construction was knocked down and Vignon designed a simple and majestic, though somewhat clumsy, Greek temple.

During the Restoration, the temple reverted to its Christian function, but the still-unfinished church yet again faced threats of another transformation: there was a suggestion that it should be the first disembarkation platform for the Paris-to-Saint-Germain-en-Laye railway line. The plan was quickly dropped, and the church of Sainte-Marie-Madeleine was finally consecrated in 1842.

VISIT

The architecture of La Madeleine follows the design of a **Greek temple** in every aspect, apart from its size being larger; 52 Corinthian columns 66 feet/20 metres high surround the church, which includes a single nave. In the pediment, there is a sculpture of the Last Judgement by Lemaire. Having strictly followed the Greek design, the only interior lighting is provided by three cupolas above the nave. Because of the inadequate lighting, it is difficult to distinguish the **sculpted groupings** in the vestibule, or the Apostles by Rude, Pradier and Foyatier on the pendentives. **La Madeleine** is clearly the least religious of the big Parisian churches — it does not even carry a cross on its pediment! The **Boulevard de la Madeleine** leads on to Boulevard des Capucines. On each side of this wide street there are businesses of every kind. The *Trois Quartiers* department store continues to be patronized by successive generations of wealthy Parisians; its functionalist design (1932) makes it the forerunner of present-day supermarkets. All around, there are boutiques, travel agencies and terrace cafés.

In 1847 **Alphonsine Plessis,** immortalized by Alexandre Dumas junior as "La Dame aux Camélias", died at n° 15 Boulevard de la Madeleine.

On **Boulevard des Capucines,** the *Scribe* (n° 14) occupies the place of the *Grand Café* where, in 1895, the Lumière brothers organized the first public film projection — 33 spectators each paid one franc to see 10 two-minute flickering films. Nearby, opposite n° 19 Boulevard des Capucines, Stendhal collapsed in the middle of the road in 1842, struck down with apoplexy. N° 35 used to be the artist Nadar's studio, and it was here in 1874 that a group of young artists held the first exhibition of their works. They earned their nickname of "Impressionists" from one of the paintings exhibited — *Impression Soleil Levant* by Claude Monet. Finally the **Olympia,** the Parisian music-hall of the 1950s and 1960s was host to innumerable aspiring musicians, including the French star Johnny Hallyday, the Beatles and the Rolling Stones.

Cognacq-Jay Museum*, 25 Boulevard des Capucines *(Open daily ex. Mon and Public hols. 10 am – 5.45 pm, tel: 47 42 94 71).* Here, you can delve into the interest-

---

Place de la Madeleine

Fauchon and other high-priced gourmet shops, all hallmarks of French quality, may be found in the square surrounding the church, making it one of the most luxurious commercial centers in Paris.

In the Cité Berryer, at n° 27 Rue Royale, the atmosphere becomes less rarefied. A small market opens every morning and, on fine summer days, a fashionable crowd saunters around the sunny terraces during the lunch hour.

ing universe of the great collectors, though its founder **Ernest Cognacq,** (who established, with the help of his wife **Louise Jay,** the *La Samaritaine* department stores), does not conform to the conventional image of an art lover. Too short-sighted to appreciate the paintings offered to him, he employed a secretary to choose and buy them. Prudently, his wife preferred, "for the good of his health, that the money go to art dealers rather than a mistress." This millionaire couple assembled an exceptional collection of **paintings, furniture** and **objets d'art** all devoted to the memory of libertine **18th-century** France. The voluptuous beauties by Boucher are placed beside Fragonard's

boudoir scenes, Chardin's subtlety, the velvet faces painted by Greuze, the fine **drawings by Watteau** and the masterly lighting by La Tour *(Self-Portrait*)* or Guardi.

Rue Daunou, situated behind the museum, offers one of the district's liveliest night spots, famous for its beautiful and expensive ladies of the night.

At n° 5, the renowned *Harry's Bar* attracts its share of Americans, and others who wander in the vicinity; here, Hemingway, Richard Burton and film director Von Stroheim used to stay up until all hours of the night.

Place de l'Opéra

In the Place de l'Opéra, Baron Haussmann showed how the squares he built differed from the royal ones, such as the Place Vendôme or the Place des Victoires. His square is not a theatrical setting, but a center of communication where lanes of traffic intersect, linking the railway stations of Saint Lazare (Rue Auber), Nord and Est (Rue Lafayette), the Stock Exchange (Rue du 4–Septembre), the Louvre (Avenue de l'Opéra) and the theater district (les Grands Boulevards). Grandeur has yielded to functionalism.

Around this central square, shops selling luxury goods continue to attract shoppers. The *Grand Hôtel*, with its 39 feet/120 metres facade, is built on the site of what used to be a kitchen garden during Louis XV's era. The fabled terraces of the *Café de la Paix*, with its rooms decorated according to Charles Garnier's designs, provide a unique vantage point from which to observe the life of the boulevard.

The Opéra ●

Metro: Opéra, Chaussée d'Antin   R.E.R.: Auber   **Map 2,**
Bus: n°s 20, 21, 22, 27, 29, 42, 52, 53, 57, 66, 68, 95   **(D-E 5)**

The Opéra is a gorgeous piece of work. Its spectacular architecture, the great staircase and foyer, and the brilliant decoration of the auditorium make it perhaps the most successful monument of the Second Empire, an era dominated by an extraordinarily wealthy bourgeoisie.

▬▬ *HISTORY*

The fire in the hall of the Palais-Royal in 1781 forced the Paris Opéra to move from one theater to another, the rebuilding plans never materializing. Finally, at the end of 1860, the Minister of Fine Arts held a competition to build an opera house on the site laid out by **Haussmann,** at the intersection of the Grands Boulevards and an avenue which would link it to the Louvre. The entry of an unknown architect,

The Paris Opéra.

Charles Garnier, only 35 years old, was unanimously acclaimed. He was more original than all the other architects of his time; he parodied the great Classical styles and combined them to create a singular mixture of architectural history. Chided by the Empress for his style being "neither Greek, Louis XIV or even Louis XVI", Garnier coolly replied: "These styles have had their day, it is now the period of Napoleon III."

The first stone was laid in 1862, but the existence of an underground stream, a branch of the Grange-Batelière, forced the architect to build a huge vaulted tank, acting as a cradle, which supports the whole building. This gave birth to the legend of the underground lake popularized by Gaston Leroux in his *Phantom of The Opera*. The Opéra was inaugurated in 1875 by President MacMahon.

Its great successes should be remembered: the glamorous balls; the performances of Taglioni and Yvette Chauviré, celebrated by the Bolshoi "as the greatest living dancer"; Caruso and Chaliapin; the rivalry between Maria Callas and Renata Tebaldi. One tragic incident in the Opéra's history has left an indelible trace: on the evening of May 20th, 1896 a large chandelier fell on a child ballerina on the thirteenth step of the great staircase and killed her. The crack in the marble where it fell still remains.

The Opéra and the Grands Boulevards.

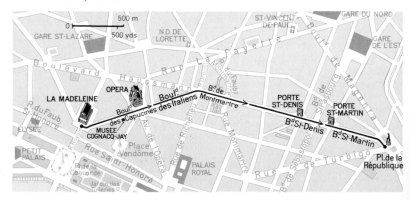

Supporters and detractors of the Opéra

Originality breeds controversy and the Opéra was no exception. Théophile Gautier saw it as a "secular cathedral of civilization", and Victor Hugo found it "comparable to Notre-Dame". But not so Claude Debussy who in 1901 blasted it in the *Revue Blanche:* "Everybody knows the Paris Opéra ... at least by repute. To my regret, I have been able to assure myself that it has not changed; to the ignorant passer-by it still looks like a railway station; inside it is very much like a Turkish bath. Odd sounds, called music by those who have paid to hear, are still produced there...its going up in flames would be no bad thing but for the harm the innocent people would undeservedly suffer."

▬ VISIT

The principal facade of the Opéra along with the Place's big buildings, form an ensemble of remarkable unity.

There is a wide staircase inset with arcades which frame groups of statues, the most remarkable being **The Dance** by Carpeaux, on the right. A petition described it as "an insult to public morals" and during demonstrations, a bottle of ink was smashed over it; the stains have never been completely removed. Threatened by the elements, *The Dance* was transferred to the Louvre and replaced with a copy by Paul Belmondo.

Visits can be made to the main rooms in the Opéra outside rehearsal times. *(Entry through the main door. Open daily 11 am – 5 pm, tel: 42 66 50 22.)*

The great staircase, 33 feet/10 metres wide at the base, rises into an open space, surrounded by superimposed galleries, which provide easy movement for the public and a perfect view of the surroundings.

The foyer also portrays the ideal of Imperial solemnity. Notice the mosaics adorning the arch of the Avant-Foyer, an extremely eclectic use of decorative motifs from all styles. As for the shimmering color and light, Garnier achieved this by a skilful use of polychrome marble (from quarries all over France) and of colored stone.

You may be surprised by the **small size of the auditorium** which only has 2200 seats (La Scala in Milan can seat 3600); five tiers of boxes encircle an Italian-style stage, 120 feet/37 metres deep. An enormous chandelier weighing over 6 tons hangs under the dome. In 1964, Chagall painted a controversial ceiling, based on themes of famous operas and ballets.

The library and small Opéra Museum are housed in the Emperor's pavilion in Rue Scribe *(open daily ex. Sun, Public hols including the 15 days of Easter).* All the scores of performances given at the Opéra since 1669 are preserved in the library. Displayed in the little museum are busts of great composers and performers, costumes and models of the sets, recreating the magic of the grand evenings at the Opéra de Paris.

From dressmakers to divas

The 1000 people working at the Opéra make up a universe of a fascinating complexity. In 1974, the dressmakers produced 2428 costumes; while the workshops were capable of making 415,000 sq feet/38,500 sq metres of scenery using 28,700 lbs/13,000 kilos of paint and 10 tons of plaster for a single set. The permanent company of the Opéra has ten soloists and a chorus of about a hundred, who have forty-two rehearsals, performances or other engagements each month. The celebrated ballet company, directed by Rudolf Nureyev, has 160 dancers. The 20 star dancers are chosen by the administrator. The orchestra is made up of 146 musicians selected through competition.

The Grands Boulevards

The Boulevard des Capucines continues towards the east after crossing the Place de l'Opéra; among the numerous places of entertainment of note, on the left at n° 2, is the large *Paramount cinema,* beside which runs **Rue de la Chaussée-d'Antin.** This street, very fashionable in the 19th century (Madame de Staël and Rossini lived here), has preserved a number of post-Revolutionary "Directoire" buildings, although unfortunately spoiled by the shops in the area between Boulevard Haussmann and La Trinité church.

The Boulevard des Italiens deserves the nickname "Theater Boulevard" more than the others, not only because it derived its name from the *Théâtre des Italiens*, the present *Salle Favart*, but also because it was the meeting place of well-known critics, theatrical directors, as well as young and pretty actresses in search of roles and partners for the evening. The **Palais Berlitz,** at n° 31, was constructed in the 30s on the site of the charming pavilion of Hanover, the boulevard's finest building, which has since been reconstructed in the Sceaux Park in the southern suburbs. In the **well-known restaurants,** *Le Café Anglais, la Maison Dorée, Le Tortini* and *le Café Riche*, the wealthy young men used to imitate the most extravagant leaders of fashion. During the Directoire, they would escort their provocative "Merveilleuses" (lady companions), dressed in transparent gauze. After the Restoration, this walkway was named the **Boulevard de Gand,** and the elegant young men were called "gandins". These dandies aroused curiosity often mixed with irony. The Second Empire with its businessmen, bankers and traders, and the sober and more restrained dress of the *Belle Époque*, put an end to their sartorial extravagances.

The Crédit Lyonnais (n°ˢ 17–23), was built between 1878 and 1882 with an iron structure by Eiffel, intended to represent the security and seriousness of the banking institution; the staircase is a copy of that at

Chambord. Almost opposite, n° 22 used to be the site of the *Café Tortini*. At n° 20, the Banque Nationale de Paris has fortunately preserved the elegant facades of the *Maison Dorée*, Balzac's favorite Parisian restaurant; note the famous gilded balconies in Rue Laffitte.

The Opéra Comique or *Salle Favart*, reconstructed in 1898, occupies the place where the Duc de Choiseul received the actors when they left their former headquarters in the Hôtel de Bourgogne in 1782. This type of show, parodying grand opera, used to link the humor of Middle Ages farce to lyrical works from the Italian *opera buffa*. Méhul, Cherubini and Léo Delibes displayed this unique French style, which disappeared with the success of the 19th-century Italian operas, although its spirit has been preserved in operetta. Today, Paris' second opera house, the *Salle Favart*, is devoted to performances of the French repertoire.

The Boulevard des Italiens ends after the Passage des Princes, at the intersection of Rues Richelieu and Drouot. The *Café Cardinal* is situated on the site of the house from which, around 1700, the poet Regnard used to look out at the windmills of Montmartre, the surrounding countryside and see in his garden "the sorrel and lettuce happily growing". On the other side of the Boulevard, the *Café Drouot* has, for 20 years, welcomed the famous **Golf-Drouot,** where the fans of Johnny Hallyday and The Wild Cats would come to concerts to scream their hearts out.

At the new Drouot, similar feelings of hope and rage also prevail among a number of the regulars of the **Hôtel des Ventes** (Auction Hall), at n° 9 Rue Drouot *(11 am – 6 pm ex. Sun and Aug. Info. 42 46 17 11)*. The three levels welcome auctioneers, appraisers, collectors, agents and experts, but also allow room for amateurs and the simply curious. Surrounding the auction rooms there are numerous antique shops, galleries and stamp sellers.

On the Boulevard Montmartre. The *Théâtre des Variétés* (n° 7) was, from 1807, the temple of the French spirit which was immortalized by Flers and Caillavet, Offenbach, Tristan Bernard and Sacha Guitry. Today, large numbers of visitors discover the scenes and historical personalities exhibited in the **Grévin Museum.** *(10, Bd Montmartre; open daily, 1 – 6 pm, tel: 47 70 85 05)*. In 1882, the caricaturist Grévin

---

Musset's View

The 19th-century poet Alfred de Musset wrote in praise of the Grands Boulevards: "Dusty and muddy as it is, this spot is one of the most pleasant in the world. It is one of the rare places on earth where pleasure is concentrated. Parisians live here, it attracts people from the provinces and remains in the memory of the visiting foreigner as does Via Toledo in Naples, or the Piazzetta in Old Venice. Restaurants, cafés, theaters, baths, gambling houses, everything is to be found here ... the whole universe is here. Beyond the curb lie the Great Indies."

established this museum of wax figures, where surprising lighting devices and mirrors contribute to the magic.

Boulevard Poissonnière derived its name from the fishmongers who used this road to reach Les Halles. It is dominated by the spectacular facade of the *Grand Rex* cinema which has a seating capacity of 2800. The Boulevard Bonne-Nouvelle, where the small *Théâtre du Gymnase* is situated, continues as far as the **Porte Saint-Denis** — a spectacular triumphal arch 78 feet/24 metres high, designed by Blondel in 1672, commissioned by the City of Paris to commemorate Louis XIV's successful campaign on the Rhine.

Boulevard Saint-Denis links Porte Saint-Denis and Porte Saint-Martin, on each side of one of the big Parisian crossroads, where the Boulevards de Strasbourg and Sébastopol meet. Music hall fans lament the decline of the establishments so well-known in their day, such as *l'Eldorado*, *Le Casino Saint-Martin* or the *Midi-Minuit*. (Bd Bonne-Nouvelle). Porte Saint-Denis and the nearby Porte Saint-Martin, were offered to Louis XIV by the city of Paris to commemorate the capture of Besançon in 1674. Apparently the city's funds were low when the second arch came to be built. Pierre Bullet entrusted the decoration of this 56-foot/17-metre high arch to the artists of Versailles, who fulfilled the contract — apparently without much enthusiasm.

With the **Boulevard Saint-Martin,** then the **Boulevard du Temple,** begins the most impoverished section of the old road. In front of the theatrical facade of the adjoining playhouses *La Renaissance* and *La Porte Saint-Martin* where Sarah Bernhardt acted, we must recall the great days of the theaters, opera and the Parisian music halls which were all situated around here. In front of the audience, which was as likely to catcall as to cheer, the actor Frédérick Lemaître had a great success at *L'Ambigu-Comique*. The most accurate portrayal of the era was recreated by Marcel Carné in his unforgettable film *Les Enfants du Paradis*.

The huge Place de la République was laid out by Haussmann in 1854, providing space for troops to be drilled and popular uprisings crushed, within rifle shot of the turbulent suburbs in the east. The Vérine barracks replaced a diorama where Daguerre used to reconstruct historical scenes on transparent panels and work on photographic processes. **Baron Haussmann** perhaps believed that the Imperial order would rule forever, but it is a huge statue of the Republic which stands on top of the monument, erected in 1883 by Morice. On the pedestal are bronze bas-reliefs by Dalou, illustrating the *History of the Republic* from the revolutionary pledge of the *Jeu de Paume* until the declaration, in 1880, of July 14th as a national holiday.

══ *RECOMMENDED FOR REFRESHMENT* ══

Le Grand Café, 8 Bd des Capucines, 75002 (tel: 47 42 75 77). Open 24 hrs. a day Mon to Sun. Recalls the Boulevards of the *Belle Époque*.

Club Haussmann, 3 Rue Taitbout, 75009 (tel: 42 46 85 33). Open noon – 5 pm Mon to Fri.

Le Square, 6 Square de l'Opéra, 75009 (tel: 47 42 78 50). Open noon – 2.15 pm, 8 pm – 1.15 am Mon to Fri. Open Sat noon – 2.15 pm, Sun 8 pm – 1.15 am. Pretty terrace.

Bouillon Chartier, 7 Rue du Faubourg-Montmartre, 75009 (tel: 47 70 86 29). Open 11 am – 3 pm, 5 – 10.15 pm Mon to Sun.

MONTMARTRE

Montmartre is an incredible world of contrasts, dreams and reality — land of good and bad. There are the memories of Picasso, Piaf and Utrillo and, with some luck, you may still make startling discoveries. But it is also full of the commonplace, the garish and the sleazy.

Around the **Place Clichy** the contrasting aspects of the capital are more starkly revealed than elsewhere; the bourgeois fortresses in the Quartier de l' Europe, artists and shady characters around Pigalle, and immigrants, sometimes poverty-stricken, who have come down from the hovels or workers' houses at La Fourche, form an incredible kaleidoscope of the human condition.

Special note! Do not confuse La Butte Montmartre with the Metro station "Rue Montmartre" which will drop you on the Grands Boulevards … quite a distance from La Butte.

Montmartre Cemetery

Metro: Place de Clichy, Blanche   Bus: n⁰ˢ 80, 95   **Map 2, (A 5)**

You can stop to pay your respects to the memory of some of the greatest French writers, painters, composers and actors by visiting the cemetery. To the right, as you enter, lie Lucien and Sacha Guitry; on the left, the austere Cavaignac sculpted by Rude. Beyond are Stendhal, Berlioz, Greuze, Degas, Offenbach and the Goncourt brothers. The tall chestnut trees, the sleeping cats in the empty fountain basins and the open chapels all contribute to a sense of peace. And if we are to remember one "shade", let it be Alphonsine Plessis, the "Dame aux Camélias" immortalized by Alexandre Dumas junior and by Verdi as Violetta in *La Traviata*.

■■■ *SURROUNDINGS*

The Boulevard de Clichy continues towards the Place Blanche and the *Moulin Rouge*; note, on the left, the little **cité Véron,** with its shrubs, houses and workshops, the first of these cities or "Montmartroise" villas clinging to the side of La Butte which have preserved their former charm.

The Place Blanche and the road bearing the same name are a thriving center of night-life. They are sited on the road which was used for centuries by quarry carts transporting chalk from the Butte Montmartre. The *Moulin Rouge* is a temple of the French can-can and the quadrille, immortalized by Toulouse-Lautrec. Farther on, to the left, follow **Rue Lepic** which inclines steeply up the slopes of the Butte. Its famous market is one of the capital's most lively and also one of the few where there are still fresh

vegetable barrows. It is a center enlivened by the "Montmartroise" spirit, where artists, newcomers, tramps, "night people" and the district's pensioners all gather.

The Montmartre carts

When there was a toll-gate in the middle of the Place Blanche (White Square), the heavy traffic of carts covered the houses and walkways with the white dust which gives the square its name.

These carts were so numerous that they literally wore away the surface of the Butte. Thus Montmartre escaped widespread renovation and construction projects, since it is almost impossible to lay sound foundations in its crumbling subsoil.

The Basilica of Sacré-Coeur.

The cafe at n° 8 is worth a brief stop: behind the bar, in the style of the *Belle Époque*, there is a mosaic depicting Sacha Guitry at the entrance of the *Moulin Rouge*. **At Rue des Abbesses,** Rue Lepic bends sharply to the left around a wide bend which makes the slope less steep. At **n° 54, Van Gogh** shared a small apartment with his brother, Theo, for several years, before heading south in the agonizing search for color which took him as far as Arles. Higher up, on the left, do not hesitate to climb the steep steps which lead to some private mews, where artists' houses, old follies, 19th-century workshops and sheds of the 30s still remain.

●● La Butte Montmartre

Map 2, Metro: Blanche, Lamarck-Caulaincourt   Bus: Montmartrobus
(A 5-6) (from Place Pigalle to the Place du Tertre via the Mairie)

La Butte Montmartre is also a place of contrasts. Boulevards are to be found alongside calm village streets, stone steps lead to open terraces, and the devout, on their way to the Sacré-Coeur, often run into night-club habitués.

▬▬ HISTORY

Renoir, together with Corot, Utrillo, Van Gogh, Willette and Toulouse-Lautrec, portrayed the dance hall, the entrance of which used to be at n° 79. During the renovation operation, the mill, named *Blute-Fin*, was preserved, as was its neighbor, *Le Radet*, thereby retaining the character of the era.

These mills — there were 30 of them in the time of Louis XV — were used to press grapes, grind grain, and crush stone. When the quarries were exhausted, the mills went out of business, the produce of the cornfields and vineyards not being sufficient to support them. The mills were then converted to cabarets which gained a dubious reputation. The king's attention was drawn to this, and he demanded a police report. To his amusement, this stated that "worldly" women who frequented them caused, in the company of the miller-proprietors, "considerable damage to the wheat and rye".

▬▬ VISIT

The narrow **Rue d'Orchampt,** on the right, bends back on itself and then opens out into a village road. How these houses came to be here remains a mystery. A fine example is n° 5, which was the Swedish pavilion in the Universal Exhibition of 1889. The three glass-fronted workshops of n° 1 have not changed since they sheltered the bohemians of Montmartre at the beginning of the century.

In the **Place Émile-Goudeau,** with its Wallace fountain and country-like appeal, it is easy to forget that it was witness to the most important art revolution of the 20th century. It was here, in these uncomfortable lodgings, better known as the **"Bateau-Lavoir",** that Picasso painted *Les Demoiselles d'Avignon* in 1907, the painting which introduced Cubism.

The Bateau-Lavoir
In a period of hardship in Montmartre, Max Jacob and Picasso used to share the same bed — one would sleep during the day, the other at night; Van Dongen, Modigliani, Juan Gris and many others lived here, from 1890 to 1920, when most of the Parisian

ainters grouped together in Montparnase. A fire in 1970 totally destroyed the ateau-Lavoir.

The **present building** has followed the ayout of the Bateau-Lavoir and has reained the gardens (entry by Rue Gareault).

From the Place Émile-Goudeau, **Rue Ravignan** runs to the tourist's Montmarre with its gift shops, souvenirs, galleries nd "artists" of the Place du Tertre. Most of he painters have deserted it for the Left Bank, but the tradition of cabarets and ingers lives on. **Rue des Saules** winds own between high walls as far as the **Lapin Agile** (on the right). On the lower evel of the Montmartre **vineyard,** where he festivals of the grape-harvesting season re held each year (September), stands a mall, peaceful house, the *Lapin Agile*, one of the main sites of old Montmartre.

The Lapin Agile

Owned by **Aristide Bruant,** who used o trade insults there with his friends, to the elight of an audience of curious ourgeoisie; then by "Père Frédé", legendry figure of the Butte, who revitalized an nspired but penniless bohemia. The *Lapin gile* was frequented by Apollinaire, Pissaro, Max Jacob and Vlaminck. Here, the rich nd fashionable used to mix with the mall-time hoods depicted by authors rancis Carco and Mac Orlan (*Quai des rumes*).

his cabaret was also the scene of the high pirits of old Montmartre: Dorgelès made a onkey paint *Sunset on the Adriatic* mocking icasso; the candidates at the elections of he **Free Commune** of Montmartre vied vith each other with their whimsical proositions for policies, such as the transormation of the Sacre-Coeur into a swiming pool. Today the decor has hardly hanged and the paintings are still piled gainst the walls.

Rue de l'Abreuvoir leaves Rue des aules and comes out into **Allée des rouillards*** — a surprising path beween private gardens, as romantic as one ould wish. At the entrance is the Château es Brouillards, an elegant folly of the 18th entury, where poet Gérard de Nerval ved in 1846. The path provides a pleasant stroll, and the whole of this part of the Butte can be covered on foot without seeing a car. Crossing the Avenue Junot (at n° 15, Tristan Tsara's house, by A. Loos) you reach the passages and steep steps of the Cité des Artistes and come out into Rue Lepic.

Rue Saint-Vincent which crosses Rue des Saules by the *Lapin Agile*, was immortalized by Bruant's verses which relate the tragic destiny of a credulous shop assistant. At n° 17 is the oldest house on the Butte which belonged to the actor Rosimond of Molière's company. It is now the small **Museum of Old Montmartre** (*open daily ex. Tue 2.30 – 5.30 pm*); at the top of a terrace garden; posters and drawings recall the good old days of the music hall and beside them is the restored *Café de l'Abreuvoir*, whose best customer was undoubtedly Utrillo.

Rue du Mont-Cenis is appropriately named after an alpine pass. Crossing Rue Saint-Vincent, there is a tiring climb of 422 feet/130 metres to the top of the Butte. From here, you can look over the rival hills of Montagne Sainte-Geneviève and the Buttes-Chaumont 419 feet/129 metres. Opposite the little cemetery which adjoins Saint-Pierre's church, is Rue Saint-Rustique which was the main village road since the 17th century. On the corner is the cabaret *La Bonne Franquette* which provided the inspiration for Van Gogh's *Guinguette*.

The Moulin Rouge

"Pour qui mouds-tu, Moulin-Rouge?
Pour la mort ou pour l'amour?
Pour qui mouds-tu jusqu'au jour?"

"For whom do you keep on turning, Moulin-Rouge, for death or for love? For whom do you keep on turning until dawn?"

The lament was heard by Toulouse-Lautrec, who painted the singers, clowns and dancers — among them La Goulue — who frequented the *Moulin Rouge*. The *Moulin* was transformed into a music hall in 1900 and is today divided into a cinema and dance hall. It still puts on shows which feature the famous can-can.

•

Saint-Pierre de Montmartre

Map 3, Metro: Anvers, Abbesses   Cablecar   Bus: Montmartrobus (see p. 154)
(A 1)

The little church of Saint-Pierre-de-Montmartre, both unassuming and
rustic, is overshadowed by the Sacré-Coeur but it is one of the oldest
sanctuaries left in Paris.

HISTORY

Some of the columns of this little church may have come from a Roman
temple dedicated to Mercury. The last bay of the nave, in which appear
the first pointed arches, help locate the former abbey, which was
founded by Queen Adelaide of Savoy, and consecrated in 1174. Legend
has it that the young Abbess Claude was the mistress of Henri IV while
he was besieging Paris in 1590. The last Benedictine abbess of the
Montmartre Abbey, named Mont Marat during the Revolution, died on
the scaffold in 1794, even though she was blind, deaf and 96 years old.

VISIT

The dark and austere interior of the
Church of Saint-Pierre gives a strong
impression of unity and harmony; a very
elusive unity because it is impossible to
distinguish the different elements of successive centuries . Amateur students of the
Cabal and the occult will be intrigued by
the strange motifs of the capitals. The site
did not reveal all its secrets until excavations led to the discovery of a Merovingian
cemetery, some sarcophagi and funerary

accessories on the site of the old cemetery
(door to the left, in front of the church
open Nov. 1st and 2nd only) and of the
Calvary garden, formerly the abbey
cemetery and garden. *(Not open to visitors)*

Rue St-Rustique, the main road of the
Montmartre village, is now very quiet
although, towards the end of the century,
the corner of this road and Rue des Saules
was the unofficial meeting-place of artists

From Saint-Honoré to the big department stores and Montmartre.

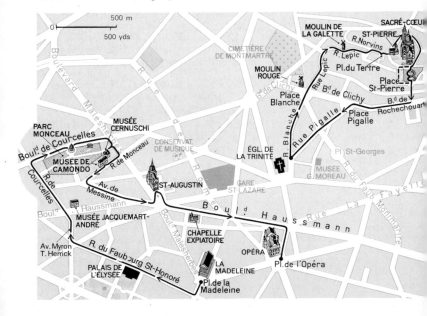

The Sacré-Cœur

Metro: Anvers, Abbesses   Cablecar   Bus: Montmartrobus   **Map 3, (A 1)**

The people of Montmartre, while remaining fond of Saint-Pierre-de-Montmartre, are supremely indifferent to the Sacre-Coeur. A little delving into history explains why...

HISTORY

The conservative National Assembly, at the beginning of the Third Republic, ordered the construction of this enormous white building as an atonement for the crimes of the Paris Commune. It must be remembered that it was the commune of Montmartre which effectively started the insurrection, by opposing the Generals Lecomte and Thomas on March 15th, 1871. The fierce resistance of the tiny population of the Butte against the troops of Versailles has still not been forgotten.

Abadie, a colleague of Viollet-le-Duc and known for his restoration of the Cathedral of Saint-Front in Périgueux, began the construction in 1876. Inspired by his past success, the plans he drew for the new basilica were Graeco-Byzantine in character. He died in 1884, when only the foundations had been laid; the church was completed in 1910 and consecrated in 1919. The unusual bell-tower, 308 feet/94 metres high, accentuates the Graeco-Byzantine style of the building.

VISIT

The Sacre-Cœur has no great aesthetic merit; its aim is to impress, rather than please, and in this it succeeds. Its massive proportions may be gauged from the bell, La Savoyarde": it weighs almost 39,098 lbs/17,735 kg, one of the biggest ever cast, and it took 28 horses to pull it to the top of the Butte. Behind the bronze doors is a vast rotunda and, in the apse, an immense mosaic. From the top of the dome there is a wonderful view of the whole of Paris. *Visit to dome and crypt: Mon to Sun, 10 am - 5 pm, payment on entry.)*

On the terrace in front of the Sacré-Cœur, people from all over the world gather; many young people often spend the night on the steps to watch the magnificent sunrise. In the evening, the quiet of the small Place du Calvaire offers a refuge from the noise and the crowds.

To the east of the Sacré-Cœur, from Rue Lamarck, the stairs of the picturesque and deserted streets descend steeply (Rues Muller and Fautrier, Passage Cottin, Biron stairs and Rue de la Bonne).

The old Place du Tertre, the former village square, has become one of the best-known and most visited spots in the capital. It is best to come in the early morning or out of season to appreciate its

The steps of La Butte Montmartre.

Map 2, Metro: Pigalle, St-Georges   Bus: n°s 67, 74
(B-C 6)

Sacré-Cœur
and the writers

There were some violent reactions to the building of the basilica. Zola wrote:

"One cannot imagine a more ridiculous and meaningless project. Paris, our grand Paris, crowned, dominated by a temple built for the glorification of absurdity."

André Breton, however, preferred to ignore it altogether:

"Early in the morning one should go to the top of the Sacré-Cœur hill in Paris, and see the city gradually freeing itself from its splendid veils before stretching out its arms ... At this hour, Beauty reaches its peak, (it is) confounded with innocence."

---

full beauty. Paris feels far away, and the rustic houses seem straight out of a naïve painting. Here you can experience the charm of this miraculously-preserved island on the "roof-top" of Paris, just as Renoir, Utrillo and many others have done before. Nearby, on the small square of the Place du Calvaire, is a wax museum with reconstructions of picturesque scenes from Montmartre's history. (Open Apr-Nov daily 10 am – 12 pm and 2.30 – 5.30 pm; Dec-March: Wed, Sat, Sun and Public hols; tel: 46 06 78 92.)

Going down from the top of Montmartre and plunging into the fever of Pigalle, take either the cablecar or Rue Ravignan, a fantasy walk which rejoins **Rue des Abbesses,** the center of local life, where the cafés and bars still attract their share of artists from the neighborhood. Now times have changed; the engravers have been replaced by designers and the song writers by video shops. Following Rue des Abbesses, to the left, you come to the small **Place des Abbesses,** where the Metro station has preserved its Art Nouveau glass entry (by Guimard).

The brick facade of **the Church of Saint-Jean-l'Évangéliste,** completed in 1907 by de Baudot, today appears very dull. It was, however, the first church to be built with reinforced concrete.

The Chapelle des Auxiliatrices is on Rue Yvonne-le-Tac. St Denis and his two companions were probably beheaded on this site. It was here, in 1534, that Ignatius Loyola and St Francis-Xavier founded the Society of Jesus which became the Jesuit Order in 1540.

Take **Rue des Trois-Frères** on the right, then turn into Rue Yvonne-le-Tac which leads down to **Place Charles-Dullin,** an area to which tourists still flock. In the small theater dating back to the Restoration Charles Dullin revitalized the art of directing between 1920–40. The theater was named after his company, thus becoming the Théâtre de l'Atelier. Rue des Trois Frères then rejoins **Boulevard Rochechouart** with its constant activity. Before continuing along the Boulevard in the direction of Pigalle, note n° 72 on the left, the facade of the Élysée-Montmartre which retains its Belle Époque brilliance in spite of the abundant posters advertising karate films.

Even though nothing remains of the Chat Noir, at n° 84, the cinema **La Cigale** has kept its lobby, ticket booth and flight of stairs, characteristic of the monumental style of decorative art favored by the Bauhaus School.

Pigalle worries official guides. The fact is that this is the principal red-light district of Paris, full of peepshows, sex shops and cinemas showing erotic films, not to mention a few hard-core theaters and a number of predatory street-walkers. Visitors be forewarned: prices in bars increase steeply as the "hostesses" are paid by percentage, and the "professionals" of the night, although pleasant with clients, may react aggressively towards intruders. Finally note, as Henry Miller did, the filthy but fetching little fountain in the square.

New Athens

"Nouvelle Athènes", with its hint of snobbery, was the name given between 1820 to 1850 to the area beyond the intersection of Rue Notre-Dame-de-Lorette and La Rochefoucauld.

HISTORY

Towards the end of the 18th century, the area between Rue Blanche and Rue des Martyrs and between the Trinité Church and Boulevard Clichy was the home of theatrical stars such as Mesdemoiselles Mars and Talma. They were succeeded by painters (**Delacroix**), architects (**Ballu** — the mansion at n° 58 is named after him) and **Viollet-le-Duc**. This district, which now sadly lacks distinction, was once comparable to the Faubourg-Saint-Germain. In the 1840s **Chopin** and **George Sand** lived out their amorous years there.

VISIT

Although the festive spirit has long since disappeared, this area is a treasure-trove of early 19th-century architecture. Particularly noteworthy are the Rue de la Tour-des-Dames (buildings date from the Restoration), Rues La Bruyère and d'Aumale (superb Directoire buildings), Rues Henner and Ballu (unusual neo-Renaissance and neo-Gothic mansions).

Some of the courtyards and interior gardens of the buildings have retained their romantic decor of fountains, porticos and groves, although it is often difficult to go in and see them. However, one can visit the unique mansion of the painter **Gustave Moreau** at n° 14 Rue de La Rochefoucauld.

The Gustave-Moreau Museum
Map 2 (C 6); Metro: Trinité; *Open daily ex. Tue & Sun 10 am – 1 pm and 2 – 5 pm.* This small museum is devoted to the visionary artist who was the master of Matisse, Rouault and Marquet, recognized today as the innovator of Fauvism and Abstract art.

Other sights

The Church of Notre-Dame-de-Lorette; it is from here that St Denis and his companions probably set off on their way to martyrdom: the busy Rue des Martyrs, with its excellent and well-patronized market, follows the path of their supposed journey. The Church's austere Greek temple facade, built around 1830, hides a richly decorated interior.

The Villa Frochot*: gardens and houses date from the *Belle Époque*. On the corner of Rue Frochot is a superb stained glass window.

The Renan-Scheffer Museum is situated in the mansion of the painter, Ary Scheffer, at n° 16 Rue Chaptal *(Open daily ex. Tue 10 am – 5 pm)*. It evokes the artists who lived in the neighborhood between 1830 and 1940, as well as the Impressionists, who lived nearby and who made a café in the Place Pigalle, *La Nouvelle Athènes*, their stronghold during their battle against Academism.

RECOMMENDED FOR REFRESHMENT

Au Clair de la Lune, 9 Rue Poulbot, 75018 (tel: 42 58 97 03). Open noon – 2 pm, 7 – 11 pm Mon to Sat. The only genuine village address on the Butte.
Chez Ginette, 101 Rue Caulaincourt, 75018 (tel: 46 06 01 49). Open noon – 3 pm, 7.30 pm – 2 am Mon to Sat.
Aux Négociants, 27 Rue Lambert, 75018 (tel: 46 06 15 11) Open 11.30 am – 8 pm Mon to Fri.

●●●
THE LOUVRE MUSEUM

Map 4, Metro: Palais-Royal, Louvre, Tuileries
(A-B 6) Bus: nᵒˢ 21, 24, 27, 34, 48, 67, 69, 72, 73, 74, 76, 81, 85, 89

The Museum's collection displays the artistic creations of all major
civilizations, with the exception of that of the Far East. It is claimed that
it provides a universal vision of Man and Art, that it dissolves the
frontiers of space, language, culture and time, and seeks to create a
"City of Humanism". By that, we mean a unity in Man's eternal
questioning, his search for identity and his common destiny. Such
profound reflections aside, the Louvre provides one of the richest
artistic experiences in the world.

▬ HISTORY

The Louvre Museum may be said to have begun with the dispersion of
Charles V's "modest collection". François I assembled twelve Italian
masterpieces in his palace — among them Leonardo da Vinci's *Mona
Lisa* — and various copies of Graeco-Roman works. Henri IV allowed
artists to live in the Louvre, and they enriched the royal collection. The
most notable among them were the painters Simon Vouet, the Coypels,
Boucher, Chardin, Greuze, Fragonard, the sculptors Dupré, Coysevox,
Girardon and Pigalle, and the cabinet-maker Boulle.

The main acquisitions were made by Louis XIV through his
powerful minister, Colbert. When Louis came to the throne, there were
barely 200 paintings. By 1710, they had increased to 1500 including the
collections of Cardinal Mazarin and the banker Jabach. Nearly all the
major works now to be seen in the Louvre were already there except
those of the Flemish and Dutch masters whose merit had yet to be
recognized. Their works were acquired by Louis XVI. The Royal
Academy of Painting attracted attention; from 1737, exhibitions were
held regularly in the Salon Carré while, from 1750, a large number of
paintings were put on permanent exhibition in the Luxembourg Palace.

Plans for setting up a public gallery were being considered when
the Revolution broke out. The Convention opened the Grand Gallery to
the public, enriching it with works brought back from Versailles. The
artistic treasures acquired by Napoleon's conquests and displayed in the
Louvre made it the finest museum in the world. These had to be
returned at the end of the Napoleonic era on the insistence of the Allies
but the kings who followed, Louis XVIII, Charles X and Louis
Philippe, continued an acquisition policy. The *Venus de Milo* was
brought back by Dumont d'Urville; the Greek and Egyptian rooms were
opened by Charles X, and Louis Philippe created the Assyrian Museum.
In 1848, the Louvre became State property and, since then, it has been
the beneficiary of legacies from private collections (Thiers, Rothschild,
Moreau-Nélaton, Caillebotte, Niarchos, Beistegui).

▬ VISIT

*Open daily ex. Tue and Public hols 9.45 am
— 6.30 pm. Entry free — Wed & Sun.
Guided tours: daily ex. Sun 10.30 am and 3
pm, with lecturers from the National*
*Museums. Departure at the information
desk, situated in the Salle du Manège. Guided
tours for groups or schools: Sat 10.30 am,
Nov – Apr. Audioguides with tape recorders).*

Once again, the Louvre is in the process of being completely transformed; the transfer of the Ministry of Finance to Quai de Bercy from its Rue de Rivoli premises which have been taken over by the Museum, will enable a general reorganization of the display of the collections; the works already exhibited will be supplemented by works drawn from reserves. Entrance will be through a glass pyramid erected in front of the Pavillon de l'Horloge, which will contain the ticket office. This office will sell catalogs, books and reproductions and provide information and study services. The following information is given subject to changes, as rooms are occasionally closed temporarily for reasons of maintenance or security (particularly between 11.30 am – 2 pm). Since drawings and pastels are displayed in rotation and because of the frequency of temporary exhibitions, visitors interested in particular works, are advised to telephone 42 60 39 26 ext. 3588 or inquire at the information desk in the Salle du Manège.

Lines (queues) at the Louvre can be very, very long. Avoid Sundays and Wednesdays and try to arrive early, before opening time.

ORIENTAL ANTIQUITIES

Major works

Stele of the Vultures — 1
Statues of Gudea and his son
Ur-Ningirsu — 2
Statue of Intendant Ebih-II — 3
Stele of Naram-Sin — 4
Stele of the Hammurabi Code — 5
Winged Bulls from the Palace
of Khorsabad — 6
Bas-Reliefs from the Palace of Sargon — 7
Frieze of the Archers — 8
Frieze of the Lions — 9

This collection, one of the richest in the world, consists mainly of discoveries made by French archeologists at the beginning of the 19th century in Mesopotamia and Iran. **Sully Crypt** — In the first bay, **antiquities from Palestine.** In the center, Qumran jar (1st century A.D.) which contained some of Dead Sea Scrolls; **lintel*** sculpted during the Roman occupation of Gebel Druse.

Rm. I. — Stele of the Vultures*** (1) (middle of the 3rd millennium B.C.), this stele commemorates for eternity a victory by the King of Lagash, one of the most prosperous Sumerian cities.

Rm. II. — Stele of Naram-Sin*** (4) (2250 B.C.) — Fine stele in pink sandstone depicting the King of Akkad climbing a mountain and trampling on the corpses of his enemies.
Statues of Gudea and of his son Ur-Ningirsu*** (2) displayed alternately at the Louvre and at the Metropolitan Museum of New York for periods of three years, are masterpieces of Sumerian art. Gudea, who reigned around 2050 B.C. over Lagash was, at the same time, a conqueror, legislator and a great builder.

Rm. III. — Statue of the Intendant Ebih-II*** (3) (2600 B.C.). This senior official of the city of Mari dedicated his effigy to the goddess Ishtar; depicted seated and dressed in the animal skin skirt of the Sumerians, his tufted fleece rendered with great realism, he stares at the outside world with a fascinating intensity and humor.

Rm. IV. — Stele of the Code of Hammurabi*** (5). Hammurabi was the king who conquered Sumer and founded the **Empire of Babylon** (1792 – 1750 B.C.). The famous stele is a block of basalt, 8 ft/2.5 m high, representing Hammurabi receiving the code from the god Shamash, the code being engraved in cuneiform below. The 280 laws regulated every aspect of social life and provide evidence of the advanced culture attained by Babylon, which developed a brilliant civilization over a period of nearly 1500 years. (Objects and alabaster statues displayed in the showcases.)

Rm. V. — The Iranian pottery from the 4th millennium, originating from **Susa,** dated back to a time when decoration and writing almost merged. Notice in particular the **goblet with the salukis** on which a greyhound race is admirably represented. Also see the jewelry boxes and **ceramics from Ismailabad;** in the center of the room, beautiful Achemenian silverware (6th century B.C.).

Rm. VI. — The Elamite civilization produced objects of rare delicacy in the second millennium B.C. such as the statue of Queen Napir Asu, made of bronze and weighing 3,850 lbs/1,750 kg; these polychrome funerary heads of the 12th and 13th centuries reveal a skill unknown in Sumer.

Rm. VII. — The marble **Capital of the Bulls**** (12th century B.C.) from **Darius' palace,** the first to be built in stone, evokes an image of its immense rooms. In contrast, the decoration was of glazed-brick bas-reliefs.

Rm. VIII. — **The Frieze of the Archers**** (8), from the palace of Susa, dates from the 6th century B.C. These soldiers were called the "Immortals" by the Greeks because regardless of their casualties, they always numbered 10,000.

Rm. XI. — **Luristan bronzes** (2500-800 B.C.) found in the tombs of Iranian mountain nomads.

Rm. XII. — Christian antiquities, such as the **Khatchkar stele,** mosaics from the Bichapur palace and Islamic ceramics reveal the many influences which spread through the Persian Empire between the 3rd and 8th centuries B.C.

Marengo Crypt (Rms. XIII and XIV). — The works from **Phoenicia** and **Palmyra** reveal the privileged position of Syria and Lebanon which were the crossroads of the many civilizations in the Mediterranean basin and Mesopotamia. The sarcophagus of King Eshmunazar of Syria (5th century B.C.) was brought from Egypt. The funerary reliefs from Palmyra stiffen Greek and Roman forms in the oriental mould.

Rm. XVI. — Greek Phoenicia and Roman Lebanon, the latter represented by bronzes from Baalbek dedicated to Jupiter.

Rm. XVIII. — **Phoenicia: primer from Ugarit*** (1300 B.C.); for the first time, an alphabet, here in cuneiform, replaced syllabic writing. Gold cup with hunting scene; stele of Baal with a thunderbolt; very rare **painted cup,** ancient example of Cretan ceramic.

Rm. XIX. — **Vase of Amathus**** (500 B.C.) came from Cyprus as did the vases and statues which surround it: very free in style and carefully decorated.

Rm. XX. — **Anatolian civilization.** The tablets from Cappadocia are written in cuneiform script. The funerary steles depict the dead and their tools.

Rms. XXI to XXIV. — **Assyrian art,** in which human faces are stiff and expressionless, while animals are portrayed with an admirable realism.

Rm. XXII. — **Bas-reliefs from the Sargon palace in Khorsabad***** (7). **The Winged Bulls***** (6) with human faces and five legs (so that four legs could be seen either from the front or from the side) used to guard the palace entrance.

Rm. XXIII. — Bas-reliefs from the Assurbanipal palace at **Nineveh** (7th century B.C.); the hunting scenes portray the absolute power of the sovereign.

EGYPTIAN ANTIQUITIES

Major works
The Seated Scribe — 1
Mastaba of Akhet-hotep — 2
Tanis Sphinx — 3
Gebel-el-Arak knife — 4
Akhenaton and Nefertiti — 5
Salt Head — 6

Crypt of the Sphinx — **The colossal sphinx from Tanis**** (3) (2nd millennium B.C.), in pink granite, is flanked by two bas-reliefs depicting Ramesses II offering incense to the Giza Sphinx which, with its massive size, dominates the steles of officials and soldiers.

Rm. 135. — **Mastaba (or tomb) of Akhet-hotep**** (2) (2500 B.C.). This funerary chapel of a high Egyptian dignitary, built in limestone, is covered with handsome sculptures in bas-relief depicting life on a big estate 4500 years ago. Stewards presenting their accounts bow before the squire, donkeys thresh wheat by trampling on the sheaves, fishermen pull in their nets, servants carry geese and ducks to the banquet. This decoration was designed to perpetuate the daily existence of the deceased in the hereafter.

Rm. 133 — Prehistory and Thinite period (3rd millennium B.C.): **Gebel el-Arak knife**** (4). The ivory handle decorated with hunting and battle scenes prefigures the art of the bas-relief. The **stele of the Serpent-King**** dates back to the Archaic period (before 2700 B.C.). The falcon, representing the god Horus, is associated with the serpent, the image of the king. The funerary statues of Nesa and Sepa* represent the couple in a pose which served as a model for the next 3000 years.

Rm. 131. — King Djedefri's Head is made of red sandstone. In this face crowned with the symbolic head-dress, the profoundly human features are accentuated by a smile of gentle melancholy. Beside it are statues of the King's family; superb pink granite columns* with capitals in the form of palm leaves.

Rm. 129. — The Seated Scribe*** *(1)* (2450 B.C.), a masterpiece of Egyptian art discovered by François Mariette in 1850. The right hand held the reed (broken and lost) with which the scribe was ready to write. The face is attentive, almost alive. However, the fascination of this statue largely stems from the colored stones (quartz and crystal) used for the eyes giving his expression a look of troubling intensity.

The Seated Scribe

The limestone group of Raherka and Mersankh**, in the corridor, demonstrates a perfection in the modeling of the bodies. There is great charm in the serene faces and the simplicity of the traditional pose.

Rm. 128. — In the different **statues of Sesostris III** (Middle Kingdom, c. 2000 B.C.) the Pharaoh's features progressively change as he ages. Likewise, in the different statues of officials and viziers, the obesity of these respectable notables has not been concealed. Hapydjefai's statue is one of the most important wood sculptures of this period.

Rms. 127 and 126. — In the well of the Percier staircase are sarcophagi and examples of funerary art of the Middle Kingdom. The treasure from Tod was discovered in the foundations of the temple; the bronze chest contained gold and silver ingots and silver cups.

Henri IV Gallery (XI). — The Egyptian gods and goddesses are represented with their terrestrial servants. In the center: the **God Amun Protecting King Tutankhamun****; statues of Sekhmet, the lionheaded goddess. **The sarcophagus of Ramesses III** (13th century B.C.) depicts the nocturnal journey of the sun; sarcophagus and capitals; group of baboons adoring the sun.

Osiris Crypt. — Sarcophagi, funerary objects, statue of the cult of Osiris and zodiac from the temple of Hathor at Denderah.

Rms. XII to XIV. — Coptic Art. From the 2nd century B.C. to the 12th century A.D., ancient forms are given new life, first under Greek, then Roman influences before finally being Christianized. Notice the famous **Veil of Antinoüs*** with its Dionysian scenes; basket-shaped capitals of the chapel of the St-Apollo monastery transferred from Baouit; delicately colored textiles.

The visit to the Egyptian antiquities continues on the first floor.

Escalier Percier: in the staircase, **statue of the bull Apis;** on the landing, the god Bes; at the top, **bust of Amenophis IV,** husband of Nefertiti, he created a new religion and gave back to Egyptian art its vigor and freshness; an extremely beautiful granite sphinx.

First floor: rooms devoted to small sculptures, objects and pieces of jewelry displayed according to chronology and theme.

Rm. A. — Furniture from private tombs. The big wooden statue of chancellor Nakhti (2000 B.C.) is very lifelike. *The Woman Bearing Offerings*** has a slim and elegant body. In the next showcase are faience hippopotami.

Rm. B. — 18th Dynasty (15th century B.C.). Sculpture reaches a high degree of refinement, its apogee represented by the statue of Queen Tiye** made of stone with a green glaze; portraits of Amenophis III.

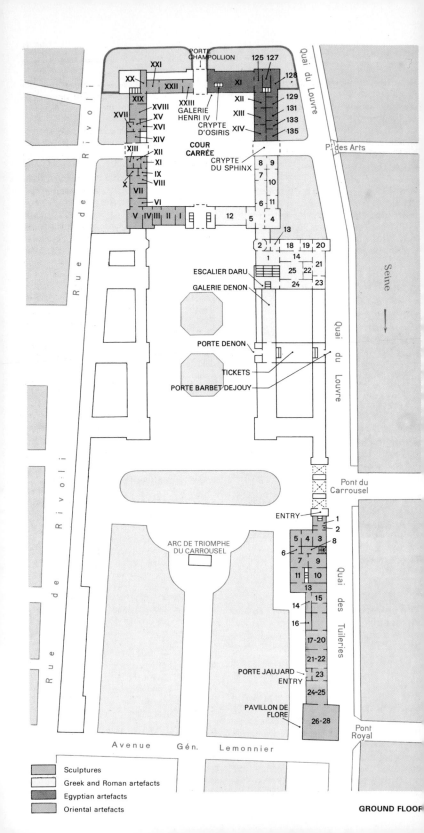

GROUND FLOOR

Rm. C. — New Kingdom. Toilet articles, furniture, musical instruments, hunting and fishing implements.

Rm. D. — The Amarna style of the brief reign of Amenophis IV (14th century B.C.) resulted in beautiful bas-reliefs. The limestone bust of the pharaoh* exudes a powerful mysticism. The symmetrical and taut features, following the rules of the Amarna school, exemplified in showcase 9 by the small group representing **Akhenaton holding Nefertiti by the hand**** (5), has an intimate simplicity rarely seen in Egyptian art. The **Salt Head**** (6), enigmatic and very true to life, is one of the finest and most realistic of Egyptian works.

Rm. E. — Deir el-Medineh. Objects discovered in the craftsmen's village of the Valley of the Kings. In the showcase facing the Cour Carrée, there is a remarkable set of jewelry; cup, head made of glass paste; look specially at the breast-plate of Ramesses II** made of gold and glass paste, and at the *Triad of Osiris* in gold and lapis-lazuli.

Rm. F. — The damascened bronze statue of **Queen Karomama*** conveys a somewhat haughty elegance.

Rm. G. — Exquisite small blue-glazed pottery statues representing **Egyptian gods;** torso of King Nectanebo I; a black basalt healing statue covered with magic signs.

Rm. H. — Following the conquest of Egypt by Alexander the Great (343 B.C.), art was influenced by Greek, then Roman styles while, at the same time, retaining its traditional forms, as seen in the statue of the **god Horus** (in the center), or in the little group thought to express the Memphite theology. On the right, two mummies, a funerary bed, and vases that were meant to contain embalmed entrails.

GREEK, ROMAN AND ETRUSCAN ANTIQUITIES

In the **Denon Gallery** (closest to the entrance), sarcophagi and Roman statues alternate. Go down the staircase on the left.

Rm. 1. — The **Lady of Auxerre***** (7th century B.C.) has a surprising relief. This is the first example of a draped standing female figure; her arm attempts a slight movement but the head remains rigidly in line with the torso. Two generations later, growing prosperity led to the flowering of a more graceful and very feminine art. From this period, known as Ionian, the **goddess Hera***** (2) (6th century B.C.) is one of the few original statues which have survived, Greek sculpture being primarily known through Roman copies. The shape of the goddess is still that of a column, but in 50 years, Greek art has progressed from the stiff, hieratic style to a much more fluid one. The face of the **Rampin Horseman***** (3) (mid-6th century B.C.) is lit by a happy smile, while the tilt of the head marks a final break with frontality. The Attic style equally suffuses the *kouroi* (young men) and the *kore* (draped women), as well as the lively drawings which decorate the ceramics from Athens and Corinth.

Rm. 2. — Severe Period. In the Torso from Miletos, there is an attempt at representing movement and anatomical details. The Apollo from Piombino*, modeled with great softness, prefigures the Classical style. Among the funerary steles, notice the graceful style of the stele called *Exaltation de la fleur.*

Rm. 4. — The Parthenon is the temple of Athena built between 447 and 432 B.C. on the Acropolis in Athens at a time when Greek Art had reached its apogee. The **Panathenaic Frieze***** (4) used to surround the temple; it depicts a procession of young women coming to offer a veil to the goddess. Sculpted by Phidias and his pupils, it included 350 human figures and 200 animals.

The **Laborde Head***** (5), designed with extraordinary purity and most probably by Phidias, summarizes the ideal of classical beauty.

Rm. 7. — Hellenistic period (3rd-1st century B.C.). In the late works, there is increasing concern for movement and dramatic expression. The **Venus de Milo***** (6), one of the greatest masterpieces of all time, dates back to that period. Found in 1820 on the island of Melos, this 2nd century B.C. statue of Aphrodite is one of the most perfect representations of feminine beauty, emphasized by the suppleness of the twisted body and the elegance of the drapery. The *Kaufmann Head* is delicately modeled.

Rm. 8. — The *Borghese Gladiator*, his body stretching along a diagonal axis, and the pathetic *Dying Gaul* are other examples of Hellenistic art.

Rm. 9. — Following the sculptors of the 5th century, Myron, Polycletus and Phidias, Praxiteles created, at the beginning of the 4th century, a new and more natural type of beauty illustrated by the *Diana of Gabies**. His **Cnidian Aphrodite***** (8) caused a scandal, not only because of its sensual nudity, but also because the model was a famous courtesan. This statue, of which hundreds of copies were made, was one of the most famous of all Antiquity. The *Apollo Sauroctonus** is a replica of a bronze by Praxiteles.

Rm. 11. — The *Barberini Supplicant*** is a moving work which puzzles specialists unable to understand its meaning. The skilful harmony of the drapery and the nobility of the face demonstrate the absolute mastery of the sculptor. The *Athena Parthenos** is a Roman replica of Phidias' most famous work, the 39 ft/12 m Athena in gold and ivory which stood inside the Parthenon.

Rm. 12. — Salle des Caryatides: the name of this former great hall of the old Louvre palace comes from the four statues by Jean Goujon which support the musicians' tribune. The sculptor Lysippos (4th century B.C.) devoted himself to the study of athletic musculature and elongated the proportions of the human body. He made several portraits of Alexander, including the one known as the *Azara Head*. The lively *Diane de Versailles* belongs to the same school. With the evolution of taste, it was no longer athletes who were represented but children and old men: *The Child with a Goose* or the *Wounded Galatea* are examples of this tendency towards realism.

Etruscan Art. Rms. 13 and 14. — Influenced by the Greeks, Etruscan art was the mainly funerary art of a mysterious people who lived in Tuscany in the 9th century B.C., and was a prelude to Roman art. The Cerveteri *Sarcophagus*** (6th century B.C.) is remarkable not only for the quality of its execution but also because, for the first time, a woman is represented next to her husband during the holy banquet. Look also at the paintings on the tombs (*Deux Vieillards*) and notice the way ceramics and jewelry evolve.

On leaving the Etruscan rooms, turn left to reach the former apartments of Anne of Austria and the **Roman Art** collection.

Rm. 18. — The Republican Period (1st century B.C.–1st century A.D.). The relief of Domitius Ahenobarbus is one of the first examples of Roman historical reliefs; the sacrifice of three animals in honor of Mars can be seen on the right.

Rms. 19-21. — Portraits occupy a very important place in Roman art. Look at those of the Emperors Caligula, Nero, Trajan, Hadrian and Marcus Aurelius and members of their families, Messalina, Livia, et al.

Rms. 22-24. — Objects from late Antiquity including mosaics from North Africa: *Triomphe de Neptune et d'Amphitrite**.

Rm. 25. — Cour du Sphinx: monumental sculptures and mosaics.

End the visit by climbing the Daru staircase to the first floor. Dominating the stairs, the **Winged Victory of Samothrace***** (6) appears to be swept by an irresistible momentum. This work, discovered in 1863, seems to exist beyond the bounds of time and style; it is one of the greatest masterpieces of Hellenistic art.

First floor. The **Salle des Bijoux** (Jewel Room, 1), opening onto Apollo's rotunda to the left of the *Victory of Samothrace*: under frescoes from Herculaneum, the Boscoreale Treasure is displayed. This is a unique collection of silver objects decorated with religious scenes, flowers and fruits rendered with acute realism. This treasure was found in Pompeii, in a house destroyed by the eruption of Vesuvius in 70 A.D. Turn left in the next room to reach the **Henri II Gallery** (ceiling painted by Braque in 1953). In the **Clarac Gallery:** pottery from Crete and Cycladic idols whose style prefigures abstract art. The bell- and violin-shaped idols provided the inspiration for Picasso's archaic style.

Rm. II. — Bronzes. Near the entrance, the magnificent *Agde Ephebe** was only discovered in 1964. The head of the **Athlete from Benevento**** (7) is one of the rare originals displaying the technical perfection of Greek bronzes in the 5th century B.C. Certain works come from Roman Gaul: the *Apollon de Lillebonne*, in gilded bronze, and the *Apollon de La Courrière* are not, however, as interesting as the small bronze animals which the Gauls became past masters at making. These are part of the small legacy left by a civilization which is less known than, for example, that of the Sumerians.

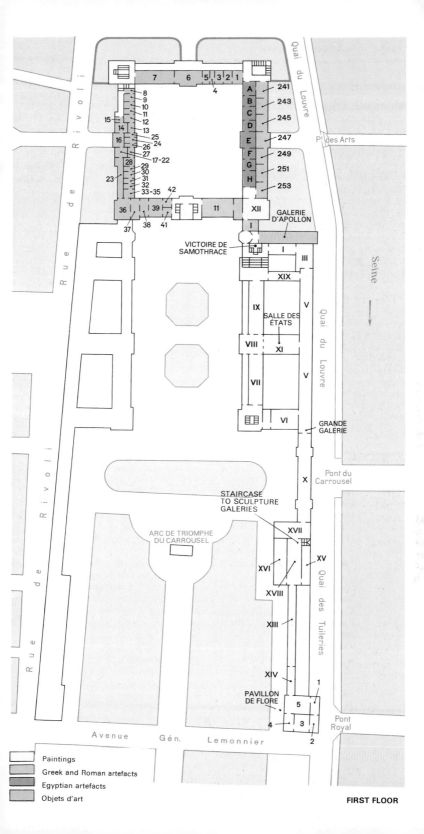

FIRST FLOOR

To the South of the Cour Carrée, the rooms are devoted to Greek ceramics.
Campana Gallery (Rms. 241-253). The geometric decoration gives way to representations of birds and horses, then hunting and mythological scenes (*Theseus'* goblet and the bowl of *Antaeus*).
In the group of hydriae from Cerveteri, an Ionian artist portrayed different episodes in the lives of gods and heroes with humor and fantasy. In the middle of the 6th century B.C., forms became much freer: vases were given the shape of eagles' or doves' heads or even of two heads facing backward and forward, their features standing out against a black glazed background. Purity of style, harmony of form and color are the hallmarks of Greek ceramics at their best. **(Rm. 243)** In the middle of the 5th century B.C., leaders of the Classical movement returned to a greater sobriety, forms having been debased by the over-abundance of heavy composition in the 4th century B.C. **(Rm. 239)** The village of Tanagra specialized in these female figurines which are perfect, exquisite replicas of the great sculptures rich Romans fought over.

PAINTINGS

Where to find:

French school	14th C.	Salle Duchâtel
	15th-16th C.	Salon Carré
	17th-18th C.	Grande Galerie Mollien wing — 2nd floor west
	19th C.	Salles Mollien, Denon, Daru — 2nd floor south
	Beistegui Coll.	Flore wing — 1st floor
Italian school	Primitives	Grande Galerie
	16th C.	Salle des Etats
	17th C.	Salle des Sept Cheminées
	18th C.	Flore wing — 1st floor
Flemish and Dutch schools	Primitives 16th-17th C.	Petits Cabinets — Seine side Tuileries side Salle des Sept Mètres, Salle Van Dyck, Galerie Médicis
Spanish school	14th-18th C.	Pavillon de Flore
German school	15th-16th C.	Petits Cabinets — Seine side
English school	17th-19th C.	2nd floor

FRENCH SCHOOL

Major works

The Avignon Pietà — 1
François I (Jean Clouet) — 2
Les Bergers d'Arcadie (Nicolas Poussin) — 3
Le Repas de paysans (Le Nain) — 4
St Joseph charpentier (Georges de la Tour) — 5
Embarquement pour l'île de Cythère (Watteau) — 6
Gilles (Watteau) — 7
Le Sacre de Napoléon (David) — 8
Le Bain turc (Ingres) — 9
Les Massacres de Scio (Delacroix) — 10
Le Radeau de la Méduse (Géricault) — 11

Salle Duchâtel (I): 14th century. The portrait of **Jean le Bon** (1360), who was king when the Hundred Years' War started, is the first of a French king. Despite the stiffness of the pose, the portrait does not lack natural expression or liveliness. In the Narbonne Altar-Cloth*, a typically French treatment appears for the first time through foreign influences. It was commissioned by Charles V whose portrait, along with that of Jeanne de Bourbon, can be seen on either side of the Crucifixion.

Salon Carré (III): 15th century. — Opposite the rich *Altarpiece of the French Parliament*, the **Avignon Pietà**** (1), Enguerrand Quarton, is a masterpiece of 15th-century painting. The sorrow expressed on the three faces leaning over the body of Christ contrasts with the serenity of the kneeling donor.
Jean Fouquet's portraits of Charles VII and of Juvénal des Ursins (c. 1450) show the vigor and skill of the artists of the time; they represented their models faithfully even though they were not always flattering. The Master of Moulins, Jean Hey, (*Portrait of a Child, Madeleine de Bourgogne*) unites Gothic and Renaissance influences with great sensitivity.
In the same room, decorated with unparalleled richness, works of **16th-century French painters** are also exhibited: the

portraits of **François I**[**] (2) by **Jean Clouet,** Pierre Quthe* by Clouet's son, François (1562), and Henri III by François Quesnel testify to the birth of a typically French style, the qualities of which are objectivity and precision. This concern for human truth is also in evidence in the 28 small portraits* by **Corneille de Lyon** displayed in the side rooms overlooking the Seine. In the middle of the century, the **first Fontainebleau School** sought inspiration in Antiquity representing its gods and goddesses and giving them elongated forms and supple lines. The *Eva Prima Pandora***, the first nude in French painting, introduces with assurance a sensuality only befitting profane painting. *Diane chasseresse** gracefully idealizes the beauty of Diane de Poitiers, Henri II's mistress. *Gabrielle d'Estrées et Sa Soeur au bain* is a famous painting of Henri IV's mistress.

Grande Galerie (V): 17th century. In the first half of the century, painters were divided between the supporters of Caravaggio (Vouet, La Tour) and those of the Carraccis (Poussin) — the Baroque style or realism. After 1660, these opposing approaches were harmonized under the direction of Le Brun, resulting in Classicism. **Simon Vouet,** with his *Présentation de Jésus au Temple*, and his pupil Le Sueur, who was also influenced by Poussin and Raphael, were the 17th-century masters of the Baroque style. Thus the *Scène de cabaret** by Valentin, *Le Jeune chanteur* by Vignon and the *Muses* by Le Sueur clearly show the influence of Caravaggio at the beginning of the century.

Passionately interested in drawing, **Poussin** studied in Italy and succeeded in creating a fusion between man and nature that had never before been achieved. His paintings representing somber landscapes peopled with dignified figures create an impression of mystery. Death is present even in his **Bergers d'Arcadie*** (3), giving the scene a heart-rending tenderness akin to the melancholy which fills the Roman landscape of *Orphée et Eurydice**. Poussin's influence survived for centuries and was felt even by Cézanne. See also *Echo et Narcisse***.

Georges de La Tour, using Caravaggio's technique, specialized first in diurnal subjects and later in nocturnal ones which enabled him to produce striking effects: *Le Tricheur à l'as de carreaux, L'Adoration des bergers***, **St Joseph charpentier*** (5), *La Madeleine à la veilleuse***. His paintings,

among the most profound meditations of the 17th century, were only rediscovered by art historians between 1920 and 1930. The **Le Nain brothers** painted historical, religious and mythological scenes as well as representations of peasant life: **Le Repas de paysans*** (4), with its somber colors and almost religious solemnity, *La Charrette** with its admirable harmony of yellow and gray. *La Victoire*, is an elegant allegorical figure, notable for the simplicity of its composition.

Claude Gelée, better known as **Lorrain** (*Port du mer au soleil couchant, Débarquement de Cléopâtre*) spent most of his life, like Poussin, in Rome. The exquisite golden light which suffuses his paintings makes him one of France's greatest landscape painters. Opposite, the series of paintings by Poussin entitled *Les Quatre Saisons* illustrates the various ages of Man and significant moments in the history of humanity.

Philippe de Champaigne, Louis XIII's court painter, personalized the art of the portrait, emphasizing character: the portrait of Robert Arnaud d'Andilly* (1657) is executed with great skill; *Les Échevins de Paris* is of historical value; finally, the *Ex-Voto*** depicts the miraculous recovery of the painter's daughter, attesting to the profound faith which makes him the painter of divine grace.

Opposite, *Le Chancelier Séguier* (1660) is one of the finest portraits by **Le Brun** and marks the appearance of a new, noble and decorative style which contributed to the glory of Louis XIV. The portrait of Le Brun by Largillière or that of Marie Serre by Rigaud are among the most significant works of the Classical period.

Grande Galerie and Rm. 6: 18th century. After the death of Louis XIV, the Regency and the reign of Louis XVI saw an explosion of freedom both in the arts and mores. Far from being solemn, **Largillière's** portraits attempt to reproduce the charm of the "grands bourgeois" he represented: the *Portrait du peintre, sa femme et sa fille** tells much about the new taste for the facile and the sensual.

Watteau is probably the greatest master of this brilliant period, able to render its exquisite fragility. The **Embarquement pour l'île de Cythère*** (6) (1717) portrays a melancholy vision of ephemeral happiness, as unreal and precious as the surrounding landscape. **Gilles*** (7) stands stiffly in his clown's costume; in the *Portrait d'un gentilhomme**, Watteau seems to contrast a pleasant, easy reality with a premonition of the imminent end of aristocratic society.

Boucher, child prodigy and protégé of the Marquess de Pompadour, the painter of *Le Repos de Diane**, is the much-copied master of gallant scenes. *Les Forges de Vulcain*, with its pale colors and diagonal composition, is proof of his talent as a decorator.

Fragonard, pupil of Boucher, studied in Rome before finding success in Paris with the liveliness and elegance of his intimate scenes. The portrait of Diderot*, with its warmth and precision, is more profound than such paintings as *La Toilette, La Leçon de musique** and *Les Baigneuses* which charmed his contemporaries. **Hubert Robert** who was in Italy with Fragonard, for the most part painted landscapes with ruins.

Chardin chose to devote himself to themes of daily life. *La Raie** is notable for its realism; in *Le Souffleur* and *Les Attributs des arts et de la musique*, he seems, through his rigorous composition, to want to check the frivolous exuberance of Boucher and Fragonard. Mythological themes served as a pretext for the glittering licentiousness of Lancret and Van Loo.

In **Rm. VI,** more works by Chardin can be found: *Le Bénédicité, La Mère laborieuse*, and the superb *Jeune homme au toton**. They reveal an intimate and subtle art. The still-lifes by Desportes and the hunting scenes by Oudry owe their realism to Chardin and the Flemish painters.

Beside these great masters, we should point out the little-known portraits by Perronneau and the moralizing compositions by **Greuze** which were much admired by Diderot and J.-J. Rousseau: *L'Accordée de village**, *La Malédiction paternelle* (Mollien wing).

Salles Mollien, Denon and Daru (VII-IX): 19th century. — Just as the Revolution and Empire were a reaction to the *Ancien Régime*, so, too, did art undergo a change. Frivolous sensuality gave way to a cold and pompous academism exemplified by **David:** *Le Serment des Horaces*. This marked the beginning of neo-Classicism, while the **Sacre de Napoléon I** *(The Coronation of Napoleon 1st)*** (8) is a historical document of great interest. The *Portrait de Mme. Récamier** is moving in its truthfulness; as for his Antique nudes, they inspired the classical nudes of Girodet (*Les Funerailles d'Atala*). David tried to impose his theories on **Gros** whose vigorous

nature thrilled to the Napoleonic epic: *Les Pestiférés de Jaffa* announces the great romantic tragedies; unable to identify with a movement which advocated a return to Classicism, Gros committed suicide. As for the even-tempered **Prud'hon,** favorite of Josephine whose *Portrait à la Malmaison* he painted, he was one of the precursors of Romanticism. He was a man of great culture as proved by works such as *L'Enlèvement de Psyché* which shows the influence of Correggio.

The incompatibility between neo-Classicism and Romanticism is exemplified by the conflict which opposed **Ingres** and **Delacroix.** Ingres considered drawing to be the basis of painting. His Classical compositions (*Apothéose d'Homère*) should not overshadow his *Grande Odalisque** or *La Baigneuse** in which he gave free rein to his sensuality, and his portraits in which he achieved supreme mastery (*Monsieur Bertin**). Finally, **Le Bain turc**** (9) combines the purity of Classical drawing with unavowed Romantic tendencies (2nd floor). Delacroix gave priority to color over drawing. **Les Massacres de Scio**** *(10)*, *La Liberté guidant le peuple, La Mort de Sardanapale**, bursting with color, violence and life, violated all the rules and provoked passionate arguments, making Delacroix the leader of the Romantic School. **Le Radeau de la Méduse**** *(11)* by Géricault, whose theme was inspired by an actual shipwreck, is a moving portrayal of despair.

ITALIAN SCHOOL

Major works

Grande Galerie (Rm. X): 13th, 14th and 15th centuries — the **Vierge aux anges****(1) by **Cimabue** (c. 1280), which shows oriental influences, faces **Giotto's St Francis**** (2) (c. 1310) in which a landscape features and where the characters are expressive. Another innovation lies in the three-dimensional quality of the figure of the saint. Notice the Madonnas by Lorenzo Monaco, Paolo Veneziano and Sassetta, Le Portement de Croix by Simone Martini, the Vierge et l'Enfant adorés par Lionello d'Este by J. Bellini and especially **Le Couronnement de la Vierge**** (3) by **Fra Angelico,** which is exceptional because of the use of perspective and the beauty of the colors.

As early as the beginning of the 15th century, there is a perceptible contrast between the conventional representation of religious scenes and the realism, for example, with which **Piero della Francesca** portrayed Sigismondo Malatesta without disguising the brutality of his expression. The composition of the Bataille de San Romano** by **Paolo Uccello** is of unusual boldness (1432). The evolution in the art of the portrait and in composition is felt in **Mantegna's St Sebastian**** (4) and in Christ bénissant by the Venetian painter **G. Bellini.** Firmness of drawing underlies the lightness and grace of **Botticelli's** Vierge à l'Enfant. In the portrait of the Condottiere* by **Antonello da Messina,** the authority and intelligence of this adventurer are most effectively rendered. The richness of color and the majestic composition of La Prédication de St Étienne* by **Carpaccio** announce the Venetian masters of the 16th century. **Perugino** had an understanding of perspective, while **Ghirlandaio** (La Visitation, Portrait d'un vieillard et de son petit-fils) allies an almost Flemish precision to Florentine calligraphy.

Rm. XI: 16th century. — Florence became the center of a new form of art which soon spread beyond the frontiers of Italy; in the world of the Renaissance, Man was the principal subject.

The **Mona Lisa***** (5) occupies the place of honor in the Salle des États. It is the most universally known work in the Louvre. **Leonardo da Vinci** used his extraordinary technical skill to give this portrait a mystery emphasized by the enigmatic smile and the gentle sadness of the gaze. The unreal landscape in the background, painted as if seen from the air, testifies to the range of his preoccupations and experiments with perspective. The Vierge aux rochers and the Bacchus are suffused with this strange atmosphere which, in Leonardo's works, borders on the supernatural.

La Vierge, l'Enfant Jésus et sainte Anne*** (6), is a masterpiece of composition in which the three figures are arranged in a pyramidal shape. The development of the painter's technique leads him to represent volumes modeled by light, gradually eliminating color.

The **Portrait de Balthazar Castiglione**** (10) is the most remarkable work by **Raphael** in the Louvre. Also in this room: La Belle Jardinière, Le grand St Michel and the Portrait de Jeanne d'Aragon.

Titian was, above all, an extraordinary colorist. In **L'Homme au gant**** (7), the light that radiates from the face contrasts with the deep blacks of the rest of the composition. St Jérôme dans le désert and even more, **Le Concert champêtre**** (9), long attributed to Titian's master, Giorgione, vibrate with color and life and have a peculiar charm stemming from the harmony between the figures and the natural surroundings in which they are represented. Intensity of expression makes the portrait of François I and the **Femme à sa toilette** outstanding pieces.

Two Venetians who excelled at vast rich compositions: **Tintoretto** (Suzanne au bain and Le Paradis, a sketch made for the decoration of the ceiling of the Doges' Palace in Venice) and, even more so, **Veronese.** In the latter's **Noces de Cana**** (8), 132 figures represent contemporaries such as Soliman II, François I, Charles V, Titian, and Tintoretto, and the painter has even included himself as a cello player. This enormous painting was completed in one year.

Le Sommeil d'Antiope** (11) by **Correggio,** a disciple of Leonardo, is an audacious diagonal composition; a great sensuality emanates from the rounded forms of the nude bodies painted with a skill which announces the Baroque.

In the ante-room of the Salle des Etats, situated behind the Noces de Cana, look also at the Portement de Croix by Lorenzo Lotto and various portraits by disciples of Leonardo.

Rm. XII: 17th century. — In this vast room with its seven fireplaces, the correct, cold and already Classical art of the **Carraccis** (fishing and hunting scenes) contrasts with **Caravaggio's** realism which is enhanced by violent lighting effects. **La Mort de la Vierge**** (12) was rejected by the churchmen who had commissioned it on the grounds that it was indecent, but it won the admiration of the painters of the time. Guido Reni, Giordano,

Piazzetta and Guercino played with light in a manner never seen before; in the four scenes he painted on the theme of Hercules, **Guido Reni** displayed the influence of Classical nudes.

Rm. XIII. — Flore wing. 17th century. — Caravaggio freely interpreted traditional iconographic themes and used audacious lighting effects. The *Diseuse de bonne fortune*, with its light colors, is an early work. The peaceful landscapes of Domenichino belong to the classical tradition of Poussin's country scenes. Works from various Italian schools: Bologna, Genoa and Naples.

Rm. XIV: 18th century. — In that century (known as the Age of Reason or Enlightenment), Venice was extremely prosperous. **Guardi** took pleasure in painting its festivals; the picturesque street scenes of **D. Tiepolo** are full of life. Finally, with the decline of Italian painting, artists like **Crespi** (*La Puce*) attempted a renewal by seeking inspiration in the Dutch School. The **Beistegui collection,** donated to the Louvre in 1953, has a number of major works: *La Mort de Didon* by Rubens, the *Portrait du Général Bonaparte* by David, and the *Portrait de la Marquesa de la Solana* by Goya.

SPANISH SCHOOL

Major works

Le Christ en croix (El Greco)— 1
Le Jeune mendiant (Murillo)— 2
La Marquesa de la Solana (Goya)— 3

Works by 16th-century Spanish painters are exhibited in the **Pavillon de Flore (Rms. 1 and 2).** Important religious themes are often treated with dramatic force. *L'Homme au verre de vin***, by a 15th-century Portuguese artist, broke new ground with its simplicity and life-like expression. At the end of the 16th century, **El Greco,** who originally came from Crete, gave Spain a national painting style. This mystic has paintings of elongated bodies, twisting them like flames; a dark violence pervades his **Christ en croix adoré par deux donateurs**** (*1*).

Rm. 3: Works of **the Golden Age:** the style of **Ribera** contrasts with El Greco's mannerism: *Le Pied-bot** and the *Adoration des bergers* show his tendency towards realism and liking for dramatic scenes.
Le Jeune mendiant** (*2*) **(Rm. 4)** by

Murillo is a vigorous work distinguished by beautiful light; it is in sharp contrast to the set of solemn paintings on the life of St Bonaventura by **Zurbarán** with their geometrical shapes. **Velázquez** portrayed with great subtlety, members of the Spanish aristocracy such as the Infanta Margareta.

Goya (Rm. 14) is represented in the Louvre by some of his early works; the **Marquesa de la Solana**** (*3*) reveals his gift for sumptuous color which is also to be admired in his *Dame à l'éventail**, the *Portrait de la Marquesa de la Cruza* and the *Christ au jardin des oliviers*.

FLEMISH AND DUTCH SCHOOL

Major works

Vierge du chancelier Rolin
(Jan Van Eyck)— 1
La Nef des fous (Hieronymous Bosch)— 2
La Bohémienne (Frans Hals)— 3
Le Prêteur et sa femme
(Quentin Matsys)— 4
Les Joueurs de cartes
(Pieter de Hooch)— 5
La Dentellière (Vermeer)— 6
La Kermesse (Rubens)— 7
Histoire de Marie de Médicis
(Rubens)— 8
Portrait of Charles I (Van Dyck)— 9
Self-Portraits (Rembrandt)— 10
Les Pèlerins d'Emmaüs (Rembrandt)— 11

Rms. 1-5. — Flemish painting, which was late in ridding itself of Gothic influences, must be distinguished from the Dutch masters who attained perfection in the art of portraiture, still-life, landscape and, above all, genre scenes.

Petits Cabinets, Seine side. — The **Rolin Madonna**** (*1*) by **Jan Van Eyck** is noteworthy for the expressiveness of the faces and the precision with which details are treated, a quality also found in other early Flemish works: Rogier van der Weyden's *Braque Family Triptych* (1450) and *La Salutation angélique* or even the *Floreins Madonna* by Memling. Realism reaches its peak in **La Nef des fous**** (*2*) by **Hieronymous Bosch. Le Prêteur et sa femme**** (*4*) by **Quentin Matsys** (1514) does not depart from tradition, but the beauty of the faces and the intimate character of the scene point to the influence of Van Eyck. *Les Mendiants** by Brueghel the Elder, and the sad-faced *Nain* *du Cardinal de Grandvelle** by **Anthonis Mor** belong to the realist manner.

Petits cabinets, Tuileries side. — (17th century). Works by artists influenced by Rembrandt: G. Dou (*La Femme hydropique*) is skilful in giving the illusion of reality to the objects he paints; P. Potter specialized in animals.

Vermeer, rediscovered in the 19th century, is one of the great masters of Dutch painting. The delicately rendered woman in **La Dentellière**** (6) seems to exist outside time; *L'Astronome*** (1668) belongs to the same period and is another example of this "silent world" of light and color.

In the next rooms: sketches by Rubens, works by Teniers, Paul Bril, and "Velvet" Brueghel represent the various tendencies present in the 17th century.

Rubens (1577-1640) dominated Flemish painting in the 17th century. An aristocrat who occasionally dabbled in diplomacy, he devoted a **set of 21 paintings** to the story of **Marie de Médicis**** (8) exhibited in the **Galerie Médicis (18).** His dazzling **Kermesse**** (7) **(Rm. 17)** or the portraits of his second wife, Helen Fourment, full of tender emotion, demonstrate his genius as a colorist and his ability to render life.

Rm. 17. — The truculent Jordaens and Snyders owe their technique mainly to Rubens. Van Dyck, with his elegant and precise manner, chose the role of official painter of the English Court; his portraits of **Charles I**** (9) and others were admired by his contemporaries for their nobility and the perfection of their technique. The 16th century saw the golden age of Dutch painting. The **Bohémienne**** (3) by **Frans Hals,** striking in its spontaneity, is one of the masterpieces of a school of realistic portraitists. Ruysdael, whose landscapes usually feature a vast sky, is the master of a genre also illustrated by Van Goyen (*Le Patinage*) and Van de Velde (*Canal glacé*).

In **Les Joueurs de cartes**** (5), *La Buveuse* and *L'Intérieur d'une maison hollandaise*, **Pieter de Hooch** relies for his effects on geometrical flagstones and vistas viewed through open doors and windows.

Rembrandt, like Vermeer, also touched on the unknown regions of the subconscious. However, through his use of *chiaroscuro*, he revealed a darker passion. In his **self-portraits***** (10) he first appears as a young man basking in success but his face changes gradually, marked by poverty, grief and the feeling of being misunderstood. With **Les Pèlerins d'Emmaüs**** (11), he abandoned the style of a fashionable painter (*Portrait à la toque et à la chaine d'or*) to become the painter of the inner world (*Le Philosopher en méditation**, *St Mathieu inspiré par l'ange***).

GERMAN SCHOOL

Petits cabinets, Seine side. — Self-portrait painted by **Dürer** (1493) at the age of 22, on the occasion of his engagement. The influence of the Middle Ages is still visible in this realistic portrait of the painter holding a thistle symbolizing fidelity. However, the fact that he has chosen to be his own model is proof of his need for self-knowledge and gives this work an important place in the history of art. Look also at the luminous water-color of a Tyrolean landscape.

In the *Vénus dans un paysage** (1529) by **Lucas Cranach,** the elongated body of the naked goddess is an example of Mannerism in which the influence of the Italian Renaissance is tempered by a typically German stiffness and realism. *Le Chevalier, la femme et la Mort* by **Hans Baldung Grien,** with its violent colors, remains deeply Gothic in spirit.

The portrait of Erasmus* by **Holbein** (1523) is probably the most perfect of the works by this painter of European aristocracy; the sharp profile and the air of concentration of the humanist writer are rendered with deep psychological understanding.

Cabinet des dessins (Department of Drawings). On the 2nd floor of the Pavillon de Flore, the Louvre collection is, with that of the Albertina in Vienna, the richest in the world.

FRENCH SCHOOL

Second floor (reached through the Department of Egyptian Antiquities). Works by the neo-Classic painters David, Gros, Prud'hon are exhibited in **Rm. 1.**

Rm. 2. — Remarkable portraits by **Ingres;** *Le Bain turc** represents the ultimate result of his variations on this theme.

Rm. 3. — Landscape painters. The tendency towards realism is evident in the landscapes painted by **Corot,** whose *Cathédrale de Chartres** was one of Proust's favorite paintings; it is also noticeable in the famous *Angélus** by **Millet** and even more so in the works by the painters of the **Barbizon school (Rms. 6 and 9)** who paved the way for Impressionism.

ENGLISH SCHOOL

Rm. 12, second floor. Painting in England was, at first, the work of foreigners like Holbein and Van Dyck. In the 18th century, English painters began producing land-scapes and portraits of note. The portrait of Sir Charles William Bell by Lawrence is a perfect example of the coldness of the neo-Classical style, whereas Julius Angerstein and his wife* (1792) look on from their portrait with an air of more engaging simplicity. *Master Hare*, by Reynolds, was considered the masterpiece of English painting, and thousands of copies were made of it. In the portrait of Lady Gertrude Alston or *Conversation dans un parc*, as it is entitled here, Gainsborough was more interested in representing the exterior of his models than in studying their character; he had a great talent for rendering fabrics and lace. Finally, the vitality expressed in *Captain Robert Hay of Spot* by Raeburn contrasts with these rather conventional works.

DECORATIVE ART

Major works

Crown Jewels — 1
Harbaville Triptych — 2
Tapestries: Hunts of Maximilian — 3
Portraits on enamel — 4
Furniture by Boulle — 5
Furniture by Charles Cressent — 6

Galerie d'Apollon (reached by going up the Daru staircase, on the left of the *Victory of Samothrace*). Two superb **gates** dating from 1650 form the entrance to this gallery, magnificently decorated under the direction of Le Brun after it was burned in 1661. The ceiling boasts a vast composition by Delacroix, **Apollon vainqueur du serpent Python***. The showcases contain what is left of the fabulous **treasure** of the kings of France. Portraits of famous paint-ers and architects can be seen in medallions on the walls.

Showcase 1: Jade vases, lapis lazuli, jasper from collections belonging to Louis XIV.
Showcase 2: Crowns worn by Louis XV and Napoleon I for their coronations.
Showcase 3: objects made of rock crystal.

Showcase 4: the **Crown Jewels*** (*1*): the *Regent***, an exceptionally pure 136-carat diamond bought by the Regent in 1717; the *Côte-de-Bretagne* ruby*, cut in the shape of a dragon in the 18th century reducing its weight to 105 carats; the *Hortensia**, a rare 20-carat pink diamond; the *Sancy*, a 54-carat stone; 19th-century reliquary brooch; the *Plaque de l'Ordre du Saint Esprit*, a decoration given by Louis XV to the Duke of Parma; lastly, a recent acquisition, a set of sapphires and dia-monds which belonged to Queen Hor-tense, Napoleon III's mother.
Showcase 6: 5th-century oriental porphyry vase mounted with a silver gilt eagle, presented to Abbot Suger of Saint-Denis Basilica.
Showcase 7: Coronation regalia previously kept in the Saint-Denis Basilica; *la Vierge de Jeanne d'Evreux* (1339).
Return to the entrance of the Galerie d'Apollon and, on the right, go through the rooms devoted to Egyptian Antiquities until you reach the Champollion staircase.
Salles de la Colonnade (1-7). — Under the gilded coffers of the ceiling, four ceremonial cloaks of the Ordre du Saint-Esprit.
Romanesque room (4). — Between two porphyry columns from the old basil-ica of Saint Peter's in Rome there are artefacts from Christian Rome (the Barber-ini ivory), Byzantium (the 10th-century **Harbaville Triptych*** (2) and objects from the Romanesque period (reliquary of Charlemagne's arm). The bronze eques-trian statuette in the central showcase might be of Charlemagne.
Rm. 5. — **Ivories. Reliquary casket of St Potentin,** 13th-century work from the Rhine valley. Gothic spirituality appears in the **ivory statues.** The amazing skill of the 13th- and 14th-century artists can be admired in the **Limousin enamels.** Also notice the large Embriachi altarpiece made of wood and ivory.
Rm. 6. — **Renaissance bronzes.** Humanism, born in Italy, provided the inspiration for the bronzes from Florence, the work of the Paduan artist Riccio, and the medals by Cellini and Pisanello.
Rm. 7. — **Tapestries, enamels.** Superb set of 12 tapestries representing the **Hunts of Maximilian*** (3) woven in Brussels for Charles V around 1510. The **portraits on enamel*** (4) displayed in the central showcase show the amazing technical mastery of the Limoges crafts-men.

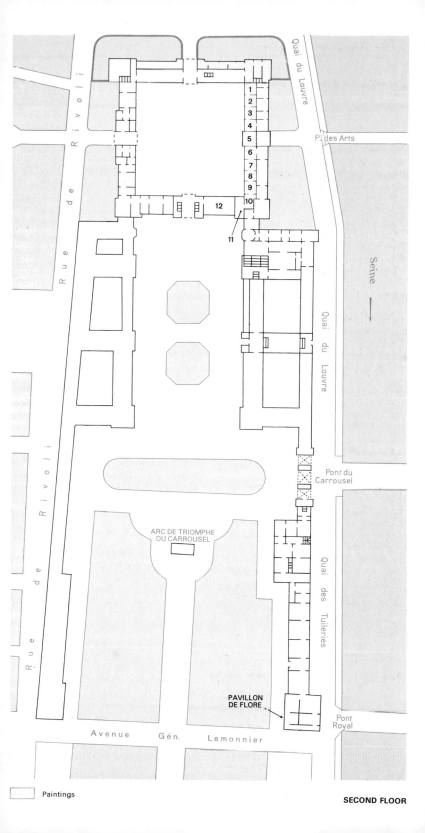

SECOND FLOOR

Paintings

Bernard Palissy decorated his plates with colorful motifs in relief; Italian artists created masterpieces in faience and glass; notice the blue goblets from Murano, the beautiful colors of the works from Deruta and Gubbio and the rich compositions of Faenza.

Rms. 8 and 9. — French tapestries from the 16th and 17th centuries.

Rm. 10. — Jewelry, medallions, watches and clocks from France, Germany, Italy and Flanders.

Rm. 11. — Tapestries woven in the Louvre workshops, before the creation of the Gobelins.

Rm. 12. — In the room of Maréchal d'Effiat, there is a simple and elegant display of Louis XIII furniture.

Rms. 13-15. — The richness and majesty of the "Grand Siècle", Louis XIV's reign, are reflected in the splendid **furniture**** (5) made by **André-Charles Boulle** (1642-1732) and his sons. These pieces, sometimes overly decorated, with tortoise shell and copper inlays, harmonize beautifully with the big Gobelins tapestries.

Rm. 16. — The furniture** (6) made by **Charles Cressent** during the Regency has curved and complicated lines; the sensuous fantasy which characterizes them resulted in the Rococo style; the taste for chinoiseries, widespread at the time, is visible in the faience **(following rooms)** and porcelain **(Rm. 20)**.

Rms. 28-34. The **trademarks** of the most famous French cabinet-makers, Leleu, Oeben, Riesener and Jacob, are on the pieces displayed in this room, most of which were part of the royal furniture. The discreet and elegant Louis XVI style was succeeded by the solemn and somewhat cold Empire style. See the **throne*** of Napoleon I and the cradle of the King of Rome, his son.

Rms. 35-42. — Furniture and objets d'art assembled by the great collectors of the last century.

SCULPTURE

Major works

Rm. 1 — The evolution of **Romanesque art** can be traced from the crude style of the old church of Sainte-Geneviève-des-Bois to that of the Christ de Lavaudieu, and the sorrowful Christ détaché de la Croix (13th century).

Rm. 2. — The greatest **Gothic sculptures** are those for which the human body again served as model, nature inspiring the floral motifs.

Rm. 3. — The **Vierge de la Celle**** (1) (14th century) is one of the most beautiful of all the statues produced in the Ile-de-France workshops. The effigies of **Jeanne de Bourbon** and **Charles V** are two remarkable 14th-century portraits.

In the corridors: Virgin and Child in gilded polychrome stone from Cîteaux; **Tête d'apôtre*** by Jean de Cambrai.

Galerie haute (Upper gallery). — Beside 13th-, 14th- and 15th-century works in wood, there are numerous statues originating from Germany and the Netherlands. The passionate faces in the moving **Vierge à l'Enfant d'Isenheim**** (2) announce Grünewald's Expressionism. The deep, forcefully rendered draperies are also found in most of the religious figures sculpted in the workshops of the Rhine Valley and Bavaria (**Portement de Croix, Mise au Tombeau, Vierge de l'Annonciation*** in painted and gilded marble by **Riemenschneider**). The **altarpiece from Coligny*** (16th century) in painted and gilded wood was made in an Antwerp workshop.

Rm. 4 — Faces take on a greater individuality as in the recumbent tomb effigies of **Pierre d'Evreux and Catherine d'Alençon.** Under the mutilated high-reliefs of the rood-screen* from the Cathedral of Bourges (13th century) recumbent statues and statues of saints are exhibited, demonstrating the increasing refinement of provincial sculpture.

Rm. 5. — The impressive **tomb of Philippe Pot***, Grand Seneschal of Burgundy, carried by eight hooded mourners, is one of the masterpieces of the 15th century.

Rm. 6. — The first French Renaissance, marked by the strong personality of **Michel Colombe** (Gaillon altarpiece: St George Fighting the Dragon), did not renounce the Gothic heritage.

Rm. 7. — French Renaissance. — The statue known as the **Diane d'Anet** decorated the castle at Anet which belonged to Diane de Poitiers, mistress of Henri II. Its qualities of fullness and sensitivity are also found in the **Trois Grâces**** (3) by **Germain Pilon** whose statues of the **Chancelier de Birague** and of his wife are proof of his mastery and vigor. **Jean Goujon,** who sculpted the bas-reliefs of the old Louvre, disregarded the Italian influence. His pure and simple style, inspired by ancient Greece, gives great charm to the **Nymphs of the Fontaine des Innocents**** (5). The almost Roman vigor of the *Amiral Chabot* by Jean Cousin contrasts with the elegance of the tombs of the Montmorency family by Prieur.

Grande salle italienne (great Italian room) and **galerie basse** (lower gallery) **(Rm. 11)** — Italian sculpture evolved from the static stiffness of the *Vierge de Ravenne* (13th century) to the already feminine **Vierge de l'Annonciation*** by Pisano (14th century) and further with the *Seated Virgin* by Jacopo Della Quercia, the delightful small angels by Verrocchio and the admirable bas-relief of the *Virgin and Child*** by **Donatello** who dazzled Europe. This evolution culminated at the end of the 15th century in Florence in a style illustrated by Duccio's Madonna and the great altarpiece by the **Della Robbias.** Above the door, the **Nymphe de Fontainebleau** by **Benvenuto Cellini,** was a source of inspiration for the numerous French artists who represented Diana. From the rooms where **Mediaeval and Renaissance sculpture** is exhibited, you reach **rooms 12-21** through the Portal of the Palazzo Stanga and an underground passage; **17th-, 18th- and 19th-century sculpture** is displayed below.

Rms. 13-17. — 17th century. Works in the Mannerist style of the beginning of the century (reign of Henri IV); Baroque and Classical works from the time of the Sun King; tombs by Guérin and Anguier; monumental works created for Versailles and Saint-Cloud by Marsy and Legros. There are also impressive mythological pieces by **Puget** such as *Hercules Resting, Milo of Crotona, Perseus Liberating Andromeda,* and *Alexander and Diogenes.*

Rms. 18-22. — In the beginning of the 18th century, because of **Versailles** and other royal residences, sculptors were encouraged to create works for display in the open air; Coysevox, the Coustou brothers, and Lemoyne were officially commissioned to execute works the themes of which were often borrowed from mythology. Look at the groups executed for the Grande Cascade at Marly by Coysevox, the statue of Marie-Adélaïde de Savoie as Diana and the beautiful maquette of the **Chevaux du Soleil*** by the Marsy brothers for the Grotto of Thétis at Versailles. The exquisite allegories by Falconet have a piquancy; the other sculptors of Louis XV's time, such as Pigalle, Allegrain or Pajou, went back to the Classical style and created works as lifelike and expressive as those of antiquity.

Rm. 22. — Houdon succeeded in accurately rendering the character of his models, the acerbic irony of Voltaire, the spontaneity of the Brongniart children, the worried expression of Rousseau, the middle-class solidity of Washington.

Rms. 23 and 24. — Neo-Classicism is represented by a master in the person of **Canova.** His creations are full of life and perfectly executed. The statues that were officially commissioned, such as the busts of Napoleon, are easily distinguished from the others which are freer in character and almost libertine (*Baiser de l'Amour à Psyché**).

Rm. 25. — Romantic Room. On the wall there are plaster studies for the **Marseillaise**** by Rude, bursting with romantic fervor. *Le Pêcheur napolitain**, by the same artist, has a naively trusting smile. David d'Angers gives a lively firmness to the faces of his subjects.

Rm. 26. — Galerie Barye. The artist, having lost interest in the human figure, portrayed **animals** with a keen sense of observation. Some of his groups representing wild animals fighting have a force bordering on violence.

Rms. 27 and 28. — Salles Carpeaux. Carpeaux was the only great master of the Second Empire who did not conform to academism without incurring the disapprobation of official circles; the famous **Danse**** (7) was commissioned for the Paris Opera. Behind the spontaneity and dash which characterize his works, a tragic anxiety announcing Rodin may occasionally be sensed, for example in the bronze group of Ugolino and his sons.

In the Basement, the **two Slaves**** (8) by Michelangelo were meant to represent the Liberal Arts bemoaning the death of their protector, Pope Julius II; they are a powerful expression of the soul of the artist, tortured by his genius and excessive nature.

The original **Marly horses**** by G. Coustou are also here, casts having replaced them on the Place de la Concorde.

PARIS' MAIN MUSEUMS

The main museums of Paris presented here cover the history of Western, and particularly French art, from its origins to the latest trends of today. The Louvre Museum (*see p. 160*) spans the period from Antiquity to the early 19th century, the new Orsay Museum continues up to the beginning of the 20th century, and the Pompidou Center is devoted to contemporary art. Other museums offer major collections of art from the Far East, Africa and the South Seas.

The National Museums are open daily except Tuesday; some are also closed on holidays.

●

Musée des Arts Africains et Océaniens

(National Museum of African and Oceanic Arts)

**Map,
East
Paris
(E 4)**

Metro: Porte-Dorée   Bus: nᵒˢ 46, PC
Entrance: 293 Av. Daumesnil, 75012 (on the edge of the Bois de Vincennes)

— *Open daily, ex. Tue and Public hols, 10 am – noon and 1.30 – 5 pm, tel: 43 43 14 54.* — Exhibited here are artistic works from countries constituting the former French Colonial Empire. The building, which has a sculpted frieze, was erected for the **Colonial Exhibition of 1931.** Even the most jaded viewer is likely to be charmed by the display, which is animated by a shared magical and spiritual purpose, without any consciously aesthetic intent.

▬ *VISIT*

On the ground floor and on the right of the main hall, there are collections of **Oceanic art;** bark paintings by Australian aborigines, masks from New Zealand, dance costumes and unusual funerary figures whose heads are made from skulls.

On the first floor and on the left of the main hall: masks and fetishes, hangings and statues in wood, ivory and bronze evoking all the vehement cosmogony of **Africa.** These illustrate how much modern art owes to early Black art.

On the second floor, the art from the **Maghreb** regions offers an almost familiar aspect; calligraphy and delicately subtle embroidery, rugs, jewelry, arms and brocades, furniture inlaid with ivory and mother-of-pearl — all the refinements of a civilization which suddenly appears to be very near to us after the secret and gaudy world of African and Oceanic arts.

The museum has a large **underground tropical aquarium** and a water-world of fish, tortoises and crocodiles.

●●

Musée des Arts Decoratifs
(Museum of Decorative Arts)

**Map 4,
(A 6)**

Metro: Palais Royal, Louvre   Bus: nᵒˢ 21, 24, 27, 67, 72, 81, 85, 95
Entrance: 107 Rue de Rivoli, 75001

— *Open daily ex. Mon and Tue, 12.30 – 6.30 pm and on Sun 11 am – 5 pm, tel: 42 60 32 14.* — The Museum of Decorative Arts has been given a completely new look. The five-year renovation has opened 100 rooms, spread over six floors, displaying several thousand artifacts for those who are curious to know about daily life from the Middle Ages to the present day.

▬ VISIT

The Museum of Decorative Arts goes fearlessly back in time. On the **first floor,** (on the Rue de Rivoli side), six rooms, stark and white, pay homage to the decorators and creators of contemporary style, as well as to its originators: Breuer, Le Corbusier and Mies Van der Rohe. On the Tuileries side, some treasures of Art Nouveau and Art Deco are revealed, such as the beautifully-shaped blown-glass vases with bubbles, or the 1920 chair by Clément Rousseau ... not to mention Guimard and Gallé or the superb apartment of Jeanne Lanvin.

The **second floor** walls are covered with unpolished stone which provides the setting for the display of objects from the Middle Ages to the Renaissance: enamels, ivories, bronzes, sculptures and tapestries; among the masterpieces, a Venetian goblet in blown glass, embossed plates and bronze anatomical models.

On the **third floor,** the great styles from Louis XIII to Louis XV, follow one another in an almost rarefied atmosphere, in such a profusion of line, workmanship and decoration that they become almost trite.

On the **fourth floor,** there are two new rooms, one devoted to tableware from Rouen and Saint-Cloud, the other to rare gold and silver items of the 17th and 18th centuries.

On the **fifth floor,** a center of arts and crafts is open to the public.

On the **sixth floor,** there is a permanent exhibition of the collection donated by the painter Jean Dubuffet.

Musée des Arts et Traditions Populaires ●●
(Museum of Popular Arts and Traditions)

Metro: Sablons, Porte-Maillot   Bus: nos 73, PC
Entrance: 6 Route du Mahatma-Gandhi, 75016

Map, West Paris (B 3)

— *Open daily ex. Tue, 10 am – 7 pm, tel: 47 47 69 80.* — The aim of this museum is to give a general view of the whole of **rural society** as it was before the Industrial Revolution and as it still is in some French provinces. Displayed here is a miscellany of traditional shows, games, dances and music, along with local handicrafts, now recognized as having intrinsic artistic merit. They include pottery, crockery, tools and even a fascinating almost abstract, collection of skittles in carved wood.

▬ VISIT

In the ground floor gallery, the large display cabinets vividly show the different **lifestyles** in rural France, from the shepherds' huts of the Aubrac to the mountain pastures of Savoy and from the Camargue to the thatched cottages in Brittany.
In the **Study Gallery (Galerie d'Études)**, situated underground, rural objects are classified and studied according to their function and use. Musical instruments, games, implements and tools of various kinds ... so many handcrafted objects which are sometimes little masterpieces. Audio-visual displays are available for visitors.

••
Musée Guimet
(Guimet Museum)

Map 1,   Metro: Iéna   Bus: n°˙ 32, 63   Entrance: 6 Pl. d'Iéna, 75016
(D 5)
— *Open daily, ex. Tue, 10 am – noon and 1.30 – 5 pm.* — This museum was started from the collections of Emile Guimet, industrialist, musician and untiring traveler who fell under the spell of the **Asiatic arts.** Bequeathed to the State in 1884, they form the heart of this magnificent museum. Renovated and modernized, it is one of the richest in the world.

▬▬ *VISIT*

On the ground floor of this museum, in the first room, visitors are welcomed by the monumental **Khmer statues** which create a peaceful, almost religious atmosphere. These 11th–13th-century statues are followed by the smiling faces of the **Bayon style** (12th century), meditating behind half-closed eyes. Both the pinnacle and the demise of Khmer art are represented here, recreating the powerful magic and mystery of Angkor.

The art of central **Vietnam** appears more Baroque and expressive, seen in the fantastic Makara dragon (12th century) and the 10-armed Champan *Seated Siva.* A row of very beautiful banners from **Tibet** and **Nepal,** highly-colored gouaches and ritual objects illustrate the art of the Lamas. **Thai** art is recognized by its Buddhas with their original flame-shaped hairstyle and by very characteristic leather art. Finally, the **Island of Java** in the 8th and 9th centuries, developed a high standard in its bronzes, particularly evident in the standing statue of *Avalokitesvara* displaying various cult objects in his 10 hands.

The first floor is devoted to the evolution of **art in India,** from the 3rd century B.C., up to modern day. Notice the beautiful collections of Buddhist high and low reliefs, the noble *Magaradja,* from the school of Mathura, in the 2nd century, representing the Serpent-King, the very realistic series which the Amaravati school

devoted to incidents in Buddha's life. Among the numerous bronzes of this prodigious period, the admirable **Dancing Siva*** (11th century) stands out. The **Mogul miniatures** concentrate on describing, in surprising detail, the court life of powerful kings who, for several centuries, subdued the whole of North India.

At the crossroads of East and West, **Afghanistan** and **Pakistan** were influenced by Greek art, evident in the Treasure of Bengram and particularly in *The Genie with Flowers.*

On the same floor, there is also a display of ceramics, bronzes, jewelry, furniture and Chinese lacquerware.

In the David-Weill room, the Treasure of Li Yu is exhibited. Dating from the 5th century B.C., it contains objects inlaid with turquoise.

On the second floor, silk paintings and flags evoke the ancient "silk road" of Central Asia; the *Portuguese Screen,* painted in Japan in the 16th century, is a humorous illustration of the arrival of the Portuguese. However, the important pieces here are the **Chinese ceramics**,** which are among the most beautiful to be seen anywhere. Notice the dazzling, three-color **Ming vases,** the celadons, the delightful harmony of the 18th-century **Famille rose,** which was to make all Europe marvel.

••
Musée Marmottan
(Marmottan Museum)

Map 1,   Metro: Muette   Bus n°˙ 32, 52, 63
(E 1)   Entrance: 2 Rue Louis-Bailly, 75016

— Open daily ex. Mon, May 1, Dec 25, 10 am – 6 pm, tel: 42 24 07 02. —
This museum was set up in the exquisite, typically 19th-century
mansion where the art historian, Paul Marmottan, used to live. He
bequeathed it to the State, along with his collection of *objets d'art* and
furniture which date from the Renaissance, the Consulat and the
Empire. An exceptional collection of works by **Monet** has since been
added, particularly a series of **65 canvases painted at Giverny** at the
beginning of the century.

Among the other treasures of this museum are works of art as
varied as 16th-century **Brussels tapestries,** *The Toper* by **Frans Hals,**
grand portraits of important figures from the reign of Napoleon I, and
the Wildenstein donation of splendid 13th-16th-century **miniatures** in
which the perceptive viewer will find scenes ranging from the lives of
saints to agricultural activities. The explosion of bright colors which sets
alight Monet's work, makes the Marmottan one of the most important
centers of Impressionism in Paris. The famous *Impression, soleil levant,*
which gave the Movement its name, painted in 1872 and exhibited at
Nadar's gallery in 1874, hung here until it was stolen in 1985. There are
also works by Sisley, Guillaumin and Boudin. After this, plunge into the
winding universe of the underground gallery to experience the fantasy of
the paintings, where water, light and flowers blend and mingle together
in complete pictorial ecstasy; in the Giverny garden, through the work
of the almost-blind master, Impressionism truly became the style of
painting which expressed a perfect happiness.

Musée de l'Orangerie
(Orangerie Museum)

●●●

Metro: Concorde   Bus: nᵒˢ. 24, 72, 73, 84, 94   **Map 2,**
Entrance: Place de la Concorde   **(F 4)**

— Open daily ex. Tue, 9.45 am – 5.15 pm. — The building in which the
Nymphéas by Monet are displayed, is identical to the Jeu de Paume and
has been completely renovated, allowing the impressive **Walter-
Guillaume collection** to be seen in natural light. There are 144
masterpieces, mainly from the 1920s assembled by Domenica Walter
and her two husbands, Paul Guillaume and Jean Walter. The 22
paintings by Soutine, 24 by Renoir, 14 by Cézanne and 9 by Douanier
Rousseau are incomparable. The aim of the presentation is to preserve
the unity of a collection in which each work represents a significant stage
in the evolution of modern art.

Nearly all the works exhibited have become classics: **Le Vase
paillé, Le Rocher rouge, Dans le parc du château noir** by Cézanne; **Le
Noce** and **Le Carriole du père Junier** by Douanier Rousseau; still-lifes
as well as the **Grands nus dans le paysage** and the *Arlequins* by Derain,
who was Picasso's rival; the pink and red Odalisques by Matisse, the
Enfants au piano, the *Soeurs Larolle, Claude en costume de clown* and the
series of *Nus de Gabrielle* by Renoir. Also to be found here are Utrillo's
naively poetical paintings, works by Modigliani (fine portrait of Paul
Guillaume), De Chirico and Van Dongen and paintings by Picasso from
the pre-Cubist period and the years 1921-23, when the unusual *Géantes*
announced the arrival of Surrealism.

●●●
Musée d'Orsay
(Orsay Museum)

Map 4,   Metro: Solférino-Bellechasse   R.E.R.: Gare d'Orsay   Bus: n°s 63, 68, 83, 84
(B 4)   Entrance: I Rue de Bellechasse

— *Open daily ex. Mon, 10.30 am – 6 pm; Thu 10.30 am – 9.45 pm; Sun 9 am – 6 pm, tel: 45 49 48 14.*

▬ HISTORY

The decision to create the **Musée d'Orsay** was taken in 1977. Its purpose was twofold: to save a threatened monument, the **Gare d'Orsay** (designed by the architect Laloux in 1900), and to create a **museum of 19th-century art,** covering the period between the closing years of Romanticism and the advent of Modern Art. In other words, it would form the vital link between the Louvre and the Pompidou Center.

The main priority of the Musée d'Orsay is to enable the visitor to view the ensemble of artistic output during the second half of the 19th century and the first years of the 20th century: painting, sculpture, decorative arts, graphic arts, architecture and town-planning, photography and cinematography. The Musée d'Orsay is a highly original concept, in that all these features are displayed within the complex framework of their links with literature, music and poetry, and with the various political, social and economic movements that characterized the period between 1848 and 1914.

The works on display are drawn from the national collections covering the period, previously housed at the Louvre, the Jeu de Paume and the Palais de Tokyo. In addition, there is material from museum reserves, donations and many other sources which had previously been widely dispersed. This basic collection has been supplemented by a continuing policy of acquisition, assisted by the Société des Amis du Musée d'Orsay (The Friends of the Orsay Museum).

▬ VISIT

The former station has been adapted lengthways from the main entrance, in such a way as to make maximum use of the immense hall that formerly contained the railway platforms. The grand floor and the station foyer are now occupied by a complex of rest areas and information points designed to prepare the visitor. This leads to a small auditorium, surrounded by a display of objects, pictures and texts illustrating the period between 1848 and 1914; the auditorium itself shows films that place the art of the 19th century in a historical context. The next area is devoted to instructing children about the museum. Nearby is the main auditorium in which films of 19th-century art history are continuously projected. Audiovisual projections can also be viewed at various stages throughout the building. These enable the visitor to visualize the milieu in which 19th-century artists developed, how the

Salons worked, the world of art enthusiasts and dealers, even the faces and voices of the artists themselves. (*Some of these projections have to be specially requested.*)

The collections themselves are exhibited in highly diversified rooms, generally in chronological order. Various itineraries are available: the visitor can select the rooms he wishes to see, in the order that he wishes to take them.

From the reception area, a staircase leads down to the former railway platform level, where it opens onto a broad walkway that covers the length of the building, with two wide areas at each end. There, and in a series of side rooms, works from 1848-1870 are displayed.

At the end of the walkway, escalators lead to the upper floor of the museum; this direct access to the 4th floor is designed to acilitate the chronological presentation of the collection.

The intermediate level is devoted to the period 1870-1914. It is organized around a series of terraces overlooking the main walkway, with display rooms of various sizes. From these three levels, the visitor can reach the five-floor Amont pavilion, the two towers overlooking the terraces, and the glassed-in passages of the station's west side.

Painting Section

The **Painting Section** is representative of every trend, from a selection of **Romantic works** which links the Musée d'Orsay with the later works in the Louvre, to the entire **Impressionist collection**, formerly housed in the **Jeu de Paume**, and supplemented with recently-acquired works by **Renoir, Monet** and **Bonnard.** Other acquisitions, in the form of drawings and pastels by **Merson** and **Degas**, have been added, along with a number of paintings by foreign artists like **Klimt, Burne-Jones, Knopff** and **Munch.**

On the **ground floor,** in the rooms to the right of the main central walkway: Romanticism, Eclecticism, Symbolism: some post-1850 paintings by **Ingres** and **Delacroix** (the bulk of their work remains in the Louvre.) Then **Chassériau, Gérome, Cabanel, Regnault, Puvis de Chavannes, Gustave Moreau** and **Degas** (pre-1870).

In the rooms to the left of the main walkway: Realism (**Daumier, Corot, Millet, the Barbizon School, Courbet**), landscapes (**Daubigny, Jongkind, Boudin**), then **Manet** and the first Impressionists (**Monet, Bazille,** and pre-1870 **Renoir**).

On the **upper level,** in the **Galerie des Hauteurs,** there are works from the post-1870 period when Impressionism was at its zenith (**Manet, Degas, Monet, Renoir, Sisley, Pissarro, Van Gogh, Cézanne.**) The **Bellechasse Gallery** which follows, is devoted to post-Impressionism (**Seurat, Signac, Cross, Gauguin, the Pont-Aven School,** and the **Nabis,** with **Maurice Denis, Bonnard** and **Vuillard**).

At the **intermediate level,** the last rooms exhibit the new 20th-century paintings (**Klimt,** the **Fauvists, Matisse**) which make the transition between the Musée d'Orsay and the Musée d'Art Moderne at the Pompidou Center.

Sculpture Section

On the **ground floor,** along the main walkway, there are works by **Rude, Barye, Préault,** and **Pradier.** At the end, there is a sculpture by **Carpeaux,** which forms a link with the rooms devoted to **Garnier,** the Paris Opera and Haussmann's town planning.

At the **intermediate level,** there is a kind of "sculpture garden" directly below the huge skylight of the hall. Every tendency is represented here, from 1870 to 1914 (**Rodin, Maillol, Bourdelle, Dalou**).

Decorative Arts Section

Second Empire decorative art is shown on the **ground floor,** in the rooms facing the Rue de Lille.

At the **intermediate level,** three series of rooms are reserved for Art Nouveau (**Horta** and **Van de Velde** in Belgium, **Guimard** in Paris, **Gallé** and **Majorelle** at Nancy).

The Graphic Arts

Chronologically ordered, the graphic arts occupy various areas on the **ground floor** and **intermediate levels.**

Photography and Cinema

Photography and cinematography are here admitted to a French art museum for the first time.

A number of rooms on the **ground floor** and **upper floor** are exclusively devoted to photography, chiefly displaying 19th-century work. The museum's collections, most of which are drawn from existing reserves, have been greatly enriched by acquisitions of an international selection of photographs (**Emerson, Stieglitz, Cameron, Fenton, Steichen**), as well as works by French photographers (**Atget, Carjat, Nadar**).

The birth of cinematography is displayed on the **intermediate level,** covering the period up to its development on an industrial scale. Permanent projection of "primitive" motion pictures.

Architecture and Town-Planning

The **Amont Pavilion** is entirely devoted to architecture and town-planning, with scale-models, drawings, reproductions and original elements of construction.

A permanent display area is reserved for the Universal Exhibitions (Paris, 1878, 1900), which testify to the confrontation between art and industry which took place in the second half of the 19th century.

Of the two towers which rise above the terraces, one is dedicated to architect **H. Guimard,** while the other shows turn-of-the-century town planning and architecture in France and abroad (**Augustin Perret, Tony Garnier, Wagner** in Vienna, **Burnham** in Chicago).

The Press and Illustrated Book ex-hibitions occupy glassed-in areas on the 2nd and 3rd levels, which trace their appearance in the mid-19th century, and their subsequent vital role in the development of a new collective imagination.

The Musée d'Orsay's original presentation, its many temporary exhibitions, and its vivid audiovisual depiction of its own historical context are bound to give this huge new project a prominent place among the cultural assets of Paris.

The visit should end with a stop at the upstairs café, (**Café des Hauteurs**), which offers a magnificent view of the city.

●●● # Musée Picasso
(Picasso Museum)

Map 5,   Metro: St. Sébastien Froissard   Bus: n°s 20, 29, 65, 96
(B 4-5)   Entrance: 5 Rue de Thorigny

— *Open daily ex. Tue, 9.45 am – 5.15 pm.* — Opened in September 1985, the Picasso Museum is in the Salé mansion, built in 1656 by Aubert de Fontenay, a salt-tax collector. The classical building, exceptionally well restored, is in keeping with the painter's fondness for old houses. Some 64,584 sq. feet/6000 sq. metres of space have been cleared, and Diego Giacometti, the famous sculptor's brother, designed the furniture and lighting.

Containing 203 paintings, 158 sculptures, more than 3000 drawings and prints, 16 collages and 88 ceramics, this remarkable collection was made possible by a law allowing payment of death duties to the State in the form of works of art. This unique collection allows us to appreciate the range and variety of the work of one of the greatest artists of the century. In addition, Jacqueline Picasso donated the artist's private collection (paintings and drawings by Renoir, Cézanne, Rousseau, Derain, Braque, Matisse and Miró).

══ *VISIT*

At the foot of the grand staircase the *Man with a Sheep* (bronze from 1943) invites the visitor to discover the world of Picasso spread over three stories. The Director of the museum, Dominique Bozzo, decided on a chronological order mixing sculptures, paintings and drawings to clearly define each period.

On the **first floor** are works from the blue, pink and Cubist periods and from the 1920s, when Picasso flirted with the Surrealist movement. There is also a group of paintings by Matisse, Cézanne, Derain, and Douanier Rousseau for which he had a special liking.

On the **second floor** is the rest of his private collection (paintings by Corot, Le Nain, Modigliani) and rooms for temporary exhibitions.

On the **ground floor,** works from the 1930s are exhibited, as well as sculptures in a garden. There is also a cafeteria.

Ceramics and works painted at the time of *Guernica*, during the war and in the 1950s are exhibited in the **basement**.

●●●

Pompidou Center (National Museum of Modern Art)

Metro: Hôtel-de-Ville, Rambuteau   R.E.R.: Châletet-les Halles
Bus: n°s 21, 29, 38, 47, 58, 67, 69, 70, 72, 74, 76, 81, 85, 96
Entrance: On the 3rd and 4th floor of the Pompidou Center

Map 5, (A-B, 2-3)

— *Open daily ex. Tue, May 1st, Dec 25th, noon – 10 pm; Sat and Sun 10 am – 10 pm.* — The Pompidou Center's Museum of Modern art was modernized and reorganized at the beginning of 1985; the new display of works traces more clearly the succession of schools and trends which have appeared during the 20th century, making it one of the most important museums in the world. It houses the collections which were previously exhibited in the Palais de Tokyo and in the National Center of Contemporary Art, as well as donations from numerous artists (Vasarely, Adami, Hartung ...).

A series of temporary exhibitions, highlighting the links between Paris on the one hand and Berlin, Moscow and New York on the other, put into perspective the role played by Paris in the history of the plastic arts of the 20th century.

HISTORY

The first movement to be born at the dawn of the 20th century was that of the **Nabis**. Sérusier, Bonnard, Vuillard and Vallotton renewed the art of posters and theatrical decor and helped to open the door to modern art.

More influenced by Van Gogh, the **Fauves** opposed the neutral colors of the Nabis' style with the boldness of pure colors. Gathered around the pupils of Gustave Moreau, Matisse, Marquet and Manguin, were painters such as Vlaminck, Derain, Dufy, Braque, then Van Dongen. Following the **Salon d'Automne of 1905,** the Fauves intensified the horrified reaction by applying their tubes of paint directly onto canvas, banishing all shadow and perspective, in a feverish search for pure color.

Cubism. Did it originate from the discovery of Black primitive art which fascinated Vlaminck or from Cézanne's famous statement: "Everything can be reconstructed in the shape of a cylinder, cone or sphere"? Whatever its origin, its first example and striking manifesto was Picasso's *Les Demoiselles d'Avignon*, painted in 1907 at the same time that Braque, in Marseilles, was endeavoring to convey mass through geometric shapes. A group formed around them, with Juan Gris, Gleizes, Metzinger, La Fresnaye, then about 1911, Léger, R. Delaunay and Villon. The effect of Cubism spread rapidly after the war and persisted nearly 50 years, influencing all decorative arts, from architecture to furniture.

In opposition to the preceding movements which concerned only painting, **Surrealism** was born from the "Dada" protest against an Establishment which had allowed the horrors of war, although it was originally aimed to express the unconscious. To do this, it mingled objects, people and scenery which it changed or recreated according to its needs, thereby giving the painting the dimension of a dream, a question or even a provocation. This trend is well illustrated by Max Ernst, De Chirico, Dali, Tanguy, Miró and Duchamp.

Expressionism was never a school but rather a trend which belonged to all eras. Its importance in the 20th century led many painters who did not have much in common to accept the label. They included Modigliani, Rouault, Soutine, Munch and Kokoschka, all of whom depicted a world which was usually tragic and tormented.

Abstract art contrasts with the other schools by rejecting any form of representation or expression of reality. Originating around **Kandinsky** and Paul Klee, and demonstrated particularly by Mondrian, Manessier and De Staël, it experienced an almost universal development in the 1950s.

Pollock's experiments, action painting, and poetic abstraction can be associated with it. Figurative painting, although rejecting some of its original fluency, reappeared in the 1960s. Whether called "New Figurative" or "Hyper-realism", representational art still seems to have a long future ahead of it.

▬▬ VISIT

3rd Floor
The works of the **Fauves** are recognizable by their violent, almost strident, colors. **Vlaminck,** a colossal Fleming, who used to boast that he was a "gentle barbarian" did not hesitate to paint *Un Paysage aux Arbres Rouges.* His friend **Derain** variegated in red and green his *Two Barges.* Also note the intensity **Marquet** gave to the *Pont Saint-Michel.* **Matisse** evolved a more decorative style, based on arabesques and harmony of colors, already evident in *Le Luxe* which, however, dates back to his Fauve period. Similar, yet different in tone, are *La Tête rouge* by **Modigliani** and the realistic *Montmartre* by **Utrillo.**
The birthplace of the greatest revolution in pictorial art of the 20th century, Paris owed it to itself to have a museum displaying an exceptional collection of **Cubist works. Braque** achieved complete mastery of this new form of expression with *Le Guéridon* (1911), *La jeune fille à la guitare* and *l'Homme à la guitare* (1914). **Picasso's** style was in continuous change from *La Femme Assise dans un Fauteuil* (1909) to the *Joueur de guitare* (1910). Also note the works by Léger (*La Noce*) and La Fresnaye (*L'Homme assis*), as well as *Le Petit déjeuner* by Juan Gris. Accepting this influence, but attaching great importance to color research, *Improvisations* by **Kandinsky** and *La Ville de Paris* by R. Delaunay (1911) mark the future importance of abstract art immediately before the War.

On the 4th floor, post-World War I works are displayed.

On the terrace a *Machine* by **Tinguely** has been placed close to sculptures by **Max Ernst.**

On the same side as the Saint-Merri Church (South), the evolution of Cubism and abstract art has been retraced. Notice, in particular, the very pure nudes by **Matisse,** the *Grand intérieur rouge*** and *La Blouse roumaine*** which achieve, through strictly limited means, a powerfully decorative effect. Through his arabesques and use of bright color, **Dufy** became the painter of the good life between the two wars: racetracks, music and boats. The intimate scenes of ordinary life and the nudes by **Bonnard** and **Vuillard** make a pleasant contrast to the painful Expressionism of Pascin and especially of **Soutine,** seen in his startling *Groom*.* A series of tragic and disjointed women painted by **Picasso** carried Cubism to the edge of Expressionism; his evolution thus changed considerably from the style of Braque seen in his *Guéridon noir,* or in *La Nature morte à la table en marbre.* Notice, too, the abstract works by Paul Klee, Kandinsky, Mondrian and the enormous power of **Fernand Léger** (*Composition avec deux perroquets***).

In the center, various paintings by the **School of Paris** are displayed next to the major works of Dadaism and, in particular, **Surrealism** from around 1925: Max Ernst Magritte, Tanguy, Miró, Victor Brauner, Salvador Dali.

On the Rue Rambuteau side (North), it becomes difficult to identify a major direction in the explosion of contemporary art. The *Salon,* created by Agam for President Pompidou, intrigues as does the **Boutique de Ben**; Mathieu's style is easily recognizable (*Les Capétiens Partout*) as are the styles of **Giacometti** (*Femme Debout*), Dubuffet and Pollock.

WALKS IN AND AROUND PARIS

The Albert-Kahn Gardens ●●

Metro: Pont-de-Saint-Cloud, Pont de-Sèvres   Bus: n°ˢ 52, 72
Map, West Paris (E 1)

1 Rue des Abondances, or 5 Quai du 4-Septembre, Boulogne-Billancourt.
Open daily from Nov 15th to May 15th, 9.30 am – 12.30 pm and 2 – 6 pm.

Albert Kahn, a multi-millionaire of the *Belle Époque*, had a curious and expensive passion for collecting typical "sights" from all over the world. He built a garden (in a town better known for the Renault factory) in which he juxtaposed the dells of an English garden, a French park, a jumble of rocks from the Vosges Forest, blue cedars surrounding a lake, and Japanese houses in the middle of a Japanese garden. It is hardly surprising that Mr Kahn died penniless.

The Maison de la Native, in which temporary exhibitions are organized around ecological themes, is open to the public. There is also a museum of photography and cinema, currently open only on weekends, when films are shown. However, by the end of 1987, the museum plans to stage a major exhibition presenting the work of the seven photographers and two cinema directors sponsored by Albert Kahn. The artists in question took over 72,000 plate photographs and shots over 87 miles/140 km of black and white footage on a succession of world tours.

At Boulogne-Billancourt, see the Cook House designed by Le Corbusier (1926), 6 Rue Denfert-Rochereau.

The Arsenal Library

Metro: Sully-Morland   **Map 5, (D 4)**

1 Rue de Sully, 75004. Open Tue and Thur at 2.30 pm ex. Sept 1st-15th.

The Arsenal Library, situated in the former residence of the Grand Master of the Artillery and Henri IV's Minister, Sully, contains 14,000 manuscripts, 120,000 prints and 1,000,000 printed volumes.

■■ *HISTORY*

On the ruins of an ammunition depot which was destroyed by lightning, Sully had a new arsenal built by **Philibert Delorme**. Under Louis XIV, production of arms and gunpowder ceased, and the building was converted into a warehouse and later, into a court of justice.

Then, at the end of the 18th century, it became the repository of the collection of manuscripts of the Comte d'Artois, the future King Charles X; in 1797 it became a public library where Charles Nadier, the librarian, received Dumas, Musset, Lamartine, Vigny and Victor Hugo. At the end of the century, José Maria de Heredia established the **Salon des Parnassiens,** frequented by Verlaine and Mallarmé.

■■ *VISIT*

You can visit **Mme. de Meilleraye's** room, painted by S. Vouet, her oratory and a music room which has superb Louis XV paneling with the top of the doors depicting the Four Seasons by Bouchardon. The Boulevard Morland extends along the wing of the arsenal, which was added by Boffrand around 1720 in order to double the size of the Henri IV building, and leads to the Pont Morland. To the right, with a view over the Seine, is the Quai Saint-Bernard and its promenade, with an open-air sculpture museum, as well as the Austerlitz port and docks; to the left, is the **Arsenal Pleasure Port**. This dock, for a long time unused, can today accommodate more than 200 pleasure boats of 20 feet/6 metres to 46 feet/14 metres. The east side has been laid out with very pleasant terraced gardens, together with children's playgrounds; in good weather, the dock has a sea-side atmosphere.

From Auteuil to Jasmin: Art Nouveau and Art Deco

Map, West Paris (D 3)

Auteuil, now integrated into the 16th arrondissement, retained its rustic character well into the 19th century. Rich Parisians had fanciful cottages and Gothic-style houses built here which they used as second homes. It was only after 1860, that architects started to build proper urban *hôtels particuliers* in the area.

VISIT

Even more spectacular for those who come upon it from the Quai Citroën or the Quai de Grenelle is the **Maison de la Radio** (*Av. President-Kennedy — Metro: Passy, Ranelagh. Open daily ex. Mon, 10 am – noon and 2 – 5 pm, tel: 42 36 21 80*). Its circular mass has force and harmony; a crown with a circumference of 1,640 feet/500 metres and dominated by a tower 230 feet/70 metres high, was constructed in 1963 to a design by Henry Bernard. Judged at the time as a building of the future, today it has become part of the scenery of the Right Bank.
Via Rue de Boulainvilliers, go around the Maison de la Radio and follow **Rue La Fontaine** on the left, to enter the domain of Hector Guimard and Art Nouveau. It was here that this master of modern art created his principal works (1895–1910), characterized by constant repetition of plant-life forms and the choice of varied and contrasting materials (brick, stone, metal, ceramic). At n° 14 Rue La Fontaine, the **Béranger Castle** (1894–98) is perhaps Guimard's major work; he designed all the furniture himself, right down to the smallest detail. Following this success, he received numerous orders, which included the entrances to the Metro stations. Other buildings designed by Guimard between 1910–11, are n°s 17-21 Rue La Fontaine, n° 11 Rue François-Millet, n° 60 Rue La Fontaine and, at n° 25 Rue La Fontaine, the famous Studio Building de

Sauvage (1926). Leave Rue La Fontaine on the right to follow Rue George-Sand, then, to the left, take **Avenue Mozart** N° 2 Villa Flore is a house by Guimard (1926), while at n° 122 Av. Mozart, is the mansion he constructed for himself in 1910.

Via Rue Raffet on the right, one enters the kingdom of **Art Deco,** the style which dominated architecture in the 1930s.
At n° 18 Rue Raffet, is a beautiful 1925 house; n°s 30 and 40 Rue Jasmin are the unusual "Maison Triptyque" and the "Pink Building" by Morosolli (1930).

On the right of Rue Raffet, **Rue du Docteur-Blanche** is an amazing sanctuary of Art Deco; it was at n°s 8 and 10, Square du Docteur-Blanche, that architect A. Jeanneret applied, for the first time, the theories of his brother, Le Corbusier; n° 12 houses the **Le Corbusier Foundation***. Farther up, the **Impasse Mallet-Stevens*** comprises a collection of houses entirely conceived by Mallet-Stevens in 1927. Notice the importance given to volume, the total absence of all decoration, and the fine relationship with Cubism which featured in the **"manifesto" of Art Deco**. Farther up, at n° 5 Rue Docteur-Blanche, P. Patout's house (1928) owes its originality to the black mosaic which covers its base. (*Open daily ex. Sat, Sun, Public hols and Aug. 10 am – 1 pm and 2 – 7 pm, tel: 42 88 41 53. Exhibition of maps, library, photographs.*)

Place de la Bastille

Metro: Bastille **Map 5, (C 5)**

The Place de la Bastille entered into history on July 14th, 1789. Until the middle of the century it was, for Parisians, the center of rowdy night life, both disreputable and rough, as offered by the small dance-halls in the Rue de Lappe.

▬ HISTORY

The Bastille dominated the whole of the east of Paris for more than four centuries. Originally built at the Porte Sainte-Antoine in the fortifications of Charles V, it was completed in 1382; the fortress, about 230 × 100 feet/70 × 30 metres had eight towers and a moat. Louis XIII converted it into a prison for political offenders: here were incarcerated Bassompierre, who wrote his memoirs in captivity, the great orator Mirabeau, the poisoner La Voisin, the mysterious "Man in the Iron Mask", the young Voltaire and the adventurer Latude who escaped three times during his 28-year sentence. One of the last prisoners was the Marquis de Sade who was moved on July 3rd, 1789 to a lunatic asylum.

The Government was considering the Bastille's demolition because of the expense of maintaining it and the small number of prisoners there, when, on July 14th, 1789, it was stormed by the people of Paris who saw it as a major symbol of royal absolutism. They found only seven prisoners, among them four forgers and one madman, who were locked up again the next day. Legend has, however, made the taking of the Bastille one of the most important events of the Revolution.

Eight hundred workmen took part in the demolition of the walls, after which the site became a fashionable walk, and the stones were used for the Pont de la Concorde. Since then, there is dancing on the open square every July 14th.

▬ VISIT

Today, only the slender July column, crowned by the figure of Liberty, stands in memory of Parisians killed during the July 1830 riots. Plans for another opera house on the site of the old Bastille station promise a new future for the area.

Belleville and Ménilmontant

Metro: Belleville, Ménilmontant **Map, East Paris (B-C 3)**

Belleville and Ménilmontant were, at one time, choice areas. However, due to recent changes, a pedestrian who wanders along their boulevards would find this difficult to believe. On the one side, an immigrant population, on the other, a vast complex of new low-income housing which is, at best, commonplace. Between the two, you will search in vain for Maurice Chevalier's "Ménilmuche" or for the villages sung about by Édith Piaf and Charles Trénet at a time when it was thought that to come from Belleville made one particularly Parisian.

You should, however, leave the boulevard and climb the steep slopes of Paris' highest hill (after Montmartre), to discover the little provincial streets whose topography fortunately discourages property developers.

A walk to be recommended is that of Rue Ménilmontant to Place de la Mare, continuing on to the left up the picturesque Rue de le Mare.

Rue des Cascades, on the right, has remained one of the better preserved areas, with its large paving stones and its irregular, winding layout. Go back along **Rue des Amandiers,** a wide road of the old "village" which goes around the hill. Some shops and cafés have kept their old signs; alleyways and passages sneak between old houses, then disappear into courtyards and small yards, or become steps which ascend towards roads with names reminiscent of ancient paths: Mûriers (blackberry bushes), Pruniers (plum trees). Not a single house stands straight as the ground is so uneven; on one side are a few acacias, a multitude of pigeons and children playing; on the other, concrete houses. Between the two is old Ménilmontant which is gradually disappearing, and will soon no longer exist, except in songs and films about old Paris.

Bercy, the new frontier

**Map,
East
Paris
(E 3)**

Metro: Bercy   Bus: n⁰ˢ 24, 62

Until the end of the 1970s, the docks, depots and 19th-century houses along the Quai de Bercy seemed to be out of step with their modern surroundings; a large proportion of the capital's supply of raw materials used to arrive there. A spectacular renovation operation has totally changed all that.

The **Palais Omnisports de Bercy** (1983) represents the most important recent work carried out by the municipal authorities of Paris. Despite the daring features of the architecture (such as the famous grassy slopes around the sides of the construction) and the high costs of operation, this "palace" is a great success, mostly due to the flexibility of its design, which makes it an infinitely variable "geometric" hall. It can accommodate 17,000 people around a wooden cycling track and athletic track and can also be converted into a concert hall or a motorcycle racing track. The Six-Day Paris Cycling Race is held here each year.

The transfer of the **Ministry of Finance** from the Louvre to the Quai de la Rapée, beside the Palais Omnisports, should contribute towards the complete transformation of the district. The project of architects Chemetov, Devilliers and Duhart-Harosteguy takes the form of a gigantic arch 1148 feet/350 metres long, which spans the embankment in order to sit on the same bank of the Seine. Its 1,940,000 sq feet/180,000 sq metres of floor space will be occupied by the Ministry's staff at the end of 1988.

Between the Ministry and the Palais de Bercy, a **park** of about 30 acres/12 hectares will form a kind of Parisian Tivoli with games, fountains and terraces.

The Bois de Boulogne

**Map,
West
Paris
(B-C-D,
2-3)**

The Bois de Boulogne serves many purposes. On weekends, Parisian families invade 2137 acres/865 hectares of woods, lawns and gardens which are lungs of the west of the capital. Every Sunday, race-goers hurry to the Auteuil and Longchamp courses. As soon as night falls, and in spite of the marked police presence, the street-walkers carry on a brisk trade in the woods.

HISTORY

The wood, previously called the Rouvre Forest because of the numerous red oak (*rouvre*) trees, owes its name to the woodcutters' **pilgrimage,** from Boulogne-sur-Mer to Notre-Dame, which took place in the 14th century. Because of the number of thieves who hid in the woods and attacked unfortunate travelers, Henri III had it enclosed in 1556 by a massive rampart with eight gates, two of which are Maillot and La Muette. Later, Louis XIV opened the park to the public and made it one of his favorite walks. **Colbert** outlined its rectilinear routes, crossing each other in the shape of stars, and this arrangement has been maintained. Sumptuous pavilions were soon built there, such as the Bagatelle, the Château de la Muette and the Folie Saint-James. At the time of the **Second Empire,** the wood was replanted and felling was controlled; it was also embellished, according to the taste of the day, with artificial lakes, winding pathways and amusement parks.

VISIT

The lakes and the Pré Catelan

The Lower Lake provides pleasant boat trips to the islands or to a coffee house-restaurant which welcomes walkers and courting couples at its tables.

The Upper Lake swarms with small boats; from here, you can go deep into the wood via the Grande Cascade, then circle the grounds of the Racing-Club de France. By taking the Croix-Catelan road, you reach the beautiful park where a court minstrel from Provence was murdered during the reign of Philippe Le Bel. Note the magnificent copper beech in the center of the garden with its branches shading nearly 5,380 sq feet/500 sq metres.

The Bagatelle Park*, hidden in the heart of the wood, (*entrance opposite the Longchamp training ground*), was, for a long time, associated with love and gallantry — the Regent Philippe d'Orléans used to meet the prettiest ladies of the Court there. Today it is a maze of flowerbeds and rose gardens.

In springtime, the lawns spreading over 20 acres/8 hectares, are covered with broad swathes of color, formed by some 1,500,000 tulips, daffodils and crocuses. In May, the walled iris garden comes into bloom, followed by water-lilies, dahlias and all kinds of forest and water plants. An exceptional **arboretum** at Bagatelle combines cedars from Libya, tulip-trees from Virginia, black walnut trees from America, sequoias and araucarias. However, the park's main attraction is the **rose garden** covering an area of 2½ acres/1 hectare, where there are nearly ten thousand different varieties forming an incredible rose museum. The best time for the roses is mid-June to mid-July and September to the end of October.

The Municipal Floral Nursery* (*Metro: Porte d'Auteuil; Entrance 3 Av. de la Porte d'Auteuil, open daily Oct – March, 10 am – 5 or 6 pm.*)

In the tree nursery and the hothouses, built by Fonnigé in 1898, a million plants are cultivated each year to decorate public parks and official receptions. The best time to see the azaleas is in the latter half of April and the chrysanthemums in late October.

The Roland-Garros Stadium, near the nursery, stages one of the "Grand Slam" tennis championships of the professional circuit; all the great players of the world compete in this tournament held at the end of May every year. The Molitor swimming pool in the Avenue de la Porte Maillot is decorated with beautiful Art Deco stained glass.

Jardin d'Acclimatation

(*Map 1, A1 Entrance: Sablons crossroads — Open daily 10 am – 6 pm. Special attractions during school holidays, Wed, Sat, and Sun.*)

A miniature railway runs through this park for children. The park derived its name from the exotic animals which are acclimated there. Despite the monkeys, bears and sea-lions, many people prefer the chickens, rabbits and sheep of the Normandy farm, where picnics are permitted. The **Musée en Herbe*** contains workshops and temporary exhibitions for children; the big doll's house comprises six furnished rooms and contains antique dolls.

The Buttes-Chaumont

Map,
East
Paris
(B 3)

Metro: Buttes-Chaumont   Bus: nᵒˢ 26, 60, 75

The Second Empire transformed one of the most sinister areas in Paris into one of the most picturesque of Parisian parks.

■■■ HISTORY

Previously, the Buttes-Chaumont, completely bare (which is how it earned its name of "Mont Chauve" or "Bald Mountain"), was, for a long time, an area of quarries and rubbish dumps. **The Montfaucon gallows,** with its forked gibbet, was in constant use and described with horror by Villon and Clément Marot.

    In 1864, Napoleon III and Haussmann decided to transform the Buttes into a park covering 2,475,720 sq feet/230,000 sq metres. Alphand and Barillet created one of the most beautiful parts of the area by constructing a lake and massing huge rocks there.

■■■ VISIT

Nothing is missing in this park. There are streams, waterfalls, and jagged rocks; an island 167 feet/50 metres high rises out of the lake, crowned with a small temple which can be reached either by a foot-bridge or by the "Suicides' Bridge".

Those who like walking may prefer the plain grassy slopes, the wood with its beech and fir-trees, or the little roads leading off various parts of Rue du Général-Brunet, where houses, gardens and workshops have been preserved. There is also **the Avenue Secrétan covered market,** constructed by Baltard, and the French Communist Party's headquarters built by Niemeyer at the **Place du Colonel-Fabien**.

Charonne

Map,
East
Paris
(C 4)

Metro: Gambetta, Porte de Bagnolet   Bus: nᵒˢ 26, 76, 351

For a long time, Charonne remained the last of the Parisian villages, forgotten in the heart of the 20th arrondissement. Then property developers swarmed down the little roads, small squares, cul-de-sacs, arched porchways and the houses with adjoining workshops, many of which had retained their gardens and even their vegetable patches. When they had finished, only the old main village road and church were preserved, together with some picturesque alley-ways.

    In **Rue Saint-Blaise,** which goes down towards Montreuil, there are some old houses: nᵒˢ 6, 12, 21, 23 (beautiful courtyard) 31, 46, (18th century). In Rue de Bagnolet, note the little Hermitage pavilion at n° 148 (1734) and the house at n° 137 (18th century) which can be seen before reaching the **Saint-Germain-de Charonne*** Church, with its sturdy 12th-century bell-tower standing in the middle of the little village cemetery. Rebuilt in the 15th century, it was again renovated in the 18th and 19th centuries. The sculpted foliage which decorates the inside pillars, and the bunches of grapes symbolizing the Charonne vineyards, date back to the 15th century.

La Défense

R.E.R.: La Défense Bus: n° 73 **Map,
West
Paris
(A-B 2)**

The district of La Défense was built on the modest hill of Courbevoie and Puteaux, old villages of Ile-de-France. They have been completely transformed by the towers which have been springing up since 1964 and continue to do so today.

▬ HISTORY

La Défense officially came into existence in 1958. The first complex to be inaugurated was the National Center for Industry and Technology (CNIT) in 1964, with the Esso building becoming its first occupant in the same year. Since then, 33 buildings have been constructed, representing half the total of the planned office space — 161,460,000 sq feet/1,500,000 sq metres. In the towers are the offices of such important companies as Elf, Électricité et Gaz de France, Mobil Oil, Crédit Lyonnais, etc., which employ more than 80,000 people.

▬ VISIT

Other than the comings and goings of office employees, the exterior of La Défense is surprisingly lifeless. The main interest in visiting it is to see modern town-planning and new and rather controversial architectural styles.

The Palais du CNIT, a concrete building in the shape of a triangle with three points of support, designed by Zehrfuss, Camelot and Mailly, covers an area of 968,760 sq feet/90,000 sq metres; its arches span 722 feet/220 metres! Among exhibitions which are held there each year are the Boat Show (January), Home-making Exhibition (March), SICOB (office equipment and computers, etc.; Sept) and the Childhood Exhibition (Nov). In front of the center, note the sculpture by Miró, *Les Deux Personnages*, and in the square, Calder's red mobile. Among the towers, the following should be particularly noted: the Fiat Tower (1974) which is the tallest at 584 feet/178 metres; the Winterthur and Franklin Towers with their tinted glass facades, and the Manhattan Tower comprising 4000 panes of glass which reflect all the changes of the sky. The GAN Tower, in the form of a Greek cross, is built entirely from metal, except for its main core of concrete.

A walk along the open terraces reveals an amazing view over the Pont de Neuilly and the Étoile. Various **temporary exhibitions** are also held here. Also to be seen are works by Agam, (monumental fountain), Moretti (*Le Monstre,* on the lower level), a bronze fountain by Louis-Leygue (Place des Corolles), and a fresco by Attila. Meanwhile, the huge wings of the mechanical bird by Philolaos spread out over the Terrasse des Reflets.

The Seine embankment

Metro: Bel-Air, Javel **Map,
West
Paris
(D 3-4)**

Between the Quais de Grenelle and Citroën, the Rues de Javel and Dr-Finlay.

The Seine embankment was the object of one of the largest town-planning operations carried out in Paris during the 1970s. Over an area of 62 acres/25 hectares — which was occupied by factories and depots, as well an enormous complex of houses, offices, hotels and public facilities was built — the most spectacular of which are the sixteen 30-storied tower blocks. The commercial center of Beaugrenelle, with a public library and swimming pools, was also built in this area which has three levels of traffic lanes.

Also worth visiting are:

– La Ruche, the old rotunda from the wine pavilion of the Universal Exhibition of 1900, designed by Eiffel. Returning along Passage de Dantzig (*Metro: Convention*), one reaches an area of artistic creation which attracted Fernand Léger, Zadkine, Soutine, Blaise Cendrars and many others.

– Georges-Brassens Park*, constructed on the site of the old Vaugirard slaughter-houses where Ernest Moreau's pavilions (1897) can still be seen.

●

"Galeries" and covered arcades

Map 2,
(E-F 6)
Map 3,
(E-F
1-2)

The itinerary suggested here is not designed for a quick exploration of Paris. It is like going on a ramble, with numerous detours, designed to reveal the fantasy and mystery of this wonderful city.

Here you will find dusty glass ceilings painted with birds and flowers in the Modern style; innumerable walking sticks and curios; a second-hand bookshop established in 1780, selling antique books in tarnished gilt bindings — in short, the "real" Paris, otherwise flawed by modern offices, fast-food reataurants and supermarkets.

Sunless and secretive beneath their translucent sky-lights, with their flaking plaster figurines, the covered arcades of Paris have a charm that is all their own.

▬▬▬ *HISTORY*

The increase in the number of covered arcades in Paris, during the **first half of the 19th century,** can be explained by the new architectural possibilities opened up by the iron industry and by the irritation of pedestrians caused by the traffic, already considered excessive.

The oldest arcades are those in wood, constructed by Victor Louis in 1786 in the area of the **Palais-Royal,** comprising two walkways between three rows of shops lit by glass roofs. A few were opened during the Revolution and the Empire, but it was after 1823 that they multiplied in accordance with the new fashion. Haussmann's town-planning, with its emphasis on large open road axes, put an end to the development of arcades which were only to reappear much later along the Champs-Élysées (in particular with the Galerie du Lido), during the Art Nouveau period.

▬▬▬ *VISIT*

Galerie Véro-Dodat — *from 19 Rue J.-J. Rousseau to 2 Rue du Bouloi* — Two pork butchers, Véro and Dodat, opened this arcade in 1826, immediately achieving unprecedented success because of the luxury of its marble and mirrors, as well as its gas lighting, then a great novelty. Today it is still one of the most beautiful "galeries" and one of the most intriguing, with its

boutiques in which dark woods, bronzes and curios contribute to a very distinctive atmosphere, unreal and sensual.

Galerie Vivienne — *from 4 Rue des Petits-Champs to 6 Rue Vivienne* — Opened in 1823, the Galerie Vivienne represents a beautiful example of the neo-Classical style. Note the decorations on the semi-circular windows and the rotunda adorned with nymphs and goddesses. This arcade has had a new lease of life since the re-opening of the tea-rooms, which do not at all disturb the venerable Petit-Giroux bookshop, at this address from the very beginning.

Passage Choiseul — *from 44 Rue des Petits-Champs to 23 Rue Saint-Augustin* — The entrance of this arcade in Rue Saint-Augustin, is the beautiful facade of a mansion built in 1655. Under the dignified interior tribune, with its four Ionic columns, French poets hurried to the printer, Lemerre (at n° 23). Céline spent a large part of his childhood in this arcade about which he left a powerful and unforgettable account in *Mort à Crédit* (*Death on the Installment Plan*).

Passage des Princes — *from 5 Bd des Italiens to 97 Rue de Richelieu* — Opens under one of the most famous palaces of the era and is the last of the great Parisian arcades. It has retained certain elements of its Napoleon III decor, especially the shop front of the *Écume de mer* where artisans still skilfully carve Meerschaum pipes in view of the public.

Passage des Panoramas — *from 10 Rue Saint-Marc to 11 Bd Montmartre*. This passage owes its name and former success to the two panoramas which were set up in the big rotundas on the boulevard. The invention of the panorama, a huge painting depicting towns, the countryside and historical scenery, was brought to France by Fulton, together with his underwater schemes. A distinguished public used to crowd into this arcade when, in 1817, it became one of the first places to install gas lighting. Chateaubriand, Dumas and Delacroix were regular visitors. From the other side of the Boulevard Montmartre, it extends into **Passage Jouffroy** and **Passage Verdeau** — *from 10 Bd Montmartre to 6 Rue de la Grand-Batelière*.

Passage du Caire — *2 Pl du Caire* — This arcade exemplifies the Egyptian style which was so popular in Paris following Bonaparte's return from Egypt. It is now dominated by wholesale ready-to-wear clothes shops.

Passage du Grand-Cerf — *from 145 Rue Saint-Denis to 10 Rue Dussoubs* — This passage was only covered in 1825. The metal frame, bridgings of forged metal and high vault make it one of the most spectacular of Paris arcades, but unfortunately, it is also one of the most deserted.

Passage du Prado — *from 18 Bd Saint-Denis to 12 Rue du Faubourg-Saint-Denis* — Created in 1785 under the name of Passage du Bois-de-Boulogne. A very popular dance hall here attracted throngs until 1929. Since then, it has been nearly abandoned to numerous ethnic restaurants.

Parc Montsouris and the Cité Universitaire

●

Metro: Cité Universitaire   R.E.R.: Cité Universitaire

Map, East Paris (F 1)

The second Empire made the Parc Montsouris the green belt of south Paris. Today it has been completed by the complex of the Cité Universitaire whose 37 buildings are now spread around the 530,560 sq foot/40,000 sq metre park, where students from all over the world are lodged.

On the Montsouris hill, which had long been quarried and where windmills used to turn, **Haussmann** designed a park in 1868 in the style of an **English garden;** the very uneven site enabled the development of fine grass slopes. At the top of the park, one comes upon the unexpected reproduction of the **Bardo** (the Bey of Tunis' palace) made for the 1867 Universal Exhibition. On the east side of the park is a large lake fed by a waterfall, a very peaceful spot.

All around the park, numerous roads and housing developments commemorate the artists who used to work there: Rue de l'Aude, Rue Saint-Yves, and, at n° 11, the Cité du Souvenir seems to have escaped 20th-century Paris. Braque had his studio in the road which is named after him, not far from that of Douanier Rousseau. Ozenfant's studio, at n° 53 Av. Reille, was designed by Le Corbusier; opposite, a glass roof dating from the turn of the century conceals the **Montsouris reservoir.** In the 30s, André Lurçat built a beautiful series of mansions in the Villa Seurat and Rue Nansouty.

At n° 21 Bd Jourdan is the main entrance of the **Cité Internationale Universitaire de Paris,** inaugurated in 1925. At this time, the Cité consisted only of the E. and L. Deutsch-de-la-Meurthe Foundation, built in the Anglo-Saxon style. Dudok, a follower of Frank Lloyd Wright, then built the Netherlands College with the free lines of Art Deco. Le Corbusier added a manifesto of modern architecture in the Swiss Foundation and the Brazil House. The Iranian pavilion, with its enormous staircase, suspended floors and black steel girders, is a fine example of French architecture of the 60s.

There are also two complexes in a somewhat "Parisian" style: the bucolic **Villa Floréal** and the surprising workers' town of **Rue Daviel** (n° 10), containing 40 country houses in the heart of Paris.

Place de la Nation

**Map,
East
Paris
(D 4)**

Metro: Nation   Bus: n⁰ˢ 56, 86

The huge crossroads of the Place de la Nation, which even the largest public demonstrations do not manage to congest, firmly retains its place in Republican folklore.

▬ *HISTORY*

The square was originally called "Place du Trône-Renversé", literally, "Square of the Overturned Throne", and had a guillotine erected in it by the Convention. In July 1848, following the escape of Louis-Philippe, it was once again the scene of a monarch's fall. In 1880, during the celebrations of July 14th, the Third Republic gave it the more peaceful name of "Nation". In 1899, the monumental work by Dalou, the *Triumph of the Republic,* was erected in the middle of the square. It was originally intended for the Place de la République and thus appears rather large for its present site.

▬ *VISIT*

On each side of the Avenue du Trône rise two columns, bearing statues of St. Louis and Philippe Auguste. The two **toll houses designed by Ledoux** are among the last remaining in Paris. For over 1000 years, the Avenue du Trône was the location of a Gingerbread Fair which was transferred to the Bois de Vincennes in 1965.

The small **Picpus Cemetery** (*entrance — 35 Rue de Picpus. Open daily ex. Mon, 2 – 6 pm and until 4 pm from Oct–Apr*) – preserves the memory of some 1300 victims of the guillotine. The family of one of them, the Prince of Salm, bought the ground where the bodies had been thrown and made it into the cemetery of the old French nobility.

The Palais des Congrès

**Map,
West
Paris
(B 4)**

Metro: Porte-Maillot   Bus: n⁰ˢ 73, 82

In 1984, Paris claimed to be the city holding the largest number of international conferences, a fact made possible by the construction of a huge conference center at the end of the '70s by Gillet, Guibout and Maloletenkov.

From the outside, the building's most striking feature is the opposition of the center's horizontal lines to the vertical lines of the hotel tower which dominates it. Inside, two levels of shops and restaurants surround a large auditorium.

Paris during the age of iron and steel

In the 19th century, the massive works by Haussmann and the introduction of cast iron changed the face of Paris.

Cast-iron was used in the hothouses of the Jardin des Plantes (1833) and triumphed in Les Halles, designed by Baltard. However, Haussmann had to fight hard to prevent his architect from covering the cast-iron frame, thought to be undignified, too military, in short, too industrial. This attitude continued throughout the century.

This reticence was not shown in the covered **markets,** such as Saint-Quentin (85 Bd Magenta, 75010. Metro: Gare de l'Est); Saint-Martin (Rue Château-d'Eau, 75010. Metro: Château-d'Eau) and Secrétan (46, Rue de Meaux, 75010. Metro: Bolivar.)

Nor was it the case for the Industrial Center of the 1878 Exhibition, for the Eiffel Tower, or for the gallery of machinery by Contamin in 1889, whose dimensions are comparable to the Eiffel Tower (1,313 $\times$ 377 $\times$ 157 feet/400 $\times$ 115 $\times$ 48 metres high); these are utilitarian buildings, trading or temporary units. Boileau's pronouncement: "Hangars — this is the future for metal" was ardently followed by architects who strove to conceal the use of metal in all the buildings, particularly in **railway stations,** regarded as prestigious sites, representing the gateways of Paris. The cast-iron structure of the **Gare de l'Est** (1847) designed by Duquesnoy, with its trusses extending 985 feet/300 metres, is concealed behind a massive stone facade. In comparison, the **Gare du Nord,** designed by Hittorf, contains all types of neo-Greek columns and pillars which surround its huge, glass arcade, while the 17th-century facade of the **Gare Saint-Lazarre,** designed by Lisch, leaves no doubt about the use of the building. The struggle by architects to outdo engineers, and reintroduce cast iron, reached its height with the **Gare d'Orsay;** Laloux, around 1898-1900, overwhelmed the facades under the grandiosity of clock pavilions, sculpted pediments and enormous statues.

The **great department stores** also contributed to this tendency.

Brightness, luxury and fantasy were the criteria applied in three different styles. At Place de la République, Davioud began the **Magasins Réunis** in 1865. He was inspired by the Louvre for the forecourt and lateral pavilions, covering the facade with Classical style stonework but giving the store what he called "a commercial outlook" by very bright interior lighting. An identical style was used for the first **Bon Marché** by Boileau; however, in his extension in 1876, he did not use stone except for the supports of the facade — cast iron was no longer concealed. This is even more visible in the masterpiece of this style: **La Samaritaine*,** in Rue de la Monnaie (1905), in which Frantz Jourdain achieved total harmony between function and aesthetics, the simplicity of the elements of steel which carry the six stories of glass flooring balancing a facade made totally of glass. In contrast, **Le Printemps** designed by Sédille in 1882, uses stone in all styles, experimenting with shapes and effects, sphinxes and polychrome materials, and introducing some remarkable innovations, such as the hollow pillars which contain all the cables.

The same interaction of historical references is visible in the **grand hotels:** the *Louvre* (1855), the *Grand Hôtel* (1867) and the *Continental* (1878) which all resemble blocks of flats. For churches such as **Saint-Augustin,** Baltard borrowed a few features from all the "respectable" styles in order to compensate for the boldness of the surprising structure which supports the building. Among the different categories of buildings described here, the famous reading room of the **Bibliotheque Nationale** should be cited. In it, Labrouste created a prime example of the style, floating nine glass cupolas on thin, cast-iron columns, without any of it being visible on the outside. At the turn of the century, when reinforced concrete was about to appear, the use of steel was still shunned. It only gained acceptance in Paris by being masked as pseudo-Gothic, pseudo-Roman, pseudo-Renaissance and pseudo-Byzantine.

Rue de Paradis

Map 3,   Metro: Gare-de-l'Est, Poissonnière, Château-d'Eau   Bus: n° 32
(D 2-3)

The proximity of the Gare de l'Est, where porcelain arrives from Nancy, Lunéville and Strasbourg, has made this street the center of tableware. The International Tableware Center at n° 30 displays the products of the main manufacturers of porcelain and crystal. Ceramics not only adorn the shop windows but also the walls of buildings, some of which are among the more successful examples of Art Nouveau.

══ VISIT

Crystal Museum (Musée du Crystal; *30 bis Rue de Paradis. Open daily, ex. Sat, Sun and Public hols. 9 am – 5 pm; tel: 47 70 64 30).* Also known as the Baccarat Museum, this institution celebrates the dazzling virtuosity of French master glass-makers. For 150 years, the Baccarat establishment has worked for the greatest European families, from the Hapsburgs to the Romanov Czars, and has provided for the heads of State and embassies. Displayed here are a few of its most beautiful works. The other shop windows in the district are consequently somewhat overlooked.

The Museum of Advertising * (Musée de l'Affiche; *18 Rue de Paradis. Open daily ex. Tue, noon – 6 pm, tel: 42 46 13 09).* Since the 1970s, the interest in styles of art for posters and advertisements has increased markedly. In the former china and porcelain shop of Choisy-le-Roi, which has preserved beautiful ceramic panels in its courtyard and interior, some 70,000 exhibits of the museum are displayed on a rotating basis. Besides the posters, it has recently expanded to show television advertisements and audio-visual methods. Works by Toulouse-Lautrec, refined and flowing floral works by the masters of Art Nouveau, the new styles by Colin, Segonzac, Jacno and Morvan, right up to the posters which made walls "speak" in May 1968, are all allocated a place in this incomparable museum. There is also a library and video equipment for use by the public.

● Père-Lachaise cemetery

Map,   Metro: Père-Lachaise, Gambetta   Bus: n⁰ˢ 26, 61, 69, 76
East Paris
(C 3-4)   *Open 7.30 or 8.30 am – 5 or 6 pm, depending on the season.*

On the slopes adjoining the Buttes-Chaumont and Belleville, the 116 acres/47 hectares of Père-Lachaise cemetery offer one of the capital's finest walks. It is the world's most-visited cemetery, as remarkable for its illustrious residents as for its sumptuous foliage.

HISTORY

This site is named after **Louis XIV's confessor,** who embellished it and had various buildings erected on the site which was bought by the Jesuits in 1626. At the beginning of the 19th century, the city of Paris decided to convert the area into a cemetery, and the architect, **Brongniart,** organized the layout of the park with great flair.

The opening of the cemetery was promoted in a somewhat unique fashion; to popularize it, the supposed graves of the tragic lovers Héloïse and Abélard were transferred there, as well as the graves of Molière and La Fontaine, no doubt with a view to attracting future "customers".

VISIT

The Père Lachaise cemetery, where Balzac and Chopin, Delacroix and Sarah Bernhardt, Proust and Maurice Thorez, Colette and Jim Morrison are all buried, would fill a fashionable address book with the names of its residents. An incredible **museum of 19th-century French statuary** can be found here. In the extravagant monuments, lyricism competes with bombast. Sentimental poetry and solemn epitaphs carved in marble, make some graves unintentional masterpieces of the art of the pompous, while naked muses, goddesses of pagan charm and languorous widows suggest that many of the deceased wanted to take the memory of earthly affections and pleasures with them to eternity. **A chapel** at the very top of the main pathway commands a fine panorama over the south of Paris.

The Federates' wall (*Mur des Fédérés*), in the far corner of the cemetery beside Rue des Pyrénées, witnessed the last days of the Paris Commune when fighting took place among the graves. Finally cornered, the last Communards were shot against this wall on May 28th, 1871. Each year on May 1st, Trade Union processions still pay homage to these 147 fighters.

Paris' quays and bridges

On sunny days, the Seine, with its quays, perfect for walks, its barges and pleasure boats, its tramps sleeping under bridges and its preoccupied fishermen, is one of the most pleasant features of Paris. And so it should be. Not only was the river the *raison d'être*, but also the sustainer and provider of Paris. For two thousand years, the Seine brought grain, timber, wine and building materials to the city, sometimes inconveniencing it by floods and by facilitating Norman raids. There is no better way of viewing the splendor and diversity of Paris than a walk along its banks.

Austerlitz Viaduct, built in 1904 by J.C. Formigé, is reserved for the Metro; its 459-foot/140-metre arch holds the record as the longest span in Paris.

Pont d'Austerlitz, built in 1855 and enlarged around 1886, suffers from the worst traffic jams, after the Pont de la Concorde.

Quai Saint-Bernard, between the Ponts d'Austerlitz and Sully, has recently been developed into a promenade with games, lawns, terraces and an open-air sculpture museum.

Pont Sully, built in 1876, rests on the tip of the Ile Saint Louis, offering a fine view of Notre-Dame, the Cité and the Ile Saint-Louis.

Pont de la Tournelle is protected by a

statue of St Geneviève sculpted by Landowski. In 1928, it replaced a wooden bridge which had been destroyed several times by ice and floods. On the quay of the same name at n° 15, rises *La Tour d'Argent*, the restaurant which has been renowned for its cuisine since 1502. Henri IV is credited with having introduced the use of the fork in this restaurant. Notice the fine 17th-century mansions at n°s 27, 37, 47 (Museum of National Assistance) and n° 55.

Pont Marie was constructed by Christophe Marie, the property developer of the Ile Saint-Louis, starting in 1614. The houses which used to stand on it were destroyed in the 18th century.

Quai de Montebello was used during the Middle Ages as a warehouse for storing firewood and timber which was floated down the river. In the 17th century, an annexe of the Hôtel-Dieu was built there linked to the main building by the Pont-au-Double.

Pont d'Arcole, built in 1828, was renovated in 1888.

Le Petit-Pont. In Roman times, this was a wooden footbridge which extended the Orleans road. In 1185, Maurice de Sully built it in stone, but it often caught fire due to the combustible wooden housing adjoining it.

Pont Notre-Dame was the first bridge in Paris. Formerly lined with houses which were numbered in gold (the first attempt at street-numbering in Paris), the king would begin his state procession into Paris from this bridge which has been rebuilt several times, most recently in 1913.

Pont Saint-Michel was reconstructed in the 19th century. It offers beautiful views of the city and access to the **second-hand book-stalls,** venerable institutions of Paris' quays. Lovers of old bindings and first editions should not be too hopeful about making priceless discoveries here!

Pont-au-Change owes its name to the money-changers and gold- and silversmiths who set up their houses there in the 14th century. Parisian bird-catchers used to release thousands of birds on this bridge to greet the arrival of kings.

The Pont-Neuf*, despite its name meaning "new", is the oldest bridge in Paris. Its construction was begun in 1578 by Androuët du Cerceau and was completed in 1604. Merchants, entertainers and

tooth-pullers used to set up shop there. On the Right Bank, Henri IV and Sully had an enormous pump built, depicting the **Samaritan** giving Christ a drink; the name is echoed by the big department store nearby (*La Samaritaine*).

Quai des Grands-Augustins, the construction of which was started by Philippe le Bel in 1313, is the oldest quay in Paris. At first, a convent of the same name stood there, then it became a poultry market and finally the offices of the Paris omnibuses. Today it is a major book-center with numerous publishers and bookshops. Note the 17th-century mansions at n°s 51 and 35.

Pont des Arts*, offers a delightful view of the successive quays of the Seine, the Louvre, the Mint and the Institut. Napoleon, First Consul at the time, decided on its erection based on new techniques of metal construction. Completed in 1804, this was the first cast-iron bridge in Paris. Due to frequent damage by barges hitting its pylons and thus weakening its roadway, part of it was renovated by Visconti and Lefuel (1855, then 1872), before being completely reconstructed between 1982–84. The new Pont des Arts has only five arches, and steel was used in place of cast iron, but every detail has been reproduced including the decorations, street lamps and benches.

Pont-Royal, built around 1685 by Gabriel to Hardouin-Mansart's designs, is, without question, Paris' most beautiful bridge.

Pont Alexandre-III*: Czar Alexander II laid its first stone but it was not inaugurated until 1900 by his successor. It is a characteristic example of cast-iron art and of the *Belle Époque*, with its winged horses, twisted candelabras and pompous garlands. It has a superb view of Les Invalides.

Pont Iéna, enlarged in 1936, has preserved its eagles and equestrian statues celebrating Napoleon's victories.

Pont Mirabeau was constructed in 1895. Its fame seems to depend more on the immortal references of Apollinaire than to its own qualities:
"Sous le pont Mirabeau coule la Seine et nos amours.
Faut-il qu'il m'en souvienne
La joie venait toujours après la peine".
("Under the Pont Mirabeau flows the Seine, and our loves.
I must remember the joy always followed the pain".)

Rue Réaumur:
The age of iron and glass

Metro: Réaumur-Sébastopol   Bus: nᵒˢ 20, 39   **Map 3, (E-F, 1-3)**

The Third Republic executed the plans of the Second Empire; the Rue Réaumur was bulldozed between Rue Saint-Denis and Rue Notre-Dame-des-Victoires. This road, opened in 1897, was quickly taken over by wholesale cloth merchants, and a competition was organized for the design of its facades. Architects who took part combined the traditional stone with cast-iron and glass, creating a harmonious whole.

Note in particular **n° 118,** inspired by the precepts of Art Nouveau and **n° 122** dating from 1898. Attributed to Chedanne, perhaps incorrectly, the building at n° **124** (1903) achieved the ideal of a commercial building, at once dignified and modern, which, for the first time, gave iron an expressiveness through the simplicity of its structure, without using any of the usual decoration. Also note nᵒˢ 126, 130 (1898–99), 132 (1910), 69 (1895) and 61 (1896).

Near the establishment of the silk merchants Marion-Ladonne, 95 **Rue Montmartre** (built by S. Périssé in 1898) is one of the first Parisian examples of a facade made entirely of glass and decorated with glazed bricks. At n° 37 **Rue du Louvre,** the *Figaro* building adopted the "cruise liner" style which was in fashion in the '30s.

The Faubourg-Saint-Antoine

Metro: Bastille, Ledru-Rollin   Bus: nᵒˢ 45, 76, 86, 91   **Map 5, (C 5, D 6)**

Rue du Faubourg-Saint-Antoine, between Bastille and Nation, holds an important place in the social and political history of 19th-century Paris: heart of a working people's district, it was in the vanguard of all the century's uprisings.

Today, it remains the symbol of Paris before the industrial revolution, a Paris of artisans and small householders, fiercely individualistic, adhering to the libertarian ideas of Proudhon and Blanqui. Today it is a stronghold of the socialist party.

▄▄▄ *HISTORY*

The Faubourg-Saint-Antoine was built around the ancient royal abbey of Saint-Antoine, founded in 1198 for the salvation of "repentant girls". Louis XV granted the Faubourg's artisans a considerable privilege, excluding them from the authority of the guilds. Free to use new materials and to invent styles and motifs, the Faubourg's joiners and cabinet-makers became increasingly successful. They were the first to use mahogany and ebony, bronze ornaments and marquetry, and became the appointed suppliers for the king and the court.

Some of these craftsmen succeeded even before the industrial revolution. Réveillon, the pioneer of wallpaper, had up to 400 employees working in his workshops at 31 Rue de Montreuil. His technique of paper-joining enabled Pilâtre de Rozier to make the first ascent in a paper balloon in the courtyard of the workshop on October 19th, 1783.

Today, working conditions have greatly changed, but the traditions of the Faubourg remain much the same. Furniture-makers of all styles prosper, and the last of the great cabinet-makers still survive.

The Quinze-Vingts Hospital (off n° 50, Passage de La Boûle-Blanche) which was built by St Louis for 300 blind people, is worth noting; barracks constructed by Robert de Cotte (17th century) also deserve notice. Other places of interest here are the Trogneux fountain (1710), a row of picturesque alleys, the Marché Aligre and the second-hand dealers.

•• The Saint-Denis Basilica

Metro: Saint-Denis-Basilique; S.N.C.F: all Paris-Nord lines, ex. Crépy-en-Valois Bus: n°s 156, 177

The town of Saint-Denis has all the characteristics of a Paris suburb – factories, high-rise apartments and subsidized housing – but the old center is the Gérard-Philipe theater which creates great local excitement during the Summer Music Festival. More importantly, Saint-Denis is not just another suburban town; it is the necropolis of the kings of France, with a notable Gothic church.

▬▬ HISTORY

We owe the Saint-Denis Basilica, built in the 12th century, to Abbot Suger. Legend has it that St Denis, who was beheaded on the Butte Montmartre, chose this spot for his burial "carrying his own head in his hands". From the 6th century, French kings, beginning with Dagobert, had chosen Saint-Denis for their interment. King Dagobert was also a benefactor of the abbey founded by St Geneviève. With the exception of Hugues Capet, all the kings of France were buried here for over a thousand years. The Basilica was sacked during the Revolution, although some of the most precious tombs were saved.

▬▬ VISIT

The construction of the huge Gothic nave was executed under Suger between 1135–1145 and partly reconstructed by Pierre de Montreuil in the 13th century. It inspired all the 12th- and 13th-century architects who were building cathedrals. Note, in particular, the beautiful **south portal** on which one can still make out the theme of the Last Judgement (1259), the **narthex** where Suger raised the first pointed arches, the high nave, the immense transept (13th century) and the **Romanesque crypt** (12th century). Along the sides are the impressive series of **royal tombs**** which forms a remarkable panorama of French sculpture from the Merovingian era to the Renaissance: Dagobert's monumental tomb erected in the 13th century and restored by Viollet-le-Duc, those of Henri II and Catherine de Médicis by Germain Pilon, the recumbent statues of Charles Martel and Pépin le Bref, and monuments by Philibert Delorme.

• Saint-Martin Canal

Map 3, (B-C 5) Metro: République, Jaurès Bus: n°s 46, 75

Visit: La Patache, "Eautobus" with about 20 seats, offers a half-day cruise on the Seine and Saint-Martin Canal. Departure: 9 am, Quai Anatole-France, in front of the Deligny swimming pool carpark, and 2 pm, Quai de la Loire, in front of the coffee shop 'Les Palmiers'. Daily ex. Mon and some public hols, April – Oct. Reservations only — tel: 48 74 75 30.

The basins which link the Ourcq canal to the Seine provide an unexpected scene in the capital: the iron footbridges, hotels, barge-workers' coffee-shops, workshops and warehouses on the northern side, come straight out of 19th-century industrial Paris. More than 4000 barges use this 2.8 mi./4.5 km waterway (divided by nine locks) each year. Notice the beautiful **Pont de la Rue de Crimée,** worked by a hydraulic system on Place Stalingrad; the **Villette Rotunda,** one of the pavilions constructed by Ledoux for the Paris toll; and the Louis XIII-style buildings of the big Saint-Louis Hospital, situated behind the Quai de Jemmapes. On the footbridge which crosses high above the canal near the small Square des Récollets and Rue de Lancry, the actress Arletty uttered the famous words "Atmosphere, atmosphere", in Marcel Carné's film *Hôtel du Nord.* This same hotel, which is nearby, is soon to be restored.

Rue de Sèvres

Metro: Sèvres-Babylone, Duroc, Rennes   Bus: n°ˢ 39, 70, 87   **Map 4, (D-E, 3-4)**

This quiet residential district has become one of the centers of Parisian fashion: women's shoes and boots of the highest quality are to be found around the Croix-Rouge intersection and at the top of Rue des Saints-Pères.

▬▬ VISIT

Rue de Sèvres, now lined with shops as far as Rue Vaneau, crosses what was, for a long time, the exclusive domain of religious orders. The beautiful **Hôtel Choiseul-Praslin*** (1732) is set back opposite the **Fellah Fountain** (1806), an example of Egyptian style at the beginning of the 19th century; Saint Vincent-de-Paul's Chapel at n° 95 contains the shrine displaying the body of the philanthropic chaplain Monsieur Vincent (1585-1660), founder of the "Enfants Trouvés" (orphanage). Not far away, at n° 140 Rue du Bac, is the chapel of the Sisters of Saint-Vincent-de-Paul, which is still a place of pilgrimage. The **Laennec Hospital** (1878) replaced the Hospital for Incurables. However, today it is the *Bon Marché* department store which dominates the street and represents the main attraction. On the site of what had once been a leper-house, a shrewd shop manager bought a small novelty shop in 1852. Twenty years later, he was the head of the first department store in Paris. The present buildings were constructed in 1873, and Eiffel and Moisant designed the metal structure.

The Sèvres-Raspail intersection, at the end of Rue de Sèvres, is dominated by the grand *Hôtel Lutetia*. To the left by Rue de Sèvres, Rue Récamier leads to the **Récamier Theater,** a characteristic work by

the pioneers of reinforced concrete, Blondel and Hennebicque (1908). Near the Croix-Rouge intersection, the street becomes more youthful and lively, abounding in fashion, linen and fancy goods shops. Also nearby, at n° 21 Rue du Vieux-Colombier, French theater became widely recognized when, in 1913, Jacques Copeau with the help of Louis Jouvet, L.P. Fargue, G. Gallimard and R. Martin du Gard, founded the Vieux Colombier company.

Via Rue Cassette and Rue de Vaugirard, one comes to the Catholic Institute which incorporates the former Carmelite Convent. **Saint Joseph's Church** marks the appearance, in 1620, of the Jesuit style in Paris; note the Louis XIII decoration in the chapels, as well as the beautiful Virgin by Bernini.

Also worth seeing ...

The handsome 18th-century mansions in Rue du Cherche-Midi, and The Hébert Museum, 85 Rue du Cherche-Midi *(open daily ex. Tue and Public hols. 2 – 6 pm, tel: 42 22 23 82).* The Montmorency-Bours mansion (1743) has one of the least-known museums in Paris. In its refined rooms, among the portraits of noblewomen and the delicate watercolors, are the works of Antoine Hébert, a painter of the end of the 19th century.

Villages in the 16th arrondissement

**Map 1,
(E-F,
1-2-3)** Passy, La Muette, Ranelagh and Avenue Foch are names suggestive of solid wealth and elegance. Their other striking quality is that they still retain the semi-rural charm of the old villages on the outskirts of Paris.

▬ VISIT

Passy *(Metro: Trocadéro, Passy)*. This was only a poor village of woodcutters when iron-rich spring waters, discovered there in the 18th century, made it a wealthy place. However, it was not the water which made Rues Vineuse and des Vignes famous, but the wine which the local friars used to produce, now remembered in the **Wine Museum.** *(Entrance: n° 5 Rue des Eaux. Open daily 2 – 6 pm. Wine-tasting sessions).* At n° 8 Rue Franklin, the **Clemenceau Museum** is housed in the "Tiger's" apartment. *(Open daily, ex. Mon, Wed, Fri, 2 – 5 pm.)*

La Muette and the Ranelagh gardens *(Metro: La Muette)* The vast domain of French kings has been replaced by Rue de Passy's shops, a lively market and the "Petite Ceinture" railway, charmingly anti-quated with its provincial station, and beautiful homes in private mews (Avenues Vion-Whitcomb, O.-Cruz, des Chalets).

The Balzac-Museum — *(entrance: 47 Rue Raynouard. Open daily ex. Mon and Tue, 10 am – 5.30 pm)* — has been set up in the charming country house in which Balzac lived between 1840-47.

●● Château and Bois de Vincennes

**Map,
East
Paris
(E-F,
5-6)** Metro: Château-de-Vincennes   Bus: n°ˢ 46, 56, 86

The Vincennes Château, bordering the wood of the same name, is a towering Valois keep beside majestic classical buildings; these were the forerunners of Versailles.

The Château de Vincennes was built by the Valois family, from Philippe VI to Charles V. The feudal site, completed in 1370, was extended by Mazarin according to plans by Le Vau; the pavilions of the King and Queen face each other across the large main courtyard. King Louis XIV spent his first months of married life (1660) in this splendid residence. Shortly afterwards, the King put Superintendent Fouquet under house-arrest here, guarded by d'Artagnan.

For a century, the château was used as a **prison,** before Bonaparte assigned it to the army in 1804. Extensive restoration has finally removed all the damage caused by 150 years of military occupation, returning it to its original beauty.

▬ VISIT

The Château is in the form of a huge rectangle, enclosed by a high wall and a wide moat. The ramparts used to include nine towers which have now been leveled. **Inside the ramparts***(open daily ex. public hols).* There are two distinct sections: one mediaeval and the other 17th-century, exemplifying the skill of Classical artists.

The Royal Chapel was constructed under Charles V and completed by Phi-

libert Delorme. Its flamboyant facade, narrow nave, very elegantly decorated consoles and the frieze at the foot of its windows, make it a very beautiful Gothic building. However, the stained-glass win-dows of the choir reveal a style already marked by the Renaissance.

The Keep (Donjon) is defended by fortified ramparts and the drawbridge by a barbican: it has four floors, each divided into a main chamber with vaulting that rests on a central pillar and four small rooms in the turrets, which were used as prison cells. This palace-fortress serves as a museum retracing its own history.

The north portico, enclosing the main courtyard, opens onto the **royal pavilions** which form a Classical ensemble. Mazarin died in the King's Pavilion in 1661.

Bois de Vincennes
The Royal Forest of Vincennes was laid out under the **Second Empire** by Alphand and Barillet-Deschamps. Excluding the artillery area and the drill ground, the two architects were given complete freedom to make it into an **English-style park,** by including many different points of interest.

Zoological garden *(Metro: Porte-Dorée, Av. Daumesnil. Open daily 9 am – 5.30 pm).* The Vincennes Zoo, the largest in France, covers 35 acres/14 hectares and has about

600 mammals and 700 birds.

Lac Daumesnil, with its two islands, is very popular with Parisians for outings on sunny days. *(Rowing boats and bicycles for hire.)* To the south of the lake, the **Buddhist Temple** of Paris *(Open daily ex. Tue, Wed and Fri, 9 am – noon and 2 – 4 pm)* is housed in one of the four pavilions constructed for the Colonial Exhibition of 1931. 18,000 tiles made from chestnut wood shelter a gilded Buddha, 29 feet/9 metres tall.

The Indochinese Memorial Temple is situated on the east side of the Lac des Minimes, behind a Chinese pavilion from the 1906 Colonial Exhibition of Marseilles.

The Paris Flower Garden (Parc Floral), near the Château *(entrance: Route de la Pyramide. Open daily 9.30 am – 5.30 pm).* This garden, covering an area of 70 acres/ 28 hectares, offers a variety of gardens and pavilions containing different flowers.

Parc de la Villette

●●

Metro: Porte de Pantin

Map, East Paris (A-3)

La Villette is a French showpiece of the latest technology. This vast 136 acre/55 hectare park, beside the Ourcq and Saint-Denis canals, was once the site of slaughterhouses; it proposes to give the French an understanding of the latest developments in modern technology. The architects Adrien Fainsilber (museum), Bernard Tschumi (garden), Bernard Reichen and Philippe Robert (the Grande Halle) have together created a real town-within-a-town.

VISIT

Opened in January 1985, the Grande Halle is now used for exhibitions, conferences and shows. It is an example of cast-iron techniques, enormous in size and flooded with light. It was built in 1867 by Mérindol, covering an area of 5 acres/2 hectares and can accommodate 16,000 people.

The Géode is an enormous sphere of polished steel, 119 feet/36 metres high. It is possibly the most striking aspect of the park which is constantly reflected in its mirrored walls. It is also a total cinema auditorium, which plunges its 380 viewers into a gigantic image, projected onto a semi-circular screen measuring 10,562 sq ft/1,000 sq metres *(Open Tue, Thur, Sun 11 am – 6.30 pm, Wed, Fri, Sat, 11 am – 11.30 pm. Closed Mon.)*

The City of Science and Industry opened its doors in the Spring of 1986. Covering an area of 322,920 sq feet/

30,000 sq metres, it combines the exhibition techniques from the Palais de la Découverte and the collections from the Conservatory of Arts and Crafts. It is hoped that visitors will be inspired to change from simple observers into discoverers and active technicians. It will provide a paradise for children and the opportunity for adults to at last understand "How it works", or to delve into the fantastic media library of 20,000 audiovisual aids and 250,000 books.

The City of Music, which should open in 1988, will contain the National Conservatory, a concert hall devoted to contemporary music and a Museum of Instruments. For the moment, the gardens which wind around the Grande Halle, museum, and Géode, the pavilions designed by Bernard Tschumi, and the huge Zenith concert hall are sufficiently enticing to visitors.

THE PALACE OF VERSAILLES

●●●

For most visitors, the name "Versailles" evokes the epic historical events which have taken place within the walls of this great palace: the glorious reign of Louis XIV, the tragic destiny of Marie-Antoinette, Benjamin Franklin's visits, the first flight of a Montgolfière in the presence of the King of Sweden, Gustave III, the proclamation of the German Empire in the Hall of Mirrors and the 1919 peace treaty. More recently, the palace has been the setting for receptions given in honor of Queen Elizabeth and President Reagan. As soon as Louis XIV transferred his court and government to Versailles in 1682, the palace immediately became a magnet for foreign heads of state and other curious spectators anxious to visit and emulate the magnificent edifice. The brilliant reign of the House of Bourbon and the courtly etiquette which prevailed under Louis XIV should not obscure the fact that Versailles was, in its day, the greatest political and cultural center in Europe.

HISTORY

Versailles-au-Val-de-Galie was nothing more than a tiny hamlet amid woods and lakes when **Louis XIII** chose the setting for his hunting lodge, "to avoid sleeping out in the cold any longer", according to Saint-Simon. By 1651, as reported by the gazettes of the time, the young Louis XIV was already hunting in the area. After Cardinal Mazarin's death in 1661, the king, free at last to do as he wished, longed for a residence which would outshine the splendor of Fouquet's château at Vaux-le-Vicomte. For the young monarch accompanied by his mistress, Mademoiselle de Vallière, and the Court, Versailles became the setting for country outings, hunting parties and receptions. Initially, the King contented himself with improving his father's lodge and the park surrounding it, which he had enlarged by Le Nôtre, "designer and landscape artist of all the royal gardens".

Colbert and Le Brun organized academies to enable different craftsmen to work closely together and to train younger artists. Orders were placed with factories to embellish the royal quarters. As building superintendent, **Colbert** was in charge of studying architectural projects, presenting them to the King, ordering materials and supervising the construction work. Designs for sculptures, furniture, tapestries and paintings were submitted to **Le Brun,** who was responsible for the interior decoration of the palace. After each peace treaty signed at Versailles, the palace received a new addition. With the Treaty of Aix-la-Chapelle, **Le Vau** began work on the King's apartments (*Grands Appartements*) in the north wing and the Queen's apartments in the south wing. The Hall of Mirrors, designed by **Mansart,** was built to celebrate the Treaty of Nijunwegen. The Treaty of Ryswick gave Louis XIV the opportunity to add the finishing touch to his dream: the chapel.

In 1715, when the King died, Louis XV, his great-grandson, deserted the palace. The Regent, as well as the Court, much preferred the atmosphere of the Parisian salons to the rather stiff etiquette which regulated life at Versailles. In 1722, just before his coronation at Rheims, the King once again took up residence at Versailles. Out of respect for Louis XIV, very little was altered. New rooms, known as the *"Petits appartements"*, were fitted out for the King, overlooking an inside

View of the ornamental lake designed by Le Nôtre.

courtyard, *La Cour des Cerfs* (the Deer Court). In 1738, the architect **Gabriel** was contracted to install another private apartment, **Les Cabinets Intérieurs du Roi** (the King's Inner Chambers), farther away from the official reception rooms.

Criticized by his contemporaries for "neglecting to make any major additions to Versailles", Louis XV undertook the construction of the **Opéra** and planned to modernize the palace. In 1774, **Louis XVI** came to the throne, and, for his own part, was content to maintain the existing premises. Marie-Antoinette, however, cherished more elaborate plans. She had her private chambers and the **Salon des Nobles** entirely refurbished and fitted out several smaller, more intimate rooms.

On October 6th, 1789, Louis XVI and Marie-Antoinette appeared on the balcony of the King's chambers to face the angry crowd of Parisians who had come to take the royal couple back to the capital. Upon leaving, Louis XVI solemnly confided to the Minister of War, La Tour du Pin: "You are now in charge here. Try and save my beloved Versailles." He was never to see the palace again.

The Revolution

On June 10th, 1793, the Convention passed a law allowing the sale of the royal family's furniture and personal belongings. It took from August 25th, 1793, to August 11th, 1794 to auction off the 17,082 lots from the Palace of Versailles. The bids were paid for with *assignats* (bank notes issued during the Revolution, the value of which was assigned to property owned by the nation). The crowd of buyers was composed of those nobles who had not fled France, art dealers, former suppliers to the royal family, and people who had come out of curiosity. Many of the pieces left the country but have since been returned to France by collectors or repurchased by the State.

Under **Louis-Philippe**, the **Museum of French History** was installed to spark new life into the palace. The collection included paintings, sculptures and miscellaneous pieces displayed in chronological order from the time of the Crusades until 1848. To complete the museum, Louis-Philippe had the famous Gallery of Battles designed. The architect Nepveu completely refurbished many of the interiors but drawings of the original décor later enabled craftsmen to restore the apartments of the Dauphin and the Dauphine, Louis XV's daughter.

▬ *VISIT*

The exterior of the palace

The three large avenues leading to the palace from Saint-Cloud, Paris and Sceaux, come together at the **Place d'Armes.** Before reaching this impressive esplanade, the avenues are separated from one another by the **Royal stables**, built by Hardouin-Mansart. The "Great Stables" on the northern side were reserved for saddle horses, whereas the "Small Stables' on the southern side housed the plow horses and coach horses.

The **palace gates** open onto the **Ministers' Courtyard**, named after Louis XIV's ministers who occupied the two wings of the château on each side of it. Farther in, is the **statue of Louis XIV**, which Louis-Philippe had sculpted by Cartellier, and a second gate which marked off

the entrance to another courtyard, known as the **Royal Courtyard**. The privileged few who had access to this area were said to have "the honors of the Louvre". To the right stands the wing added by Gabriel when the château was renovated in 1772. On the left stands the Dufour Pavilion, named after its 19th-century architect. The gilded gates on each side open onto stairways leading to the royal apartments. On the northern side, the **"Ambassadors' Stairway"** (destroyed during the 18th century) led to the King's Chambers. The Queen's Stairway stands on the southern side. At the far end of the courtyard, lined by the buildings which belonged to the original château erected by Louis XIII, you will find the **Marble**

Courtyard, so named because of its black and white marble surface.

The northern and southern arcades both give direct access to the park. The **magnificent facade***** of the palace is best seen from a certain distance down the gardens. From this angle, it completely dwarfs the buildings surrounding the Marble Courtyard. With its imposing size, the facade proudly testifies to the glory of the 17th century. At the time of the palace's construction, however, the cost of such a gigantic undertaking was harshly criticized by Colbert, the Minister of Finance under Louis XIV. The foundations underlying the two lateral wings had to be entirely leveled to compensate for the sloping terrain. Perhaps the most ingenious piece of engineering at Versailles is the manner in which the horizontal plane of the facade was given depth by the colonnade of the protruding central portion. The flat roof, concealed behind a railing decorated with vases and trophies, was inspired by the Italian school of architecture.

Inside the palace

The chapel** was the last of its kind to be built inside a palace in France. Its construction was begun in 1683 but was interrupted by war. As architectural tastes changed during the interval, the king, Mansart and Robert de Cotte chose to complete the chapel in freestone rather than in marble. When it officially received the Church's blessing, the king "carefully examined it from top to bottom". The central body of the nave shows the *Holy Father* (Coypel). Above the altar is the *Resurrection of Christ* by de la Fosse. Above the gallery where the king sat during daily mass, is Jouvenet's Pentecost.

The **Hercules Salon** is the first reception room after the main entrance. Installed in 1712, it owes its name to the huge ceiling fresco painted by Lemoyne, which depicts Hercules being received among the gods. The ceiling harmonizes with Veronese's *Supper With Simon*, which was presented to Louis XIV by the Republic of Venice.

The Grand Apartments***

The Grand Apartments, the Chapel and the Hall of Mirrors accurately reveal the sumptuous lifestyle of the court from 1680 to 1700. The impressive decor has been

---

Visit to Versailles

R.E.R. (commuter train): Versailles Rive-Gauche (Left Bank) Station.
S.N.C.F: from Montparnasse or Saint-Lazare Stations.
Bus: n° 171 (Pont de Sèvres).
Parking: Place d'Armes, in front of the palace. Pay parking is available all over Versailles.
Visit: Information tel: 39 50 58 32 Wheelchairs are available for the handicapped. Animals, food and back-packs are prohibited. Closed on Mondays and Public holidays.
● **Palace**: open 9.45 am – 5.30 pm (admission until 5 pm). Reduced rates for 18 to 25 year-olds, over 60 year-olds, and on Sundays. Free admission for under 18 year-olds.
● **Grand Trianon**: open 2 – 5 pm. Closed on Saturdays and Sundays.
● **Petit Trianon**: open 2 – 5 pm. Closed on Saturdays and Sundays.
Unaccompanied visits: Entrance C (groups are admitted until 1.30 pm on Sundays). Chapel, Grand Apartments, Hall of Mirrors, the Queen's Apartments, Apartments of the Dauphin and the Dauphine, Apartments of Louis XV's daugh-

ters, the History of France Museum, 17th-century rooms (may be subject to certain restrictions), the Grand Trianon, the Petit Trianon.
Guided tours: Entrance A at the Queen's Staircase. The commentary is given in French or in English by National Museum guides. Groups of 30. Extensive tours on Saturdays at 2.30 pm from October to July. Tours are held every day at noon.
● **Palace**: King's Apartments and the Opéra from 9.45 am to 3.30 pm (last departure) from Tuesday to Friday. Entrance B. Apartments of Madame de Pompadour and Madame du Barry at 2 pm. The Queen's Inner Chambers and the Dauphine's Inner Chambers at 3.30 pm.
● **Gardens**: Open from sunrise to sunset. The fountains are turned on from May to September on the 1st, 3rd and 4th Sundays of each month. *Son et Lumière* shows in the summer. Tel 39 50 36 52.
Mass is held in the Chapel on the first Sunday of each month. Oct — March, noon, Apr — Sept, 5.30 pm.

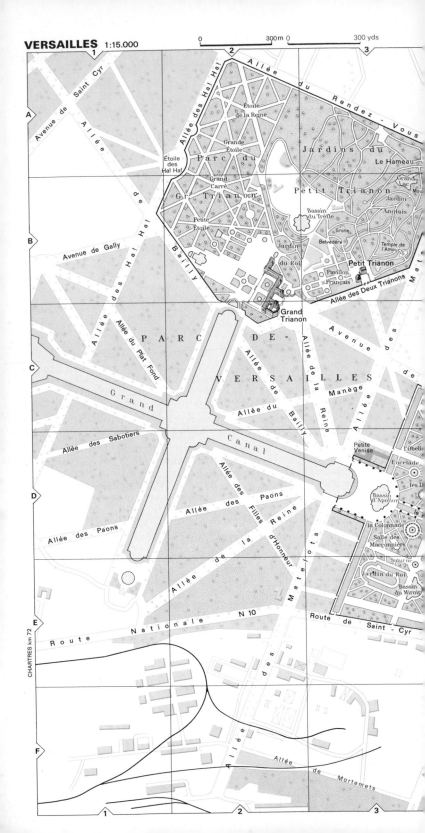

meticulously restored and testifies to the overwhelming pomp of Louis XIV's reign. The King's Stairway originally led to the Grand Apartments. Today, visitors enter through the Hercules Salon. The different salons comprising the Grand Apartments become more and more sumptuous as they near the Throne Room. Filled with a profusion of silver furniture, marble, frescos and richly-colored brocades, the ceilings were all painted on the theme of Apollo the Sun God, symbolizing the King, and the planets which gravitate around him. From 1682 on, the rooms were open only to special guests and to the court three times a week, from November to Easter. On these days, known as "Apartment Days", the King entertained his courtiers from 6 to 10 pm.

On the ceiling of the **Hall of Abundance**, the figure of Magnificence is shown drawing strength from Abundance. On "Apartment Days", hot and cold drinks, wines and sherbets were served in this room.

The fresco in the **Venus Salon** (painted by Houasse) celebrates the Triumph of Venus. Here, the courtiers could enjoy "raw fruit, lemons, oranges, fruit jellies and jams".

The Diana Salon. Here, the goddess presides over hunting and navigation. The salon was used as a billiard room.

The Mars Salon (painted by Audran). The war god's chariot is drawn by wolves. Originally designed as a guardroom, this salon was used as a ballroom, game-room and concert hall.

The Mercury Salon (painted by J-B. Champaigne). Here, the god's chariot is harnessed to roosters. After 1682, the room was used as a games-room and a ceremonial chamber for Louis XIV.

The Salon of Apollo (painted by Lafosse). The chariot is drawn by four horses, and beside the Sun God stand the four seasons. It was here that the King granted formal audiences to foreign ambassadors. The room also served as a ballroom.

The Hall of Mirrors opens onto the **Peace Salon** on one side and to its counterpart, the **War Salon*** on the opposite side. The latter was designed by Hardouin-Mansart to celebrate the military exploits of Louis XIV. The ceiling is decorated with an allegory of France and Le Brun's portrait of the Sun King. The bas-reliefs on the chimney were sculpted by Coysevox.

The Hall of Mirrors*** is 246 feet/75 metres long and 33 feet/10 metres wide. Mansart designed it in 1678 but the work was not completed until 1686. The originality of the room is the manner in which the light from 17 large windows on one side of the hall reflects off 17 mirrors, on the opposite wall. The ceiling was painted by Le Brun to celebrate the military exploits of Louis XIV's reign, especially the war against Holland. The hall was one of the busiest rooms in the palace. The courtiers used it as a meeting place, and commoners were admitted to watch the King on his way to Mass. On exceptional occasions, Louis XIV received ambassadors in the hall. For official receptions, the Hall of Mirrors was transformed into a fairyland of glittering jewels and gowns which sparkled in the light of thousands of candles. On such occasions, the monarchy must indeed have appeared to be blessed with divine powers.

The Peace Salon leads to the **Queen's Grand Apartments****. The Queen's bedroom, which has been magnificently restored, served as the master bedroom for the royal couple. In these chambers, where all the royal children of France were born in public, the Queen went through the daily ritual of rising and retiring for the night. The **Salon of Nobles** and the antechamber have been restored in the style prevailing just before the Revolution. In the antechamber, visitors should pay special attention to the admirable portrait of Marie-Antoinette and her children by Madame Vigée-Lebrun.

The King's Apartments. The Queen's Staircase leads to the King's Chambers on the first floor of the château built by Louis XIII. The suite includes a guardroom and two antechambers. The second antechamber, known as the "Bull's-eye" (*Oeil-de-Boeuf*), is decorated with a colorful frieze depicting children at play.

In 1701, Louis XIV had the famous **King's Bedroom** built at the very heart of the château. He was to die in this room on September 1st, 1715. Only certain privileged courtiers were admitted to assist the King in his daily ritual of dressing and undressing. The bust of Louis XIV on the mantel was sculpted by Coysevox. **The Council Chamber** is the last room in the apartment. The rocaille wood-work was added by Louis XV, while the silk hangings are perfect copies of the originals and were woven in the silk factories of Lyons.

The King's Inner Chambers, designed

by Gabriel for Louis XV, include the bedroom fitted out in 1738, to replace Louis XIV's bedroom, which the new monarch found much too cold. Louis XV's inner chambers are sumptuously furnished. In Madame Adélaïde's chambers, superbly decorated with Louis XV woodwork, a small boy of seven named Wolfgang-Amadeus Mozart once played the harpsichord for the King and his daughters. The room contains an exceptional cabinet which Louis XVI had designed for his gold dishes.

The King's Library*** is one of the most beautiful rooms designed by Gabriel. Some of the furnishings which were missing have only recently been restored to their proper place. The last room of the Inner Chambers is the **Porcelain Dining-room.**

The Royal Opera**, designed by Gabriel, was completed in 1770, the year Louis XVI married Marie-Antoinette. The construction, which was entirely in wood to give the Opera exceptionally good acoustics, has been entirely restored according to the original plans. The King's private box was closed off behind gilt railings. The ceiling fresco depicts Apollo crowning the artists. The bas-reliefs and sculptures at the back came from the Pajou workshop.

The Queen's Inner Chambers** lie behind the Grand Apartments. Although these rooms were originally used by Marie Leczinska, they were subsequently fitted out for Marie-Antoinette by Mique and the Rousseau brothers. The Queen used these chambers to receive her dressmaker and hairdresser and as a private music room.

The King's Small Apartments include a series of rooms which both Louis XV and Louis XVI used to escape the courtly protocol which prevailed elsewhere in the palace, as well as in the apartments of Madame de Pompadour, Madame du Barry, the Inner Chambers of the Queen, the Dauphin and the Dauphine, Louis XV's daughter.

The Grand Trianon**
This elegantly-designed château, built by **Mansart** in 1687, includes two separate wings joined by a colonnade. After the Revolution, the palace was deserted until Napoleon finally had it refurbished. Parts of the building were later renovated by Louis-Philippe. It is now decorated with Empire and Restoration period furniture. The apartments of Louis XIV were situated

in the left wing, while the right wing was successively used by Louis XIV and Madame de Maintenon, Louis XV and Madame de Pompadour, Louis XVI and Marie-Antoinette and, finally by Napoleon.

The Small Trianon* was built by **Gabriel** for Louis XV, at Madame de Pompadour's request. Both **Madame du Barry** and **Marie-Antoinette** after her, took a special liking to this rather austere residence with its beautiful facade overlooking the park. The apartments are richly furnished with 18th-century period pieces. The **English garden** to the north and east of the Petit Trianon offers a surprisingly pleasant relief from the tidy, geometrical French-style gardens elsewhere. With its ruins, the Temple of Love standing in the middle of an island, and sheep grazing peacefully in Marie-Antoinette's rustic **hamlet**, the garden earned the praise of J.-J. Rousseau and his contemporaries.

The parks and gardens of Versailles***
Today, the grounds only cover 2013 acres/815 hectares. At the time of Louis XVI, the estate included the gardens directly surrounding the palace, a secondary park of 4200 acres/1700 hectares encompassing the Swiss Pool, the zoo, the Grand Canal, the Trianons, and the main park covering 14,820 acres/6000 hectares. The 26-mile/43 km long wall which originally closed off the park was destroyed during the Revolution.

The **palace gardens**, and especially the area leading from the western facade, superbly display the art of **French landscaping** at its best. As is characteristic of this style, everything is laid out with architectural accuracy to give an overall impression of order and harmony. The original gardens planted for Louis XIII had already been designed in the same orderly manner.

As if he had foreseen the grandiose plans that Louis XIV harbored for Versailles, Le Nôtre first designed the gardens along two main axes running from east to west and north to south. All subsequent alterations to the gardens were to follow this original layout. Two ornamental pools surrounded by statues of nymphs and figures representing the rivers of France lie in front of the central body of the palace. At the foot of the stairs, from which one can see the whole park, the round pool is dedicated to **Latona**, mother of Apollo and Diana. (According to the legend, the peasants of

Lycia provoked Jupiter's anger by refusing to protect Latona, and were turned into frogs and toads). The westward axis carries on through the *Tapis Vert* (Green Carpet) until it reaches the pool of Apollo's Chariot (designed by Tuby) and the **Grand Canal** which sits at the bottom of a slope and serves as a collecting basin for run-off water. The north-south axis which crosses the canal, led to the zoo on one side (destroyed during the Revolution) and to the Grand Trianon on the other. Under the *Ancien Régime*, a flotilla of gondolas would carry the courtiers up and down the canal, or serve as a platform for musicians during open-air concerts.

From both sides of the Tapis Vert, sandy paths run through **groves of trees**. On the south side, they lead to the ballroom grove with its sloping, circular tiers which used to surround a marble dance floor, or to the elegant Colonnade. On the north side, the paths lead to the Obelisk Pool and the Pool of Enceladus with its statue of the giant buried beneath the rocks.

The northern gardens are remarkable for the **Pyramid Fountain** with its tritons and Girardon's masterful sculpture personifying **Winter**. A walkway lined with statues of children, the **Marmousets**, leads to the Dragon Pool and the **Fountain of Neptune**. The statue of Neptune with Amphitrite at his side, which Louis XV had sculpted by Sigisbert Adams, was unanimously acclaimed at the time as "creating one of the most beautiful effects one could imagine". This part of the garden is still used today for parties at night.

The landscaping of Versailles was a gigantic undertaking, but perhaps the amazing engineering feat in the creation of this magnificent park was the installation of the hydraulics system. A pump was originally installed in Clagny to drain water from reservoirs set up in the surrounding hills. When this system proved to be insufficient, Remequin Sualem, a carpenter from Liège, was brought in. With his invention, the Marly Machine: (a 14-wheel pump driven by the water of the Seine), the water was raised to the level of the 530-foot/153-metre high aqueduct which supplied Versailles.

A few statistics on Versailles

Length of the garden facade (including corners of the protruding central portion): 2198 feet/670 metres.

Hall of Mirrors: 239 feet/73 metres long, 33 feet/10 metres wide, 42 feet/13 metres high.

Surface area of the roof: 27 acres/11 hectares.

Length of the facade of the Grand Trianon: 393 feet/120 metres.

Surface area of the palace gardens: 235 acres/95 hectares.

Grand canal: 5413 feet by 203 feet/ 1650 metres by 62 metres. Circumference 3.5 mi./5.6 km. Surface area: 59 acres/24 hectares.

Main hunting park: 13,832 acres/ 5600 hectares, with 26 mi./43 km of wall.

Entire domain belonging to the palace: 20,995 acres/8500 hectares.

— 1300 rooms during the Ancien Régime (500 today).

— 1250 chimneys.

— 67 staircases.

— 2140 windows.

— 3000 orange trees housed in the Orangerie.

The stables could accommodate 2500 horses and 200 coaches. All of the three avenues leading to the Courtyard of Honor are wider than the Champs-Élysées 216 feet/66 metres. Avenue de Paris: 400 feet/ 122 metres. Avenue de Saint-Cloud: 312 feet/95 metres. Avenue de Sceaux: 275 feet/84 metres.

In 1776, Louis XVI began reforesting the park. Hubert Robert was requested to create a new grove to display Girardon's sculpture, **Apollo's Bath**. This masterpiece of 17th-century sculpture had originally stood in the Grotto of Thétis. The **Orangerie**** was built by Mansart to enhance the southern gardens. Today, it still serves as a hothouse for 1200 varieties of palm and orange trees.

PARIS ADDRESSES

Hotel ratings:

★	Basic
★★	Basic but comfortable
★★★	Very comfortable
★★★★	High class
★★★★(L)	De luxe

Restaurant ratings:

♦	Basic but pleasant
♦♦	Very pleasant and comfortable
♦♦♦	Elegant decor and service of high quality
♦♦♦♦	Exceptional

Prices

Hotels: average price for a room for two with attached bathroom, no breakfast.

Restaurants: average price for a meal inclusive of wine, coffee and tip.

❻ from 100 F
❻❻ 100-200 F
❻❻❻ 200-300 F
❻❻❻❻ 300-500 F
❻❻❻❻❻ 500 F and above

Symbols

≼ View
ℙ Parking
⋘ Park or garden
⌀ Peace and quiet
☜ No pets
▭ Swimming pool
Ġ Accessible for disabled
♪ Music
Tx Telex

Hotels and restaurants

Hotels:

★★★★(L) **Intercontinental**, 3 Rue de Castiglione, 75001, ☎ 42 60 37 80. Tx 220114. AE, DC, Euro, Visa. 500 rm including 27 apart. ⋘ ⌀ Ġ ❻❻❻❻❻ Rest. ♦♦ **La Rôtisserie Rivoli** ☜ Ġ ❻❻❻ **Le Café Tuileries**, ❻❻ Discotheque.

★★★★(L) **Lotti**, 7 Rue de Castiglione, 75001, ☎ 42 60 37 34. Tx 240066. AE, DC, Euro, Visa. 130 rm, 2 apart. ❻❻❻❻❻ Rest. ♦♦ and grill-room ♦♦ ❻❻❻

★★★★(L) **Meurice**, 228 Rue de Rivoli, 75001, ☎ 42 60 38 60. Tx 230673. AE, DC, Euro, Visa. 160 rm, 32 apart. ℙ Ġ ❻❻❻❻❻ Rest. ♦♦♦ ❻❻❻❻

★★★★(L) **Ritz**, 15 Pl. Vendôme, 75001; ☎ 42 60 38 30. Tx 220262, 670112, AE, DC, Euro, Visa. 163 rm, 42 apart. ℙ ⋘ ⌀ Ġ The favorite residence of Chanel and Hemingway, in the most prestigious square in Paris, ❻❻❻❻❻ Rest ♦♦♦♦ **L'Espadon**. Excellent cooking. Spec.: *assiette de petits hors d'oeuvre Escoffier, raviolis de fruits de mer mousse au cresson, canette de Barbarie, pêches au vin d'orange.* ❻❻❻❻

★★★★**Saint-James et Albany**, 202 Rue de Rivoli, 75001, ☎ 42 60 31 60. Tx 213031. AE, DC, Euro, Visa. 208 rm, 3 apart. ⋘ ⌀ ☜ ❻❻❻❻. Rest. ♦♦ **Le Noailles.** ❻❻

★★★ **Brighton**, 218 Rue de Rivoli, 75001, ☎ 42 60 30 03. Tx 217431. 70 rm. ≼ ☜ ❻❻❻❻

★★★ **Molière**, 21 Rue Molière, 75001, ☎ 42 96 22 01. 32 rm, 3 apart. ⌀ ❻❻❻❻

★★★ **Novotel Paris Les Halles**, 8 Pl. Marguerite-de-Navarre, 75001 ☎ 42 21 31 31. Tx 216389. AE, DC, Euro, Visa. 285 rm. ☜ Ġ ❻❻❻❻

★★ **Agora**, 7 Rue de la Cossonnerie, 75001, ☎ 42 33 46 02. 28 rm. ❻❻❻

★★ **Family**, 35 Rue Cambon, 75001, ☎ 42 61 54 84. 25 rm. Ġ ❻❻❻

★★ **Montpensier**, 12 Rue de Richelieu, 75001, ☎ 42 96 28 50. 43 rm. Ġ ❻❻❻

★★ **Sainte-Marie**, 83 Rue de Rivoli, 75001, ☎ 42 60 36 76. 51 rm. Ġ ❻❻❻

★★ **Timhotel Le Louvre**, 4 Rue Croix des Petits-Champs, 75001 ☎ 42 60 34 86. Ix 216405. AE, DC, Euro, Visa. 56 rm. ☜ ❻❻❻

Restaurants:

♦♦♦♦ Le Grand Véfour, 17 Rue de Beaujolais, 75001, ☎ 42 96 56 27. AE, DC, Euro, Visa. ❧ ♿ Closed Jul 29 – Aug 27, Sat and Sun. The historically-classified decor has been freshened up, and this enhances chef Signoret's light cooking. **❶❷❸❹**

♦♦♦ Carré des Feuillants, 14 Rue de Castiglione, 75001, ☎ 42 96 67 92. Alain Dutournier's beautiful, classy restaurant where he does his utmost to satisfy his stylish clientele. **❶❷❸❹**

♦♦♦ Gérard Besson, 5 Rue Coq-Héron 75001, ☎ 42 33 14 74. AE, DC, Euro, Visa. ♿ Closed 3 weeks Jul, 2 weeks year-end, Sat and Sun. Very good cooking, refined service. **❶❷❸❹**

♦♦♦ Hubert, 25 Rue de Richelieu, 75001, ☎ 42 96 08 47. Tx 210311. AE, Visa. ♿ Closed Sun, Mon. The 1900s decor and modern cooking are a perfect complement to each other. Good cheeses and light desserts. **❶❷❸**

♦♦♦ Le Mercure Galant, 15 Rue des Petits-Champs, 75001, ☎ 42 97 53 85. Closed Sat noon, Sun and hols. Good service in an extremely elegant dining-room. Spec: *feuilleté de langoustines*. **❶❷❸**

♦♦♦ Prunier-Madeleine, 9 Rue Duphot, 75001, ☎ 42 60 36 04. AE, DC, Euro, Visa. ♿ Spec.: *langouste au basilic, salade Prunier*. **❶❷❸❹**

♦♦ La Barrière Poquelin, 17 Rue Molière, 75001, ☎ 42 96 22 19. AE, DC, Euro, Visa. Closed Aug 1-20, Sat noon and Sun. Delightful decor for M. Guillaumin's fine light cooking. Spec: *lapin et navets Berrière; escalope de cervelle aux épinards*. **❶❷**

♦♦ Baumann Baltard, 9 Rue Coquillière, 75001, ☎ 42 36 22 00. Spec: *choucroute*. **❶❷**

♦♦ Les Bouchôleurs, 34 Rue de Richelieu, 75001, ☎ 42 96 06 86. Closed Sat, Sun noon, 3 weeks in spring, 1 week in mid-Aug. The true *moule de bouchots* from l'Aiguillon-sur-Mer, in theVendée region, is served in all its delicious forms. **❶❷**

♦♦ Chez la Vieille, 37 Rue de l'Arbre-Sec, 75001, ☎ 42 60 15 78 ❧ Closed Sat, Sun; lunch only. Very few tables (booking necessary); discover and appreciate Adrienne Biasin's authentic, generous cooking. Spec: *pot au boeuf, boeuf gros sel, rognons, côte de veau, faux-filet, tomates farcies*. If you are very hungry, unlimited helpings of *hors-d'oeuvre* and desserts. **❶❷❸**

♦♦ Chez Pauline, 5 Rue Villedo, 75001, ☎ 42 96 20 70. Visa. Closed 4 weeks Jul, 1 week year-end, Sat eve and Sun. André Genin adds light dishes to the solid traditional ones. Excellent Beaujolais wines. Spec: *raie au chou nouveau, boeuf bourguignon*. **❶❷❸**

♦♦ Escargot Montorgueil, 38 Rue Montorgueil, 75001, ☎ 42 36 83 51. AE, DC, Euro, Visa. ♿ Closed 1 week mid-Aug, May 1, Jan 1, Mon and Tue. A stunning setting; six snail specialties, and the *Montorgueil turbot*. **❶❷❸**

♦♦ Le Globe d'Or, 158 Rue St-Honoré, 75001, ☎ 42 60 23 37. Gérard Constiaux and wife Christiane will soon have gourmets flocking to try their good southwest cooking. **❶❷❸**

♦♦ Pavillon Baltard, 9 Rue Coquillière, 75001, ☎ 42 36 22 00. AE, DC, Euro, Visa. ♿ Alsace regional dishes; 12 different sorts of *choucroute*. **❶❷**

♦♦ Pharamond, 24 Rue de la Grande-Truanderie, 75001, ☎ 42 33 06 72. AE, DC, Euro, Visa. Closed Jul, Sun and Mon noon. Authentic *Belle Époque* setting. Normandy specialities. **❶❷**

♦ Au Pied de Cochon, 6 Rue Coquillière,75001, ☎ 42 36 11 75. AE, DC, Euro, Visa. ♿ "New look" for this institution which never closes. **❶❷**

♦ La Ferme Irlandaise, 30 Pl. du Marché-St-Honoré, 75001, ☎ 42 96 02 99. Irish stew and good Irish meats. **❶**

♦ La Fermette du Sud-Ouest, 31 Rue Coquillière, 75001, ☎ 42 36 73 55.. Visa. ❧ Closed Sun and Aug. Good, rich cooking from Périgord. **❶❷**

♦ Joe Allen, 30 Rue Pierre-Lescot, 75001, ☎ 42 36 70 13. Spec: American dishes, apple pie. **❶❷**

♦ Saudade, 34 Rue des Bourdonnais, 75001, ☎ 42 36 03 65. Closed Sun. Portugal in Paris: *fados* and *bacalhau*. **❶❷**

♦ Le Trou des Halles, 47 Rue St-Honoré. 75001, ☎ 45 08 80 13. **❶**

♦ Le Vieil Écu, 166 Rue Saint-Honoré, 75001, ☎ 42 60 20 14. Closed Sun. **❶**

♦ La Vigne, 30 Rue de l'Arbre-Sec, 75001, ☎ 42 60 13 55. Offers solid, traditional cooking. Spec: *oeufs en meurette à la moelle, magret de canard à l'orange, onglet de boeuf à l'auvergnate*. **❶❷**

♦ Porte du Bonheur, 8 Rue du Mont-Thabor, 75001, ☎ 42 60 55 99. AE, DC, Euro, Visa. ♿ One of the best Chinese restaurants in Paris. Fine, subtle dishes; if you go in a group, order a Chinese banquet. **❶❷**

♦ Yakitori, 34 Pl. du Marché-St-Honoré, 75001, ☎ 42 61 03 64. Delicious and inexpensive Japanese specialities. **❶**

═══════════════ *PARIS 2ⁿᵈ*

Hotels:
★★★★(L) **Westminster**, 13 Rue de la Paix, 75002, ☎ 42 61 57 46. AE, DC, Euro, Visa. 102 rm, 18 apart. Ⓟ ♨ ♿ **❶❷❸❹❺** Almost

next door to the Opéra. Rest ♦♦♦ **Le Céladon**. Closed Aug, Sat and Sun. ❻❻❻
★★★★ **Edouard VII**, 39 Av. de l'Opéra 75002, ☎ 42 61 56 90. Tx 680217. AE, DC, Euro, Visa. 95 rm, 5 apart. ℗ ⌘ 6 ❻❻❻❻❻
★★★★ **Favart**, 5 Rue Marivaux, 75002, ☎ 42 97 53 34. Tx 213126. 38 rm. ❻❻❻❻
★★★ **Ascot Opéra**, 2 Rue Monsigny, 75002, ☎ 42 96 87 66. 36 rm. ❻❻❻❻
★★★ **François**, 3 Bd. Montmartre, 75002, ☎ 42 33 51 53. 64 rm, 11 apart. ⌘ ❻❻❻❻
★★★ **Métropole-Opéra**, 2 Rue de Gramont. 75002, ☎ 42 96 91 03. Tx 212276. AE, 52 rm. 6 ❻❻
★★ **Nouveau Monde**, 98 Rue de Cléry. 75002, ☎ 42 33 22 37. 48 rm. 6 ❻❻
★★ **Timhotel La Bourse**, 3 Rue de la Banque, 75002, ☎ 42 60 05 39. AE, DC, Euro, Visa. 46 rm. ⌘ ❻❻❻❻
★★ **Vivienne**, 40 Rue Vivienne. 75002, ☎ 42 33 13 26. 44 rm. ❻❻

Restaurants:
♦♦ **Auberge Perraudin**, 164 Rue Montmartre, 75002, ☎ 42 36 71 09. AE, DC, Euro, Visa. Closed Sun. Such finesse in the restaurant of this disciple of the Troisgros brothers and Paul Bocuse. Claude Perraudin has a setting equal to his talent. Spec: *terrine de foie gras* (take-away), *saumon aux écrevisses, gigue d'agneau en chevreuil*. ❻❻❻
♦♦ **Au Lyonnais**, 32 Rue Saint-Marc, 75002, ☎ 42 96 65 04. AE, DC, Visa. 6 Closed Sun. Cooking from the Lyons region. ❻❻
♦♦ **Delmonico**, 39 Av. de l'Opéra, 75002, ☎ 42 61 44 26. Closed Sun. Modern setting for traditional cuisine. ❻❻❻
♦♦ **Le Petit Coin de la Bourse**, 16 Rue Feydeau, 75002, ☎ 45 08 00 08. Closed Sat and Sun. The inexhaustible Claude Verger runs this gourmet branch of the stock market. ❻❻
♦♦ **Le Vaudeville**, 29 Rue Vivienne, 75002, ☎ 42 33 39 31. AE, DC, Visa. 6 A beautiful old-fashioned *brasserie*. ❻❻❻
♦ **L'Amanguier**, 110 Rue de Richelieu, 75002, ☎ 42 96 37 79. AE, DC, Visa. Closed May 1. Spec: *estouffade à la menthe en cassolette*. Winter garden and patio. ❻❻
♦ **Hollywood Savoy**, 44 Rue Notre-Dame-des-Victoires, 75002, ☎ 42 36 16 73. AE, DC, Euro, Visa. Closed Sat noon. American specialties. ❻❻

══════════ *PARIS 3rd*
Hotels:
★★★★ **Pavillon de la Reine**, 28 Pl. des Vosges, 75003, ☎ 42 77 96 40. Tx 216160. AE, DC, Euro, Visa. 49 rm. ℗ ⌘ ☖ 6 Set in

beautiful surroundings, calm and elegance are part of the charm of this hotel. ❻❻❻❻❻
★★★ **Little Palace Hotel**, 4 Rue Salomon-de-Caus; 75003, ☎ 42 72 08 15. 59 rm. ⌘ 6 ❻❻❻ Rest. ♦ ❻
★★ **Hôtel du Marais**, 26 Rue Commynes, 75003, ☎ 48 87 78 27. 38 rm. ❻❻
★★ **Roubaix**, 6 Rue Greneta, 75003, ☎ 42 72 76 27. AE, DC, Visa. 53 rm. ❻❻
★ **Grand Hôtel Arts-et-Métiers**, 4 Rue Borda, 75003, ☎ 48 87 73 89. 35 rm. 6 ❻❻
Restaurants:
♦♦ **Ambassade d'Auvergne**, 22 Rue du Grenier-Saint-Lazare, 75003, ☎ 42 72 31 22. Visa. Closed Sun. The excellent cooking offered by the Petrucci family and staff is a passport to Auvergne. Spec: *charcuterie, saucisse fraîche, aligot, soupe aux choux*. ❻❻
♦ **L'Ami Louis**, 32 Rue du Vertbois, 75003, ☎ 48 87 77 48. Closed Jul-Aug, Mon, Tue, Solid, traditional cooking. ❻❻❻

══════════ *PARIS 4th*
Hotels:
★★★ **Célestins**, 1 Rue Charles-V, 75004, ☎ 48 87 87 04. 15 rm. ❻❻❻
★★★ **Les Deux Iles**, 59 Rue St-Louis-en-l'Ile, 75004, ☎ 43 26 13 35. 17 rm. Lovely 17th-century mansion. ❻❻❻
★★★ **Lutèce**, 65 Rue St-Louis-en-l'Ile, 75004, ☎ 43 26 23 52. 23 rm. ⚒ ❻❻❻
★★★ **Saint Merry**, 78 Rue de la Verrerie, 75004, ☎ 42 78 14 15. 13 rm. ⌘ ❻❻❻
★★ **Place des Vosges**, 12 Rue de la Birague, 75004, ☎ 42 72 60 46. AE, DC, Euro, Visa. 16 rm. ❻❻❻
Restaurants:
♦♦♦ **Chez Benoît**, 20 Rue Saint-Martin, 75004, ☎ 42 72 25 76. Closed Aug, Sat and Sun. ❻❻
♦♦ **Au Franc Pinot**. 1 Quai Bourbon, 75004, ☎ 43 29 46 98. AE, DC, Euro, Visa. Closed Sun and Mon. Bernard Meyruey's excellent dishes are served in the vaulted basement rooms of this 17th-century restaurant; wine-tasting at the counter. ❻❻
♦♦ **Au Quai des Ormes**, 72 Quai de l'Hôtel-de-Ville, 75004, ☎ 42 74 72 22.. Visa. ⚄ 6 Closed Sat, Sun, Aug 5–31. The Masraffs keep their numerous customers happy. Spec: *dos de st-pierre grillé, poêlée de langoustines aux artichauts*, low-calorie specials. ❻❻❻
♦♦ **Bofinger**, 5 Rue de la Bastille, 75004, ☎ 42 72 87 82. AE, DC, Euro, Visa. 6 1900s setting, seafood, *choucroute*. ❻❻
♦♦ **Coconnas**, 2 bis Pl. des Vosges, 75004, ☎ 42 78 58 16. AE, DC, Visa. ⚄ 6 Closed Dec 15 – Jan 15. Mon and Tue. ❻❻

◆◆ **Domarais**, 53 bis, Rue des Francs-Bourgeois, 75004, ☎ 42 74 54 17. Closed 1 week in winter, Sat noon, Sun, Mon noon. Surprising decor in a 15th-century chapel under an 18th-century cupola. Pleasant cooking, spec: *estouffade d'escargot à l'ail doux, saumon à la moelle de boeuf.* ◗◗

◆◆ **La Tzarine**, 36 Rue St Louis en l'Ile, 75004, ☎ 46 33 65 22. Spec: caviar, smoked salmon, blinis, *foie gras*, vodka, champagne served in a friendly atmosphere with music. ◗◗◗

◆ **Jo Goldenberg**, 7 Rue des Rosiers, 75004, ☎ 48 87 20 16. The meeting-place for the Parisian Jewish community. ◗

PARIS 5th

Hotels:

★★★★ **Collège de France**, 7 Rue Thénard, 75005, ☎ 43 26 78 36. AE. 29 rm. ◗◗◗

★★★ **Select Hôtel**, 1 Pl. de la Sorbonne, 75005, ☎ 46 34 14 80. 70 rm. ◗◗◗◗

★★ **Carmes**, 5 Rue des Carmes, 75005, ☎ 43 28 78 40. 42 rm. ✖ ◗

★★ **Les Grandes Écoles**, 75 Rue du Cardinal Lemoine, 75005, ☎ 43 26 79 23. 35 rm. ≋ 曲 ⚲ ◈ Preferable to reserve in advance in order to enjoy the calm of the flower garden and the charm of this hotel situated right in the heart of the Latin Quarter. ◗◗◗

★★ **Maxim Hotel**, 28 Rue Censier, 75005, ☎ 43 31 16 15. 37 rm. ✖ · ◗◗◗

★★ **Nations**, 54 Rue Monge, 75005, ☎ 43 26 45 24. 38 rm. ◗◗

★★ **Plaisant Hôtel**, 50 Rue des Bernardins, 75005, ☎ 43 54 74 57. 24 rm. ◗◗

★★ **Trois Collèges**, 16 Rue Cujas, 75005, ☎ 43 54 67 30. Tx 206034. AE, DC, Visa. 32 rm. ⚲ ◗◗◗

Restaurants:

◆◆◆◆ **La Tour d'Argent**, 15–17 Quai de la Tournelle, 75005, ☎ 43 54 23 31. AE, DC, Visa. ≋ ◈ Closed Mon. In his superb decor, the untiring Claude Terrail, Lord of the *Tour*, supervises everything for his demanding customers while, in the kitchen, Dominique Bouchet prepares excellent food. Duck is a specialty: *canard au sang, canard Marco Polo ...* but also *gigot de sept heures, curry de homard aux légumes.* The little wine and vineyard museum is a must, opposite the "Comptoir de la Tour". ◗◗◗◗◗

◆◆◆ **Auberge de la Bûcherie**, 41 Rue de la Bûcherie, 75005, ☎ 43 54 78 06. AE, DC ◈ Closed Mon, Jul-Aug. B. Bosque offers an excellent cellar and dishes to match. Spec: *chou farci aux langoustines.* ◗◗◗

◆◆◆ **Dodin-Bouffant**, 25 Rue Frédéric-Sauton, 75005, ☎ 43 25 25 14. DC, Visa. ◈ Closed Aug, end-of-year, Sat, Sun. The traditions of the great J. Manière live on: saltwater tank for shellfish. Spec: *fricassée de morue à la provençale, estouffade d'agneau, ragoût de canard et de ris de veau.* Unbeatable value. ◗◗◗

◆◆◆ **Duquesnoy**, 30 Rue des Bernardins, 75005, ☎ 43 54 21 13. AE, Visa. ◈ Closed Sat, Sun and Aug. Classical but constantly evolving cooking. Spec: *fondants de pieds de porcs truffés, terrine fondante de canard, agneau rôti, gratin d'artichauts.* ◗◗◗

◆◆◆ **Miravile**, 25 Quai de la Tournelle 75005, ☎ 46 34 07 78. AE, DC, Visa. Closed Sun. Spec: *filet d'agneau sous croûte de sel, crêpes soufflées à la liqueur.* ◗◗◗

◆◆ **L'Ambroisie**, 65 Quai de la Tournelle, 75005, ☎ 46 33 18 65. AE, Visa. ◈ Closed Feb school hols, Aug 10–31, Sun and Mon. There are only nine tables in this excellent restaurant, where the privileged clientele can taste dishes such as *queue de boeuf braisée en crépines, mousse de poivrons au coulis de tomates, millefeuille aux fruits.* ◗◗◗

◆◆ **Auberge des Deux Signes**, 46 Rue Galande, 75005, ☎ 43 25 46 56. AE, DC, Euro, Visa. Closed Sun and hols. Solid Auvergne-style cooking along with fish and seafood. ◗◗◗

◆◆ **Le Coupe-Chou**, 11 Rue de Lanneau, 75005, ☎ 46 33 68 69. AE, Visa. Closed Sun noon. Very "Left Bank" setting and clientele. ◗◗◗

◆◆ **Le Pactole**, 44 Bd. Saint-Germain, 75005, ☎ 46 33 31 31. Visa. ◈ · Closed Sun, Sat noon. Good cooking from Roland Magne and his young team. Beautiful terrace in warm weather. Spec: *filet de daurade à l'ail doux, faisan aux choux vinaigrette de truffes, filet de boeuf surprise.* ◗◗◗

◆◆ **Villars-Palace**, 6 Rue Descartes, 75005, ☎ 43 26 39 08. AE, DC, Euro, Visa. Closed Sat noon. La Montagne Sainte-Geneviève graced with deliciously prepared seafood. ◗◗◗

◆ **Abélard**, 1 Rue des Grands-Degrés 75005, ☎ 43 25 16 46. AE, DC, Visa. ≋ Closed Feb, Tue. Spec: *panaché de poissons au safran.* ◗◗

◆ **Balzar**, 49 Rue des Ecoles, 75005, ☎ 43 54 13 67. Visa. ✖ Closed Aug, end-of-year hols and Tue. Good simple cooking in classic French *brasserie.* Spec: *Boeuf gros sel* on Sat. *Foie de veau niçoise.* ◗◗

◆ **Chez René**, 14 Bd. Saint-Germain, 75005, ☎ 43 54 30 23. ◈ Closed Jul 26 – Sep 3, Sat and Sun. Good bistro-style cooking. ◗◗◗

◆ **Chez Toutoune**, 5 Rue de Pontoise, 75005, ☎ 43 26 58 81. Visa. Closed Sun, Mon, Aug 15 – Sep 15. Menu is a bargain. ◗

◆ **L'Estrapade**, 15 Rue de L'Es, 75005, ☎ 43 25 72 58. Closed Sat noon, Sun, Aug 7-23.

Simple, pleasant meals in this small, extremely reasonable restaurant. **☎☎**

◆ **Le Petit Prince**, 12 Rue de Lanneau, 75005, **☎** 43 54 77 26. Open eve. Left Bank atmosphere. **☎**

◆ **Salut l'Artiste**, 22 Rue Cujas, 75005, **☎** 43 54 01 10. AE, DC, Visa. ♿ Closed Sun, Aug. Enjoyable restaurant and reasonable prices. **☎☎**

◆ **Le Sunset**, 35 Quai de la Tournelle 75005, **☎** 43 25 44 42. Subdued lighting for intimate suppers. Modern cooking. **☎☎**

◆ **Vivario**, 6 Rue Cochin, 75005, **☎** 43 25 08 19. ✍ Closed Dec 25 – Jan 1, Sun, Mon. True Corsican cooking and wines in a friendly atmosphere. **☎☎**

=============== *PARIS 6th*

Hotels:

★★★★(L) **Guy-Louis Duboucheron**, 13 Rue des Beaux-Arts, 75006, **☎** 43 25 27 22. Tx 270870. AE, DC, Visa. 27 rm. ⚓ Perhaps the most beautiful bar in Paris. **☎☎☎☎** Rest. ◆◆◆ Suppers. Closed Aug. **☎☎☎**

★★★★ **Littré**, 9 Rue Littré, 75006, **☎** 45 44 38 68. Tx 203852. AE, Euro, Visa, 100 rm. ♿ Comfortable and classic. **☎☎☎☎** Rest. ◆◆ **☎☎**

★★★★ **Lutetia-Concorde**, 45 Bd. Raspail, 75006, **☎** 45 44 38 10. AE, DC, Euro, Visa. 300 rm, 17 apart. One of the largest hotels on the Left Bank. **☎☎☎☎** Rest. ◆◆◆ ♿ **Le Paris**. Commander Jacky Fréon offers you excellent cooking in the beautiful dining-room. Spec: *langoustines aux trois brunoises, filet d'agneau au curry, filet de bar homardine*. **☎☎☎**

★★★★ **Relais Christine**, 3 Rue Christine, 75006, **☎** 43 26 71 80. 51 rm. ℗ Former 16th-century cloister. **☎☎☎☎**

★★★ **Abbaye Saint-Germain**, 10 Rue Cassette, 75006, **☎** 45 44 11 52. 45 rm. ▦ **☎☎☎**

★★★ **Angleterre**, 44 Rue Jacob, 75006, **☎** 42 60 34 72. 27 rm. ✍ **☎☎☎**

★★★ **Grand Hôtel l'Univers**, 6 Rue Grégoire-de-Tours, 75006, **☎** 43 91 50 72. 34 rm. **☎☎☎**

★★★ **Saints-Pères**, 65 Rue des Saints-Pères, 75006, **☎** 45 44 50 00. Tx 205424. 40 rm. In the middle of Saint-Germain. ✍ **☎☎☎**

★★ **Balcons**, 3 Rue Casimir-Delavigne 75006, **☎** 46 34 78 50 Euro, Visa, 55 rm. ♿ **☎☎**

★★ **Les Marronniers**, 21 Rue Jacob, 75006, **☎** 43 25 30 60. 35 rm. ✍ **☎☎**

★★ **Molière**, 14 Rue de Vaugirard, 75006, **☎** 46 34 18 80. AE, Visa, 15 rm. **☎☎**

★★ **Nice**, 155 Bd. du Montparnasse, 75006, **☎** 43 26 60 24. 26 rm. ✍ **☎☎**

★★ **Pas-de-Calais**, 59 Rue des Saints-Pères, 75006, **☎** 45 48 78 74. 40 rm. **☎☎**

★★ **Perreyve**, 63 Rue Madame, 75006, **☎** (1) 45 48 35 01. 30 rm. ✍ **☎☎**

★★ **Scandinavia**, 27 Rue de Tournon, 75006, **☎** 43 29 67 20. 22 rm. ✍ **☎☎**

★★ **Seine**, 52 Rue de Seine, 75006, **☎** 46 34 22 80. 30 rm. ✍ **☎☎**

★★ **Welcome**, 66 Rue de Seine, 75006, **☎** 46 34 24 80. 30 rm. ✍ **☎☎**

★ **Verneuil** 36 Rue Dauphine, 75006, **☎** 43 26 85 34. 29 rm. **☎☎**

Restaurants:

◆◆◆ **Brasserie Lipp**, 151 Bd. Saint-Germain, 75006, **☎** 45 48 53 91. Closed Jul, Nov 1, Dec 25, Easter and Mon. **☎☎☎**

◆◆◆ **Jacques Cagna**, 14 Rue des Grands-Augustins, 75006, **☎** 43 26 49 39. AE. Visa. Closed Dec 24 – Jan 2, Aug, Sat and Sun. Quality and comfort. Spec: *salade de homard breton et de foie de canard tiède, pétoncles en coquille fumet cremé au caviar Serruga*. **☎☎☎**

◆◆◆ **Lapérouse**, 51 Quai des Grands-Augustins, 75006, **☎** 43 26 68 04. AE, DC, Euro, Visa. ♿ Closed May 1, Sat noon. A classified building (with the famous "private salons" of the *Belle Époque*.). Spec: *tourte de volaille, consommé de rougets marinés avec du foie gras, tartare de saumon et dorade, ris de veau aux langoustines*. **☎☎☎**

◆◆ **L'Apollinaire**, 168 Bd. Saint-Germain, 75006, **☎** 43 26 50 30. AE, DC, Euro, Visa. ✍ Closed Dec 18 – Jan 13. Fish specialties. **☎☎☎**

◆◆ **Brasserie Lutetia**, 45 Bd. Raspail, 75006, **☎** 45 44 38 10. A very popular, large, recently-renovated restaurant. **☎☎**

◆◆ **Chez Gramond**, 5 Rue de Fleurus, 75006, **☎** 42 22 28 89. Visa. Closed Jul 31 – Sep 3, Sun. The gourmet's annex to the neighboring Senate. Spec: *civet de lièvre* in season, fish. **☎☎☎**

◆◆ **La Closerie des Lilas**, 171 Bd. du Montparnasse, 75006, **☎** 43 52 21 68. AE, DC, Visa. ♿ Pricey, but a must for those who want to be in on the Paris world of arts and letters. **☎☎☎**

◆◆ **L'Épicurien**, 11 Rue de Nesles, 75006, **☎** 43 29 55 78. Closed Sun. An enjoyable moment in this small flower-filled restaurant. **☎☎**

◆◆ **La Foux**, 2 Rue Clément, 75006, **☎** 43 25 77 66. ♿ Closed Sun, Christmas and Public hols. A favorite publishers' haunt, with the best in Lyons-style cooking prepared by A. Guini: *pieds de mouton, gras double, tablier de sapeur*. At noon on Sat the chef serves a delicious *casse-croûte niçois*. Excellent Beaujolais wines. **☎☎☎**

◆◆ **Grégoire Xavier**, 80 Rue du Cherche-Midi, 75006, **☎** 45 44 72 72. AE, Visa. Closed Aug 1–25, Sat eve, Sun. Small rooms but excellent cooking. Astonishing 100 F menu. Spec: *salade de rougets, ris de veau à la graine de moutarde*. **☎☎**

♦♦ **La Grosse Horloge**, 22 Rue St-Benoît, 75006, ☎ 42 22 22 63. AE, DC, Visa. Spec: fish, *foie gras de canard maison*. ❻❻

♦♦ **Guy**, 6 Rue Mabillon, 75006, ☎ 43 54 87 61. Closed Aug 10-20, Sun, noon ex Sat. Brazil and its specialties: *samba, fei-joda, carioccas* especially Sat noon. ❻❻

♦♦ **Joséphine (Chez Dumonet)**, 117 Rue du Cherche-Midi, 75006, ☎ 45 48 52 40. Solid, honest cooking in a very handsome 1900s bistro. Exceptional wine. ❻❻

♦♦ **O Brasil**, 10 Rue Guénégaud, 75006, ☎ 43 54 98 56. Private restaurant-club open until 2 am. Authentic Brazilian music and cooking. *Feijoada* as in Rio. ❻❻

♦♦ **La Petite Cour**, 8 Rue Mabillon, 75006, ☎ 43 26 52 26. Visa. Closed Dec 15 – Jan 15, Sun and Mon in winter. Light cooking. Spec: *tartare de thon frais, lapereau aux pâtes fraîches* served in a Napoleon III setting. Beautiful terrace in summer. ❻❻

♦♦ **Le Petit Zinc**, 25 Rue de Buci, 75006, ☎ 43 54 79 34. Spec: *foie frais, confit de canard*, fish and seafood. ❻❻

♦ **Le Caméléon**, 6 Rue de Chevreuse, 75006, ☎ 43 30 63 43. Closed Sep, Sun, Mon, hols. Good meat, enjoyable wines at low prices. ❻❻

♦ **Chez Tante Madée**, 11 Rue Dupin, 75006, ☎ 42 22 64 56. Closed Aug 15–25, Sat noon and Sun. Very reasonable prices for good cooking. Spec: *dés de gigot d'agneau sautés aux aubergines confites, turbot sauce au citron et aux artichauts*. ❻❻

♦ **Le Palanquin**, 12 Rue Princesse, 75006, ☎ 43 29 77 66. Visa. ♿ Closed Sun. Vietnamese specialties. ❻

♦ **Polidor**, 41 Rue Monsieur-le-Prince, 75006, ☎ 43 26 95 34. Closed Sun, Mon and Jul 25 – Aug 15. Family-style meals at reasonable prices. ❻

♦ **La Porte Fausse**, 72 Rue du Cherche-Midi ☎ 43 22 20 17. Closed Sun, Mon, 1 week in Easter, Aug, Sep 1. *Tourte de blettes, pâtes fraîches, ravioli, pissaladière, sardines à la sauge, poche de veau farcie* and many other genuine Niçoise specialties. ❻❻

♦ **Saints-Pères**, 175 Bd. Saint-Germain, 75006, ☎ 45 48 56 85. Closed 1 week Feb, Aug 15 – Sep 15, Wed and Thu. ❻❻

━━━━━━━━━━━━━━━━━ *PARIS 7ᵗʰ*

Hotels:

★★★★(L) **Pont-Royal** (Mapotel), 7 Rue de Montalembert, 75007, ☎ 45 44 38 27. Tx 270113. AE, DC, Euro, Visa. 80 rm, 5 suites. ♿ The most literary bar in Paris in the heart of the publishers' quarter.. ❻❻❻❻ Rest. ♦♦**Les Antiquaires**. Closed Aug and Sun. Spec: *magret de canard au confit d'oignons*. ❻❻

★★★★(L) **Sofitel-Bourbon**, 32 Rue Saint-Dominique, 75007, ☎ 45 55 91 80. Tx 250019. AE, DC, Euro, Visa. 112 rm, 4 apart. 🅿 ♿ ❻❻❻❻❻ Rest. ♦♦♦**Le Dauphin**. ♿ ❻❻

★★★★ **Montalembert**, 3 Rue Montalembert, 75007, ☎ 45 48 68 11. 60 rm. ♿ ❻❻❻

★★★ **Lenox**, 9 Rue de l'Université, 75007, ☎ 42 96 10 95. 34 rm. ❻❻

★★★ **Quai Voltaire**, 19 Quai Voltaire, 75007, ☎ 42 61 50 91. 33 rm. ♿ ♿ ♿ Oscar Wilde and Wagner were once guests here. ❻❻

★★★ **Saint-Simon**, 14 Rue St-Simon, 75007, ☎ 45 48 35 66. 34 rm. ⚏ ♿ ♿ ❻❻

★★ **Mars**, 117 Av. de La Bourdonnais, 75007, ☎ 47 05 42 30. 24 rm. ♿ ❻❻

★★ **Royal Phare**, 40 Av. de La Motte-Picquet, 75007, ☎ 47 05 57 30. 34 rm. ❻❻

★★ **Solférino**, 91 Rue de Lille, 75007, ☎ 47 05 05 54. Visa. 34 rm. ♿ Closed Dec 22 – Jan 3. ❻❻

★★ **Vaneau**, 85 Rue Vaneau, 75007, ☎ 45 48 25 09. DC, Euro, Visa. 52 rm. ♿ ❻❻

Restaurants:

♦♦♦♦ **Jacques Le Divellec**, 107 Rue de l'Université, 75007, ☎ 45 51 91 96. AE, DC, Visa. ♿ ♿ Closed Sun and Mon. Jacques Le Divellec's restaurant in Paris is a success. Fresh fish specs in a sea-blue setting: *huîtres frémies, langoustines au foie gras, pâtes fraîches à l'encre de seiche*. ❻❻❻❻

♦♦♦♦ **Le Jules Verne**, Eiffel Tower, 2nd floor (direct elevator service), 75007, ☎ 45 55 20 24 (reservations necessary). The most stunning aerial view in Paris, in a harmonious gray and black decor designed by Slavik. Piano-bar. ❻❻❻

♦♦♦ **Bistrot de Paris**, 33 Rue de Lille, 75007, ☎ 42 61 16 83. Closed Sat noon and Sun. Michel Oliver takes the time to supervise his restaurant with talent and competence for fashionable Parisians. Spec: *côte de boeuf rôtie*. ❻❻❻

♦♦♦ **La Bourgogne**, 6 Av. Bosquet, 75007, ☎ 47 05 96 78. AE, DC, Visa. Closed Sat noon and Sun. Lionel Lesage continues the Julien family's tradition of rich cooking with the same chef. Spec: *ris de veau aux morilles*. ❻❻❻

♦♦♦ **La Cantine des Gourmets**, 113 Av. de La Bourdonnais, 75007, ☎ 47 05 47 96. AE, DC, Visa. Closed Sun and Mon. A charming welcome, and a cosy, comfortable setting in which to appreciate Régis Mahé's great light cooking. ❻❻❻

♦♦♦ **La Ferme Saint-Simon**, 6 Rue de Saint-Simon, 75007, ☎ 45 48 35 74. Visa. ♿ Closed Aug 2-26, Sat noon and Sun. Superb cooking and excellent desserts prepared by Francis Vandehende. Spec: *duo d'oursins en demi-glace, grillandine de homard*. ❻❻❻

♦♦♦ **Le Galant Verre**, 12 Rue de Verneuil, 75007, ☎ 42 60 84 56. AE, DC, Euro, Visa. ♿ Closed Sat noon and Sun. Warm comfortable setting. Spec: *jarret de veau aux pâtes fraîches.* ❻❻❻

♦♦♦ **Le Récamier** (Martin Cantegrit), 4 Rue Récamier, 75007, ☎ 42 22 51 75. DC, Euro, Visa. Closed Sun. Martin Cantegrit takes care of everything: a beautiful private terrace, fresh produce bought at Rungis, and a prestigious choice of dishes. ❻❻❻

♦♦ **Chez Françoise**, Aérogare des Invalides, 75007, ☎ 47 05 49 03. AE, DC, Visa. ♿ Closed Sun eve, Mon and Aug. A dining-room for the nearby National Assembly, frequented by ministers and deputies. Spec: *foie gras frais d'oie, filet de barbue à la mousse de truite, pigeons à la crème de petits pois.* ❻❻

♦♦ **Chez Gildo**, 153 Rue de Grenelle, 75007, ☎ 45 51 54 12. Closed Jul, Aug, Sun and Mon. Italian specialties. ❻❻❻

♦♦ **La Flamberge**, 12 Av. Rapp, 75007, ☎ 47 05 91 37. Closed Aug 8 – Sep 8, Sat noon and Sun. Spec: *salade de feuilles de chêne,* desserts. ❻❻❻

♦♦ **Florence**, 22 Rue du Champ-de-Mars, 75007, ☎ 45 51 52 69. AE, Visa. Closed Jul, Sun and Mon. The Fayet brothers offer good fresh pasta and excellent Italian-style cooking. ❻❻

♦♦ **Labrousse**, 4 Rue Pierre-Leroux, 75007, ☎ 43 06 99 39. ♿ Set in the calm of a small, almost provincial, street, fine cooking by Yves Labrousse. Spec: *langue d'agneau lie de ravigote, salmis de pintade aux girolles.* ❻❻❻

♦♦ **Le Perron**, 6 Rue Perronet, 75007, ☎ 45 44 71 51. Set in a small street, pasta and good Sicilian cooking. ❻❻

♦♦ **Quai d'Orsay**, 49 Quai d'Orsay, 75007, ☎ 45 51 58 58. AE, DC, Euro, Visa. Closed Sun, Christmas and Aug 2-25. Warm ambience and fashionably crowded for chef Bigeard's excellent seasonal cooking. ❻❻❻

♦♦ **Ravi**, 50 Rue de Verneuil, 75007, ☎ 42 61 17 28. Elegant restaurant, where Indian cooking is beautifully prepared. Delicious *tandoori, gambas,* curry. ❻❻❻

♦♦ **Relais Saint-Germain**, 190 Bd. Saint-Germain, 75007, ☎ 42 22 21 35. Spec: *saumon cru au citron et au poivre vert, marquise au chocolat.* Excellent value for money. ❻❻

♦♦ **La Sologne**, 8 Rue de Bellechasse, 75007, ☎ 47 05 98 66. AE, DC, Visa. Closed Aug, Sat, Sun. Game in season. ❻❻

♦♦ **Tan Dinh**, 60 Rue de Verneuil, 75007, ☎ 45 44 04 84. Closed Sun and Aug 15-31. The most Parisian Vietnamese restaurant; one of the best-stocked wine-cellars in Paris. ❻❻

♦ **Aux Fins Gourmets**, 213 Bd. St-Germain, 75007, ☎ 42 22 06 57. Good and inexpensive. ❻

♦ **Au Pied de Fouet**, 45 Rue de Babylone, 75007, ☎ 47 05 12 27. Closed Sat eve, Sun, Mar 23 – Apr 1, Jul 27 – Aug 31, Dec 22 – Jan 2. More *à la mode* than ever. Very good and still inexpensive. Probably the best pastries in Paris. ❻❻

♦ **Le Bistrot 28**, 28 Rue de l'Exposition 75007, ☎ 47 05 80 39. Closed Sat noon, Mon, Aug 10–25, Dec 20 – Jan 5. A delightful little restaurant in a quiet street. Good cooking at a reasonable price. ❻❻

♦ **Chez Germaine**, 30 Rue Pierre Leroux, 75007, ☎ 42 73 28 34. Closed Aug, Sat eve and Sun. Good simple home cooking. ❻

━━━━━━━━━━━━━━━━━━━━ *PARIS 8th*

Hotels:

★★★★(L) **Bristol**, 112 Rue du Faubourg-Saint-Honoré, 75008, ☎ 42 66 91 45. Tx 780961. AE, DC, Euro, Visa, 200 rm, 45 apart. ℗ ♨ ⚓ ▣ A discreet palace over looking an 18th-century cloister; greatly appreciated by its international clientele. ❻❻❻❻❻ Rest ♦♦♦ **Le Bristol** ♿ Excellent cooking. ❻❻❻❻

★★★★(L) **California** (Mapotel), 16 Rue de Berri, 75008, ☎ 43 59 93 00. Tx 660634. AE, DC, Euro, Visa, 188 rm, 5 suites ♿ ❻❻❻❻ Rest. ♦♦. Closed Sat, Sun. ❻❻

★★★★(L) **Claridge Bellman**, 37 Rue Francois-1er, 75008, ☎ 47 23 54 42. Tx 641150. AE, DC, Visa, 42 rm. ⚘ Splendid old furnishings, where the friendly atmosphere comes as an agreeable surprise. ❻❻❻❻❻ Rest. ♦♦♦ **Relais Bellman**. Closed Sat, Sun and Aug. Spec: *raviolis Royans, papillote de barbue à l'étuvée de poireaux, pavé grillé aux champignons de bois.* ❻❻❻

★★★★(L) **Crillon** (Relais et château Concorde). 10 Pl de la Concorde, 75008, ☎ 42 96 24 24. Tx 290204, 290241. AE, DC, Euro, Visa. 195 rm, 48 apart. ⚘ ♿ An aristocratic setting for Gabriel's palace (1760). ❻❻❻❻❻ Rest. ♦♦♦♦ Jean Paul Bonin and his team bring talent and art to their cooking served in this superb grand hotel setting. Delicious light dishes. ❻❻❻❻ Grill ♦♦ **L'Obélisque**. Sonia Rykiel's feminine decor, light cooking. ❻❻

★★★★(L) **George V**, 31 Av. George-V, 75008, ☎ 47 23 54 00. Tx 650082, 290776. AE, DC, Euro, Visa. 298 rm, 38 apart. ❻❻❻❻❻ Grand tradition. Superb furnishings,. Rest. ♦♦♦ ⚘ **Les Princes**. Good cooking. ❻❻❻❻

★★★★(L) **Lancaster**, 7 Rue de Berri, 75008, ☎ 43 59 90 43. Tx 640991. AE, DC, Euro, Visa. 67 rm, 10 apart ⚘ ❻❻❻❻ Rest. ♦♦. Closed Sat eve and Sun eve. ❻❻❻

★★★★(L) **Palace Maxim's**, 42 Av. Gabriel, 75008, ☎ 45 61 19 92. This hotel is entirely designed by Pierre Cardin, and is a palace of elegance and luxury. 46 apart. from 50 to 200 sq m., 2 bars, caviarteria, gymnasium, etc. ❻❻❻❻❻

★★★★(L) **Plaza-Athénée**, 25 Av. Montaigne, 75008, ☎ 47 23 78 33. Tx 650092. AE, DC, Visa, 218 rm. 44 apart. Rest. ♦♦ **Relais Plaza** (closed Dec 15–31) and ♦♦♦ **Le Régence Plaza**. Excellent cooking.❻❻❻❻

★★★★(L) **Pullman Windsor**, 14 Rue Beaujon, 75008, ☎ 45 63 04 04. Tx 650902. AE, DC, Euro, Visa. 135 rm. ⚓ ❻❻❻❻❻ Rest. ♦♦♦ **Le Clovis**, ☎ (1) 45 61 15 32. Closed Aug, Sat, Sun, hols. Spec: *fondant de légumes de Provence et ses petits rougets de roche, croûte de st-pierre à la crème d'oseille.* ❻❻❻

★★★★(L) **Warwick**, 5 Rue de Berri, 75008, ☎ 45 63 14 11. Tx 642295. AE, DC, Euro, Visa. 46 rm, 4 suites. & ❻❻❻❻❻ New but in the grand tradition,. Rest ♦♦♦ **La Couronne** & closed Aug 5-26 and public hols. ❻❻❻

★★★★ **Astor l'Horset**, 11 Rue d'Astorg, 75008, ☎ 42 66 56 56. 128 rm. 🎵 & ❻❻❻❻ Rest. ♦♦ **La Table de l'Astor.**❻❻

★★★★**Bedford**, 17 Rue de l'Arcade, 75008, ☎ 42 66 22 32. Tx 290506. Visa. 147 rm, 12 apart. & ❻❻❻❻   Rest ♦♦ & **Le Relais Victoria**. ❻❻❻

★★★★ **Castiglione**, 40 Rue du Faubourg-Saint-Honoré, 75008, ☎ 42 65 07 50. Tx 240362. AE, DC, Euro, Visa, 114 rm ❻❻❻❻ Rest. ♦♦ ❻❻

★★★★ **Roblin**, 6 Rue Chaveau-Lagarde, 75008, ☎ 42 65 57 00. Tx 640154. AE, DC, Euro, Visa. 70 rm. ⚓ ❻❻❻❻ Rest. ♦♦ **Le Mazagran**. Closed Aug, Sat and Sun. ❻❻

★★★★ **San Regis**, 12 Rue Jean-Goujon, 75008, ☎ 43 59 41 90. 43 rm. ❻❻❻❻ Snack. ❻

★★★ **Amina**, 4 Rue d'Artois, 75008, ☎ 43 59 03 19 30 rm. ✄ & ❻❻❻

★★★ **Bradford**, 10 Rue Saint-Philippe-du-Roule, 75008, ☎ 43 59 24 20. 48 rm. ✄ ❻❻❻❻

★★★ **Friedland**, 2 Av. de Friedland, 75008, ☎ 45 63 52 97. 35 rm. ❻❻❻

★★★ **Montaigne**, 6 Av. Montaigne, 75008, ☎ 47 20 92 28. 33 rm. ✄ ❻❻❻

★★★ **Résidence Saint-Honoré** (Mapotel), 214 Rue du Faubourg-Saint-Honoré, 75008, ☎ 42 25 26 27. Tx 640524. AE, DC, Euro, Visa. 91 rm. & ❻❻❻❻

★★ **Buckingham**, 45 Rue des Mathurins, 75008, ☎ 42 65 81 62. Tx 642173. AE, DC, Visa, Euro. 37 rm. ✄ ❻❻❻ Rest. ❻❻

★★ **Ceramic Hôtel**, 34 Av. de Wagram, 75008, ☎ 42 27 20 30. Tx 260717. AE, DC. 60 rm. An Art Deco hotel with an astonishing ceramic-covered facade. ❻❻❻

★★ **Élysée**, 12 Rue des Saussaies, 75008, ☎ 42 65 29 25. 32 rm. & ❻❻❻

★★ **Folkestone**, 9 Rue de Castellane, 75008, ☎ 42 65 73 09. 32 rm. ❻❻❻

★★ **Peiffer**, 6 Rue de l'Arcade, 75008, ☎ 42 66 03 07. 41 rm. ❻❻

★ **Bellevue**, 46 Rue Pasquier, 75008, ☎ 43 87 50 68. 48 rm. ✄ ❻❻

Restaurants:

♦♦♦♦ **Lamazère**, 23 Rue de Ponthieu, 75008, ☎ 43 59 66 66. AE, DC, Euro, Visa. ✄ Closed Aug and Sun. Roger Lamazère's magic cooking to delight gourmands. Spec: *foie gras, truffes, confit.* ❻❻❻❻❻

♦♦♦♦ **Lasserre**, 17 Av. F.-D.-Roosevelt, 75008, ☎ 43 59 53 43. ✄ Closed Aug 3 – Sep 1, Sun and Mon. René Lasserre deserves particular mention for his important services to great French cooking. Maîtres d'hôtel, wine waiters and a roof which opens. Spec: lobster Newburg, *pigeon André Malraux.* ❻❻❻❻

♦♦♦♦ **Laurent**, 41 Av. Gabriel, 75008, ☎ 42 25 00 39. AE, DC. 🎵 ✄ & Closed Sat, Sun and nat hols. The pearl of the Golden Triangle is the Champs-Élysées gardens. Spec: lobster salad, *côte de boeuf écossais « Angus »*, great wines. ❻❻❻❻

♦♦♦♦ **Ledoyen**, carré des Champs-Élysées, 75008, ☎ 42 66 54 77. & Closed Aug 2 – Sep 3, Easter, Mon and Sun. Tie obligatory. Spec: *fricassée de poissons à la provençale, mignon d'agneau poêlé aux corolles de courgettes et de tomates avec galette de pommes dauphines, surprise Leyoden aux fraises des bois.* ❻❻❻❻

♦♦♦♦ **Le Pavillon Élysée**, 10 Av. des Champs-Élysées, 75008, ☎ 42 65 85 10. AE, DC, Visa. 🎵 Closed Sat, Sun, Aug. G. Lenôtre's dream come true: a luxurious gourmet spot on the Champs-Élysées with the staff of *Pré Catelan* supervised by Patrick Lenôtre. On the ground floor, **Les Jardins de l'Élysée** mixes modern cooking and traditional dishes at lower prices. Spec: *foie gras, caviar, salmon.* ❻❻❻❻❻

♦♦♦♦ **Lucas-Carton**, 9 Pl. de la Madeleine, 75008, ☎ 42 65 22 90. Visa. ✄ & Closed Fri, Sat noon and Sun. In a historically-classified decor, the highly-talented Alain Senderens's inventive light cooking: *asperges meunière, canard Apicius, gâteau de riz*, superb wines. ❻❻❻❻❻

♦♦♦♦ **Taillevent**, 15 Rue Lamennais, 75008, ☎ 45 63 39 94. Closed Feb 9-16, Jul 26 – Aug 24, Sat and Sun. A temple of French cooking managed by J.-C. Vrinat with cooking by Claude Deligne. Great wines at modest prices. Early booking recommended. ❻❻❻❻

♦♦♦ **Chiberta**, 3 Rue A.-Houssaye, 75008, ☎ 45 63 77 90. AE, DC, Visa. Closed Aug,

Sat, Sun and Public hols. Beautiful modern decor for Jean-Michel Bedier's exceptional cooking: *bavarois de saumon, marbré de rougets*, great desserts and Burgundy wines. ❶❷❸❹

◆◆◆ **La Fermette Marbeuf**, 5 Rue Marbeuf, 75008, ☎ 47 23 31 31. Decorated in 1900s green ceramic, the *Fermette* is prettier than ever. Good, subtle cooking. ❶❷

◆◆◆ **Fouquet's**, 99 Av. des Champs-Élysées, 75008, ☎ 47 23 70 60. AE, DC, Visa. ♿ Closed Jul 20 – Aug 20. A meeting place for show business and the cinema. The good cooking of P. Ducroux and beautiful terrace. ❶❷❸

◆◆◆ **Lord Gourmand**, 9 Rue Lord-Byron, 75008, ☎ 45 62 66 06. AE, Visa. Closed Sat, Sun, Public hols, Aug and 1 week at Christmas. Very few chefs have as brilliant a prize-list as Daniel Météry, a pupil of the Troisgros brothers, Paul Bocuse, Michel Guérard. Spec: *bar à la vapeur en vinaigrette, souris d'agneau, tourte tiède aux pommes et abricots*. ❶❷❸

◆◆◆ **Le Marcande**, 52 Rue de Miromesnil, 75008, ☎ 42 65 19 14. AE, DC, Visa. ♨ Closed Aug 9 – Sep 2, Sat and Sun. ❶❷❸

◆◆◆ **La Marée** (Relais gourmand), 1 Rue Daru, 75008, ☎ 4/ 63 52 42. Closed Sat, Sun. Quality remains the main characteristic of this restaurant specializing in fish: *rougets grillés*, oysters, *turbot à la moutarde*. ❶❷❸❹

◆◆◆ **Maxim's**, 3 Rue Royale, 75008, ☎ 42 65 27 94. Closed Sun. Pierre Cardin imposes his style while the chef Menant and his fine team make a serious effort. ❶❷❸❹ or more. On the 1st floor. lunch and suppers. Nearby, in the Rue St-Honoré: **Minim's**. The prices are reasonable. ❶❷

◆◆◆ **Au Petit Montmorency**, 5 Rue Rabelais, 75008, ☎ 42 25 11 19. Visa. ♨ Closed Aug, Sat and Sun. Spec: *foie gras au caramel poivré*. ❶❷❸

◆◆ **L'Addition**, 10 Rue de la Trémoille, 75008, ☎ 47 23 53 53. Very good light cooking at highly reasonable prices. Spec: *sardines marinées aux baies roses, nage océan, vins d'Arbois*. ❶❷

◆◆ **Al Amir**, 66 Rue François-Ier, 75008, ☎ 47 23 79 05. ♿ The charm of the Orient, and "A Thousand and One Nights", just off the Champs-Élysées. Wonderful *mèzzès*, and Lebanese wines. ❶❷❸

◆◆ **Chez Modeste**, 8 Rue Miromesnil, 75008, ☎ 42 65 20 39. J.-P. Coffe is unique! His clientele, his good dishes and modest wines direct from the vineyards. ❶❷

◆◆ **Chez Vong**, 27 Rue du Colisée, 75008, ☎ 43 59 77 12. AE, DC, Visa. ♿ Closed Sun. A chic Chinese restaurant with a Hollywood

decor. Refined dishes, with excellent *dim-sum* (steam-cooked foods). ❶❷

◆◆ **L'Espace**, 1 Av. Gabriel, 75008, ☎ 42 66 11 70. AE, DC, Visa. Closed Sat noon. ♿ The place to see and be seen; cinema-showbiz decor, society clientele, and a special welcome for all. Buffets, daily specials, inexpensive wines. ❶❷

◆◆ **Le Grenadin**, 46 Rue de Naples, 75008, ☎ 45 63 28 92. Closed 2 weeks in Aug, Sat, Sun. The young Patrick Cirotte is a chef to follow. Spec: *lapin rôti jus à l'ail, ragoût de langoustines aux artichauts violets*. ❶❷

◆◆ **Hédiard**, 21 Pl. de la Madeleine, 75008, ☎ 42 66 09 00. AE, DC, Visa. Closed Sun ♿ Rest. ❶❷❸ Caterer, food shop and wine cellar.

◆◆ **Tong Yen**, bis Rue Jean-Mermoz, 75008, ☎ 42 25 04 23. AE, DC, Visa. ♿ A well-frequented fashionable spot. Good Chinese specialties. ❶❷❸

◆ **Le Bar des Théâtres**, 6 Av. Montaigne, 75008, ☎ 47 23 34 63. Closed Aug. For after-theater suppers. ❶❷

◆ **Boeuf sur le Toit**, 34 Rue du Colisée, 75008, ☎ 43 59 83 80. ♿ ♪ Recently reopened, a good *brasserie* with a piano-bar and oysters on display. ❶❷

◆ **Boulangerie Saint-Philippe**, 73 Av. F.-D.-Roosevelt, 75008, ☎ 43 59 78 76. Lunch only. Closed Sat and Aug. ❶

◆ **La Maison de la Vigne et du Vin**, 21 Rue Francois-Ier, 75008, ☎ 47 20 59 42. A lovely restaurant dedicated to wine, with cooking by the Layrac brothers. ❶❷

◆ **Savy**, 23 Rue Bayard, 75008, ☎ 47 23 46 98. Closed Sat, Sun and Aug. Auvergne-inspired cooking, which is good, simple, and not too expensive: *choux aveyronnais, farçou, jambonneau aux lentilles*. ❶❷

◆ **Théâtre des Mathurins**, 36 Rue des Mathurins, 75008, ☎ 42 65 98 00. Friendly cafeteria open daily till midnight. ❶

◆ **Théâtre du Rond-Point**, Av. F.-D.-Roosevelt, 75008, ☎ 42 56 22 01. ❶❷

Hotels:

★★★★ (L) **Grand Hôtel**, 2 Rue Scribe, 75009, ☎ 42 68 12 13. Tx 220875. AE, DC, Euro, Visa. 583 rm. 12 suites. ♿ ❶❷❸❹❺ Rest. ◆◆◆ **Le Patio** (noon only) ♨ ♿ Closed Aug. ◆◆ **Café de la Paix**. In the tradition of supper after the show. ❶❷❸

★★★★(L) **Scribe**, 1 Rue Scribe, 75009, ☎ 47 42 03 40. 217 rm, 5 apart and 6 duplex. ♿ ❶❷❸❹❺ Rest. ◆◆◆ **Les Muses**, ♿ Closed Sat, Sun and eve in Aug. A refined setting for thoroughly classical dishes prepared by the young P. Aracil. Spec: *baudruche de fruits de mer à la crème légère, poulet de Bresse en pot-au-feu.* ❶❶❶❶

★★★ **Leman**, 20 Rue de Trévisse, 75009, ☎ 42 46 50 66. Tx 281086. AE, DC, Visa. 24 rm. A charming and refined hotel in a quiet street. Authentic carpets and marble floors, beautiful furnishings, Italian tiles. ❶❶❶❶❶

★★★ **Moulin Rouge**, 39 Rue Montmartre, 75009, ☎ 42 81 93 25. Tx 660055. AE, DC, Euro, Visa, 50 rm. ❶❶❶❶

★★ **Blanche**, 69 Rue Blanche, 75009, ☎ 48 74 16 94. 54 rm. ⊗ ❶❶

★★ **La Bruyère**, 35 Rue La Bruyère, 75009, ☎ 48 74 03 69. AE, Visa, 31 rm. ♿ ❶❶

★★ **Lorette**, 36 Rue Notre-Dame-de-Lorette, 75009, ☎ 42 85 18 81. 83 rm. ❶❶

★★ **Migny**, 13 Rue Victor-Massé, 75009, ☎ 48 78 59 97. 54 rm. In the heart of Pigalle. ❶❶

★★ **Résidence Sémard**, 15 Rue P.-Sémard, 75009, ☎ 48 78 26 72. 41 rm. ❶❶

★★ **Royal Fromentin**, 11 Rue Fromentin, 75009, ☎ 48 74 85 93. 45 rm. ❶❶

Restaurants:

◆◆◆◆ **L'Opera**, 5 Pl. de l'Opera, 75009, ☎ 42 68 12 13. ♿ Closed Aug. Chef Gil Jouanin belongs among the greats. Under Charles Garnier's ceilings, classified historical monuments, fine traditional cooking, large wine selection. ❶❶❶❶

◆◆◆ **Auberge Landaise**, 23 Rue Clauzel, 75009, ☎ 48 78 74 40. AE, DC, Visa. ♿ Closed Aug, Sun. Spec: *foie gras chaud aux raisins, cassoulet.* ❶❶

◆◆ **Casino**, 41 Rue de Clichy, 75009, ☎ 42 80 34 62. ♿ The chef J.P. Jarrault and his associate, P. Masbatin, opened this restaurant 3 years ago, and it has turned out to be a delightful local restaurant. Spec: *salade de raie au vinaigre de cidre*, and very good desserts. ❶❶❶

◆◆ **Charlot**, 12 Pl. Clichy, 75009, ☎ 48 74 49 64. AE, DC, Visa. Fish and seafood specialties. ❶❶❶

◆◆ **Le Grand Café**, 4 Bd. des Capucines, 75009, ☎ 47 42 75 77. AE, DC, Visa. Open 24 hours. *Belle Époque.* Seafood and good cooking. ❶❶

◆◆ **Pagoda**, 50 Rue de Provence, 75009, ☎ 48 74 81 48. Visa. Closed Sun in Aug. Chinese cooking. Spec: *canard laqué, pinces de crabes frites.* ❶❶

◆◆ **Le Petit Riche**, 25 Rue Le Pelletier, 75009, ☎ 47 70 68 68. AE, Visa. Closed Aug 10-31 and Sun. Improved cooking in this 1880's setting. Recommended spec: *petit salé, boeuf gros sel, foie de veau*, Loire wines. ❶❶

◆◆ **Ty Coz**, 35 Rue Saint-Georges, 75009, ☎ 48 78 42 95. AE, DC, Visa. Closed Sun, Mon.

Seafood specialities with 20 years of tradition. ❶❶❶

◆ **Les Diamantaires**, 60 Rue La Fayette, 75009, ☎ 47 70 78 14. Closed Jul 27 – Sep 7, Mon, Tue. Good, simple Greek cooking. ❶❶

Hotels:

★★★★ **Pavillon l'Horset**, 38 Rue de l'Échiquier, 75010, ☎ 42 46 92 75. Tx 641905. AE, DC, Euro, Visa. 91 rm. ❶❶❶❶

★★★ **Gare du Nord**, 33 Rue de Saint-Quentin, 75010, ☎ 48 78 02 92. Tx 642415. AE, Euro, Visa. 49 rm. ❶❶❶❶

★★★ **Terminus Nord**, 12 Bd. de Denain, 75010, ☎ 42 80 20 00. Tx 660615. AE, DC, Euro, Visa. 225 rm. ⊗♿❶❶❶❶

★★ **Apollo**, 11 Rue de Dunkerque, 75010, ☎ 48 78 04 98. Tx 648895. AE. 45 rm. ❶❶❶

★★ **Baccarat**, 19 Rue des Messageries, 75010, ☎ 47 70 96 92. 31 rm. ▦ ⌕ ❶❶❶

★ **Chabrol**, 46 Rue de Chabrol, 75010, ☎ 47 70 10 77. 25 rm. ❶❶

★ **France**, 57 Rue des Petites-Écuries, 75010, ☎ 42 46 39 70. 40 rm. ⊗ ❶❶

Restaurants:

◆◆ **Au Châteaubriant**, 23 Rue de Chabrol, 75010, ☎ 48 24 58 94. AE, Visa. ⌕ ⊗ ♿ Closed Jul 27 – Aug 27, Sun, Mon. For more than 10 years the skilled Guy Bürrli, former chef of J. Forno, has cooked pasta and offers excellent Italian cooking. ❶❶❶

◆◆ **Brasserie Flo**, 7 Cour des Petites-Écuries, 75010, ☎ 47 70 13 59. AE, DC, Visa. Closed Aug 1–28. This 1890s restaurant is also owned by J.-P. Bucher; excellent *brasserie*-style cooking. Book by phone to avoid queuing at the bar. ❶❶

◆◆ **Chez Michel**, 10 Rue de Belzunce, 75010, ☎ 48 78 44 14. AE, DC, Visa. ♿ Closed Aug 1-25, 15 days in Feb, Dec 25, Fri, Sat. Spec: *salade de langoustines aux kiwis.* ❶❶❶

◆◆ **Julien**, 16 Rue du Faubourg-Saint-Denis, 75010, ☎ 47 70 12 06. AE, DC, Visa. ♿ Closed Jul. One of the most delightful "links" in J.-P. Bucher's chain. Good cooking in a *brasserie*. Expect an hour's wait standing and 20 min seated during peak times. ❶❶

◆◆ **Louis XIV**, 8 Bd. Saint-Denis, 75010, ☎ 42 08 56 56. AE, DC, Visa. ♿ Closed Jun 1 – Sep 1, Mon, Tue. Superb fish and seafood dishes, and game in season. Traditional *grande cuisine.* ❶❶❶

◆◆ **La Petite Tonkinoise**, 56 Rue du Faubourg-Poissonnière, 75010, ☎ 42 46 85 98. Visa. Closed Aug – Sep 15, Dec 24 – Jan 5, Sun, Mon. Excellent Vietnamese cooking. ❶❶

♦ **Pinocchio**, 49 Rue d'Enghien, 75010, ☎ 47 70 01 98. AE, DC, Visa. Closed Sat noon, Sun and Jul 31 – Aug 30. All possible kinds of pasta. Excellent, simple Italian cooking. ❻❻

Hotels:

★★★★ **Holiday Inn**, 10 Pl. de la République, 75011, ☎ 43 55 44 34. Tx 210651. AE, DC, Euro, Visa. 333 rm, 8 suites 🅿 & ❻❻❻❻❻ Rest. ♦♦♦ ❻❻

★★ **Du Nord et de l'Est**, 49 Rue de Malte, 75011, ☎ 47 00 71 70. 44 rm. ⊗ ❻❻

★★ **Royal-Voltaire**, 53 Rue Richard-Lenoir, 75011, ☎ 43 79 75 67. AE, Visa, 55 rm. ❻❻❻

Restaurants:

♦♦♦ **A Sousceyrac**, 35 Rue Faidherbe, 75011, ☎ 43 71 65 30. AE, Visa. Closed Aug, 1 week (Easter), Sat, Sun. Spec: game, *lièvre à la royale, foie gras.* Good, inexpensive wine selection. ❻❻

♦♦ **Le Chardenoux**, 1 Rue Jules-Vallès, 75011, ☎ 43 71 49 52. AE, Visa. An authentic 1900s bistro. Spec: *pudding à la moelle,* seasonal produce. ❻❻❻

♦♦ **Chez Philippe** 106 Rue de la Folie-Méricourt, 75011, ☎ 43 57 33 78. Closed Sat, Sun and Aug, nat hols. Offers fine, rich specialties from the Southwest. Good wines. ❻❻

♦♦ **Le Péché Mignon**, 5 Rue Guillaume-Bertrand, 75011, ☎ 43 57 02 51. Visa. Closed Aug, 1 week school hols in Feb, Sun, Mon. Spec: *panaché de poissons aux raviolis de St-Jacques, fricassée de ris et rognon de veau au sauternes.* ❻❻

♦♦ **Le Repaire de Cartouche**, 8 Bd. des Filles-du-Calvaire, 75011, ☎ 47 00 25 86. Visa. & Closed Jul 25 – Aug 24, Sat, Sun and nat hols. Dishes from the Southwest; rich and well served. ❻❻

♦ **Astier**, 44 Rue J.-P. Timbaud, 75011, ☎ 43 57 16 35. Closed Aug 9 – Sep 2, Dec 25 – Jan 1, Sat, Sun. A good, inexpensive bistro. The menu changes daily, and Michel Picquart knows his wines. ❻

Hotels:

★★★ **Azur**, 5 Rue de Lyon, 75012, ☎ 43 43 88 35. Tx 670038. AE, DC, Euro, Visa. 64 rm. ❻❻❻❻

★★★ **Paris-Lyon Palace** (Inter-Hôtel), 11 Rue de Lyon, 75012, ☎ 43 07 29 49. 128 rm. & ❻❻❻❻ Rest. ♦♦ **Le Relais de la Méditerranée.** ❻❻

★★★ **Terminus Lyon**, 19 Bd. Diderot, 75012, ☎ 43 43 24 03. 61 rm. ❻❻❻

★★ **Frantour**, 2 Pl. Louis-Armand, 75012, ☎ 43 44 84 84. Tx 217096. AE, DC, Euro, Visa. 315 rm. & ❻❻❻❻

★★ **Jules César**, 52 Av. Ledru-Rollin, 75012, ☎ 43 43 15 88. Tx 670945. 48 rm. ⊗ ❻❻

Restaurants:

♦♦♦ **Au Pressoir**, 257 Av. Daumesnil, 75012, ☎ 43 44 38 21. Visa. Closed Aug, Easter school hols, Sat and Sun. The freshened-up setting highlights Henri Seguin's pleasant cooking: *rougets à la purée de cresson, lapereau farci aux cèpes, mesclun aux oreilles de porc.* Good service. ❻❻❻

♦♦♦ **Le Train Bleu**, 20 Bd Diderot, gare de Lyon, 1st Floor, 75012, ☎ 43 43 09 06. Tx 220064. AE, DC, Euro, Visa. & Historically classified 1900s setting. Cooking from the Lyons and Forez regions. ❻❻

♦♦ **La Gourmandise**, 271 Av. Daumesnil, 75012, ☎ 43 44 34 26. & Closed Aug 15-31, Sat noon, Sun. Alain Denoual's efforts are praiseworthy. Spec: *cabillaud à la compôte d'aubergines, magret de canard aux navets nouveaux.* ❻❻

♦♦ **Le Trou Gascon**, 40 Rue Taine, 75012, ☎ 43 44 34 26. Closed Aug 15 – Sep 15, Sat and Sun. Good country cooking. Southwest: *jambon de pays, confit de canard à la galette de cèpes, raviolis au foie gras,* good Bordeaux wines and choice of armagnacs. ❻❻❻

Hotels:

★★ **Gobelins**, 57 Bd Saint-Marcel, 75013, ☎ 43 31 79 89. 45 rm. ❻❻❻

★★ **Véronèse**, 5 Rue Véronèse, 75013, ☎ 47 07 20 90. 66 rm. ⊗ ❻❻

Restaurants:

♦♦ **Chinatown Olympiades**, 44 Av. d'Ivry, 75013, ☎ 45 84 72 21. Chic, but reasonable prices. ❻❻

♦♦ **Le Petit Marguery**, 9 Bd de Port-Royal, 75013, ☎ 43 31 58 59. AE, DC, Euro, Visa. Closed Sun, Mon, Aug and Dec 23 – Jan 2. Bravo to the Cousyn brothers for their good humor and fine cooking. Spec: *champignons des bois,* game in season. ❻❻❻

♦♦ **Ti Koc**, 13 Pl. de Vénétie, 75013, ☎ 45 84 21 00. First Chinese nightclub in Paris. Cooking and floor show much like those of Hong Kong or Singapore. ❻❻❻

♦♦ **Les Vieux Métiers de France**, 13 Bd. Auguste-Blanqui, 75013, ☎ 45 88 90 03. AE, DC, Euro, Visa. Closed Sun, Mon. Spec: *cocotte d'oursins, sauté de langoustines maraîchères.* ❻❻

♦ **Chez Jacky**, 109 Rue du Dessous-des-Berges, 75013, ☎ 45 83 71 55. Spec: *foie gras armagnac maison, queue de langoustine tiède au pamplemousse.* ❻

◆ **Hawaii**, 87 Av. d'Ivry, 75013, ☎ 45 86 91 90. Visa. ⑁ Closed Thu. The chic Asian *brasserie*. Vietnamese spec: *nems*, grilled pork and chicken.

◆ **Sing-Sing**, 100 Av. d'Ivry, 75013, ☎ 45 82 93 17. Vietnamese specs. ❶❶

════════════ PARIS 14ᵗʰ

Hotels:
★★★★ (L) **Méridien Montparnasse**, 19 Rue du Ct-R.Mouchotte, 75014, ☎ 43 20 15 51. Tx 200134, 203518. AE, DC, Euro, Visa. 915 rm, 35 apart.   ℗ ⑁ ✲ ⑁ ❶❶❶❶❶ Rest. ◆◆. Closed Aug 4-31. **La Rûche**, ◆◆ **Le Montparnasse 1925**. ❶

★★★★ (L) **Pullmann Saint-Jacques**, 17 Bd. Saint-Jacques, 75014, ☎ 45 89 89 80. 797 rm. ℗ ⑁ ❶❶❶❶❶ Rest. ◆◆ **Café Français**. Closed Aug. Regional dishes. ❶❶

★★ **Carlton Palace**, 207 Bd.Raspail, 75014, ☎ 43 20 62 94. Tx 200183. Visa. 63 rm. ❶❶❶

★★ **Châtillon Hôtel**, 11, Sq. de Châtillon, 75014, ☎ 45 42 31. 17 rm. ⑁ Closed Aug. ❶❶

Restaurants:
◆◆◆ **Le Dôme**, 108 Bd. du Montparnasse, 75014, ☎ 43 35 25 81. AE, DC, Euro, Visa. Closed Mon. Excellent fish and seafood served in this famous setting. ❶❶❶

◆◆◆ **Le Duc** 243 Bd. Raspail, 75014, ☎ 43 20 96 30. ⑁ Closed Sat, Sun, Mon. Fresh fish feast by Jean and Paul Minchelli. Shellfish, *loup cru en vessie tartare*, *sole au vinaigre*, seafood. ❶❶❶❶

◆◆ **Auberge de l'Argoat**, 27 Av. Reille, 75014 ☎ 45 89 17 05. Closed Aug, Sun, Mon. First place goes to Brittany cooking, with such dishes as the *andouille de Guéméné aux poissons de la côte*. ❶❶

◆◆ **Gérard et Nicole**, 6 Av. J.-Moulin, 75014, ☎ 45 42 39 56. AE, DC, Euro, Visa. Closed Jul 15 – Aug 15, Sat and Sun. Gérard and Nicole continue to offer a warm welcome and very good cooking. Spec: *saumon aux feuilles de lard*, *feuilleté de pigeon à la sauce betterave*. ❶❶❶

◆◆ **Lous Landès**, 157 Av. du Maine, 75014, ☎ 45 43 08 04. Visa. An abundance of flowers and paintings, and Jean-Pierre's piano add to the excellent Landaise cooking. Spec: *maca-ronade de coquillages*, *foie gras en papillote*, *garbure*. ❶❶❶

◆◆ **Natacha**, 17 bis Rue Campagne-Première. 75014 ☎ 43 20 79 27. Closed Sun eve. *Lotte aux poireaux*, *grenadin de veau*. ❶❶

◆ **L'Assiette**, 181 Rue du Château, 75014, ☎ 43 22 64 86. Closed Aug, 1 week in May, Sat noon and Mon. Only 5 tables to sample the Southwest specs. ❶❶

◆ **Au Feu Follet**, 5 Rue Raymond-Losserand, 75014, ☎ 43 22 65 72. ⑁ Closed Sat noon, Sun, Jul 20 – Aug 20. A friendly little res-taurant, where the proprietress is hard at work in the kitchen. *Boeuf mode* and *brandade de morue* served long into the evening. ❶❶

◆ **La Cagouille**, 89 Rue Daguerre, 75014, ☎ 43 22 09 01. ⑁ Closed Sun, Mon and Jul 26 – Sep 3. The best and undoubtedly cheapest fish bistro in Paris. Spec: *moules brûle-doigts*, *rougets grillés*, *drôle de petite friture*. A magnifi-cent selection of cognacs. ❶❶

◆ **Chez Fernand**, 11 Rue G-Saché, 75014. ☎ 45 43 65 76. AE, DC, Euro, Visa. ⑁ Closed Sun. The proprietor makes his own bread, butter and *charcuterie*, and prepares his delectable camemberts. ❶❶

◆ **La Coupole**, 102 Bd. du Montparnasse, 75014, ☎ 43 20 14 20. Visa. ⑁ Closed Aug. Good, simple cooking in a 1920s setting, which draws a varied and numerous clientele. ❶❶

◆ **Leni. Restaurant**, 5 Rue de Pressensé. 75014, ☎ 45 41 06 17. Closed Mon, Tues. For movie buffs and fans of honest family-style cooking. ❶❶

◆ **Les Petites Sorcières**, 12 Rue Liancourt, 75014, ☎ 43 21 95 68. Closed Aug, 1 week at Christmas, Sat noon, Sun. Good, simple cooking and friendly service. ❶❶

════════════ PARIS 15ᵗʰ

Hotels:
★★★★(L) **Hilton International Paris**, 18 Av. Suffren, 75015, ☎ 42 73 92 00. Tx 200955. AE, DC, Euro, Visa. 79 rm, 29 apart. ⑁ ℗ ⑁ ✲ ⊠ ⑁ ❶❶❶❶❶ Rest. ◆◆◆ **Le Toit de Paris** ⑁ ⑁ Closed Jul 27 – Aug 28, Sun eve only. The top of the Hilton offers a splendid view of the capital. ❶❶❶❶ Rest. ◆◆ **Le Western**, ✲ ❶❶ ◆ **La Terrasse** (coffee-shop). ❶❶

★★★★(L) **Nikko**, 61 Quai de Grenelle, 75015, ☎ 45 75 62 62. Tx 260012. AE, DC, Euro, Visa. 777 rm, 9 suites. ℗ ⑁ ✲ ⊠ ⑁ The ultramodern masterpiece of the newly-constructed Seine water-front, ❶❶❶❶❶ Rest. ◆◆◆ **Les Célébrités**. Joël Robuchon's brilliant culinary traditions perpetuated masterfully by his successor, Jacques Sénéchal. Magnificent desserts in a spacious, modern setting. ❶❶❶

★★★★(L) **Sofitel Paris**, 8–12 Rue Louis-Armand, 75015, ☎ 45 54 95 00. Tx 200432. AE, DC, Euro, Visa. 635 rm. ⑁ ℗ ⑁ ⊠ ⑁ At the city limits, a contemporary luxury hotel with its own panoramic swimming pool. ❶❶❶❶❶ Rest ◆◆◆ **Le Relais de Sèvres**. ⑁ Closed Aug, Sat and Sun. ❶❶❶

★★ **Confort Hôtel**, 2 Rue de Casablanca, 75015, ☎ 45 58 16 08. 50 rm. ✲ ❶❶

★★ **Lecourbe**, 28 Rue Lecourbe, 75015, ☎ 47 34 49 06. 47 rm. Indoor patio. ⚓ ❻❻❻
★★ **Pacific Hôtel**, 11 Rue Fondary, 75015, ☎ 45 75 20 49. Tx 201346. Euro. 66 rm. Small and classic. ❻❻❻

Restaurants:

♦♦♦ **Morot-Gaudry**, 6 Rue de la Cavalerie, 75015, ☎ 45 67 06 85. Visa. ⚜ Closed Sat, Sun. In the "open sky," with a superb view over the roofs of Paris and the Eiffel Tower from the beautiful terrace on warm days, J.-P. Morot-Gaudry's good cooking with good wines. ❻❻❻
♦♦♦ **Olympe**, 8 Rue Nicolas-Charlet, 75015, ☎ 47 34 86 08. AE, DC, Euro, Visa. Closed Jul 29 – Aug 21, Dec 22 – Jan 2, Mon. Eve only ex Thu. High-quality cooking. Fashionable Parisian and international clientele. ❻❻❻❻
♦♦♦ **Le Pfister**, 1 Rue du Dr-Jacquemaire-Clémenceau, 75015, ☎ 48 28 51 38. ⚓ Closed Sat noon, Sun and Aug, Sep and hols. Hushed opulence in a quiet street; Catherine and Philippe offer a celestial *feuilleté d'endives au roquefort, rillettes de saumon, ragoût de tête de veau mijoté aux légumes, feuilleté aux prunes et à la cannelle*. Reasonably-priced wines. ❻❻
♦♦ **L'Aquitaine**, 54 Rue de Dantzig, 75015 ☎ 48 28 67 38. AE, DC, Euro, Visa. Closed Sun, Mon. Christiane Massia's dishes inspired by the Southwest. ❻❻❻
♦♦ **Au Petit Mirabeau**, 3 Rue de la Convention, 75015 ☎ 45 77 95 79. Closed 15 days in Aug, Dec 25–Jan 1, Sat, Sun and nat hols. Good traditional French cooking. Spec: *gâteau de foies blonds, pâtes aux foies de volailles, rognons de veau, desserts en soupière*. ❻❻
♦♦ **Aux Trois Horloges**, 73 Rue Brancion, 75015, ☎ 48 28 24 08. AE, DC, Euro, Visa. Real *pied-noir* cooking in the great tradition. *Couscous, paëlla, méchoui*. Home catering service. ❻❻
♦♦ **Chez Maître Albert**, 8–10 Rue de l'Abbé Groult, 75015, ☎ 48 28 36 98. AE, DC, Euro, Visa. Closed Sat noon. Artists from the Beaux-Arts exhibit while M. Civel serves little masterpieces. Spec: *bouillabaisse en filets, escalope de saumon frais Maître Albert*. ❻❻
♦♦ **Le Clos de la Tour**, 22 Rue Falguière, 75015 ☎ 43 22 34 73. AE, DC, Euro, Visa. Closed Aug, Sat noon, Sun. Small, selective menu. ❻❻
♦♦ **La Gauloise**, 59 Av. de La Motte-Picquet, 75015, ☎ 47 34 11 64. AE, DC, Euro, Visa. ⚜ ⚓ Closed Sat and Sun. It's worth trying out the next-door annex, *La Gitane*, for pleasant, inexpensive bistro cooking. ❻❻
♦♦ **La Maison Blanche**, 82 Bd. Lefèvre, 75015, ☎ 48 28 38 83. ⚓ Closed Sat noon, Sun and Mon. Young, fashionable clientele at José Lampreia's restaurant. ❻❻❻

♦♦ **Napoléon et Chaix**, 46 Rue Balard, 75015, ☎ 45 54 09 00. Closed Jul, 2 weeks in Sep, Sat noon and Sun. Simple, enjoyable, varied meals. ❻❻❻
♦♦ **La Petite Bretonnière**, 2 Rue de Cadix, 75015, ☎ 48 28 32 39. AE, Visa. ⚓ Closed Aug 5 – Sep 2, Dec 24 – Jan 7, Sat noon, Sun. Southwest specs: *foie gras frais au torchon, terrine de St-Jacques aux artichauts* (in season). ❻❻
♦♦ **Pierre Vedel**, 19 Rue Duranton, 75015, ☎ 45 58 43 17. ⚜ ⚓ Closed Sat and Sun from Jul 9 to Aug 8. Pierre Vedel has kept the tradition of good Sete region cooking, *bourride*, fish, but also *tête de veau Vaugirard, côte de boeuf*; pleasant and low-priced wines. ❻❻❻
♦♦ **Le Restaurant du Marché**, 59 Rue de Dantzig, 75015, ☎ 48 28 31 55. Excellent specs from the Landes: wine from Chalosse. ❻❻❻
♦ **Le Caroubier**, 8 Av. du Maine, 75015, ☎ 45 48 14 38. Closed Sun eve and Jul 15 – Aug 21. Excellent *couscous*, prepared in all possible ways, good *merguez* and *pastillas*. ❻❻
♦ **Moulin de la Boulange**, 70 Rue de Vouillé, 75015 ☎ 48 28 81 61. AE, DC, Euro, Visa. Closed Sat and Sun. Specialties from the Beaujolais region, excellent wines: Beaujolais and Coteaux du Lyonnais. ❻❻
♦ **Le Tout Alger**, 364 Rue de Vaugirard 75015, ☎ 45 32 78 26. Closed Sun, Mon and Aug. *Couscous, paëlla, brochettes, merguez*. ❻❻
♦ **Le Pacifico**, 50 Bd. du Montparnasse, 75015, ☎ 45 48 63 87. Closed Dec 25 – Jan 1, Mon noon. For the "Chicanas" and Mexican spec: *tacos, enchiladas, guacamole*. ❻❻
♦ **Le Volant**, 13 Rue B.-Dussanne, 75015 ☎ 45 75 27 67. Visa. Closed Aug, Sat noon and Sun. Frequented by competition racing drivers. Simple, tasty dishes under the direction of the ex-driver proprietor, G. Houel. Superb meats. ❻❻

PARIS 16ᵗʰ

Hotels:

★★★★ **Baltimore**, 88 *bis* Av. Kléber, 75016, ☎ 45 53 83 83. Tx 611591. AE, DC, Euro, Visa. 119 rm. ⚓ ❻❻❻❻❻ Rest. ♦♦♦ **L'Estournel**. Closed Sat, Sun and Aug. Enjoyable cooking. ❻❻❻
★★★★(L) **Raphaël**, 17 Av. Kléber, 75016, ☎ 45 02 16 00. Tx 610356. AE, DC, Euro, Visa. 87 rm, 4 suites. ⚓ ❻❻❻❻❻ Rest. ♦♦. Closed Sun. ❻❻
★★★★ **Résidence du Bois** (Relais et châteaux), 16 Rue Chalgrin, 75016, ☎ 45 00 50 59. 20 rm. ⚓ ❻❻❻❻❻

★★★ **Muette**, 32 Rue de Boulainvilliers, 75016, ☎ 45 25 13 08. AE, DC, Euro, Visa. 13 rm. Closed Aug. Former 18th-century mansion.

★★★ **Régina de Passy**, 6 Rue de la Tour, 75016, ☎ 45 00 23 45. AE, DC, Euro, Visa. 30 rm. ❶❶❶❶

★★★ **Résidence Impériale**, 155 Av. Malakoff, 75016, ☎ 45 00 23 45. AE, DC, Euro, Visa. 30 rm. ❶❶❶

★★ **Exelmans**, 73 Rue Boileau, 75016, ☎ 42 24 94 66. 53 rm. ♿ ❶❶❶

★★ **Villa d'Auteuil**, 28 Rue Poussin, 75016, ☎ 42 88 30 37. 17 rm. ❶❶

★ **Trocadéro**, 21 Rue Saint-Didier, 75116, ☎ 45 53 01 82. 27 rm. ❶❶

Restaurants:

♦♦♦♦ **Faugeron** (Relais gourmand), 52 Rue de Longchamp, 75016, ☎ 47 04 24 53. Closed Aug, end Dec, Sat and Sun. Henri Faugeron successfully blends Corrèze regional recipes with modern light ones. ❶❶❶

♦♦♦♦ **Jamin**, 32 Rue de Longchamp, 75016, ☎ 47 27 12 27. Closed Jul, Sat and Sun. Joël Robuchon is still the leader of the great young French chefs. In a new setting, his preparations have reached the highest standards: *raviolis de langoustines, morue fraîche aux aromates, agneau rôti en croûte de sel*, great wines. ❶❶❶❶ Early booking is highly recommended.

♦♦♦♦ **Le Pré Catelan**, Rte de Suresnes, Bois de Boulogne, 75016, ☎ 45 24 55 28. Tx 614983. AE, DC, Euro, Visa. ♿ Closed Feb, Sun eve and Mon. Beautiful restaurant in the heart of the Bois de Boulogne. Light, inventive cooking. ❶❶❶❶

♦♦♦♦ **Le Vivarois**, 192 Av. Victor-Hugo, 75016, ☎ 45 04 04 31. AE, DC, Euro, Visa. Ⓟ ♿ Closed Aug, Sat and Sun. An ultra-modern decor for traditional cooking based on market-fresh produce. Spec: *huîtres chaudes au curry, pâte de canard F. Point, pied de porc farci aux légumes et aux truffles, coq ivre de pommard*, good wines. ❶❶❶

♦♦♦ **Le Chandelier**, 4 Rue P. Valéry, 75016 ☎ 47 04 55 22. AE, DC, Euro, Visa. Closed Jewish hols, Fri and Sat eve May to Sep. A luxurious kosher restaurant in an 18th-century mansion, run by the Beth-Din of Paris. Light cooking. ❶❶❶

♦♦♦ **La Grande Cascade**, Bois de Boulogne, 75016 ☎ 45 06 33 51. AE, DC, Euro, Visa. Ⓟ ♿ Closed Dec 20 – Jan 20; noon and eve May 15 – Oct 15; noon only the rest of the year. A pastoral setting for an extremely Parisian restaurant. ❶❶❶

♦♦♦ **Guy Savoy**, 28 Rue Duret, 75016, ☎ 45 00 17 67. ♿ Closed Sat and Sun. Guy Savoy makes a great effort to satisfy his demanding customers. ❶❶❶❶

♦♦♦ **Jean-Claude Ferrero**, 38 Rue Vital, 75016, ☎ 45 04 42 42. AE, DC, Visa. ♿ Closed Aug 15 – Sep 1, Dec 24 – Jan 5, Sat and Sun. In his beautifully-restored private mansion, J.-C. Ferrero's mushroom specs, exceptional menus. ❶❶❶❶

♦♦♦ **Paul Chêne**, 123 Rue Lauriston, 75016, ☎ 47 27 63 17. AE, DC, Visa. Closed Sat, Sun and Aug. Paul Chêne is, thanks to his reliable and inspired cooking, one of the greatest ambassadors of French cooking. Spec: *beignets de brandade à la rouille, merlan frit en colère*, game in season. ❶❶❶

♦♦♦ **Le Petit Bedon**, 38 Rue Pergolèse, 75016, ☎ 45 00 23 66. AE, DC, Visa. Closed Sat, Sun, and Aug. Beautifully redecorated, this pleasant restaurant is devoted to simple but great cooking. Prices have not increased. Spec: *tourte au frais, homard cocotte*. ❶❶❶

♦♦♦ **Prunier Tratkir**, 16 Av. Victor-Hugo, 75016, ☎ 45 00 89 12. AE, DC, Visa, ♿ Closed May 1, Mon and Tue. A restaurant-fishmarket since 1915; traditions continue, seafood dishes being the specialty of the house. ❶❶❶

♦♦♦ **Le Toit de Passy**, 94 Av. Paul-Doumer, 75016, ☎ 45 24 55 37. Visa. ♿ Ⓟ Closed Sat noon, Sun, Public hols, Dec 22 – Jan 5. Above the roofs of Paris, a small gourmet's paradise. Modern decor with a terrace for Yann Jacquot's good cooking. Spec: *blancs de poireaux à la vinaigrette de truffes, rognon de veau rôti entier, poulet de Bresse à la crème d'estragon*. ❶❶❶

♦♦ **Brasserie le Stella**, 133 Av. Victor-Hugo, 75016, ☎ 47 27 60 54. Closed Aug and 1 week Feb. An attractive, highly fashionable *brasserie*; the proprietor buys his wines directly from the vineyard. ❶❶

♦♦ **Conti**, 72 Rue Lauriston, 75016, ☎ 47 27 74 67. Visa. Closed Sat, Sun, Public hols and Aug. Excellent Italian specs. ❶❶❶

♦ **Aux Trois Obus**, 120 Rue Michel-Ange 75016, ☎ 46 51 22 58. *Brasserie*-style. ❶❶

PARIS 17

Hotels:

★★★★(L) **Concorde La Fayette**, 5 Pl. du Gal-Koenig, 75017, ☎ 47 58 12 84. Tx 650892, 650905. AE, DC, Euro, Visa. 1 000 rm, 25 apart. Ⓟ ♿ A very modern complex dotted with boutiques, conference rooms theaters, accommodation and restaurant facilities, ❶❶❶❶❶ Rest. ♦ **L'Arc-en Ciel**, ♿ ❶❶ ♦♦♦ **L'Étoile d'Or**, ❶❶❶ ♦♦ **Les Saisons** (coffee-shop), ❶❶ Panoramic bar on the 33rd floor. ❶❶❶

★★★★(L) **Méridien Paris**, 81 Bd. Gouvion Saint-Cyr. 75017, ☎ 47 58 12 30. 1 027 rm

16 apart. 🅿 ❺❺❺❺❺ Rest. ♦♦ **Le Clos Longchamp**, ❺❺❺ ♦♦ **Le Yamato** (Japanese dishes), ❺❺ ♦ **La Beaujolaise**, ♦ **Arlequin** (coffee-shop). ❺

★★★ **Belfast**, 10 Av. Carnot, 75017, ☎ 43 80 10. 59 rm. ∮ 🅿 ♿ Close to the Arc de Triomphe. ❺❺❺

★★★ **Regent's Garden**, 6 Rue Pierre-Demours, 75017, ☎ 45 74 07 30. 40 rm. ❺❺❺

★★ **Deux Acacias**, 28 Rue de l'Arc-de-Triomphe, 75017, ☎ 43 80 01 85. 31 rm. ❺❺

Restaurants:

♦♦♦ **La Barrière de Clichy**, 1 Rue de Paris, 92110 Clichy, ☎ 47 37 05 18. AE, DC, Visa. Closed Sat noon, Sun. Market-fresh preparations. Superb wines. ❺❺❺

♦♦♦ **Le Bernardin**, 18 Rue Troyon, 75017, ☎ 43 80 40 61. AE, Visa. Closed Sun, Mon and Aug. A pleasant setting where Gilbert Le Coze takes care of his regulars. Fresh fish selected nightly at Rungis (the largest fish market in France). ❺❺❺❺

♦♦♦ **Chez Georges**, 273 Bd Pereire, 75017, ☎ 45 74 31 00. Closed Aug. Open till 11 pm. A leg of lamb is carved before you in the dining-room once a week. Dishes on the other days include: *train de côte de boeuf*, memorable fresh chips. The cellar is well looked after by the proprietor, Roger Mazarguil. ❺❺

♦♦♦ **Ma Cuisine**, 18 Rue Bayen, 75017, ☎ 45 72 02 19. AE, DC, Visa. ♿ 🅿 Closed Sun. A new setting to enhance the meat and fish dishes prepared by Alain Donnard. Glorious desserts. ❺❺❺

♦♦♦ **Le Manoir de Paris**, 6 Rue P.-Demours, 75017, ☎ 45 74 61 58. AE, DC, Visa. Closed Jul 5 – Aug 5, Sat, Sun. Francis Vendehende (*La Ferme St-Simon*) and his chef, P. Groult, give a daily demonstration of their competence and talent in this charming restaurant. ❺❺❺

♦♦♦ **Michel Rostang** (Relais gourmand, Relais et châteaux), 29 Rue Rennequin, 75017, ☎ 47 63 40 77. Visa. Closed July 26 – Aug 26, Sat noon, Sun. The restaurant is becoming more and more beautiful, which makes you further appreciate Michel Rostang's good cooking. Spec: *soufflé léger de homard, tarte chaude aux escargots*, good wine selection. ❺❺❺❺

♦♦ **Apicius**, 122 Av. de Villiers 75017, ☎ 43 80 19 66. Closed Aug 8-24, Sat, Sun. In a handsome new decor: *tête de veau rémoulade, ragoût de homard et de turbot à l'ail*, modest, enjoyable light wines. ❺❺

♦♦ **La Braisière**, 54 Rue Cardinet, 75017, ☎ 47 63 40 37. Closed Sat noon, Sun. Good cooking from the Breton B. Vaxelaire. Spec: *braisière de canard poëlée de lotte*. ❺❺❺

♦♦ **Chez la Mère Michel**, 5 Rue Rennequin, 75017, ☎ 47 63 59 80. Visa. ♿ Closed Aug, Sat, Sun, hols. The temple of *beurre blanc sauce* perpetuated by M. Gaillard in his authentic little bistro. ❺❺❺

♦♦ **Chez Laudrin**, 154 Bd. Pereire, 75017, ☎ 43 80 87 40,. AE, Visa. ♿ Closed Mar 24 – Apr 1, Sat and Sun. Solid cooking and good wines (billed according to amount consumed) are offered by Jacques Billaud, ably seconded by chef Benoît Teillet. Spec: *pétoncles farcies, bourride de baudroie, bavette* and delicious chips. ❺❺

♦♦ **La Côte de Boeuf**, 4 Rue Saussier-Leroy, 75017, ☎ 42 27 73 50. AE, DC, Visa. Closed Sat, Sun, 1 week Easter, Aug 3–31 and Christmas hols. A superb joint of beef, along with excellent dishes inspired by Fernande Allard, the chef's mentor for 12 years. ❺❺

♦♦ **La Coquille**, 6 Rue du Débarcadère, 75017, ☎ 45 74 25 95. Visa. Closed Aug, Dec 25 – Jan 1, Sun, Mon. C. Lausecker continues the fine tradition of Paul Blache's cooking. A festival of seafood in season. ❺❺❺

♦♦ **Guyvonne**, 14 Rue de Thann, 75017, ☎ 42 27 25 43. Closed Dec 24 – Jan 5, Jul 14 – Aug 4, Sat and Sun. Carefully-prepared dishes made to order, and served in the calm of the Parc Monceau. ❺❺❺

♦♦ **Lajarrige**, 16, Av. de Villiers, 75017, ☎ 47 63 25 61. Visa. Closed Aug 4 – Sep 1, Sat noon, Sun. Musketeer J.-C Lajarrige receives you in his 17th-century setting. Regional cooking by E. Marrottat. Spec: *foie gras en papillote à l'émincé de homard, cuisse de canard confite et fumée*. ❺❺

♦♦ **Michel Comby**, 116 Bd. Pereire, 75017, ☎ 43 80 88 68. A new restaurant. Spec: *cassolette de queues d'écrevisses*. ❺❺

♦♦ **Paul et France**, 27 Av. Niel, 75017, ☎ 47 63 04 24. AE, DC, Visa. Closed Jul 14 – Aug 15, Sat and Sun. Members of the Paris-St-Germain football club dine here. Excellent fresh produce. ❺❺❺

♦♦ **La Petite Auberge**, 38 Rue Laugier, 75017, ☎ 47 63 85 51. DC, Visa. Closed Aug, Sun, Mon. Discover the fine cooking of Léo Harbonnier. Spec: *turbot C. Renault, millefeuille*. ❺❺❺

♦♦ **Le Petit Colombier**, 42 Rue des Acacias, 75017, ☎ 43 80 28 54. Visa. ♿ Closed Sat and Sun noon, Dec 25 – Jan 3, Jul 25 – Aug 17, Bernard Fournier's pleasant small country-style inn. Spec: *foie du veau, terrine de mousserons à la julienne de truffes*, selected wines at reasonable prices. ❺❺❺

♦♦ **Le Relais d'Anjou**, 15 Rue de l'Arc-de-Triomphe, 75017, ☎ 43 80 43 82. DC, Visa. Closed Aug, Sat noon, Sun. Excellent Angevine cooking. Spec: *charlotte de crabe et* *d'avocat au coulis de tomate.* ❸❸❸

♦♦ **Le Santenay**, 75 Av. Niel, 75017, ☎ 42 27 88 44. Closed Jul 30 – Aug 16, Sun eve and Mon. An extensive choice of classic dishes; highest quality cooking prepared by the chef Francis Vallot. ❸❸❸

♦♦ **Sormani**, 4 Rue du Gal-Lanrezac, 75017, ☎ 43 80 13 91. Closed Aug 1–25, 1 week at Easter, Dec 25 – Jan 1, Sat, Sun. In a setting of blue velvet, Pascal Fayet offers you the finest Italian gourmet festival in Paris. Accept recommendations. Pasta, *raviolis, carpaccio,* ham, *rougets* Great chiantis. ❸❸❸❸

♦♦ **La Toque**, 16 Rue de Tocqueville, 75017, ☎ 42 27 97 75. Visa. Closed Jul 14 – Aug 15, Christmas hols, Sat and Sun. Alain Donnard gives the full measure of his ability. Spec: *boeuf à la ficelle, paillard de veau.* ❸❸❸

♦♦ **Verger Pereire**, 275 Bd Pereire, 75017, ☎ 45 74 33 32. Prix fixe menu includes a *faux-filet grillé sauce anchoïade* and excellent chips. ❸❸

♦ **Le Beudant**, 97 Rue des Dames, 75017, ☎ 43 87 11 20. Closed Jan 15–30, Sat noon, Sun. It's quite small, but you'll appreciate the excellent regional cooking. Spec: *salade de moules, poulet au vinaigre,* Loire wines. ❸❸❸

═══════════════ *PARIS 18ᵗʰ*

Hotels:

★★★★ **Mapotel Terrass**, 12 Rue Joseph-de-Maistre, 75018, ☎ 46 06 72 85. Tx 280830. AE, DC, Euro, Visa. 108 rm, 19 apart. A remarkable view of Paris from the upper floors. ❸❸❸❸❸ Rest. ♦♦ **Le Guerlande**. ❸❸

★★★ **Résidence Montmartre**, 10 Rue Burq, 75018, ☎ 46 06 45 28. 46 rm in a typical Old Montmartre street. ❸❸❸

★★ **Prima Lepic**, 29 Rue Lepic, 75018, ☎ 46 06 44 64. AE, DC. 38 rm. ⊗ ❸❸

★★ **Royal Montmartre**, 68 Bd. de Clichy, 75018, ☎ 46 06 22 91. 51 rm. ⚐ ❸❸ Brasserie *Le Chat Noir.* ❸

★★ **Timhotel Montmartre**, 11 Pl. Emile-Goudeau, 75018, ☎ 42 55 74 79. Tx 650508. AE, DC, Euro, Visa. 61 rm. ❸❸

Restaurants:

♦♦♦♦ **Beauvilliers**, 52 Rue Lamarck, 75018, ☎ 42 54 19 50. Visa. ⊗ ♿ Closed Sep 1-15, Sun, Mon noon. Édouard Carlier welcomes you in his beautiful Montmartre restaurant as if you were a surprise guest. Superb fresh bouquets, refined cooking. Green terrace in nice weather. ❸❸❸❸

♦♦♦ **Les Fusains**, 44 Rue Joseph-de-Maistre, 75018, ☎ 42 38 03 69. Visa. ♿ Closed Sun, Mon and Sep. Eve only. Spec: *feuilleté léger de petits-gris et champignons des bois, aiguillettes de canard au miel et au vinaigre, gratin de fruits rouges au champagne.* ❸❸❸

♦♦ **Clodenis**, 57 Rue Caulaincourt, 75018, ☎ 46 06 20 26. AE, DC, Visa. Closed Sun. The second "great" restaurant on the Butte. Spec: game in season, *foie gras de canard, turbot aux algues.* ❸❸❸

♦♦ **La Crémaillère 1900**, 15 Pl. du Tertre, 75018, ☎ 46 06 58 59. AE, DC. A picturesque 1900s *brasserie.* ❸❸

♦♦ **Les Semailles**, 3 Rue Steinlen, 75018, ☎ 46 06 37 05. AE, DC, Visa. Closed Feb 1-15, Aug 15-31, Sun, Mon. Jean-Jacques Jouteux's recital for gourmands: *cigale de mer et cresson de fontaine au basilic, suprême de pigeonneau "Mozart".* ❸❸❸

♦ **Le Bateau-Lavoir**, 8 Rue Garreau, 75018, ☎ 46 06 02 00. Good food at reasonable prices. ❸❸

═══════════════ *PARIS 19ᵗʰ and 20ᵗʰ*

Restaurants:

♦♦♦ **Relais des Pyrénées**, 1 Rue du Jourdain, 75020, ☎ 46 36 65 81. AE, DC, Euro, Visa. Closed Aug, Sat. Spec: *piperade, garbure, saumon frais au champagne, poulet basquaise sauté.* ❸❸

♦♦ **Au Cochon d'Or**, 192 Av. Jean-Jaurès, 75019, ☎ 46 07 23 13. AE, DC, Euro, Visa. ♿ Spec: beef, fish. ❸❸❸

♦♦ **La Chaumiere**, 46 Av. Secrétan, 75019, ☎ 46 07 98 62. AE, DC, Euro, Visa. Closed Aug and Sun. Spec: *tartare de langue de veau, barbue à la crème d'oursin.* ❸❸

♦ **Aux Becs Fins**, 44 Bd. Ménilmontant, 75020, ☎ 47 97 51 52. Closed Aug 10–26, Sun. Laurent Lefèbvre serves good helpings of wholesome food in his little bistro. Spec: frogs, *terrines gras-double, cassoulet.* ❸❸

♦ **Dagorno**, 190 Av. Jean-Jaurès, 75019, ☎ 46 07 02 29. AE, DC, Euro, Visa. Closed Sat. Spec: home-smoked salmon, *foie gras de canard maison.* ❸❸❸

Recommended Addresses

Organized by arrondissement

Delicatessens:

Kraker's, 9 Rue d'Aboukir, 75002, ☎ 42 26 57 68. *Gambrinus*, 13 Rue des Blancs-Manteaux, 75004, ☎ 48 87 81 92. *King Henry*, 44 Rue des Boulangers, 75005, ☎ 43 54 54 37. *Cantin Mariane*, 12 Rue du Champs-de-Mars, 75007, ☎ 45 50 43 94. *Charcuterie Vignon*, 14 Rue Marbeuf, 75008, ☎ 47 20 24 26. *La Carte des Vins*, 80 Bd. R.-Lenoir, 75011 ☎ 43 38 74 99. *Kayyam*, 9 Pl. Félix-Eboué

75012, ☎ 43 43 18 50. *Ma Cave*, 105 Rue de Belleville, 75019, ☎ 42 08 62 95.

Fine foods, caterers, specialties:

Battendier, 8 Rue Coquillière, 75001, ☎ 42 36 95 50; *charcutier*–caterer, take-aways (Mme de Gaulle's favorite caterer!). *Le Coq St-Honorè*, 3 Rue Gomboust, 75001, ☎ 42 61 52 04; selected poultry game in season. *La Maison des Foies Gras*, 9 Rue Danièle-Casanova, 75001, ☎ 42 61 42 36. *Verlet*, 256 Rue Saint-Honorè, 75001, ☎ 42 60 67 39; the oldest tea and coffee house in Paris; tasting and sales. *Paul Corcellet*, 46 Rue des Petits-Champs, 75002, ☎ 42 96 51 82; the most exotic fine foodstuffs. *Legrand*, 1 Rue de la Banque, 75002, ☎ 42 60 07 12; traditional fine foods; excellent wines. *Coesnon*, 30 Rue Dauphine, 75005, ☎ 43 54 35 80; one of the best *charcutiers* in Paris. *Poilâne, Lionel*, 8 Rue du Cherche-Midi, 75006, ☎ 45 48 42 59; always a queue to buy the rye bread, *croissants, tartes aux pommes*. *Bon Marché*, 38 Rue de Sévres, 75007, ☎ 42 60 33 45; the best grocery store among the large department stores. *Fauchon*, 26 Pl. de la Madeleine, 75007, ☎ 47 42 60 11; an impressive array of produce, with prices to match the house's very high reputation. *Pétrossian*, 18 Bd. de Latour-Maubourg, 75007, ☎ 45 51 59 73; the Parisian Mecca for caviar and smoked salmon. *Androuet*, 41 Rue d'Amsterdam, 75008, ☎ 48 74 26 93; fine cheeses to savor there or take-away. *Hédiard*, 21 Pl. de la Madeleine, 75008, ☎ 42 66 44 36; specializes in exotic fruits, jams and fruit jellies; good selection of wines. *Cantine Christian*, 2 Rue de Lourmel, 75015; a master of cheese who upholds tradition. *A l'An 2000*, 82 Bd. des Batignolles, 75017; open until 1 am; *charcuterie*–caterer; take-away dishes.

Tea-rooms:

Cador, 2 Rue de l'Amiral-Coligny, 75001, ☎ 45 08 19 18; view of the Louvre Colonnade. *Fanny Tea*, 20 Pl. Dauphine, 75001, ☎ 43 25 83 67. *Pandora*, 24 Passage Choiseul, 75002, ☎ 42 97 56 01. *Le Flore-en-l'Ile*, 42 Quai d'Orléans, 75004, ☎ 43 29 88 27. *Le Jardin de Thé*, 10 Rue Brise-Miche, 75004, ☎ 42 74 35 26; near Beaubourg; excellent tarts. *Le Lys d'Argent*, 90 Rue St-Louis-en-l'Ile, 75004, ☎ 46 33 37 39. *Paris*, 2 Pl. Ed-Rostand, 75006, ☎ 43 29 31 30; overlooking the Luxembourg Gardens.

Cakes and pastries:

Christian Constant, 26 Rue du Bac, 75007, ☎ 42 96 53 53; lemon meringue tarts, chocolate biscuits. *Dalloyau*, 101 Rue du Fg-Saint-Honoré, 75008, ☎ 43 59 18 10. *Lenôtre*, 51 Av. V.-Hugo, 75016, ☎ 45 01 71 71.

Ices:

Berthillon, 31 Rue St-Louis-en-l'Ile, 75004, ☎ 43 59 18 10. *Le Bac à Glaces*, 109 Rue du Bac, 75007, ☎ 45 48 87 65. *Jean Saffray*, 18 Rue du Bac, 75007, ☎ 42 61 27 63. *Baggi*, 38 Rue d'Amsterdam, 75009, ☎ 48 74 01 39. *Raïmo*, 59 Bd. de Reuilly, 75012, ☎ 43 43 70 17. *Glacier de France*, 48 *bis* Av. d'Italie, 75013, ☎ 45 80 23 75. *La Sorbetière*, 12 Rue Gustave-Courbet, 75016, ☎ 45 53 26 91.

Wine bars:

L'Echalote, 14 Rue Chabanais, 75001, ☎ 42 97 47 10. Delicious daily dishes: *bavette, onglet, pavé* ... are accompanied by the best Beaujolais. Also fresh Irish salmon to take away. Meals for around 100 F.

Le Rubis, 10 Rue du Marché-Saint-Honoré, 75001, ☎ 42 61 03 34. Closed Sat, Sun, Aug. Good, reasonably-priced Beaujolais.

Taverne Henri IV, 13 Pl. du Pont Neuf, 75001 ☎ 43 54 27 90. Closed Sat, Sun, Aug, Christmas, Easter, nat. hols. Beaujolais, Touraine and Muscadet wines, regional products, sandwiches and snacks.

Au Duc de Richelieu, 110 Rue de Richelieu, 75002, ☎ 42 96 38 38. Closed Jul 28 – Sept 1, and Sun. Sandwiches made from regional products.

Entre Deux Verres, 48 Rue Ste. Anne, 75002, ☎ 42 96 42 26. Good selection of Bordeaux wines, regional snacks and grilled meat.

La Cloche des Halles, Rue du Coq-Héron, 75003, ☎ 42 36 93 89. Closed Sun. Good wines (Brouilly, Fleurie, Aloxe Corton), and quiche, ham on the bone.

Gaité Bar, 7 Rue Papin, 75003, ☎ 42 72 79 45. This bar proves that wine-tasting has a great future. An inimitable setting. Beaujolais, Bordeaux wines.

La Tartine, 24 Rue de Rivoli, 75004, ☎ 42 72 76 85. Closed Tue, Aug. The regulars fully appreciate the extensive selection of good wines, the strongly-flavored cheeses and the *crottins de Sancerre*.

Bernard Pantonnier, 19 – 21 Rue des Fossés-Saint-Jacques, 75005, ☎ 43 26 80 18. Closed Sat, Sun, Aug. In the heart of the Latin Quarter, the most popular wine bar in Paris. Reasonable prices. Touraine, Champagne, Beaujolais, sandwiches with Landes ham and a delicious camembert de Sainte-Mère-Eglise.

Le Soleil d'Austerlitz, 18 Bd. de l'Hôpital, 75005, ☎ 43 31 39 36. Visa; closed Aug, Sat. Excellent wines at the counter, sandwiches, a daily special.

Le Beverly, 9 Rue de l'Ancienne-Comédie,

75006, ☎ 43 26 78 48. Closed Sundays.
Wines selected by the owners: Menetou-
Salon, Reuilly, etc., with delicious regional
dishes: *boudin*, home-made *charcuterie*, etc.
Le Café Parisien, 15 Rue d'Assas, 75006, ☎ 45
44 41 44. Closed 15 days in Aug, 1 week in
winter, eve, Sun, Mon. Excellent regional
wines, a daily special.
Le Millésime, 7 Rue Lobineau, 75006, ☎ 46 34
22 15. Closed Sun. Quality French wines, and
occasionally less convincing wines from elsewhere. Gypsy guitarist in the evenings.
Le Petit Bacchus, 13 Rue du Cherche-Midi,
75006, ☎ 45 44 01 07. Closed Sun and Mon.
Charcuterie, cheese, pastries and wine by the
glass or take-away.
Le Sauvignon, 80 Rue des Saints-Pères, 75007,
☎ 45 48 49 02. Closed Sun, Aug. A veritable
institution, despite its limited floor space. The
clientele come here for the finest sandwiches
in Paris, and for the Beaujolais, Bordeaux and
Sancerre wines.
Vin sur Vin, 20 Rue de Montessuy, 75007, ☎
47 05 14 20. Closed Sun. Under the shadow
of the Eiffel Tower, in a quiet street. Tastings
and food served 11 am – 11 pm. This is an
excellent little restaurant with a talented
young chef. Excellent food and 120 wines to
sample.
Bistrot du Sommelier, 97 Bd. Haussmann,
75008, ☎ 42 65 24 85. Closed Dec 25 – Jan
1, Sat eve, Sun. Selection of wines direct from
the estates.
Le Blue Fox, Cité Berryer, 75008, ☎ 42 65 08
47. Numerous tourists. Fashionable and expensive.
La Boutique des Vins, 31–33 Rue de l'Arcade,
75008, ☎ 42 65 27 27. Closed Sat, Sun and
Aug. One of the newest wine bars, and the
first run by a woman, who prepares a
different special every day. Wine by the glass,
by the bottle, and to take away.
Ma Bourgogne, 133 Bd. Haussmann, 75008, ☎
45 63 50 61. Closed Sat, Sun and Aug.
Remarkable value for money. Brasserie and
restaurant at noon in a bar that stocks genuine
Beaujolais and Burgundy wines.
Le Val d'Or, 28 Av. Franklin-Roosevelt, 75008,
☎ 43 59 95 81. Closed Sun. Brasserie and
restaurant at noon. Terrines and home-cured
ham on the bone. All Beaujolais wines and
superb Aloxe Corton.
La Cave Drouot, 8 Rue Drouot, 75009, ☎ 47
70 83 38. Closed Sun. Daily special and wines
at the counter, rigorously selected by the
owner. Auction room atmosphere. Beaujolais, Bordeaux, Côtes-du-Rhône, Madiran.
L'Oenothéque, 20 Rue St-Lazare, 75009, ☎ 48
78 08 76. Visa; closed Sat, Sun, hols. Delicious
cooking which enhances the wines.

Relais Beaujolais, 3 Rue Milton, 75009, ☎ 48
78 77 91. Closed Sun, Aug. Small restaurant
(luncheons, dinners). A tiny counter fre-
quented by the locals. Beaujolais, Loire wines.
La Devinière, 70 Rue Alexandre-Dumas,
75011, ☎ 43 73 22 97 Visa; closed Aug 5 –
Sept 5, Sun, Mon. Good selection of Loire
wines, *tartines* and a daily special.
Jacques Melac, 42 Rue Léon-Frot, 75011, ☎
43 70 59 27. Closed Sun and Mon. Quality
French wines and snacks at the counter.
Gypsy guitarist in the evenings.
Le Rallye, 6 Rue Daguerre, 75014, ☎ 43 22 57
05. Closed Sun, Mon, July 17 – Aug 15.
Auvergne *charcuterie*.
La Royale, 80 Rue de l'Amiral-Mouchez,
75014, ☎ 45 88 38 09. Closed Sun, Aug.
Restaurant with a daily special at noon. The
owner offers advice for those wishing to taste
Touraine and Beaujolais wines.
Les Caves Angevines, 2 Pl. Léon-Deubel,
75016, ☎ 42 88 88 93. Well-chosen wines
bottled by the owner. Six tables for his
delicious daily specials.
Au Père Tranquille, 30 Av. du Maine, 75015, ☎
42 22 88 12. Closed Sun, Mon. A true wine
club, not always accessible to the general
public. Priority is given to Touraine wines. A
number of tables reserved for the regulars;
beautiful terrace in summer. Daily special at
noon.
Le Pain et le Vin, 1 Rue d'Armaillé, 75017, ☎
47 63 88 29. Annex of the *Toques Gour-
mandes* (Fournier, Dutournier, Faugeron,
Morot-Gaudry). Daily special, wine by the
glass and by the bottle, sandwiches, fresh
charcuterie, open noon – 2 am.
La Winstub, 11 Av. de la Grande-Armée,
75017, ☎ 45 00 13 21. Solid food at low
prices and a magnificent selection of wines,
cervelas, roll-mops, *jambonneau*.
Aux Négociants, 27 Rue Lambert, 75018, ☎
46 06 15 11. Closed Jul 15 – Aug 15, Dec 25,
Jan 1, Sat, Sun. Good Beaujolais and Bourgueil
wines, low-priced daily specials.

Wine cellars and wine merchants:

La Galerie des Vins, 201 Rue Saint-Honoré,
75001, ☎ 42 61 81 20. *Lucien Legrand*, 1 Rue
de la Banque, 75002, ☎ 42 60 07 12.
Gambrinus, 13 Rue des Blancs-Manteaux,
75004, ☎ 48 87 81 92. *Lescène-Dura*, 63 Rue
de la Verrerie, 75004, ☎ 42 72 08 74. *King
Henry*, 44 Rue des Boulangers, 75005, ☎ 43
54 54 37. *Mon Vignoble*, 43 Rue Poliveau,
75005, ☎ 47 07 22 91. *Cave Jean-Mermoz*, 25
Rue Jean-Mermoz, 75006, ☎ 42 56 07 49;
for all objects to do with wine. *Georges
Duboeuf*, 25 Rue Marbeuf, 75008, ☎ 47 20 71
23. *Steven Spurrier*, 25 Rue Royale, 75008, ☎

42 65 92 40. *L'Oenophile*, 30 Bd. Voltaire, 75011, ☎ 47 00 69 45. *Kayyam*, 8 Pl. Félix-Eboué, 75012, ☎ 43 43 39 71. *Cave des Gobelins*, 56 Av. des Gobelins, 75013, ☎ 43 31 66 79. *Réserve et Sélection*, 119 Rue du Dessousdes-Berges, 75013, ☎ 45 83 65 19 (depot). *Caves de Passy*, 3 Rue Duban, 75016, ☎ 42 88 85 56. *Centre de Distribution des Vins de Propriétés*, 13, Bd. Ney, 75018, ☎ 42 09 61 50. *Caves Lepic*, 19 Rue Lepic, 75018, ☎ 46 06 18 50. *Ma Cave*, 105 Rue de Belleville, 75019, ☎ 42 08 62 95. *Divinord*, 10 Rue Morice, 92110 Clichy, ☎ 47 30 30 56.

Piano-bars:

Le Montana, 28 Rue St-Benoît, 75006, ☎ 45 48 93 08. From midnight until 6, snacks and jazz.
Le Clair de Nuit, 9 Rue Deparcieux, 75014, ☎ 43 20 25 54. Closed noon. For small appetites and large thirsts at night.

Beer:

Le Trappiste, 4 Rue St-Denis, 75001, ☎ 42 33 08 50.
Le Manneken Pis, 4 Rue Daunou, 75002, ☎ 47 42 85 03.
L'Académie de la Bière, 88 *bis* Bd. de Port-Royal, 75005, ☎ 43 54 66 65.
La Gueuze, 19 Rue Soufflot, 75005, ☎ 43 54 63 00.
Le Bar de la Marine, 59 Bd. du Montparnasse, 75006, ☎ 45 48 27 70.
Pub Saint-Germain, 17 Rue de l'Ancienne-Comédie, 75006, ☎ 43 29 38 70.
La Taverne de Nesles, 32 Rue Dauphine, 75006, ☎ 43 26 38 36.
Bar (belge) du New Store, 63 Champs-Élysées, 75008, ☎ 42 25 96 16.
Au Général La Fayette, 52 Rue La Fayette, 75009, ☎ 47 70 59 08.
La Taverne Kronenbourg, 24 Bd. des Italiens, 75009, ☎ 47 70 16 64. Brasserie 11 pm – 3 am.
La Taverne de la Bière, 15 Rue de Dunkerque, 75010, ☎ 42 85 12 93.

Video-bars:

Le Look, 49 Rue Saint-Honoré, 75001, ☎ 42 33 44 98. Reasonably-priced drinks.
Hall-Catraz, 72 Rue Quincampoix, 75003, ☎ 42 71 39 02. Very *à la mode*: salads and giant screen.
Le Casablanca, 41 Rue Quincampoix, 75004, ☎ 42 78 82 69. Video, electronic games, small sandwiches.
Le Studio, 15 Rue Quincampoix, 75004, ☎ 42 78 73 90. Video, billiards, restaurant, lots of noise.

Cabarets:

Paradis Latin, 28 Rue du Cardinal-Lemoine, 75005, ☎ 43 25 28 28.
Alcazar, 62 Rue Mazarine, 75006, ☎ 43 29 02 20. An entirely new show, setting and atmosphere, thanks to J.-M. Rivière's long-awaited return to the Alcazar.
Don Camillo, 10 Rue des Saints-Pères, 75007, ☎ 41 60 25 46.
Crazy Horse Saloon, 12 Av. George-V, 75008, ☎ 47 23 32 32.
Lido, 116 *bis* Av. des Champs-Élysées, 75008, ☎ 45 63 11 63. A perfectly organized show with astonishing special effects, lavish costumes and, of course, the famous Bluebell Girls.
Folies-Bergères, 32 Rue Richer, 75009, ☎ 42 46 77 11. A huge theater (seats 1600) for lasting memories of Paris nightlife.
Moulin-Rouge, Pl. Blanche, 75009, ☎ 46 06 00 19.
Michou, 80 Rue des Martyrs, 75018, ☎ 46 06 00 19.

Clubs, discotheques:

La Scala, 188 *bis* Rue de Rivoli, 75001, ☎ 42 61 64 00. A huge discotheque, where the dancers vibrate to an electronic setting and light shows.
Bains-Douches, 7 Rue du Bourg-l'Abbé, 75003, ☎ 48 87 34 40.
Caveau de la Huchette, 5 Rue de la Huchette, 75005, ☎ 43 26 65 05. A jazz institution.
Cherry Lane, 8 Rue des Ciseaux, 75006, ☎ 43 26 28 28. Left Bank disco; young, often foreign clientele.
Chez Castel, 15 Rue Princesse, 75006, ☎ 43 26 90 22. As exclusive as it is famous.
Apocalypse, 40 Rue du Colisée, 75008, ☎ 42 25 11 68.
Atmosphere, 45 Rue François-1er, 75008, ☎ 47 23 70 72.
Club 79, 79 Av. des Champs-Élysées, 75008, ☎ 47 23 68 75.
Élysées-Matignon, 2 Av. Matignon, 75008, ☎ 42 25 73 13. Oil magnates, showbiz Parisians, the high-fashion world ... a luxury haunt.
Le Garage, 41 Rue de Washington, 75008, ☎ 45 63 21 27.
Keur Samba, 79 Rue La Boëtie, 75008, ☎ 43 59 03 10. African music, one of Paris' liveliest night-spots.
Régine's Club, 49 Rue de Ponthieu, 75008, ☎ 43 59 21 60. A brilliant night-spot.
Le Palace, 8 Rue du Faubourg-Montmartre, 75009, ☎ 42 46 10 87. Still one of the most "in" night-spots in Paris.
Bus Palladium, 4 Rue Fontaine, 75009, ☎ 48 74 54 99.
Royal, 2 Rue des Italiens, 75009, ☎ 48 24 43

88. "Retro" dancing with orchestra for older couples. Young on Tues eve.

New Morning, 79 Rue des Petites-Ecuries, 75010, ☎ 45 23 51 41. Jazz.

La Resserre aux Diables, 94 Rue St-Martin, 75010, ☎ 42 72 01 73. Restaurant-rock club complex.

Adison Square Gardel, 23 Rue du Com. Mouchotte, 75014, ☎ 43 21 54 58. From the genteel 5 pm "tea and dance-floor" to the Fri night American style.

Utopia Jazz Club, 79 Rue de l'Ouest, 75014, ☎ 43 27 27 36. One of the last clubs for progressive jazz.

L'Ecume des Nuits, 81 Bd. Gouvion-St-Cyr (Hotel Méridien), 75017, ☎ 47 58 12 30.

La Main Jaune, Pl. de la Porte-de-Champerret, 75017. ☎ 47 63 26 47. Disco dancing ... on roller skates!

Fashion addresses:

Castelbajac, 31 Pl. du Marché-Saint-Honoré, 75001.

Elisabeth de Senneville, 3 Rue de Turbigo, 75001.

Kenzo, Jungle Jap, 3 Pl. des Victoires, 75001.

Thierry Mugler, 10 Pl. des Victoires, 75001.

Ventilo, 27 bis Rue du Louvre, 75001.

Anne-Marie Béretta, 24 Rue Saint-Sulpice, 75006.

Chantal Thomass, 5 Rue du Vieux-Colombier, 75006, and Forum des Halles.

Emmanuelle Khanh, 2 Rue de Tournon, 75006.

Giorgio Armani, 31 Rue du Four, 75006.

Issey Miyaké, 201 Bd. Saint-Germain, 75006.

Mic-Mac, 13 Rue de Tournon, 75006.

Pierre Cardin Diffusion, 185 Bd. Saint-Germain, 75006.

Saint-Laurent Rive Gauche, 6 Pl. Saint-Sulpice, 75006, and 38 Rue du Fg-Saint-Honoré, 75008.

Sonia Rykiel, 6 Rue de Grenelle, 75006.

Azzedine Alaia, 60 Rue de Bellechasse, 75007.

Chloé, 3 Rue de Gribeauval, 75007, and Rue du Fg-Saint-Honoré, 75008.

Angelo Tarlazzi, 67 Rue du Fg-Saint-Honoré, 75008.

Cacharel, 34 Rue Tronchet, 75008, and Forum des Halles.

Cerruti 1881, 15 Pl. de la Madeleine (women), and 1 Rue Royale (men).

Chanel, 21 Rue Cambon, 75008.

Dior, 15 Av. Montaigne, 75008.

Dorothée Bis, 10 Rue Tronchet, 75008.

Givenchy, 3 Av. George-V, 75008.

Guy Laroche, 30 Rue Fg-Saint-Honoré, 75008.

Lanvin, 22 Rue du Fg-Saint-Honoré, 75008.

Nina Ricci, 17 Rue François-1er, 75008.

Per Spook, 18 Av. George-V, 75008.

Chic and inexpensive clothes:

Most of the top designers have boutiques and warehouses where they sell models from previous years for half-price.

Courreges, 7 Rue de Turbigo, 75001.

Emmanuelle Khanh, 6 Rue Pierre-Lescot, 75001.

Rodier, 11 Bd. de la Madeleine, 75001.

Pierre Cardin, 11 Bd. de Sébastopol, 75001.

Pierre d'Alby, 60 Rue de Richelieu, 75002.

Givenchy, 3 Av. George-V, 75008.

Nina Ricci, 39 Av. Montaigne, 75008.

Dorothée Bis Stock, 76 Rue d'Alésia, 75014.

Mic-Mac, 13 Rue Laugier, 75017.

Cacharel Stock, 171 Rue de Belleville, 75019; 114 Rue d'Alésia, 75014.

Paris-Nord Diffusion (Daniel Hechter Dépôt), 62 Rue de Pelleport, 75020. Most of the sales depots are situated near the Rue Saint-Placide (75006), and in the 10th, 15th and 16th arrondissements. The main sales depot is the *Réciproque*, 95 Rue de la Pompe, 75016.

Shoes:

Bally, 11 Bd. de la Madeleine, 75001; 12 Rue du Four, 75006.

Laurent Mercadal, 3 Pl. des Victoires, 75001.

Accessoire, 6 Rue du Cherche-Midi, 75006.

Charles Jourdan, 62 Rue de Rennès, 75006.

Maud Frizon, 83 Rue des Saints-Pères, 75006.

Sacha, 24 Rue de Buci, 75006.

Pucci Verdi, 40 Rue de Verneuil, 75007.

Stéphane Kélian, 62 Rue des Saints-Pères, 75007.

Gli Rossetti, 54 Rue du Fg-Saint-Honoré, 75008.

Walter Steiger, 49 Rue du Fg-Saint-Honoré, 75008.

Weston, 124 Av. des Champs-Élysées, 75008.

English bookshops:

Galignani, 224 Rue de Rivoli, 75001, ☎ 42 60 76 07.

W. H. Smith, 248 Rue de Rivoli, 75001, ☎ 42 60 37 97.

Brentano's, 37 Av. de l'Opéra, 75002, ☎ 42 61 52 50.

Shakespeare & Co., 37 Rue de la Bûcherie, 75005.

BIBLIOGRAPHY

Belloc, Hilaire: *Paris 1900* (Methuen, London, 1929)

Brassaï: *The Secret Paris of the 30's* (Thames and Hudson, London, 1976; and Pantheon, New York, 1977).

Carr, P: *Days with the French Romantics in the Paris of 1830* (Methuen, London, 1932)

Chastel, A: *Paris* (Thames and Hudson, London, 1971)

Dorsey, H: *The Belle Epoque in the Paris Herald* (Thames and Hudson, London, 1986)

Evenson, Norma: *Paris, a Century of Change 1878 – 1978* (Yale University Press, New Haven, 1979)

Fitch, N.R: *Sylvia Beach and the Lost Generation. A History of Literary Paris in the 20's and 30's* (Souvenir Press, London, 1984)

Gajdusek, Robert E: *Hemingway's Paris* (Charles Scribners and Sons, New York, 1982)

Gosling, N: *Paris 1900 – 1914: The Miraculous Years* (Weidenfeld and Nicholson, London, 1978)

Horne, A: *The Fall of Paris: The Siege and Commune 1870-1871* (Penguin, New York, 1964; and Macmillan, London, 1965)

Jennett, S: *Paris* (B.T. Batsford, London, 1973)

Morton, B.N: *Americans in Paris: An Anecdotal Street Guide* (Olivia and Hall Press, Michigan, 1984)

Porter, D: *Frommer's Guide to Paris* (Prentice Hall Press, New York, 1983)

Reehling, B (ed): *A Touch of Paris Guide: A Selective Guide in Plain English* (Geneva, Traders and Travellers, 1985)

Roth, C: *The Book of Paris* (Angus and Robertson, London, 1979)

Russell, J: *Paris* (Thames and Hudson, London, 1983)

Shaw, I and Searle, S: *Paris! Paris!* (Weidenfeld and Nicholson, London, 1977)

Shaw, I: *Paris/Magnum: Photographs 1935 – 1981* (Aperture Inc., New York, 1981)

Sutcliffe, A: *The Autumn of Central Paris, The Defeat of Town Planning* (Edward Arnold, London, 1970)

Thomson, D: *Renaissance Paris, Architecture and Growth 1475 – 1600* (A. Zwemmer Ltd., London, 1984; and University of California Press, California, 1984)

Wells, P: *The Food Lover's Guide to Paris* (Workman, New York, 1984; and Methuen, London, 1985)

White, S: *Sam White's Paris* (New English Library, London, 1983)

Wiser, W: *The Crazy Years, Paris in the Twenties* (Thames and Hudson, London, 1983)

Zeldin, T: *The French* (Flamingo, London, 1983; and Pantheon, New York, 1983)

General Index

Index of people

Printed in Singapore by Tien Wah Press
Dépôt légal: 3803-1-1987
ISBN 0-13-331331-X